Life and Death in the Third Reich

Life *and* Death
in the
Third Reich

PETER FRITZSCHE

The Belknap Press of
Harvard University Press
Cambridge, Massachusetts
London, England

A Caravan book. For more information,
visit www.caravanbooks.org

First Harvard University Press paperback edition, 2009.

Library of Congress Cataloging-in-Publication Data

Fritzsche, Peter, 1959–
Life and death in the Third Reich / Peter Fritzsche.—1st ed.
p.   cm.
Includes bibliographical references and index.
ISBN 978-0-674-02793-0 (hardcover : alk. paper)
ISBN 978-0-674-03465-5 (pbk.)
1. Germany—History—1933–1945.   2. Germany—Ethnic
relations—History—20th century.   3. National socialism.
4. Holocaust, Jewish (1939–1945)—Germany—Causes.
5. Collective memory—Germany.   I. Title.

DD256.5.F747 2008
943.086—dc22   2007040552

Pg. 119-42
Pesecution of Jews, oct. 30

Germans + the Nazi Movement - Oct. 6
pg. 1-75

Contents

Preface

I open this book with descriptions of how Nazis divided communities, families, and individuals. In the 1930s, Germans both pushed back and tugged at National Socialism. Many Germans despised the Nazis though they made compromises along the way. Yet most people identified with the Third Reich, and most believed that the Nazis had healed the wounds of German history. At the end of the war, it was very difficult for Germans to come to grips with their initial political desire for the Nazis and their later feelings of betrayal or to evaluate the parts they and their fellow citizens played in the construction of racial community and in the pursuit of war and genocide or even to recognize the fundamental, revolutionary aims of National Socialism. Postwar debates and discussions preoccupied families for decades and spilled from one generation to the next. I know this well, since my own parents were born in Weimar-era Berlin. These conversations have now become part of the historical record, which, in turn, recognizes the efforts that Germans from all backgrounds and generations have, in the end, made to examine their pasts. This work has been difficult. It is also admirable, even exemplary.

Given my own family connections to Germany, this book has been many decades in the making. In the last years of researching and writing, I have been honored by support from the University of

Konstanz, the Center for Advanced Study at the University of Illinois, and the Research Board of the University of Illinois. I thank my former student Jim Wrzosek for his research help. I am also grateful for the criticisms of the German Colloquium at Illinois, the extensive readings by Jeff Hayton, Joe Perry, and Jonathan Huener, as well as the engagement of Jonathan's undergraduate class at the University of Vermont in the winter of 2007 and especially of the interlocutors Katherine Rendall and Jessica-Lyn Wagar. Thanks to my brave students, Annamarie Stone, Erin Blaze, and Jesse Glim, for leading a discussion of a draft chapter in front of their teacher in Urbana. My wife, Karen Hewitt, also read and commented helpfully on the manuscript. Harvard University Press found superb, critical readers and provided expert editorial guidance. All in all, I have many intellectual debts, from Chicago to Philadelphia, Tel Aviv, Berkeley, and Berlin. Therefore I dedicate this book to my indispensable teachers over the past forty years, Ruth Marx, Anne Wheeler, Earl Bell, Thomas Childers, and Gerald Feldman.

Life and Death in the Third Reich

Introduction

A popular book published in Germany in 1940 came close to describing the early stages of the Holocaust. It scrutinized ruthless violence against civilians and scouted the psychological dynamics among perpetrators. The time is the beginning of the war after authorities have put neighborhoods under guard, assigning the population color-coded identity passes (red, pink, and white) to classify political reliability. As a church burns, soldiers arrive to round up men, women, and children in the marketplace before marching them to the East. The guards confiscate the last possessions of the deportees. They lock the civilians up in barns, which they threaten to burn down. At one point, soldiers debate the morality of killing women, which one pointedly refuses to do. Children are shot with the justification that "in ten years they will be men." Later on, soldiers "liquidate" stragglers at the end of the column. Frightened prisoners whisper to each other, "Take off your glasses!" for the commander intends to "destroy our entire intellectual class" by killing the men wearing them. When two columns of deportees meet, one of the prisoners remarks: "That is how we look . . . but unfortunately no one else sees us"; evidently, public opinion around the world has ignored the plight of the deportees. The book described in detail how other ethnic groups deliberately manhandled, beat, and otherwise abused the prisoners.

1

In his fictionalized reportage *Death in Poland,* Edwin Erich Dwinger anticipated many elements of the systematic murder of Jewish civilians carried out by mobile killing units, or *Einsatzkommandos,* under the command of the SS beginning in the summer of 1941, after the German invasion of the Soviet Union. Dwinger also incorporated specific features of the German occupation of Poland such as the imprisonment and execution of intellectuals. However, the subject of *Death in Poland* is not German killers, but ethnic Germans whom Polish soldiers and paramilitaries have deported or slaughtered. Although his account of Polish atrocities during and after "Bloody Sunday" in Bydgoszcz, or Bromberg, on 3 September 1939, two days after the German invasion of Poland, is almost completely fictional, Dwinger portrayed modern war as a characteristically genocidal enterprise in which civilians are regarded as the primary targets. One of the ethnic Germans who have been liberated by the Wehrmacht reflects on what will happen to Poland: "whether its cities will be entirely destroyed, or whether its intellectual class falls in battle, or whether one-third of its population perishes in the hail of bullets—I can't think of any consequences of the war that I would regard as unjust." Of course, Germany's invasion of Poland and its occupation forces had in fact accomplished much of this agenda before readers even opened Dwinger's book.

On one level, *Death in Poland* provided a justification for the destruction of the Polish nation by transforming specific atrocities into a general condition of war. Dwinger's report became one of the star texts in seminars and workshops that the Nazis' elite military guard, the Schutzstaffel, or SS, organized to prepare units for deployment in Poland and the Soviet Union. In one 1940 seminar, the speaking points for the book emphasized: "it was not just the rabble that was behind these crimes; the Polish intellectual class took part, and representatives of the Church tolerated it. Conclusion: the truly guilty: England (the Jew). No matter how severe, every German measure in the East is justified. The discipline to be hard in thought and feeling!"[1] The shift in targeting from Polish intellectuals to "the Jew" anticipated the escalation of Germany's war against the nations and people of Europe. Since the Germans did in fact assume almost exactly the cruel roles that Dwinger had assigned to the Poles, *Death in Poland* feels like an instruction manual. Dwinger had clearly thought through quite carefully the dynamics of murdering civilians. In this regard, he had written a very useful book for German invaders.

However, *Death in Poland* also attentively embellished a fantasy of German victimhood in which Germans imagined themselves to be the victims of the very crimes they subsequently carried out against Poles, Russians, and Jews. The specifically German context is important to keep in mind. Although Dwinger had initially won acclaim for "diaries" detailing his experiences during the Russian civil war in 1918–1921, he did not recycle earlier material. In fact, he denied that the atrocities had a Communist or Bolshevik origin. Among the Germans featured in *Death in Poland* is a figure based on Dwinger himself, the "old Siberian" who distinguishes the deportations he witnessed in the Russian civil war from his own persecution in Poland twenty years later: warring Russian armies had "thousands shot, but let ten thousand die. It is on the word 'let' that the emphasis falls here. Epidemics . . . That is the big difference." The old man goes on to say that the Bolshevik "Jew-commissar" issued orders for the wounded "White" he had captured to be bandaged: "Have you ever heard that, from a single Pole, ever?"[2]

Since the Nazi-Soviet Non-Aggression Pact still applied in 1940, the point is not that Dwinger deliberately withheld blame from the Communists, but rather that he expended such effort to build up a specifically anti-German perpetrator. *Death in Poland* recapitulated a National Socialist version of post–World War I history. The Nazis believed that Germany was mortally threatened by a cluster of military and geopolitical dangers, by Poland, and by the Treaty of Versailles, which had redrawn Germany's borders to Poland's advantage, but also by political and social conflicts and racial degeneration that Germany's unexpected defeat in 1918 had exposed. National Socialism believed its historical mission was to revitalize Germany as a racial compact in order to make permanent the nationalist solidarities of 1914 and thereby check the "stab in the back" that it had suffered in 1918.

The Nazis considered political life in crude Social Darwinist terms, as constant struggle between peoples. This was the premise for the war of conquest and plunder they waged throughout Europe in the years 1939–1945. But the concept of life as struggle does not capture the drastic way the Nazis interpreted the world around them. As *Death in Poland* demonstrated, the peril that Germans both inside and outside the Third Reich imagined they faced was extreme and had a specific historical context. The Nazis were haunted by Germany's defeat in World War I and by the 1918 "November Revolution" that had broken out in its aftermath. Even as they built up a militarized racial state, which appeared almost unassailable to its opponents, they repeatedly imagined the demise of Germany at the hands of Poles, Bolsheviks, Jews, and other enemies. Figures of Germans threatened with sterilization or exterminated and reduced to ashes littered Nazi propaganda.[3] This embattled vision of history, which Nazis shared with many other Germans, helps explain the fantasies of extreme violence the Nazis harbored. The National Socialists completely mobilized the ground on which they stood.

Life and death were thus deeply entangled in the Third Reich. The ways in which Nazism promoted an ideal of German life were inextricably linked to the near-death they believed Germany had suffered in 1918. The Nazis delivered upon their enemies the very destruction they imagined awaited Germans. The violence of the Nazis was so excessive and their feeling of liberation from conventional morality so complete that any attempt at explanation falters.

But a context of macabre premonitions of German death makes the mindset of perpetrators more comprehensible. With their invasion of the Soviet Union in 1941, the Nazis waged a war that conformed almost exactly to their unconditional ideas. It posed the question of life or death, national survival or annihilation, in the most radical terms. However, mastery and jeopardy existed in a diabolical relationship with each other throughout the twelve years of the Third Reich. Political activity was premised on both supreme confidence and terrifying vulnerability; both states of mind coexisted and continuously radicalized Nazi policies. The sense of "can do" was wrapped in "must do." This combination released enormous energies as millions of Germans participated in public life to renovate, protect, and preserve the nation. At the same time, the Nazis' sense of urgency made their policies more lethal, since they believed that the only way to ensure the preservation of "worthy" lives was to destroy what they considered to be "unworthy" lives, including the genetically "unfit," "asocials," and Jews. The following pages explore the Nazis' ambition to regenerate national life in Germany and the allied conviction that to do so they needed, on an increasingly gigantic scale, to annihilate life.

Adolf Hitler and his Nazi followers started, escalated, and fought a brutal world war until the bitter end in May 1945. National Socialism promised Germans a life of security and prosperity, and attempted to fulfill that promise by wrecking other nations and sentencing other people to death. Forty million people died in Europe as a result of World War II—nearly 10 percent of the total population of the continent. More than half of these casualties were civilians, mostly in eastern Europe. The dead included six million Jews, about two-thirds of the total number living in Europe in 1940. These figures are difficult to fathom, but they indicate that the greater German empire the Nazis set out to create rested on the intention to violently remake "lands and peoples" into "spaces and races."⁴ National Socialism was as murderous as it was not because it was modern or efficient or bureaucratic but because it saw itself to be the specific resolution of German history in which an imperiled people tried to make themselves unassailable.[5]

As a project of social renovation and imperial conquest, National Socialism made extraordinary claims on the German people. This was not just a matter of taxation or conscription. Nazism aimed at animating the German people to act as a self-conscious ethnic union. It deliberately set about revising the way Germans looked at each other so that they would recognize the national community they belonged to as an active subject in world history. Indeed, one purpose of Dwinger's book had been to assert the primacy of ethnic destinies by exposing the mortal danger in which Poles had placed Germans. In many ways, the political success of Nazism rested on whether individual Germans came to see the world through the lenses of racial comradeship and racial struggle. Thus inevitably a further aim of this book is to explore the ways in which the German people identified with and collaborated in the new racial order of National Socialism. In other words, to what extent did Germans become Nazis in the years 1933–1945?

The nature of the relationship between the two collective nouns, "Germans" and "Nazis," is a vexed but critical historiographical issue. For a long time historians used them to denote degrees of mutual exclusion rather than kinds of equivalence. Although the existence of a core of fanatical Nazi loyalists had always been acknowledged, historical studies stressed the shallowness of political support for the Nazis in Weimar-era elections and the hollowness of their claims for the *Volksgemeinschaft,* or people's community, after 1933. Scholars concluded that key constituencies such as workers and farmers, and even parts of the middle classes, displayed little enthusiasm for the new regime. They acknowledged Hitler's popularity, but argued that the Nazi party itself and many of its social and economic policies lacked basic legitimacy.[6] In this view, Nazis resembled predators while most Germans appeared to be politically opportunistic or morally weak but not, in the main, ideo-logically complicit. Political models such as totalitarianism, which never caught the interest of historians, arrived at similar conclu-sions from a different direction. More recent treatments of German society in the Nazi period, particularly "histories of everyday life," have shown that more active though still limited collaborations oc-curred as citizens negotiated with Nazi authorities to acquire bene-fits, resources, and breathing space.[7] Even in this view, the Nazis are surprisingly autonomous from the German people; leaders pursued plans for war and conquest while ordinary citizens worried about their own lives.

In the past twenty years, as part of the "cultural turn" in the study of human behavior, historians have reconsidered the ideologi-cal traffic between "Germans" and "Nazis," pointing to shared cul-tural and political dispositions dating to the nineteenth century, the self-mobilization of professional groups, particularly in the bio-medical realm, and the overall legitimacy of the people's commu-nity and its racial precepts.[8] Recent work also pays more attention to the ways in which Nazism was actively built from below. The participation of broad sectors of German society in the Nazi project created an array of complicit relationships. To some extent, the shift in debate amounts to seeing the glass as half full instead of half empty. Real limits to the success of the Nazis should not obscure the dramatic political transformation they oversaw or the loyalties they realigned in a short period. However, few scholars have accepted the sweeping claim that most Germans shared an "exterminatory" anti-Semitic consensus with Nazi leaders, who simply dared to im-plement preconceived ideas.[9]

My argument is predisposed to the second line of interpretation, but my aim is not simply to make the case that more Germans were Nazis and Germans more National Socialist than was previously thought. It is also necessary to examine how Germans in this period struggled with the Nazi revolution in various keys of desire, fascination, and dismay. As a vast project for social, political, and racial renewal, National Socialism offered the German people a range of ways in which to participate. Germans approached Nazi policies out of fear, opportunism, and careerism, as well as varying degrees of ideological conviction. The list can be extended: citizens were also lazy, indifferent, and ignorant. These various motivations need to stay in view. However, National Socialism exerted strong pressure on citizens to convert, to see the credibility of the people's community, and to recognize one another as "racial comrades." The Nazis designed institutional settings, especially in community camps through which millions of Germans passed, to produce this conversion. What this meant was that individuals debated for themselves the whole question of *becoming*—of becoming a National Socialist, a comrade, a race-minded German, of remaining true to the old or joining the new. They grappled with questions about the importance of fitting in, the convenience of going along, and the responsibilities the individual owed to the collective. Thus the careful differentiations that scholars have made as to motivation were themselves objects of scrutiny in Nazi Germany. There was also considerable discussion about the morality of anti-Jewish policies, euthanasia, and the conduct of war. The outcomes of these examinations varied from person to person, but the *process* gave them an ideological inflection. This struggle is what Germans came to share in the Third Reich.

Moreover, the dire economic circumstances at the end of the Weimar Republic, when six million people could not find work or secure futures for themselves, and the humiliations of military defeat and the Versailles Treaty, which seemed to be linked in the popular imagination to a whole series of recurring national calamities from the Great Inflation in 1922–23 to the Great Depression in 1930–1933, made Germans more receptive to the idea of converting to a new set of ideas and more willing to accept the violence that new beginnings might require. Even before 1933, a catastrophic vocabulary of beginnings and endings insistently posed the alternatives of new choices. More than one-third of all German voters had already cast ballots for the National Socialists before 1933; others had participated in various nationalist insurgencies against the Weimar Republic. Millions of people were open to ideas of national regeneration.

Letters and diaries provide valuable insights into the effort Germans made to come to terms with National Socialism. They are not representative, perhaps, but they are telling. I have used them extensively because they capture something of the conversations Germans had with one another. They expose the fears, desires, and reservations of contemporaries, and they show how they fitted National Socialist words and concepts into everyday life. As a genre, diaries also corresponded to the autobiographical work that the Nazis themselves encouraged in the community camps they established across Germany. The National Socialist revolution intensified self-scrutiny. Writing a diary or a private letter could fortify individual outposts of liberalism, or it could justify and harden National Socialist ideas.[10] By working with political concepts, diarists and other correspondents brought them into the field of possibility. Thus Karl Dürkefälden sketched out how Social Democratic workers in the Lower Saxon town of Peine explained to themselves their "adjustment" to National Socialism. Lore Walb's diary discussed what it meant to be a "comrade." Elisabeth Brasch's 1940 autobiography weighed the good and bad of the Reich Labor Service experience. In her letters, Elisabeth Gebensleben attempted to justify to her incredulous daughter the persecution of German Jews. Her own son struggled to square his National Socialist convictions with his love for a *Mischling,* or "half-Jew" (someone with one or two Jewish grandparents). In his diary entries, Erich Ebermayer made sense of his joy over Anschluss with Austria. Franz Göll's diary recorded the deep impression that Otto Dix's triptych *Der Krieg* made on him after he visited the exhibit on "Degenerate Art" in

Berlin. The sight of Erich Maria Remarque's *All Quiet on the Western Front* on a bookshelf launched countless arguments about the nature of war. Letters from the front testified to the demands of total war, including orders to shoot innocent civilians. Toward the end of the war, the diarist Lieselotte G. worked strenuously not to let her reservations about Hitler get the best of her. Autobiographical texts reveal different and nuanced opinions, and show how the activity of reflection persistently put opposing positions into play. Diaries transcribed the strain of conversion.

The debates that Germans conducted on war and peace are particularly interesting because they went over the same historical terrain as Nazi ideologues did without necessarily arriving at National Socialist resolutions. Friends and families disagreed sharply over *All Quiet on the Western Front,* which signaled both suspicion that Remarque's sober account remained relevant, even though the Nazis had banned the "pacifist" author, and desire to find some redemptive meaning to the war that had ended in Germany's defeat. The frenzied celebrations that took place whenever one more plank was ripped out of the Treaty of Versailles—Saar, Wehrmacht, Austria, Sudetenland—did not abridge the public's strong aversion to another European conflict. During World War II itself, Germans desperately wanted the war to end quickly, but they also fought on in order to avoid what they believed to be a devastating national collapse as in November 1918. It is striking how often conversations returned to the specter of 1918, particularly after 1943 and Germany's defeat at Stalingrad. However, this obsession with 1918 was the product of Nazi history, not the lingering effect of original traumatic experience. One of the great triumphs of the Nazis was the standardization of the "Stab-in-the-Back" legend.[11]

One look into the interior of a dentist's waiting room in Dresden confirmed the unsettled state of opinions about German history: "in the bookcase below the obligatory picture of Hitler, the complete Heine, Remarque, *All Quiet on the Western Front,* muster roll of his student fraternity, several World War histories and that of an infantry regiment." Victor Klemperer, the Jewish diarist who rendered the scene, concluded about the doctor: "certainly no Nazi." But the arrangement might have been more dynamic than Klemperer suggested, the picture of Hitler less obligatory, the world war histories as poignant as Remarque's novel.[12] Or take the example of the novelist Heinrich Böll. As a Wehrmacht soldier in his twenties, he argued against euthanasia, but he also preferred the nationalist writer Ernst Jünger to Remarque, and although he hated the Nazis for making him a killer, he wished for a German victory in the war. November 1918, Versailles, German rearmament, Hitler's wars, and the prospect of victory or defeat outlined a kind of *Sonderweg,* a special path of national tribulation that preoccupied millions of Germans from 1933 to 1945. The answers they found were not always consistent with National Socialism, but the questions they posed indicate how strongly they identified their lives with the collective fate and collective trials of the nation. This identification gave Nazi propositions about the people's community considerable legitimacy.

Germans who commented on the year 1933 frequently made note of Nazi violence, the arrest of political opponents, and the establishment of concentration camps. However, these were introduced as new but somewhat remote elements on the horizon; diaries and letters generally did not describe an atmosphere thick with fear. They do not leave behind traces of a terrorized society. And while diaries mention Hitler, note his birthday on 20 April, and often come to refer to him as "the Führer," Hitler was not the central figure that one might think for people living in the *Führerstaat.* The political scene in most diaries involves the local activities of the National Socialists and their auxiliary organizations, the SA, the SS, the women's groups, the Hitler Youth, and the Reich Labor Service. The Nazi project, not Hitler's charisma, was the main point of orientation, Nazi ideas and not Hitler's words the guiding maxims.

One more thing is striking: the radio was always on. The sights and sounds of the national revolution swept up both skeptics and sympathizers. The media choreographed what so many Germans desperately desired: the evidence of national political regeneration. Contemporary accounts indicate that Germans generally approached their neighbors as people who mobilized themselves, considered and moved toward Nazi positions, and occasionally, like one of the pouty characters in an Irmgard Keun novel, switched off the radio when Göring came on "because I always have the feeling of being scolded."[13] The diaries show not only how social pressures operated—Nazism, the Jews, and the war were frequent subjects of conversation—but also the ways in which friends and relatives felt the attractions of National Socialism and its social activism. Diarists retreated in an "inner emigration" from the dictates of public life, but they also embellished narratives of Germany's suffering since 1918. These autobiographical texts, along with other supporting materials, confirm that Germans were self-conscious, deliberate subjects, as much so in the Third Reich as in the Weimar Republic. National Socialism did not succeed through seduction or paralysis or hypnosis. It was by turns unsettling and meaningful to millions of people. Indeed "the willingness of most people . . . to discuss their political experiences" struck visitors to the Third Reich.[14]

German Jews ended up looking from the outside in, and in many ways they were much more astute observers. They, too, attempted to figure out the nature of Nazism and its appeal to other Germans. The diary of Victor Klemperer, a German Jew who converted to Protestantism as a young man and, until the Nazis forced his retirement in 1935 at the age of fifty-four, taught French literature at the Technical University in Dresden, documented in rich detail his shifting evaluations of the Nazis. Although Klemperer became increasingly convinced that National Socialism rested on a broad basis of popular support, he remained more alert than most non-Jewish diarists to small gestures and turns of phrase that suggested that Germans were not completely enamored of National Socialism. If there is a unifying theme to his diaries, it is Klemperer's continual effort to put himself in a position where he would be able to reconcile himself with Germany after the fall of Nazism. He recognized the appeal of Nazi ideas, but stressed the elements of fear, conformism, and skepticism.

At one point during the war Klemperer realized that Nazi Germany would be defeated, but, like other Jewish diarists across Europe, he was not certain that Jews would survive to see their liberation. The knowledge Jews acquired about Nazi war aims and the Holocaust was inevitably much more comprehensive than what most Germans understood. However, the war trapped most of Europe's Jews. Many of their wartime diaries end abruptly, mute testimony to the deportation and murder of the diarists. Non-Jewish Germans had more choices. They could even begin to prepare themselves psychologically for the end of the war and the downfall of Nazism. Reflecting on the 1943 firebombing of Hamburg, in which he lost most of his possessions, the writer Hans Erich Nossack refused to feel sorry for himself. "The ones to be pitied," he explained, were "those who still stand at the edge of the abyss, doubting that they can surmount it, because they are still thinking the way one had to think on the other side, squeezed in between yesterday and tomorrow." If the rest of Germany was still tied to the future of the Third Reich, Nossack occupied another "present" or had slipped away from "the precincts of time" altogether.[15] Yet at one point or another in the last year of the war, millions of Germans did cross Nossack's abyss and terminate their emotional investments in the Nazi regime, the people's community, and Germany's victory. This shift was often experienced as humiliation, for it involved canceling out all the years of effort and energy invested in the Nazi project. After 1945, a combination of shame and cynicism made it much less likely that postwar memories would reconstruct the paths of political conversion that led Germans into the disastrous war in the first place.

Nossack's term "abyss" is illustrative of how many Germans ended up displacing knowledge about the war and the Holocaust. While Klemperer, who picked over words very carefully, accumulated critical knowledge, Nossack dissolved what he saw into an overwhelming natural catastrophe that left him empty-handed. The choice, he himself acknowledged, had been to either "confess or forget, there is no third option."[16] The use of diaries and letters allows me to pursue a final aim in *Life and Death in the Third Reich*: an analysis of what Germans knew about the campaign of genocide against the Jews and what Germans and Jews could have known and were able to comprehend about events that we now think about as the Holocaust. The approaching end of the war produced a sense of futility, powerlessness, and even victimization among the German people. Germans often described the defeat in 1945 as the complete "collapse" of national life. It was many decades before a more precise understanding of the articulation of the Nazi racial state, the Holocaust, and the active participation of individuals in National Socialism emerged from imagery of "the abyss." In many ways, the final furious end to World War II, from Normandy to Berlin, overshadowed study of the Holocaust. Even so, Nossack's solitary figure on the other side of the "abyss" was fundamentally different from Dwinger's imaginary victims, because Nossack no longer looked to German history to redeem loss while Dwinger still did. This perspective made critical judgments about the course of Germany's history much more likely.

Images such as "abyss" and "collapse" are deceptive. They indicate how difficult it is to write about or comprehend the Holocaust and to account for the accumulation of individual actions that led to mass murder. National Socialism delivered a traumatic blow to Western thought; not even a thinker as radical as Friedrich Nietzsche could have imagined the Holocaust. Information about the

Nazi war against the Jews was known and collected, but it was not easily transformed into knowledge about genocide. Indeed, the whole phenomenon of Nazism represents a fundamental challenge to explanation, since conventional social and political categories do not seem adequate to account for it. An analysis of class relations, social milieus, and material deprivations goes only so far. Dictatorship and terror do not explain public enthusiasm or the individual's effort of conversion. The Nazis themselves argued that their movement was different precisely because National Socialism was rooted in collective racial thinking. Whereas Karl Marx maintained that being *(Sein)* influenced consciousness *(Bewusstsein)*, the Nazis assumed that the proposition could be run in reverse, so that consciousness determined being.[17] In other words, worldviews could bring a world into view. Insofar as the Nazis redescribed the world, and got the German people to go along some of the way, scholars need to take seriously National Socialist ideology and its concepts of community, nation, and race. It is important to know how Germans at the time struggled with and made sense of the new vocabulary. As a result, attempts to understand National Socialism are necessarily entangled in the political premises and linguistic categories of National Socialism itself—an unsettling thought. The Nazis are frightening because they expanded notions of what is politically and morally possible in the modern world.

My argument rests on an earlier interpretation that National Socialism evolved out of a dynamic that existed in German politics since 1914, in which war and revolution mobilized the German people in national projects of revitalization.[18] These projects raised the fortunes of Social Democrats and other republican forces at the beginning of the Weimar Republic, but they also sustained an ultranationalist insurrection against both the nations that had defeated Germany in World War I and the old monarchist elites who had failed to achieve victory. A longing for a new order dominated Weimar's political horizon and ultimately worked in favor of the

National Socialists, who combined populism, racism, and nationalism in a youthful, energetic way. The political and economic emergencies at the end of the Weimar Republic fortified the notion that only a new course could rehabilitate Germany.

Between 1930, at the beginning of the Great Depression, and 1933, when the National Socialist German Workers' Party came to power, the majority of voters who switched parties moved either to the Nazis, who peaked with 37 percent of the vote in July 1932, or to the Communists, who nearly overtook the Social Democrats with 17 percent in November 1932 during the last free elections. This parallel ascendancy set the stage for the brutal assault that the Nazis launched against the Communists and other Marxists after Hitler came to power on 30 January 1933. The urgent sense of crisis also meant that the Nazis had to make good on their election promises of "Work and Bread." The first steps the Nazis took to resolve Germany's dire political and economic problems was a violent assault against political enemies. But it is important to remember that the Nazis had also amassed considerable political capital. Nazi victories in the early 1930s had been overwhelming and sustained by the party's ability to draw voters from all social groups, including Catholics and industrial workers. Millions of Germans recognized the Nazi seizure of power in 1933 as a "national revolution" that marked a fundamental break in German history, something that emboldened sympathizers and paralyzed opponents. With a steadily improving labor market in 1933 and 1934, the National Socialists' ideal of the people's community came to enjoy broad legitimacy.

After 1933, more and more Germans participated in the Nazis' racial project of national renewal. The National Socialists very effectively connected the misfortunes of individual Germans in the Weimar years to the misfortunes of the nation, which they claimed had been mauled by any number of internal and external enemies—Jews, Communists, and the Allies. This linkage made credible the idea of the nation as an organic, if imperiled, unity whose renovation would improve the lives of individuals from all social backgrounds. More and more Germans came to believe that only national unity guaranteed social peace and economic stability. As a result, social and political realities were increasingly interpreted through the lens of community rather than the lens of class. People felt a greater sense of equality as Nazi propaganda and social activism, guided by the ideal of the people's community, delegitimated conceits of status and birth. Social equality remained incomplete, but the sheer forcefulness of social welfare and other reconstruction work strengthened the notion that national life could and would be remade.

However, emergency conditions defined the process of renovation at every step. The Nazis never believed that it would be possible to guide Germany to a safe sanctuary; in their view, collective life always remained imperiled, from both within and without. This sense of jeopardy had the effect of accelerating the restless mobilization of society. It helps explain the relentless, destructive, and ultimately self-destructive dynamic of Nazi Germany. Indeed, with the concept of race, National Socialists dramatized each of the elements in the equation of national renewal. Once racialized, dangers appeared to be more frightening, while solutions became more drastic and the mobilization they required more complete, and more likely to end in war. For the Nazis, race worked as an exponential power.

Chapter 1, "Reviving the Nation," explores the appeal of the people's community and the ways in which the distorting images of national acclamation were both misleading and appealing. The ambition of the Nazis to recompose the nation as a racial compact and the efforts of Germans to adjust to new racial identities are the subject of Chapter 2, "Racial Grooming." Here the analysis shifts to the subjunctive tense of politics, the struggle to fashion a new ethic consistent with racial comradeship: adhering to new standards of egalitarianism, segregating out "unworthy" life, and assaulting the interests and well-being of Jews in Germany. The most complete realization of National Socialism occurred during the war, which the Nazis regarded as a permanent state of being in order for the German race to expand and survive. Chapter 3, "Empire of Destruction," examines both the new imperial order that the Nazis set about to establish in the territories they conquered in Poland and the Soviet Union and the dynamic of unconditional destruction that led to the Holocaust. Given these aims, German life meant death. Chapter 4, "Intimate Knowledge," investigates how Germans and Jews understood the war, the Holocaust, and the prospect of the defeat of Nazi Germany. The chapter considers questions of comprehensibility and interpretation to ask what victims thought they were seeing. It also examines the ways in which the guilty knowledge of Germany's crime was entangled with fears of total collapse.

Central to my argument is an analysis of the effort that Germans made to become Nazis. I examine the appeal of National Socialist ideas—the desire to accept National Socialist standards of conduct, but also the difficulty in doing so—and the extent to which Germans made deliberate, self-conscious, and knowledgeable political choices in the Third Reich. Indeed, the morality of choice was a key theme in the intellectual lives of citizens. The goal of the Nazis was to create a new national and racial self-consciousness among Germans and thereby to make them aware of and complicit in new racial designs. This audacious, murderous, and self-destructive collaboration in the name of a new, revived Germany is the subject of the chapters that follow.

1

Reviving the Nation

"Heil Hitler!"

In September 1938, as the Sudeten crisis was heating up over Hitler's demand to annex the German-speaking territories of Czechoslovakia, Victor and Eva Klemperer took a drive from Dresden to Leipzig. Along the way, they took a break at a truck stop: "huge vehicles outside . . . huge portions inside." They walked inside just as the radio began to broadcast speeches from the Nazi party rally in Nuremberg: "Introductory march, roars of triumph, then Göring's speech, about the tremendous rise, affluence, peace and workers' good fortune in Germany . . . But the most interesting thing about it all," Klemperer noted, "was the behavior of the customers, who all came and went, greeting and taking their leave with 'Heil Hitler.' But no one was listening. I could barely understand the broadcast because a couple of people were playing cards, striking the table with loud thumps, talking very loudly. It was quieter at other tables. One man was writing a postcard, one was writing in his order book, one was reading the newspaper. And landlady and waitress were talking to each other or to the card players. Truly: Not one of a dozen people paid attention to the radio for even a single second, it could just as well have been transmitting silence or a foxtrot from Leipzig." "The behavior of the customers"—this is the fundamental topic Klemperer was trying to figure out as he observed daily

life. He was constantly on the lookout for what he called "vox populi" to provide him clues about popular support for Hitler and the
Nazis, but the voices were never definitive. "What is real, what is
happening?" Klemperer wondered about the Third Reich.[1]

Scholars have been asking the same question ever since. With the
publication in 1995 of the diaries of Victor Klemperer, historians
possess one of the most detailed firsthand accounts of life in Nazi
Germany, and yet, like Klemperer, they are not sure how to read
the evidence. What is more telling: the unselfconscious "Heil Hitler" greeting of the truckers or their disregard of the radio broadcast? Klemperer introduced the new sights and sounds of the Third
Reich, but was not sure whether the rituals really had changed the
attitudes of Germans. The scene at the truck stop perfectly captures
two sides of the debate about National Socialism. On the one hand,
historians stress the degree to which non-Jewish Germans accepted
Nazism as the normal condition of everyday life and even celebrated the new order. On the other hand, they point to evidence
that Germans simply went about their business, taking care to in-
tersect as little as possible with the Nazi party apparatus.

It is worth examining more closely everyday interactions and
how they changed in the years after Hitler's seizure of power. A few
months after January 1933, there was hardly a single person who
had not on occasion raised the right arm and exclaimed "Heil Hitler!" Most people did so several times every day. Berlin's "Guten
Tag," Hamburg's "Moin," and Bavaria's "Grüss Gott" could still
be heard, but "Heil Hitler!" worked itself so closely into the vocabularies of citizens that the final end to Nazism in 1945 was often remembered as the moment when "we never have to say Heil Hitler
again!" As early as July 1933, civil servants were required to use the
greeting in official communication. Schoolteachers "heil hitlered"
their students at the beginning of class, conductors on the Deutsche
Reichsbahn "heil hitlered" travelers when checking tickets, and
post office clerks "heil hitlered" customers buying postage stamps.

Klemperer himself was astonished to see "employees constantly raising their arms to one another" as he walked through the buildings of his university in the summer of 1933. Erika Mann, daughter of the novelist Thomas Mann, estimated that children saluted "Heil Hitler!" 50 or maybe 150 times a day, in any event "immeasurably more often than the old neutral greetings." But what did it mean to call out "Heil Hitler!"? What does the greeting, the raised arm, the casual reference to "the Führer" say about the relationship between Germans and Nazis in the Third Reich? How Nazi were Germans, really?[2]

That the Hitler greeting was compulsory for civil servants confirms the dictatorial power of the regime. After the war, many Germans testified that they felt coerced or bullied into saying "Heil Hitler!" Especially in the early months of the new regime, Nazi loyalists were quick to demand that citizens use the greeting in public. In the summer of 1933, visitors to the tourist destination of Weimar would have seen signs in stores, restaurants, and hotels bearing the "encouraging command: 'Germans Greet Each Other with Heil Hitler!'" In October 1933 the "German greeting" was made mandatory in the Leipzig theater where Erich Ebermayer worked. "Who cannot go along?" he confided to his diary; for this opponent of the Nazis, "Heil Hitler!" "is now my greeting at work." As more Germans said "Heil Hitler!" to one another, it became harder not to respond in kind. This dynamic makes it difficult to know whether huge numbers of people were really converts or merely conformists. It is also clear that many Germans did not go along at all. Individuals recalled abruptly crossing the street to avoid the greeting or remembered downgrading public shows of loyalty with "inaudible mumbles and feeble hand gestures." Visitors to the heavily Catholic regions of southern Germany or to Social Democratic and Communist neighborhoods would have heard "Heil Hitler!" less frequently. Jehovah's Witnesses refused outright to use the greeting. "Do you already know the new greeting?" someone asked a few months after Hitler had come to power: "forefinger in front of your lips."[3]

Yet for all the people who felt pressure to conform, there were others who applied pressure and insisted on the greeting. With "Heil Hitler!" Nazi party members attempted to recompose the body of Germans; the arc of the right hand raised at an angle in front of the body drastically expanded the physical claim of National Socialists to public space. The assertive gesture was accompanied by an unambiguous political declaration. Unlike "Guten Tag," which sought to reconcile neighbors without further ado, the hortatory "Heil Hitler!" constituted an assertive attempt to create and enforce political unity. "Heil Hitler!" expressed the desire of many Germans to belong to the national community and to participate in national renewal. They undoubtedly included the male and female nurses whom a friend of the Klemperers watched in April 1933 as they sat "around the loudspeaker" in the hospital lounge. "When the Horst Wessel Song is sung (every evening and at other times too), they stand up and raise their arms in the Nazi greeting."[4]

"Heil Hitler!" could also be used to make a claim for social recognition because it replaced more deferential greetings in everyday life. When the mailman greeted neighbors with an ostentatious "Heil Hitler!" he put them on notice that he was a *Volksgenosse,* or people's comrade, and their equal. In similar fashion, the boss who stood at the doorway of the factory canteen welcoming with a "Heil Hitler!" workers who had previously been excluded was not wiping away social differences, but he was acknowledging the new entitlements enjoyed by his employees. Even in the private space of the home, friends and relatives greeted each other with "Heil Hitler!," indicating the extent to which loyalists wanted to recognize the place of Hitler's national revolution in their own personal lives. With the aggressive upward, outward movement of the arm, "Heil Hitler!" occupied new social and political space and made it available to the Nazi movement. It enabled citizens to try on new political and racial identities, to demonstrate support for the "national revolution," and to exclude Jews from daily social interactions. To put the words "Heil Hitler!" only in the mouths of fanatics is to miss how Germans more and less willingly adjusted themselves to the unitary ideal of the people's community.

Since it was Hitler who was hailed, the greeting poses the question of the role of the German Führer in creating political consensus. Loyalty to Hitler strengthened the regime in critical ways, but it also set limits to what party activists could achieve, since support for Hitler did not necessarily imply support for Nazi policies. In other words, "Heil Hitler!" might well have covered up differences among Germans and covered for those who were not sympathetic to the Nazis. But precisely those people who considered "Heil Hitler!" nothing more than an ordinary greeting of the day or used it to disguise their own misgivings made it more commonplace. They thereby enhanced the sense of acclamation. To an outsider, it looked as though everyone was turning into a Nazi, a view that stepped up pressure to conform. Yet insiders were never sure whether support for the regime was genuine or halfhearted; the border between true believers and mere opportunists was not clear. For Jews, however, the distinction between apparent and real Nazis did not make much difference, since they, unlike other Germans, could not join in for the sake of appearance. Not able to "pass," they stood out all the more plainly in the Third Reich.

There is plenty of evidence to suggest that after the initial period of revolutionary mobilization waned, fewer people greeted each other with "Heil Hitler!" In Berlin, in particular, visitors in the mid-1930s expressed surprise that they did not hear the "German greeting" more often. In Munich, "they've completely stopped saying 'Heil Hitler,'" claimed CBS radio correspondent William Shirer in 1940.[5] Whether this shift indicated a weakening of support for the Nazis or simply the return to more relaxed conventions is not certain. In the third month of Germany's war with the Soviet Union, in September 1941, Klemperer reported that in Dresden "Good morning" or "Good afternoon" was said to be increasing. To see for himself, he set out to count "how many people in the shops say 'Heil Hitler' and how many 'Good afternoon.'" The results: "At Zscheischler's bakery five women said 'Good afternoon,' two said 'Heil Hitler'"; but at Ölsner's grocery store "they all said 'Heil Hitler.'" "Whom do I see, to whom do I listen?" Klemperer continued to wonder. As Germany's defeat became more certain, however, the balance undoubtedly shifted in favor of "Good afternoon." In February 1944 Franz Göll, an employee in a Berlin print shop, confided: "you seldom hear the greeting 'Heil Hitler' any more," or "you make a joke out of it" by saying "Heilt Hitler"—"heal Hitler" rather than "hail Hitler." To say it "at home" was "actually frowned upon," he continued, a reminder, of course, that Göll's friends and relatives had once upon a time greeted one another with "Heil Hitler!"[6]

"Heil Hitler!" illustrates both the coerced and self-assertive aspects of the national revolution in January 1933. It raises questions about the illusory nature of acclamation: since once everyone said "Heil Hitler!" the greeting no longer reliably indicated support for the regime. But much of the power of Nazism rested on the appearance of unanimity, which overwhelmed nonbelievers and prompted them to scrutinize their own reservations. Each raised arm undermined a little bit the ambiguous relations among neighbors and built up a little more the new racial collective of National Socialism. Did that mean that sympathies for Nazism had diminished when more people once again called out "Good afternoon" on a Berlin street? Like Klemperer, historians are still counting the "Heil Hitlers" outside Zscheischler's bakery in Dresden and are still figuring out what it meant when customers said "Good afternoon" instead.

How Far Did Germans Support the Nazis?

A few years before the Klemperers drove up to the truck stop in Saxony, a young American sociologist from Columbia University arrived in Berlin by train. Late in June 1934, Theodore Abel settled in his boardinghouse, went for a walk around bustling Potsdamer Platz, and had a drink in the huge entertainment emporium Haus Vaterland, with its selection of ethnically themed restaurants. Abel himself was busy counting "Heil Hitlers," a greeting that he found was used "only in official places," while "Guten Morgen" and "Auf Wiedersehen" prevailed in "everyday contacts."[7] The reason he had come to Berlin was to launch a mammoth research project on the Nazis. His project had an interesting twist. Unlike most sociologists, who would sample the group they wanted to study and analyze it according to age, generation, and social class in order to explain political behavior by social origin, Abel wanted to ask party members directly why they had become Nazis. His was the case study method pioneered by the Chicago School of Sociology. To proceed, he devised the idea of having "old fighters," those who had joined the party in the 1920s, write their autobiographies, and for this he needed the help of the Nazi party.

At first the Propaganda Ministry, which is where Abel had his contacts, was suspicious. As he put it in his diary, they "feared that I would not do justice to the imponderables and the declaration of faith and only use the factual material." But Abel gave them assurances that "it was in order to get at the imponderables that I conceived the idea of the life-histories." In other words, Abel wanted to explore the Nazi phenomenon by way of individual testimonies rather than reduce it to general statistics. The party subsequently ran a contest and collected hundreds of autobiographical statements for Abel to use. His 1938 book, *Why Hitler Came to Power,* was the fruit of his investigation and featured six extensive autobiographies at the end. The research stands as one of the most successful attempts to assess the political motivations of the Nazis. In his conclusions, Abel acknowledged the importance of social and economic factors, but he emphasized ideology: the role of the war experience, the shock of defeat, and the determination to rejuvenate the political structures of Germany. There were not sixty million ways to Nazism.[8]

I want to adapt Abel's method and introduce three life stories, based on diaries and letters, to show in greater detail how "Heil Hitler!" and "Good afternoon" combined with each other in the Third Reich. The lives of the Gebenslebens in Braunschweig in northern Germany, the Dürkefäldens in the nearby town of Peine, and Erich Ebermayer in Leipzig reveal ways in which Germans pulled away from and pushed toward the Nazis in the years after the seizure of power. Victor Klemperer's extraordinary diary surmised how his non-Jewish neighbors might have contemplated the Nazis. At first, he assumed that the regime relied on both fear and opportunism; later, without completely abandoning his earlier position, Klemperer considered more fundamental ideological and cultural affinities. He suggested that the Third Reich made "Aryans" feel at home—*unter uns,* "just us," was the phrase he used. The letters and diaries presented here offer opportunities to evaluate Klemperer's ideas and to analyze how Germans in the 1930s discussed themselves, their relations with Jews, and the future of the Third Reich.

Elisabeth Gebensleben, a lively forty-nine-year-old and the wife of Braunschweig's deputy mayor, was an ardent Nazi supporter. Gebensleben and her children had cheered the "national opposition" to the Weimar Republic for over a decade. Like millions of other Germans, she and her husband had switched their allegiance from the monarchist German National People's Party to the National Socialists in 1930. She described herself as the sort of person who turned "first to politics, then the features" when picking up the newspaper. Her letters brimmed with political observations, and those to her daughter, Irmgard, or Immo, who had married and moved to Holland, are especially detailed. Elisabeth attempted to evoke something of the excitement of 30 January 1933: "Monday morning," the Gebenslebens' maid "suddenly called out: 'lots of Hitler flags are being hung outside'"; Frieda could see them from the window of her room. "Well then your Dad came in with the extra edition. His face was one big smile, and I smiled as well." As the news sank in, "a couple of tears rolled out": "finally, finally," after years of "struggle," "the goal has been reached." For Elisabeth, the historical moment was especially poignant because a "simple man, who fought in the trenches, is sitting where Bismarck had once sat." She believed that Hitler offered Germany social and political reconciliation.[9]

For a combative nationalist such as Elisabeth, 30 January was the culmination of years of political work. It was the repudiation of the treasonous revolution of 1918 in the name of the patriotic unity of 1914. Nonetheless, Elisabeth worried about the "battles that will now come" and even wondered whether Hitler had arrived on the scene "too late" to beat the Communists. As it was, presidential decrees gave Hitler's new government unprecedented police powers, especially after the Reichstag Fire on the night of 27 February 1933; across Germany, police and Nazi stormtroopers arrested Social Democratic and Communist activists and shut down their newspapers and trade union offices. "The ruthless intervention of the nationalist government might appear strange to some," Elisabeth commented after the 5 March elections, in which the Nazi coalition emerged victorious, "but first we have to systematically clean up." More to the point, the "Communists have to disappear, and Marxists too," an afterthought referring to the Social Democrats, the only force in Germany loyal to the republican constitution. Suspicious of Communists who "suddenly want to become National Socialists," she refused to welcome former opponents into

the "people's community" until they served "a three-year proba-
tionary period in the concentration camps." Given this terror, it is
no wonder that the "Revolution from the Right" showed "more order and discipline" than the "Revolution from the Left" had in November 1918.[10]

As the Nazis became stronger, political divisions were less obviously visible, so that the unity of the nation, though rinsed in terror,
appeared to come into view. The big celebrations of the spring of
1933—the Day of Potsdam, which on 21 March choreographed the
alliance between Hitler and Hindenburg on the occasion of the in-
augural session of the new Reichstag; Hitler's birthday on 20 April;
and finally May Day, newly recognized as an official holiday to
honor workers and symbolize their integration into the state—were
revelations. Everywhere Elisabeth saw "national enthusiasm" and
"delirious happiness" and "deepest gratitude." "Is it possible that a
single man has been able to pull this off, to weld together a people
that had been divided and impoverished?"[11] Though Hitler was important, what attracted Elizabeth's attention were the sights and
sounds of the unity of the people, cheers, marches, swastika-emblazoned flags, and the radio broadcasts, which seemed to make audi-
ble a single collective voice. She was more interested in National Socialism than in Hitler.

But what about the "mean," "horrible" "campaign against the
Jews," Immo asked from Holland, where Jewish refugees had begun to arrive from Germany. This was not the first time Elisabeth
had been forced to reflect on Nazi violence. The brutal treatment of
Braunschweig's Social Democratic mayor she blamed on the "ex-
cesses" that came with every movement (although her son admitted "quite numerous black spots" as assaults on the Left increased
dramatically after the March 1933 elections). That only "Jewish
shops" had been vandalized in Braunschweig "would allow you to
come to the conclusion" that the Nazis were at fault, but Elisabeth
knew better: "dumb kids" had smashed in the windows. How-

ever, the officially organized boycott of Jewish businesses on 1 April 1933 required a more considered answer. Elisabeth began with a concession, contrasting the *"happiness"* of the world-historical events taking place in Germany with her "sympathy" for *"the fate of the individual."* Then Elisabeth pulled herself together to justify the boycott: "Germany is using the weapon it has" to respond to "the smear campaign" from abroad. In other words, Germans were the actual victims. The next word is predictable, since discussions about Jewish suffering frequently switched to the subject of German suffering: "Versailles" had taken the "opportunities for life" away from Germans, who were now "completely understandably" fighting back on behalf of their "own sons." Elisabeth's reasoning is faulty, but she argued that the Jews should make up in 1933 for what the Allies had taken in 1919 by restricting their representation in the professions to their proportion in the population: "that is one percent." Moreover, she explained, "Jews want to rule, not serve." The proof: "have you ever heard of a Jewish maid or a Jewish laundry woman?" (Elisabeth had heard this from Frieda, a sign that "Aryan" employer and employee might be banding together against Jews.) The rhetoric in Elisabeth's letter recapitulated the work of becoming a Nazi. Elisabeth confronted Nazi terror, but after a moment of hesitation she dismissed the evidence as accidental or justified it in the name of German suffering. "Tonight Hitler speaks," she remarked in closing: "I *definitely* have to hear that" on the radio.[12]

The Gebenslebens would continue have to think about their identities as Nazis and their relationship to Jews. Elisabeth threw herself into volunteer work for the National Socialist women's organization, while her son, Eberhard, joined the stormtroopers, the SA. He deployed to training camps several times, first as a paramilitary soldier, then as a lawyer working in the Ministry of Economics. A niece became a leader in the League of German Girls. Leadership courses, training camps, paramilitary service—this was the new rhythm of life for ambitious professionals in the Third Reich. A wardrobe of uniforms, badges, certificates, and souvenir photographs documented their advances up the administrative ladder. During the war, however, Eberhard's career was jeopardized when he fell in love with Herta Euling, a pianist, who was three years older and whose grandmother was Jewish. If the two young people had married, Eberhard would have been forced out of the Nazi party, which in February 1944 rejected his appeal and even initiated an inquiry into whether his membership was still "acceptable." Eberhard's dilemma about what had the chief claim to loyalty in the Third Reich, whether love or career or ideology, was discussed openly and at length. Ultimately his family opposed the marriage but continued to think well of Herta.[13] It is clear that Eberhard was a dedicated National Socialist; one of his oldest friends broke with him over his convictions. Nonetheless, Eberhard came to see how the Third Reich might have been seen from different perspectives, Herta's first of all. As a German officer, he was also forced to see himself through the eyes of Dutch civilians when in 1941 Immo extracted from him a promise never to wear the uniform of German occupiers or to speak German in public when visiting her family. There was no final resolution to the discussions between the Nazi loyalist and his *Mischling* fiancé, whose traces have been completely lost, or between the Wehrmacht officer and his Dutch relatives. Eberhard Gebensleben was killed in Belgium in September 1944.

Elisabeth's family identified with the Nazis and took part in the task of building the National Socialist community. Karl Dürkefälden, by contrast, opposed the regime throughout the twelve years of the Third Reich. Born in 1902 to the son of a factory foreman, Dürkefälden began keeping a diary in 1932, the year in which he found himself unemployed, newly married, and living with his wife, Gerda, in his parents' house in Peine. His entries closely explored issues of the day. He documented labor struggles at the end of the Weimar Republic and, after 1933, tracked the motivations of neighbors who joined the Nazi movement or at least made peace with the new government. Later he pieced together local accounts of the pogrom against German Jews in November 1938. During World War II he carefully collected eyewitness accounts of the brutal treatment of Russian prisoners of war, who had been shipped to his region as slave laborers, and of the murder of Jews in the German-occupied Soviet territories. Karl attentively portrayed his working-class neighborhood, exposing political divisions between Left and Right that were as deep in Peine as they were in Braunschweig, just twenty-five kilometers away. But Dürkefälden was also able to describe something Elisabeth Gebensleben could not, namely, the story of how working-class conversions helped to create National Socialism.

Whereas Elisabeth regarded January 1933 as a triumphant "Revolution from the Right," Karl referred to the events more vaguely as an *Umwälzung,* a sudden, unexpected overthrow, in which many of his neighbors underwent a rapid *Umstellung,* an adjustment or conversion, to Nazism. The nature of conversion differed from family to family. Karl was dismayed at how quickly his father, mother, and sister Emma had turned into enthusiastic supporters of the Nazis. The three had even gone to Kaune's Tavern to hear the live broadcast of the ceremonies in Potsdam on 21 March. When Karl protested that local Nazis had arrested young workers in the neighborhood and seized a trade union building, his father retorted in dialect, "Ordnung mot sein," "You have to have order." As far as his father was concerned, "the Nazis could do no wrong." Meanwhile Karl and Gerda traveled to visit her parents, who lived near Hanover: "of course we also talked about the political situation. They have not yet changed their opinion." His brother-in-law, Walter Kassler, had not "adjusted himself" either. But Karl's turns of phrase indicated that many other acquaintances had converted to Nazism. Hans Kinne, the husband of Gerda's friend Irma, for example, "is now a Nazi because of his job, but only for show." Peine's barber was in the SA, but Karl thought for "professional reasons" only. His later addition of the words "not so" to the diary entry suggests that Karl initially had trouble believing that so many people converted for any other reason than opportunism. Only later did it become clear to him that conviction had played a role as well. *Umstellung* also depended on how individuals regarded the future. Another family friend, Hermann Aue "(very Left)," thought the Nazis would be gone within a year, so he was inclined to stick with the Social Democrats. But several Communists who had reportedly joined a local SA group suspected that the Nazis would be around for some time. As one put it, "with wolves you have to run with the pack."[14]

Karl left a striking image of May Day celebrations in Peine. He described the flags, the marches, the songs, the speeches honoring Germany's workers and praising Hitler. As usual, the *Waldesgrün* choir provided entertainment, but, as Karl noted, it had already cut its ties to the socialist German Federation of Workers' Choral Societies. Almost everyone seemed to be caught up in the excitement. The streets were full. Karl and Gerda, however, "stayed at the kitchen window, because we didn't want to join in shouting hail to Adolf Hitler. And I didn't want to take off my hat during the Horst Wessel Song." Karl was inside his house looking out, but politically he was on the outside looking in, and what he saw was an increasingly Nazified community in which neighbors now took notice of Karl's behavior and club members adjusted their own. What Karl was resisting as he stood alongside his wife was the pressure to conform, if only for the sake of appearances. His father told him as much the next day. He quoted what he had understood from Hitler's big May Day speech: "Hei hatte sagt, wer non ganz un gar nich wolle, vor dän in Deutschland keine Raum"—"he said there is no room in Germany for people who simply refuse to take part." "No one is supposed to be neutral," his father added, speaking this time not as a Nazi enthusiast exhorting Karl to join, but as a small-town resident warning his son of the dangers of not doing so.[15] With the word *Umstellung* Karl captured the ways in which Peine's citizens coordinated themselves. The day before Hitler's birthday, Karl's father stuck a postcard with the Führer's picture into the glass pane of the kitchen cabinet; a few months later, he came home with a framed portrait of Hitler for which he had paid 1.50 Reichsmarks, a big expense for an extended family with only one income. At the same time, Karl's brother, Willi, who had joined the SA, showed sudden interest in his wartime diaries and letters; he was reconceiving his autobiography as a German patriot. The only worrisome thing was the prospect of a new war, a topic German families discussed frequently in the years after 1933. Making his first appearance at the Dürkefäldens one Sunday, Emma's new boyfriend recalled his temporary blindness after having been shot in the head in the last war; "he doesn't want to take part in any war again," Karl reported; "he has had enough." Finally, on the occasion of another family gathering, to celebrate Gerda's birthday in February 1934, Karl's father-in-law admitted that he had "made his peace" with "the new direction." The factory in Hanover was booming, old employees had been rehired, and vacations once reserved for senior managers had been extended to ordinary workers like Friedrich Kassler. Karl and Gerda were now alone.[16]

The divisions that cut across the Dürkefäldens' kitchen table cut right through Erich Ebermayer. On 30 January 1933 the thirty-two-year-old screenwriter had listened to the radio broadcast of the celebrations in Berlin in the company of Klaus Mann, son of the novelist: "marches, marches . . . now the Horst Wessel Song . . . now shrill commando orders, drum rolls, thunderous singing." To his diary, he remarked bitterly, "we are the losers, definitely the losers." And like Karl Dürkefälden, Erich felt the enormous force of the Nazis, who seemed to sweep everything up in front of them. "There doesn't seem to be anything but 'BDM girls' and Hitler Youth on the streets. Young people don't walk anymore; they march." "Everywhere friends are professing themselves for Hitler." To live in Nazi Germany, Ebermayer wrote, was to "become ever more lonely." However, in order to be "a chronicler of this time," Erich listened regularly to broadcasts of Hitler's speeches. He switched the radio on during the Nuremberg party rally in September 1935 to find out "what satanic thing these gentlemen have conjured up." In this case it was the Nuremberg Laws, which distinguished German citizens from Jewish noncitizens: "hunting down innocent people is expanded a thousand times," he raged; "hate is sown a millionfold."[17] Erich was not a Nazi.

Yet he did something very consistent with Nazi ideas. Feeling drawn to the rural places where he had grown up, he eventually purchased a cottage in a small Bavarian village. Already in April 1934 he had returned to his hometown of Landrak in the Harz Mountains to watch the traditional bonfire on the Saturday before Easter: "We stand in the garden . . . and look up to see the flames eating through the timbers . . . The breath of fresh fields, the smell of the wood fires in the farmhouses lies in the air . . . The boys and girls up there are bounding around the fire and dancing. Singsong, loud calls, and laughter can be heard across the valley." This prompted the observation that "War, Revolution, Inflation, the System, the Third Reich have left these old customs completely untouched."[18] Interestingly, he used the Nazi term "System" to denote the Weimar Republic in his imaginary timeline. In any case, Erich Ebermayer was *not* alone; in fact, he felt very much at home. His world had not changed.

This sense of homecoming put Erich on the same emotional register as millions of Nazi sympathizers. He was also attuned to National Socialist choreography. On the Day of Potsdam, as the Gebenslebens gathered around the radio and the Dürkefäldens sat at Kaune's, the Ebermayers believed that "not even we could exclude ourselves." As Erich hauled "the old black-white-red flag from the world war" up from the basement and stored away "the good, disgraced, betrayed, never sufficiently appreciated" black-red-gold flag of the republic in its place, he conceded that a new era had begun. Upstairs, he listened to the ceremonies with his father, who was "deeply moved," and his mother, who had "tears in her eyes." Just the day before, Erich had reported on "big camps" built in Dachau and Oranienburg. Nonetheless, the desire to be part of national unity was so strong that it pulled even an anti-Nazi such as Erich into the new political community. Later he wept for joy on the occasion of the Anschluss with Austria in March 1938. "*Not* to want it," he wrote, "just because it has been achieved by Hitler would be folly."[19] Unlike Karl Dürkefälden, who remained an outsider, at crucial moments Erich willingly surrendered himself to the embrace of the national community. He repeatedly described Germany as a nation that had come home to itself. While Erich hated the Nazis, he loved the Third Reich.

What do these transcripts tell us about how Germans viewed the Nazis? The question of Nazism clearly divided neighborhoods in Peine, families like the Dürkefäldens, and even individuals such as Erich Ebermayer. Karl Dürkefälden's diary is particularly instructive because it reveals how family gatherings generated ongoing conversations about the nature of the regime, the modalities of individual conduct, and the threat of war. In the Third Reich, families hotly debated the prediction that "Hitler means war" or the excuse that "you can't make an omelet without breaking an egg" or the concession "give credit where credit is due." These disagreements confirm that Germans responded to the Nazis in contradictory ways. In Dürkefälden's milieu, it was quite clear who supported the Nazis, who "adjusted," and who kept his hat on when the Horst Wessel Song was played. Indeed, neighbors were quite self-reflective about the process of conversion and how it was qualified, as Dürkefälden's comment about neutrality or his father-in-law's testimony about peacemaking indicated. Throughout the existence of the Third Reich, people also shifted their positions, with more Germans coming round to the Nazis as Friedrich Kassler had, although some moved further away, as was the case with Karl's sister Emma, who came to distrust Hitler. Individuals themselves were ambivalent, as the example of Erich Ebermayer illustrates. Even an SA man such as Eberhard Gebensleben conceded the extravagance of Nazi violence and questioned his faith in National Socialism after he fell in love with Herta. Immo herself reminds us that simply moving to Holland could drastically alter perspectives. The ambiguities of political conviction need to stay in view. Therefore it is difficult to make neat distinctions between "Nazis" and "Germans." Readers need to remember Herta Euling as well as Elisabeth Gebensleben when considering "Nazis" and to recall Erich Ebermayer as well as Karl Dürkefälden when thinking about non-Nazis and other "Germans."

All the talk about the Nazis revealed one more thing: the effort Germans made to defend their positions and to justify their actions. Millions of people acquired new vocabularies, joined Nazi organizations, and struggled to become better National Socialists. What the diaries and letters report on is not simply the large number of conversions among friends and relatives but the individual endeavor to become a Nazi. In April 1933, Elisabeth Gebensleben, for example, felt the need to explain the Nazi-sponsored boycott of Jewish businesses, although issues about Jews had never before come up in her correspondence. This ideological work was not always easy or welcome, and new Nazi identities remained incomplete, but the majority of Germans struggled to convert in one form or another. It was the broad effort on the part of population to adjust to the coordination of public life in 1933, to new racial regulations regarding Jews later in the 1930s, and to the requirements of total war after 1941 that continuously strengthened and radicalized the Nazi regime. Even so, conversion was an ongoing process, riddled with doubt, rather than a single, final destination.

Germans converted to National Socialism out of fear and for the sake of appearances. Indeed, each diary refers to concentration camps, arrests, and other violence. Moreover, pressure to conform to Nazi expectations persisted, a fact that Karl's father tried to point out. Like Friedrich Kassler, Germans also converted because they were persuaded finally that Nazism represented a "new direction," which offered opportunities and to which citizens simply had to adapt. In addition, there were countless people who mistrusted the Nazis, misunderstood their racial precepts, and resented their hostility to the churches, but nonetheless endorsed the "national revolution" of January 1933 and the political reconciliation it appeared to achieve. In some ways, Erich Ebermayer falls into this category. Finally, Germans converted because they were genuinely attracted to the social and political vision of National Socialism and particularly to the promise of the people's community. Alongside the Dürkefäldens and Gebenslebens, most Germans came to believe that National Socialism had healed German history. It seemed to offer them a new, improved version of national life. A majority of Germans preferred the Nazi future to the Weimar past. This majority did not coalesce on every point of Nazi policy, certainly not on the deportation and murder of Germany's Jews. But millions of Germans eagerly consumed the images of national unity. They identified their own prospects for a better, richer life with the fortunes of the new order; private happiness came to be deeply entangled with the public well-being of the Third Reich. Even after the war, more people identified with the overall program of National Socialism than with Hitler himself.[20]

Historians have been uncomfortable with the proposition that most Germans *desired* the Nazis. They have been rightly skeptical about making large claims for different kinds of people. As the letters and diaries confirm, Germans frequently viewed Nazi policies with apprehension. When they followed the lead of the party or joined its auxiliary organizations they did not always do so out of conviction. Social frictions continued to contradict the claims of the Nazis about the new people's community. The Nazis also did not undo loyalties of history and emotion connecting Germans to traditional conservative values or to Social Democracy or to religious communities. Karl Dürkefälden and Erich Ebermayer testified to that. These are important qualifications, but they risk overlooking the startling success the Nazis had in drawing converts from all political camps and in tapping and creating desire for the renewal of German life. It was the experience of conversion, which left people like Dürkefälden and Ebermayer isolated, that was new and provided the Third Reich with legitimacy and energy. This is what needs to be explained.

Volksgemeinschaft, or the People's Community

The enduring popularity of the Nazis rested on the idea of the Volksgemeinschaft, or people's community. It was not a Nazi idea, and it was not perceived as something imposed or strange. On the contrary, the Nazis were credited with finally putting into place the national solidarity that Germans had long yearned for. This is an important point because many of the achievements of the "national revolution" in 1933 were cherished by citizens who did not necessarily identify with National Socialism. The legitimacy that Hitler and his regime enjoyed rested on a wider basis of goodwill. The national revolution came before the Nazis, even if the Nazis were the indispensable means for its realization.

Since World War I, the people's community had stood for reconciliation among Germans who had long been divided by class, region, and religion. Already the "August Days" of 1914, when thousands of Germans rallied in the streets to support the national cause in time of war, revealed extraordinary emotional investment in the promise of national unity. Of course, German politics did not dissolve into collective harmony, and "1914" was always more a manufactured image than an experienced reality. Nonetheless, the idea of national solidarity resonated because it seemed to offer more social equality. It showed a path to integrate workers into national life, to break down the caste mentalities of middle-class Germans, and to disarm the deference demanded by the country's elites. Its democratic or populist quality was crucial to its appeal. The people's community was also always a statement of collective strength. It expressed "the peace of the fortress" that enabled Germans to mobilize against their external enemies in World War I. This martial aspect became more important after Germany's defeat in 1918. The calamity of the unexpected surrender, the "bleeding borders" redrawn in the postwar settlement at Versailles, and the overwhelming chaos of the inflation in the early 1920s were collective experiences that made the suffering of the nation more comprehensible. During the Weimar years, the people's community denoted the beleaguered condition Germans shared, while expressing the political unity necessary for national renewal. As a result, there was always something dramatically embattled about the Volksgemeinschaft.

The Nazis took the notion of the people's community to its most radical conclusion. They seized on the evidence of German suffering and at the same time refurbished the prospects of Germany's greatness in the future. They hammered away at internal and external enemies—Jews, profiteers, Marxists, the Allies—who allegedly obstructed national regeneration. National Socialism offered a comprehensive vision of renewal, which many Germans found appealing, but they combined it with the alarming specter of national disintegration. In the Nazi view, 1914 stood for renewal and life, while 1918 threatened Germans with revolution, chaos, and ultimately death.

The opposition between 1914 and 1918 structured political thought in Germany right up to 1945. The Nazis elaborated a fundamentally embattled worldview in which only struggle guaranteed the preservation of life; indeed, struggle was a sign of life. Seen from this drastic perspective, the people's community was inescapably endangered and implicitly violent. The state of permanent emergency declared by the National Socialists helps explain the tremendous efforts that they and their followers made to reconstruct the collective body and the satisfaction they took in images of unity and solidarity. It also helps explain the violent exclusions they accepted as part of the rebuilding process. Basic elements of the Nazi worldview, including the intense fear of the complete breakdown of national life, the resolve to avoid the chaos of 1918, and the moral calculation that to preserve life might involve destroying it, circulated widely in the Third Reich. These assumptions were never the only elements in the mix, but Germans worked with them, and debated them, as they considered Nazi policies and their own behavior. Only diehard Nazis, however, followed the logic of violence as life to the bitter end in 1945.

The idea of national solidarity expressed the desires of millions of Germans who deplored the November Revolution of 1918 and who mistrusted the Weimar Republic for the power it gave to Social Democrats. It also appealed to citizens frightened by the economic insecurity and political instability of the early 1930s. For many supporters of the republic, especially among the six million Germans who for months and years had found themselves without prospects of employment, the people's community provided a tentative answer to the bitter question posed in 1933 by the novelist Hans Fallada: "Little Man, What Now?" "Something had to be done"— these were the simple, conclusive words voiced by a friend of Karl Dürkefälden's, jobless and a new convert to Nazism. His words were echoed by thousands of workers in the winter and spring of 1933; though a socialist, Karl himself understood—"it's true too," he added parenthetically in his diary entry.[21] Countless Germans identified their own impoverishment with the misfortunes of Germany and hoped that strong-armed leadership in Berlin would improve their lot. The fact remains, however, that in no free election did Nazis receive more votes than did Social Democrats and Communists combined. National Socialists made significant inroads among workers. They could count on sympathizers in other parties. But the political housecleaning they promised required breaking the power of the socialists.

On the evening of 30 January 1933, hundreds of thousands of citizens rallied around the uniformed party members who marched through Berlin's Brandenburg Gate to celebrate the Nazi victory. "Heils" and "Hochs" and "Hurrahs" resounded between the choruses of "Deutschland über Alles" and the Nazi's own anthem, the Horst Wessel Song. The crowds were reported to be as big as those in 1871, when Germans gathered to celebrate unification. Watching from the windows of the French embassy on Pariser Platz, the French ambassador, André François-Poncet, described the scene: "From these brown-shirted, booted men, as they marched in perfect discipline and alignment, their well-pitched voices bawling war-like songs, there rose an enthusiasm and dynamism that were extraordinary. The onlookers, drawn up on either side of the marching columns, burst into a vast clamor." "For hours the columns marched by," remembered Melita Maschmann, who had been at the Brandenburg Gate with her parents and twin brother: "I was overcome with a burning desire to belong to these people for whom it was a matter of life and death." Maschmann herself was drawn to the "socialist tendency" of the Nazi movement, the idea of the people's community, which she contrasted with the conservative reserve of her parents. Nonetheless, her parents were there, too. German Nationalists rather than Nazis, they had come to the city center to witness the historic event, just as they had joined patriotic crowds to celebrate the British departure from Cologne in 1925 and to honor President Paul von Hindenburg on his eightieth birthday in 1928. For the Maschmanns, for the Gebenslebens, and for millions of others, the Nazi triumph was the culmination of a nationalist uprising that had been years in the making. As a result, 30 January 1933 was never completely owned by the Nazis. Similar scenes, in which Nazis and well-wishers took over public places, occurred throughout Germany. No one could overlook the massive size of the national assembly in 1933.[22]

Yet Social Democrats had held a mammoth rally on the Lustgarten, across from the old Hohenzollern palace, the day before. One week earlier, Communists had gathered in front of the Karl-Liebknecht House, their party headquarters on the Bülowplatz. There was no reason for observers to think that the Nazis represented the entire nation. In the days that followed, socialists responded with counterdemonstrations throughout Germany. But their numbers thinned quickly. The strong presence of the police, who tended to sympathize with the National Socialists, restricted the mobility of opponents, while Nazi toughs broke into Social Democratic or trade union offices and Nazi officials banned socialist newspapers. Moreover, the accumulating wave of violence against the Left was officially sanctioned by emergency decrees that permitted the pretrial detention of citizens suspected of threatening the peace. After the Reichstag fire on 27 February, unprecedented, broad emergency powers, which President Hindenburg granted the new government to protect "people and state," enabled the Nazis to conduct massive assaults against Communists. The terror widened further after national elections on 5 March 1933. After a narrow victory, in which the Nazis and their coalition partner, the German National People's Party, received 52 percent of the vote, stormtroopers launched violent offensives against Social Democrats, Communists, and Jews, including elected officials. Thousands of opponents were incarcerated in makeshift prisons and endured beatings and humiliations. More than 100,000 Germans passed through Dachau, Oranienburg, and other concentration camps in 1933 and 1934.

The terror was revenge on the Left after years of street fights, and payback for 1918. But the fury of the violence was also tied to the fact that the Nazis recognized only *Volkskameraden*, people's comrades, and *Volksfeinde*, enemies of the people, whom they subjected to deliberate and refined cruelties in a "willful transgression of norms."[23] Nothing better illustrates the new normalcy of Nazi violence than a set of staged photographs in the Nazi magazine, *Illustrierter Beobachter*. It showed children playing a version of "Cowboys and Indians": "The SA storms the Karl-Liebknecht House." Shots depicted playmates in detention and on guard in a makeshift concentration camp. In this imaginary mobilization, the perpetrators transformed themselves into the childlike victims they always professed themselves to be. The construction of the first concentration camps to media fanfare in March 1933, and the rapid migration of the shorthand KZ, for *Konzentrationslager*, into ordinary speech, left the public well aware that Nazis recognized only friends or foes; as Karl Dürkefälden's father understood, there was no neutral ground. This knowledge kept friends in line lest they be considered foes, but also worked the other way around, reassuring friends since it was only foes who were in the camps. Violence against purported enemies of the people remained constitutive of German politics until the very end of the Third Reich; the arrest of socialists continued through the summer of 1933 and presaged Nazi assaults on "asocials," Jews, Gypsies, and other racial enemies who purportedly obstructed the healthy development of the Volksgemeinschaft. Whether one stood inside or outside the people's community, something that was not always a matter of choice, could very well be a matter of life or death.

Opponents of the Nazis were further paralyzed by the choreography of national acclamation, which had the result of pulling more and more people into the spectacle while leaving skeptics increasingly isolated. Support for the Nazis was real enough, but the Nazis worked hard to project the appearance of near-complete unanimity. Just like the sight and sound of "Heil Hitler!" these images tended to become self-authenticating; creating the illusion of inevitability, they won more people over. Moreover, since the images of unity were themselves appealing they became more real. Already on the evening of 30 January the new minister of the interior, Wilhelm Frick, imposed the live broadcast of the *Volksjubel*, or people's jubilation, in Berlin onto reluctant radio station chiefs around the country. In the national broadcast, selected party members spoke out the scripted reactions of "ordinary citizens," who, appearing from all walks of life, expressed support for Hitler.[24] This stage management of the "man on the street" would be repeated again and again. It was intended to create an undivided German voice that could be broadcast back to the nation as the mediated echo of its own desire.

The spectacle of national unity made an unusually strong impression on Germans. The diarists and correspondents in Braunschweig, Peine, and Leipzig paid considerable attention to the celebrations accompanying the Day of Potsdam and May Day. Both true believers such as the Gebenslebens and skeptics such as Ebermayer found themselves swept up in the commotion.

Held on 21 March 1933 in Potsdam's Garnisonkirche, where Frederick the Great lay buried, the Day of Potsdam aligned Hitler with revered Prussian traditions, the Hohenzollern dynasty and the founding of the German Reich some sixty years earlier, and the heroic sacrifices of the Great War, represented by the "hero of Tannenberg," President Paul von Hindenburg, whom Hitler had so vigorously opposed in presidential elections just one year earlier. Thousands of postcards depicted Hitler and Hindenburg shaking hands and sealing the union of the new and old Germany. The pageantry of military music and church bells, and the intimate scene in the Garnisonkirche, made for a great radio broadcast. This is the significance of the Day of Potsdam: the images of unity were made available for national consumption. The growth in radio ownership especially in 1933 and 1934 indicates how great the desire was to partake in Nazi spectacle, although the fact that radios remained much less common in rural areas also indicated the limits to mobilization. Two days after the Day of Potsdam, the Nazis won passage of the Enabling Act. Supported by all the parties except the Social Democrats (Communist deputies had been banned), it provided the legal framework for dictatorship.

The coupling of Hindenburg and Hitler impressed nationalists and conservatives who had been divided by the presidential campaigns of 1932, but offered socialists very little. Joseph Goebbels, Hitler's chief strategist newly installed as minister for public enlightenment and propaganda, understood that the Nazis had not gone beyond conventional nationalist iconography or projected a compelling image of what the new Germany would look like. A few days after the Potsdam ceremonies, Hitler accepted Goebbels' suggestion that the regime declare the first of May, which in 1933 fell on a Monday, to be a paid holiday and organize an elaborate commemoration to honor German workers. Socialists around the world had celebrated May Day as a festival of labor since the 1880s; but in Germany they had failed to get the official recognition the Nazis now offered. So strong were the hopes for national unity that the German Free Trade Unions welcomed the Nazi gesture and encouraged members to participate in the celebrations. May Day 1933 stood in sharp contrast to previous May Days, when workers had demonstrated as determined opponents rather than potential beneficiaries of the system. But the stunning media spectacle of the speeches and celebrations of 1 May also contrasted with 2 May, when stormtroopers sealed off and took over the operations of the socialist Free Trade Unions and incorporated them into what became the German Labor Front, an integral part of the National Socialist apparatus. This dramatic sequence of events appeared to be a typical Nazi combination of flattering words and oppressive deeds.

What was the lasting consequence of 1 May 1933? Without workers, the Nazis did not believe they would be able to banish the specter of 1918 or transform Germany into an economic and military power. National Socialist efforts to win over workers were the ultimate test of the credibility of the people's community. The elder Dürkefälden was already an insider, and his Social Democratic son always remained an outsider, but between father and son stood millions of workers who only gradually came to accept the Nazis. However, eventually most workers credited the Nazis with restoring economic stability, and many saw themselves as *Volksgenossen*. They got their first look at the people's community on 1 May 1933. "Only then was the National Socialist state on stable foundations," Goebbels recalled ten years later.[25]

Goebbels gave the cues for the May Day celebrations: "Decorate your houses and the streets of your cities and villages with fresh greenery and the flags of the Reich! The pennant of national revival should flutter from every automobile and every truck! There should not be a train or streetcar in Germany without flowers and greenery! The flags of the Reich will fly over factory towers and office buildings! No child should be without a little black-white-red or swastika flag!" The aim was to send the message that "Germany honors Labor."[26] However, May Day was not a holiday to do as one liked. Many participants such as Hanover's Friedrich Kassler were required to assemble at work before marching in formation to the parade ground. But the regime's expectations that Germans from all walks of life join in also made good its intentions to break down the hostility between workers and burghers.

May Day was an unabashed celebration of German nationalism in which German workers played the major roles. All day long, as Berliners made their way to the parade grounds at Tempelhof, the radio played the songs of "miners, farmers, and soldiers," broadcast a "symphony of work," and featured interviews with (specially selected) ordinary fellows: a dockworker from Hamburg, an agricultural laborer from East Prussia, a metalworker from the (French-occupied) Saar, a miner from the Ruhr, and a vintner from the Mosel Valley. They were the links that composed the great chain of German being. When "workers' poets" read from their work

(3:05 P.M.), they reproduced the "authentic" voice of the "man on the street" to broadcast German nationalism in an appealing vernacular. Later in the afternoon the essayist Eugen Diesel, son of the engineer, opened up a treasure chest of enchanting words to describe the hand-built landscape of power lines, factories, and fields that attested to the vitality of the Third Reich (6:20 P.M.). All the while, squadrons of airplanes overflew Tempelhof. Among the pilots was the ever-popular Ernst Udet, whom Social Democrats would have instantly recognized, since he used to perform in their ceremonies. For one hour in the afternoon, Germany's new ocean-crossing zeppelin circled over the city as part of its twenty-six-hour tour of the nation. The airshow was particularly popular in working-class circles because it displayed the mechanical skills of German laborers as part of a wider spectacle of national power. Even before Hitler spoke (8:00 P.M.), the choreography of May Day had fastened the links between workers and the nation, between machinists and machine-age dreams, between technical mastery and national prowess.[27] By repeatedly cutting from events in Tempelhof, to reportage from onboard the zeppelin, to the "songs of miners, farmers, and soldiers" in Thüringen or Franconia, to the interviews that widened the perspective to far-flung outposts of the Reich, and back again, the radio broadcast created a single audio space across Germany. Fireworks brought May Day came to an end shortly before midnight. It was "the biggest demonstration of all times," the *Berliner Morgenpost*, formerly a leftist newspaper, happily gushed the next day.[28]

Most participants did not pay close attention to Hitler's words, but his speech reveals the way in which Nazis tried to supplant the Social Democrats. Hitler repeatedly addressed workers as patriots who had built Germany's industrial strength and served honorably in the war, but who had been unjustly oppressed by liberal economic orthodoxies. He employed a rhetoric of understanding and compassion that recognized the perspective of the working class.

With his references to World War I, he sought out the historical location where the Nazis might have common ground with workers—a few weeks later, Willi Dürkefälden, for one, looked to retrieve his own war diary. Hitler implied that Germany was coming back to workers and to the wartime ideals of the Volksgemeinschaft. He attempted to dissolve class divisions in the future by acknowledging their social basis in the past. In this regard, Social Democracy figured less as an opponent of National Socialism than as a relic of an older time that had outlived its usefulness.[29]

Over the coming years the Nazis took care to align themselves symbolically with workers. Hitler registered to vote in the working-class Berlin precinct Siemensstadt, and enjoyed a great propaganda bonanza when he spoke from the floor of the Siemens factory in a nationally broadcast radio address on 10 November 1933. Hitler's success at Siemens might have given Goebbels the idea for placing leading functionaries of the regime in Germany's factories. At least two took on these roles: the propagandist Wolfgang Diewerge worked for two months at Daimler-Benz near Stuttgart, and Eugen Hadamovsky, director of radio programming, did a stint in a rubber factory near Hanover and even wrote a book about his experiences, *Hilfsarbeiter Nr. 50,000.*[30] In addition, Goebbels tried to win over proletarian celebrities. The actor Heinrich George, whose stocky build and Berlin accent made him instantly recognizable, had been associated with the Left and had starred in the movie *Berlin Alexanderplatz* in 1931. Nonetheless, he lent his prestige to the National Socialists, appearing in important films such as *Jud Süss* and *Kolberg* and drawing the camera's eye in countless newsreels. He was an extraordinarily valuable catch for the Nazis.

What made the people's community increasingly convincing was the restless activism of thousands of people mobilized to work on the body of the nation. In his diary, Karl Dürkefälden reported on the new rhythms of everyday life. The notes he made in March and April 1933 about Social Democrats and Communists arrested and beaten by Nazi stormtroopers gave way, in June and July, to accounts of his neighbors enlisting in Nazi organizations and participating in Nazi activities: "No one wants to be a Communist any more." More or less voluntarily, Peine's citizens made sandwiches or collected money for the SA and the Red Cross, attended SA festivals, and enrolled in the Nazi women's organization or the Hitler Youth. The ubiquitous fundraising made it possible for poorer people like the Dürkefäldens to participate more fully in public life: dinner or snacks were served at party events and entry fees lifted at sport competitions. Dürkefälden's sister even traveled at discounted rates to the Nuremberg party rally in September 1933. But the pressure to comply was unmistakable. Dürkefälden's father-in-law was out every night one week in August 1933 because he had to attend meetings or risk losing his garden plot. Similarly, the officers of Walter Kassler's sports club informed members that they had to come to meetings more often, undertake more military exercises, and "behave" themselves by singing the Horst Wessel Song.[31]

What Dürkefälden recorded was the extraordinary process of coordination by which the Nazis infiltrated the political machinery and the informal, vibrant social and cultural life of German towns and cities. Coordination, or *Gleichschaltung,* hit working-class associational life especially hard. "Red" gymnastic societies, soccer teams, and bicycle clubs across Germany simply disappeared. As many as one million Social Democratic and Communist athletes were forced to abandon their fields and gymnasiums. Working-class choirs had a better chance of survival if they rewrote club statutes to exclude Social Democratic activists from leadership posts. In Hanover-Linden, for example, the metalworkers who made up the choir "Teutonia" at first voted in June 1933 to dissolve their club, which dated back to 1877, but then reconsidered in September and decided to sing in the coordinated Niedersächsischen Sängerbund after all. By contrast, "Symphonia," in the same town, refused to compromise, and singers parted company for the next twelve years.[32]

National Socialists assaulted the "alternative culture" of working-class socialists in order to coordinate it, but they also attempted to overcome the very idea of "alternative," which structured the social divisions typical of Germany's neighborhoods. Most places did not resemble Goslar, which had two voluntary fire companies, one working-class, one bourgeois; but separate socialist and nationalist organizations fractured German communities almost everywhere. Typically towns had two gymnastic societies, two soccer clubs, two swim teams, one allied with the Left, the other with the Right. During the Weimar years, uniformed veterans' associations, the republican Reichsbanner and the nationalist Stahlhelm, vigilantly upheld the basic political partisanship of German communities. It was this colorful, segregated world that the Nazis aimed to coordinate in the name of national unity. As Karl Dürkefälden reported, they relied on force from above as well as voluntary and at times enthusiastic compliance from below. The Day of Potsdam and May Day indicated that there was considerable desire among Germans to participate in rituals of national renewal. Moreover, the impression that Germans were assembling behind the Nazis reinforced itself. More and more people adjusted to the "new direction" when they saw that others had done so. To the surprise of Hitler, Goebbels, and other revolutionaries, "everything is going much faster than we ever dared to hope."[33]

Just three months after the March elections, the French ambassador François-Poncet reported on what the National Socialists had "destroyed, dispersed, dissolved, incorporated, sucked up. One after the other, the Communists, the Jews, the Social Democrats, the trade unions, the Stahlhelm, the German Nationalists, the front soldiers in the Kyffhäuser, the Catholics in Bavaria, and the rest of the Reich and the Protestant churches had to submit to their law. [Hitler] has all the powers of the police in his hands. A ruthless censorship has completely tamed the press . . . The cities are administered by mayors and councilmen drawn from his movement. The governments of the states and the state parliaments are in the hands of party members. The bureaucracy has been purged. The political parties have disappeared . . . All he had to do was blow, and the structure of German politics collapsed like a deck of cards."[34] This is an accurate summary of the destruction of German democracy, but it misses the enthusiasm and energy that accompanied the establishment of the new order. Coordination was a process of dissolution *and* affiliation.

Citizens streamed onto the huge field of activity that the Nazis had opened with their commitment to remake Germany and to improve life. With a "muscular, problem-solving rhetoric," they set out an agenda to clean up factories and streets, cancerous lungs and smoke-filled venues, and also racial undesirables such as "asocials" and Jews. "People looked to Nazism as a great and radical surgery or cleansing" and therefore saw "the movement as a source of rejuvenation" in public life. Detlev Peukert has referred to a "Machbarkeitswahn," modernity's heady sense of the possible that epitomized National Socialism as it charged into the future. The medicalization of politics pulled thousands of new professionals into state service as nurses, teachers, health-care administrators. Newly opened public-health offices dotted the cities and countryside, building on the social-welfare accomplishments of the republic. Millions of volunteers aided racially worthy but impoverished Germans through the National Socialist People's Welfare, which, overseeing charitable activity, was the largest civic organization in the Third Reich. Eight million people enrolled in the Reich Air Defense League.[35]

What is particularly interesting is how these auxiliary organizations gave Germans semiofficial responsibilities as they collected donations, distributed coal, or trained as air-raid wardens. Nazi-era volunteering placed thousands upon thousands of Germans in minor leadership posts where they watched over their small patch of the people's community. The SA, Hitler Youth, and Reich Labor Front worked the same way, striving to identify a new generation of leaders drawn from all social classes; for Hitler, the exemplary model was the recruitment of priests in the Catholic church. Leaders honed their skills through special workshops, night courses, and training camps. Many of the diarists and autobiographers introduced in this book assumed such positions: Lore Walb, Melita Maschmann, and even Karl Dürkefälden, who served his machine-tool factory in Celle as a deputy air defense warden. Eberhard Gebensleben prepared to leave for a "military sport camp" in Zossen, near Berlin, in September 1933. "You can imagine," Eberhard's mother wrote to Immo, "what it was like at our house until late at night. Packing all the things, many of which were prescribed . . . then telephoning with the physician . . . finally we got the suitcases packed, and at 7:15 this morning he left with all his heavy bags."[36] Millions of such excited, nervous domestic leave-takings took place in the Third Reich.

All this busy activity resembled fighting a war in a time of peace. Not surprisingly, citizens found the constant donations of time and money onerous, but they gradually accepted the new practices, and the slew of regulations, advisories, and prohibitions associated with them, as the best way to manage collective life. And they expected neighbors to comply. Artifacts such as gas masks, "Aryan" passports, and Winter Relief badges embodied the new standards of cooperation, training, and expertise to which members of the people's community expected one another to adhere.

A glimpse into the front hall of a working-class tenement in Berlin in the summer of 1939 reveals the techniques that German citizens had to master to manage their lives. Heinrich Hauser led the way inside:

> Your eye will first be caught by a series of colorful posters next to the entrance. There is an appeal for contributions to the "Mother and

Child" fund, another appeal for the *Winterhilfswerk*. A third is a Party exhortation to visit either an anti-semitic lecture or an anti-semitic film . . . A fourth poster, in screaming red, bears the urgent question: "Fellow-countryman, have you bought your gas mask?" A fifth warns you not to throw away such garbage as tinfoil, empty tooth-paste tubes and other metals, even old razor blades, and to collect them in special containers.[37]

Tacked onto the doorways of apartments, posters, labels, and badges attested to the fact that nearly all residents belonged to the People's Welfare or contributed to Winter Relief.

The most visible manifestations of the people's community were the huge Winter Relief campaigns, the *Winterhilfswerk,* overseen by the People's Welfare Service. From October to March, over one million party members, Hitler Youth, and other volunteers fanned out with their distinctive red boxes to collect millions of marks to realize the Nazi maxim that "A People Helps Itself." These boys and boxes were among the most familiar sights of the Third Reich. Of course, all this collecting activity, *Duddelkram,* as one housewife put it after the war, was annoying and intrusive.[38] One-pot meals on the first Sunday of every month provided opportunities for party representatives to go from door to door in the evening as they collected the pfennigs that had been "saved," and to snoop. But in general, the regime's "socialism of the deed" enjoyed legitimacy. Nazi leaders regarded every year's recordbreaking receipts as an index of political satisfaction and social commitment. In the last year before the war, the revenues collected just on "One Pot Sundays," which were observed in restaurants and hotels as well as at home, totaled fifty million marks, just shy of one mark for each German. In 1943, Winter Relief collected over 1.6 billion marks. *Winterhilfe* was the largest purchaser of coal in Germany and was second only to the Wehrmacht in buying shoes and textiles. Even more important was its role in training Germans to accept their collective responsibilities as stewards of the German race.[39]

The "Day of National Solidarity" pitched the Winter Relief campaign to its high point. On the first Saturday in December, at the beginning of the holiday shopping season, prominent Nazis as well as famous actors, musicians, and military heroes appeared in public to collect money on the streets of Berlin. Newspapers reported their locations the day before so that Berliners knew that Goebbels would be in front of the Adlon, Ribbentrop in front of the Bristol, and Rosenberg at the opera. Göring collected money in the kitschy Passage on Unter den Linden, then, tellingly, in working-class Wedding, where, as reports indicated, he enjoyed surprising popularity. "Crowds became so large that in places progress was impossible and women fainted while trying to reach the collectors," reported the London *Times*. Combining celebrity and charity, the 1938 action netted one million marks in a city of four million people in two and a half hours.[40]

Winter Relief was mostly about ordinary behavior, however. Germans wore special badges to show they had donated their marks; the badges functioned so as to make citizens accountable to themselves. "On Sundays," Hauser remarked, "when collecting for the Winter-Relief Fund is going on in the streets no one would dare walk abroad without a badge pinned conspicuously to his coat." Like "Heil Hitler!," badges displayed and enforced collective participation. Yet it was just these badges of compliant "good behavior" that became hugely popular collectibles in the Third Reich. Manufactured as novelty items for sale at twenty pfennigs, "the Winter-Relief badges always offered surprises: sometimes there were brightly painted little porcelain figures in traditional costumes, or the crests of the German lands embroidered on silk, or portraits of German poets, philosophers, and musicians out of plexiglass or synthetic resin." One hundred seventy million badges were produced during the 1938–39 campaign alone—a number sufficient to give every person in Germany two, if not three, badges. In turn, popular demand for the badges revived Germany's ailing toy industry, a success story in its own right, which newsreels screened back to movie audiences, who could watch how the badges were "cast, blown, woven, cut, brushed" at "breathtaking speed."[41] In this way, Germans repossessed for themselves the sacrifices that the Nazis demanded. People always felt "forcibly volunteered" in the Third Reich, but the accent should fall on the implications of both words; consent as well as compliance structured the practices of everyday life in Nazi Germany.

The directions in the tenement also urged Berliners to buy gas masks. The Nazis very effectively introduced themselves as the most capable wardens of Germany's security by dramatizing the nation's vulnerability to air attack. Propaganda displays of bombs and bombers, and the destruction they could wreak, revealed the exposed, trembling body of the nation, which the Nazis claimed to protect through a nationwide program of air defense. Eight million Germans eventually received special training through the Air Defense League. They not only learned how to organize bucket brigades, extinguish fires, and work while wearing gas masks but they accepted positions of responsibility for their apartment buildings and neighborhoods as did Karl Dürkefälden for his factory. By the mid-1930s every street, building, and factory in Germany was required to equip itself with the necessary tools in case of air attack, a move that ignited conversations about the dangers that Germany faced and the preventive measures the Nazis proposed to introduce into every household. "Military preparedness . . . pervades every aspect of life in modern Germany," confirmed one American observer: "Every house bears the placards of an organization for defense against air attack. The language of the street, the press, the radio, the newsstand and even the library and classroom smacks of war."[42]

A jumble of Nazi acronyms (WHW, DAF, RAD, HJ), workaday abbreviations *(Bomber, Laster),* and a thoroughly militarized vocabulary, including words like *Einsatz, Sturm,* and *Kampf* (which the rest of Europe was to learn as well), designated the new techniques to recompose national life.[43] The Nazis underlined both the danger facing Germans and their capacity to contain it, thereby making necessary the air-raid exercises that reproduced almost exactly the Winter Relief campaigns and their advertisements, streetcorner fanfare, door-to-door collections, "One Pot Sundays," and "Day of National Solidarity." The public increasingly came to regard both air defense and Winter Relief as new, necessary ways to manage modern life. They represented forms of collective organization that enabled Germans to survive and prosper in the twentieth century. Interweaving economic opportunity with the dangers that might prevent it, whether it was the threat of air attack, the presence of "asocials," or the power of Jews, Winter Relief and air-defense campaigns made the premises of the people's community tangible and persuasive.

Economic prosperity

Consuming the Nation

The people's community would not have been convincing had the Nazi regime not been able to dramatically improve the material conditions of life. On the eve of the war, in 1939, most Germans experienced the Third Reich as a cherished period of economic and political stability. These were achievements that the population was determined to hold on to. Erich Ebermayer described the public mood around the time the Klemperers walked into the truck stop. "Nobody wants war," Ebermayer explained at the end of September 1938, and he went on with a list that did not apply perfectly to average Germans but nonetheless captured the general feeling of contentment: "Everyone is doing so well! We're earning our money! We have a car, a refrigerator, a record player—what is the point of war?"[44] But the popularity of the regime rested on more than improved wages or better business prospects. A more fundamental sense that Germany had recovered its future strengthened the confidence of its citizens to expect "a better life for themselves and future generations." As Norbert Frei argues, National Socialism created a sense of "new time" in which Germans contemplated any number of improvements, but not basic alternatives to the Third Reich.[45]

Long-term loyalties to the Nazis depended on the ability of the new government to create a viable economic future for German citizens, especially for the millions of people who were unemployed in January 1933. To read the situation reports prepared by security officers of the Nazi regime and by underground agents of the Social Democratic Party in exile is to win two impressions. On the one hand, disappointment in the slow pace of economic recovery, low wages, and high prices remained widespread. In part, this was due to the high expectations the Nazis themselves had raised. Although the initial drop in the number of registered unemployed in 1933 and 1934 was dramatic, from 4.8 to 2.7 million, in 1935 there were still 2.2 million Germans without work. The regime's solution to the labor crisis was a massive public works scheme in which emergency work brigades toiled for inadequate wages in poor conditions. There were nearly 400,000 such labor conscripts in 1934, many of them working on the new Autobahns. Even for regular workers, restrictions on the right to switch jobs that came with the 1935 introduction of the *Arbeitsbuch* (labor pass), a mounting *Arbeitshetze* (work speedups), in which working hours increased, and a climate of intimidation sustained a mood of resignation. Ian Kershaw sums up: the reports indicate that "workers not only *were* unfree . . . but that most of them *felt* they were unfree, exploited, discriminated against and the victims of an unfair, class-ridden society." Even during the boom years of 1937–39, "signs indicated that Nazism was further losing ground among workers."[46] This is probably an overstatement. Nonetheless the propaganda of Nazism's economic success story could not hide the large number of workers who remained impoverished or unreconciled to the regime.

On the other hand, the reports confirm that workers credited Hitler, in particular, for the restoration of economic stability. By 1937 fewer than one million Germans remained unemployed, and the number of emergency workers had fallen to 60,000. At the end of the 1930s, labor shortages opened up opportunities for women as well; though earning less than men, women made up 37 percent of the workforce in 1939, a figure that included 6.2 million married women, up from some 4 million in 1933. Incomes never rose much beyond levels already achieved in the late 1920s, but the possession of security meant more. The effect of the end of unemployment "on the stabilization of the National Socialist regime can hardly be overestimated," concludes one historian: "millions of people who had vegetated below the poverty line, for whom hunger and destitution had become daily experiences, were snatched from the crisis of their personal existence and restored to normal conditions." Victor Klemperer recorded just this restoration in his diary. Walking along Dresden's Prager Strasse at the end of November 1936, he bumped into a young man who beamed: "I've got work—the first time in three years—and good work—at Renner's—they pay well!" he exclaimed.[47]

In 1937 German households achieved the standard of living enjoyed in 1928, before the onset of the Great Depression. Life remained modest. "Germans were used to spreading their rye bread with margarine and four-fruit jam rather than with butter and sausage," reminds Frei; "in comparison with the English, French, and Americans they ate more simply, even in the 'good' years of the prewar period, but always as much as they wanted."[48] Newspaper copy advertised the shiny wares of the consumer economy, but most working-class homes lacked basic commodities such as radios or bicycles. As business turnover improved and the bureaucracy expanded, the middle classes began to spend more money; consumer items from Winter Relief badges, skin products such as Nivea, and Coca-Cola to radios and cameras made their way into German homes. Still, Germans at the start of the war could not afford vacuum cleaners, much less the washing machines or refrigerators that epitomized the promised benefits of electrification (and had been purchased by about one percent of all households).[49] Rearmament absorbed an outsized share of resources. But it was not so much durables as the promise of prosperity that was consumed. Memories of the Third Reich corresponded in large part to the Nazis' own prewar media representation of "good times" both now and to come.

The Nazis endlessly retailed the future. One of Hitler's favorite projects was to motorize Germany by making a Volkswagen, or people's car, available to ordinary citizens. Although most people would have preferred the immediate acquisition of a bicycle, there was something enormously enticing about automobiles and the Autobahns built for them. "Music of the future" was how one old Social Democrat described the Volkswagen campaign.[50] The dream of the Volkswagen seemed to promise "a new, happier age" that would make "the German people rich and Germany beautiful," as Hitler put it. Indeed, the Volkswagen functioned as a symbol for the newly won capacity to dream about the future: in this fundamental sense, the Nazis appeared as "men of the future." And there is little doubt that the Nazis genuinely anticipated the coming automobile age. The huge vacation complex that the German Labor Front very nearly completed in Prora, on the North Sea island of Rügen, included a garage for 5,000 cars, sufficiently large for each vacationing family to drive there by car.[51] It was from the driver's seat that Hitler envisioned his empire in which Autobahns, built by thousands of slave laborers, would run German motorists to Crimea and the Caucasus, while Russians would "vegetate further in their own dirt away from the big roads."[52] Even after Stalingrad, Hitler looked forward to a prosperous peace in which one million Volkswagens would be produced every year.[53]

Although workers and employees complained of flat wages, they welcomed the expansion of vacation time from seven to twelve days over the 1930s. The first good thing that Friedrich Kassler had to say about the National Socialists, for example, concerned vacations. Moreover, the experience of travel enhanced the quality of extra free time; as late as 1934, some 28,500 of 42,000 workers at Siemens in Berlin had never been on a holiday trip beyond the forests and lakes ringing the city.[54] At first the German Labor Front deliberately instrumentalized leisure time with the very fascist-sounding program "Strength through Joy." But over time, "Strength through Joy" expanded and embodied the right of every German *Volksgenosse* to travel on holiday. It suggested how Germans should be able to live; "Enjoy Your Lives" was the organization's 1936 slogan.

Subsidized by obligatory dues to the German Labor Front, which amounted to a deduction of 1.5 percent from wages, "Strength through Joy" offered discounted trips to theaters and concerts, excursions into the countryside, and, for the lucky few, cruises to Italy, Spain, and Norway on two specially built ships. While "Strength through Joy" vacations were budget affairs, third-class railway journeys to Thüringen rather than Bavaria, and parsimonious meals at second-rate hotels, they offered millions of Germans the opportunity to travel, to see the seaside, or visit the *Reichshauptstadt*—Berlin was one of the favorite "Strength through Joy" destinations. As a result, the program enjoyed great popularity. In its peak year, 1937, 1.4 million Germans took advantage of "Strength through Joy" vacation packages lasting three to seven days, another 6.8 million went off for a "Strength through Joy" weekend, and 130,000 embarked on highly promoted "Strength through Joy" cruises for as long as twenty-one days; that same year, "Strength through Joy" took 13.5 million Germans to a play and 3.5 million to a concert.[55] Especially popular among white-collar employees and single women but also among workers, "Strength through Joy" vacations became "the symbol of the 'National Socialism' represented by the NSDAP," according to one so-cialist informant.[56] The German Labor Front laid out even more ambitious plans for the future: twenty "Strength through Joy" ho-tels, ten resorts such as the one built in Prora, and as many as sixty "Strength through Joy" cruise liners.[57]

"Strength through Joy" was appealing because it offered ordi-nary Germans access to special things such as vacations that they had not had before. Promotional tips on keeping a scrapbook of trips or snapping souvenir photographs indicated the importance the Nazis put on the quality of experience. The consumption of *Erlebnis,* experience, promoted both a greater sense of social equal-ity among Germans and an abiding sense of entitlement as *Volks-genossen.* "Strength through Joy" was "no mere 'beautiful il-lusion,'" argues Shelley Baranowski; "its touristic spectacles encouraged its participants to see a cause-and-effect relationship between their own well being and the Nazi regime's attempts to re-make Germans into the master race."[58]

With its emphasis on happiness and creature comforts and its comparisons about how much better Germans had it than other Europeans, "Strength through Joy" linked the "good life" with the "new order" and strengthened the credibility of the racial Volksgemeinschaft. Indeed, one of the most popular items Germans consumed was Germany itself. "Strength through Joy" offered dis-counted travel to the annual automobile show in Berlin or to propa-ganda exhibitions such as the exhibit of "Degenerate Art." In this period the Franconian town of Rothenburg ob der Tauber acquired its role as a cozy medieval tourist destination (from which the last two Jewish residents had been hustled out as incompatible with model German life in October 1938). Vacationers added National Socialist destinations to their itineraries as well: in Munich, the House of German Art and the Temple of Honor, which commemo-rated the "old fighters" who had fallen in the November 1923 putsch; in Nuremberg, the party rally complex; and in Berlin, the

Olympic stadium, the Aviation Ministry, and the new Chancellery, which upon its completion in 1938 was toured by thousands of visitors every day. One-hundred thousand tourists came to Landsberg each year to view the Bavarian prison in which Hitler had written *Mein Kampf* in 1924. It was not mockery but intimacy on display when "Strength through Joy" vacationers struck poses as Hitler and Goebbels for souvenir photographs.[59]

German citizens enjoyed the *Erlebnis* of Nazi Germany most vividly on the occasion of Hitler's spectacular foreign-policy successes. Adam Tooze aptly refers to the red-letter dates as objects of "collective mass consumption." In January 1935, huge fanfare welcomed the Reich's incorporation of the Saar region, where over 90 percent of the population had voted for reintegration into Germany in a League of Nations referendum. "The big torchlight parade in the evening recalled the mood on 30 January [1933]," reported Social Democratic witnesses.[60] A teenager's diary reproduced the folksy media coverage of this event; it gives some sense of the emotional investment Germans had in the rehabilitation of the nation: "Saar Germans," recounted Lore Walb,

came from all over the world to profess themselves for the German Fatherland. Many came from America, one came from Bombay, one woman did not shy away from the long journey and traveled uninterruptedly for sixteen days. She started out in Shanghai, but missed her boat, was taken by plane to the Siberian Express, where she lost two days in snowdrifts, arrived on 13 January in Berlin at eight in the morning, and immediately flew to Saarbrücken in an airplane that Reich Minister Göring had put at her disposal . . . Wasn't that an accomplishment? Emotional scenes occurred during the voting: a ninety-two-year-old walked ten kilometers to the polling place. The sick let themselves be carried on stretchers to the ballot box. One woman voted and, right then and there, suffered a heart attack because of the excitement and was dead . . . An old widow was so excited that she dropped her ballot, which was declared invalid. She explained in tears that her two sons had fallen in battle and the ballot had been their voice.[61]

The text precisely captures the way many people thought of Germany: as the tenacious underdog finally asserting its rights. Two months later, crowds acclaimed the reestablishment of a mass conscription army, the Wehrmacht, recalling for observers the "August Days" of 1914. Again socialists conceded: "For the overwhelming majority, 16 March is the definitive end to a shameful past, much more so than 30 January 1933; the day marks 'the dawn of a new age.'" All this patriotic hoopla mattered; Versailles had left deep wounds, and, anyway, Germans were apt to be "childishly proud of their army." Moreover, it was in the army that most young men gained their "first hands-on experience" with trucks, cars, and other technical equipment. It mobilized the aspirations of countless individuals.[62] Hitler's own popularity and the overall prestige of the National Socialist regime reached new heights after the March 1938 Anschluss with Austria. Even opponents of the regime such as Ebermayer could not hide their satisfaction. With these foreign policy successes, Nazism succeeded in presenting itself as the resolution of German history.

However, Germans did not want the war Hitler was determined to wage in order to gain living space and empire. In a revealing anecdote from the year 1936, Hitler's architect, Albert Speer, recalled that Hitler was "jolted by the jubilation of the Berliners when the French team filed solemnly into the Olympic Stadium. They had marched past Hitler with raised arms and thereby sent the crowd into transports of enthusiasm." But when the German cheers would not stop, "Hitler sensed a popular mood, a longing for peace and reconciliation." This was also an indication of the general contentment with things as they were. Even after the successful blitzkrieg campaigns against Poland in 1939 and France a year later, the state of war continued to trouble the public, which hoped desperately to return to the "good times" of the prewar years.[63] A soldier's letter to his wife, written just before his death in August 1943, relayed the mood of satisfaction and confidence that war had foreclosed: "If only the good old days would come back again, just one more time. Why do we have to have this dreadful war, which has disrupted our peaceful lives, broken our happiness, and dissolved all our big and little hopes for a new house into nothing?" Once it was clear that Germany would not win easily, or might not win at all, however, the continuation of war to the bitter end became the only way to save any measure of the good life. The real shock came with Stalingrad in the winter of 1943, but even then nothing made the "community of fate" more compelling than "the conviction that there will no longer be future for Germany after a lost war."[64] The way Germans thought about the war was always mediated by satisfaction with the "good times" achieved in the last years of peace.

A (large) minority of Germans supported the National Socialists in 1933, but ultimately the majority of Germans found the regime to be legitimate. They credited the Nazis for putting people back to work, for promoting a greater sense of social equality with symbolic politics from May Day to Winter Relief to "Strength through Joy," and for restoring Germany's international prestige. In this respect, 1933 was "a revolution in ways of looking, acting, and perceiving—a brown revolution of the mind."[65] Hitler enjoyed massive popularity, but the sense of "new direction" and "new time" indicated the public's deeper association with National Socialism. That the Autobahns and "Strength through Joy" continued to be remembered long after the war is evidence of how thoroughly Nazi promises matched German expectations. Germans increasingly identified their own futures with the future of the Third Reich. Within just a few years, most people could no longer imagine Germany as anything but National Socialist. Social Democracy, the republic, and the whole *Systemzeit,* as even Ebermayer dismissed the 1920s, appeared to be anachronistic. Nazis themselves ridiculed opponents as "hopeless yesteryears." In this way, the Nazis were able to accomplish the almost complete seizure of German time and space. Thus, for leading opponents of the Nazis, and for the Jews and other minorities that the regime tormented, there seemed to be little alternative but to abandon Germany altogether. Since most exiles never returned, Germany's political and intellectual life continued to be structured by the Nazis long after their defeat.

Unter Uns, or Nazism's Audiovisual Space

Elisabeth Gebensleben, Erich Ebermayer, and Karl Dürkefälden all described how strongly they and their families experienced National Socialism through the medium of the radio. On the Day of Potsdam and again on May Day, radio provided Nazi ceremonies with a vast acoustical backdrop that extended across the entire nation. Radio helped to create the collective voice of the nation. The well-scripted transmissions were themselves appealing and pulled more and more people into an expanding auditory space. While sympathizers such as Gebensleben deliberately put themselves in the apron of sound, those who did not care to listen were nonetheless assaulted by the broadcasts thanks to the sheer number of listening posts in streets, restaurants, and taverns. As a result, Victor Klemperer could repeatedly "run into" one of Hitler's Reichstag speeches. "I could not get away from it for an hour. First from an open shop, then in the bank, then from a shop again."[66] Radio as well as film turned Nazism into spectacle. The mass media reproduced and heightened the effect of national acclamation.

With banners, flags, marches, and "Heil Hitler!" the Nazis produced a distinctive public choreography and accompanying sound track that seemed to affirm the unanimity of the people's community. "On every street," noted one visitor in 1936, "one sees the gray uniforms of the Wehrmacht, the black uniforms of the Hitler

Guard, the brown uniforms of the Storm Troops and the knee breeches of the Hitler Youth." Party assemblies gathered up these uniforms in serried geometric blocks in order to display the collective strength of the Volk. These were then filmed and broadcast in newsreels and, most famously, in Leni Riefenstahl's film of the 1934 Nuremberg party rally, *Triumph of the Will,* which streamlined visual impressions into an overall image of discipline, unity, and unassailability. Reiterative displays of display were the moving images that accompanied the Third Reich. The fact that the camera was in view at the rally itself, where Riefenstahl used thirty film teams, but also in advertisements for the movie did not undercut the message by the gesture toward its artificial composition. Rather, focusing the camera, going to the movies, consuming the spectacle, and identifying and recognizing the pieces in the whole were precisely the actions that reproduced the people's community.[67]

"It seems funny, but every German soldier carries a camera."[68] Reporting from the battlefields in France in the spring of 1940, William Shirer took note of the visualization of the war as a grand event that deserved to be photographed. Germans even went to war with preprinted diaries that left space for snapshots. All this was an acknowledgment of the desire to be part of and to share the German history that was being made. Long before the war, illustrated magazines featured advertisements for cameras and articles on photography as a pastime; as many as one in ten Germans owned a camera.[69] The film critic Siegfried Kracauer even claimed that the Third Reich was represented to look like a film so that the regime could smudge "the border between reality and fiction."[70] The Third Reich was "movie made" insofar as the Nazis wanted the German people to comprehend events on the order of grand history by hearing broadcasts on the radio, seeing the reassembly of marchers on film, and taking photographs of their own part in the making of the people's community.[71] The point was to get viewers to adopt the heroicizing vantage of the camera. Nazi propaganda did not aim to pass fiction off as reality but to get Germans to discern reality as camera-ready history. To see the Third Reich in such a way that individuals were apt to take photographs to record history is perhaps the best way to understand what Nazi propaganda aimed for. Visual pleasure was not simply the result of lush media spectacles manufactured by clever propagandists in Berlin. It was also the effect of individuals participating in German history "in the making."

The eventfulness of the Day of Potsdam was the reason "all three, father, mother, and Emma" Dürkefälden, had gone to Kaune's tavern, but it was also what they themselves produced by going there. Precisely to facilitate participation in the Volksgemeinschaft, the Nazis put extraordinary effort into making affordable radios available to the public. In what it touted as the triumph of "socialism of the deed" over "private capitalism" and "economic liberalism," in 1933 the Propaganda Ministry pressed a consortium of radio manufacturers to design and produce a *Volksempfänger,* or "people's radio," for the mass market. The VE 301 was an instant success at seventy-six marks; 1.5 million sets were sold in 1933 and 1934, partially, of course, because a radio was an entertaining thing to have but also because many Germans wanted to hear Hitler and to capture for themselves the sounds of the Third Reich. Only one in four households owned radios in 1933; more than one in two did so in 1939. But not even the war, and the desire for up-to-date news about the troops, pushed the density of radio ownership close to that in the United States, where radios could be found in 90 percent of households. Both the price of the sets and the monthly fee kept poorer Germans, especially in rural areas, from making the purchase. In the cities, however, almost everyone listened to radio.[72]

The Nazis had condemned radio programming during the Weimar Republic for being too intellectual and unfaithful to the "true spirit" of the medium, which was to let the community speak up. They aimed at getting listeners to recognize what they were hearing on the radio as the sounds of the people's community.[73] At first this strategy involved establishing Berlin's authority over regional radio stations, coordinating content under the direction of the Propaganda Ministry, and transmitting live as many Nazi ceremonies and Hitler speeches as possible. Through the "people's receiver," the people would be able to receive the Führer's words directly; "radio in every German home" was Goebbels' formula. Moreover, the regime encouraged schools, restaurants, and factories to install radios in order to make listening a collective and public act. Of course, it was not possible simply to pour Hitler's words into people's heads, and, in the face of diminishing interest, programmers searched for new, less political ways to broadcast the people's community. Hitler's speeches on the anniversary of the 1923 putsch or the 1933 seizure of power remained important events. On these occasions, friends and neighbors knew they would find one another in front of the radio and could later share impressions—in this sense, *Gemeinschaftsempfang*, collective reception, had been achieved. "I just heard Hitler's speech; you will have heard it sitting at home by the radio," wrote one soldier to his family on 30 January 1940, the seventh anniversary of the seizure of power.[74] But the Nazis quickly learned that the value of the radio did not lie in the transmission of political events. After 1934, expanded radio programming devoted itself to light entertainment. With the cheerful slices of German life they broadcast and the national audience they pulled together, radio plays recreated the people's community. It produced the effect of being *unter uns*, "just us."

"Heut sind wir unter uns" were words Victor Klemperer remembered from his childhood. He recalled them after seeing a caption in the Nazi paper, *Der Stürmer*, "How nice that it's just us now!" which accompanied an article noting that one more seaside resort had banned Jews. At that moment, Klemperer remembered that these were the words that a school comrade had told him the math teacher had uttered on the day, "September 1900 or 1901 in

Landsberg," when three Jewish boys, Klemperer included, were absent in observance of Yom Kippur: "Today it's *just us*." Klemperer returned to this phrase in 1937, when its full meaning had become clear to him with the banning of Jews.[75] He believed Germans felt that "it's just us now" when they lived without Jews. "Just us" also expressed the closed circle in which Germans could see and experience "ourselves" as "we are" and as "we have become." It was the space in which the daily fare of light entertainment produced a self-absorbed cheerfulness, and in which a parade of stars and hits reflected the good life of Nazi Germany. Of course, in 1937 Klemperer could have turned on the radio and listened too, but the programming was designed for untroubled, easygoing "insiders," not troubled outsiders. In September 1939, after the invasion of Poland, *unter uns* became legally enforced Aryan space when a decree prohibited Jews from owning or listening to radios; their sets were to be handed over to the Wehrmacht, but not primarily because the army needed them. "Left unsaid, but actually already self-evident, the people's receiver was meant for the German 'Aryan people,' not the population at large."[76]

By 1935 radio programming had switched over to featuring tableaus of "normal" everyday life. Radio shows continued to let ordinary Germans speak for themselves, as had been the case with the innovative transmissions of 30 January and 1 May 1933, but without explicit political frames. Programmers deliberately aimed at broadcasting "a piece of life," humor and songs and the life situations of people from locations across Germany. Radio plays such as "A German Almanac: The News from Königswusterhausen" scooped up a handful of small-town families and followed their daily routines and life aspirations, all the while weaving them into the shiny new pattern of winter charity drives, "Strength through Joy" trips, and war preparations to create "a long chain of families and kinships" that repeatedly reenacted the reconciliations of German community.[77]

The most successful program on German radio was the musical variety request show, *Wunschkonzert für das Winterhilfswerk,* which became the subject of an enormously popular film that premiered at the end of 1939. To understand how National Socialism depicted "the people" coming to its own words, it is worth examining both the radio show and the film. On the radio, *Wunschkonzert* consisted of three parts: the top-name musicians performing the requests sent in by ordinary Germans, who, in turn, made a contribution to the Winter Relief campaign; the live studio audience providing the background of laughter and applause; and the Volksgemeinschaft, which gathered around the radio to hear what were in essence its own requests and dedications. It thereby fulfilled the Nazi programming directive "From the People, to the People." The playlist consisted of a potpourri of military marches, including Hitler's favorite, "Der Badenweiler Marsch," which opened the program; selections from Wagner, Beethoven, and Mozart; as well as choirs and bands, a mix of old and new, classical and folkloric with a bit of jazz (a clarinet, but not a saxophone) thrown in. *Wunschkonzert* created a national repertoire of "pop" music that broke down distinctions between high and low culture and remained in place as "evergreens" long after 1945. In between the performances, moderator Heinz Goedecke introduced special guests—film stars such as Zarah Leander and Heinrich George, athletes such as the boxer Max Schmeling, or entertainers such as the Berlin cabaretist Claire Waldoff—and read the dedication of the person who had made the request and offered the donation. It was a compelling display of the Volksgemeinschaft: the nationally broadcast confirmation of the simple axiom that whoever made a sacrifice to the people got the *Schlager,* or hit, she wanted.

Broadcast every two weeks on Sunday afternoons, *Wunschkonzert* quickly became Germany's top radio program. With as many as 80 percent of radios tuned in, *Wunschkonzert* was credited with gathering Germans into "one big family," with Goedecke as "Radio Uncle." As a result, Germans could imagine one another in front of the radio listening to the same program: "Sunday is *Wunschkonzert,*" wrote one soldier to his family back home; "you certainly will be listening too." And: "Bobi, did you just hear *Wunschkonzert?* Are you listening to the beautiful song, 'Baby, baby, how I love you?'"[78] More than any other program, *Wunschkonzert* realized the "collective reception" that the Propaganda Ministry had hoped for since 1933. With the war, requests were restricted to soldiers, and soon thereafter, since there were so many, to divisions. Accompanied by the formula "the battlefront shakes hands with the home front," the reformatted *Wunschkonzert für die Wehrmacht* aimed to introduce a sentimentalized version of the war based on intimacy and love rather than on separation and death. *Wunschkonzert* was discontinued in 1942, when total war became too heavy for lighthearted programming.[79]

The 1941 movie *Wunschkonzert* is interesting because it featured the radio as the means to achieve national unity. Not only do Germans from all walks of life settle down on Sunday afternoon to hear *Wunschkonzert* but the radio brings them together. The movie centers on the separation and reunion of Herbert and Inge, who meet by chance at the 1936 Olympic Games in Berlin. They fall in love, but the Luftwaffe lieutenant is unexpectedly called away on a secret mission (Operation Condor in Spain) and is not permitted to post the letters he promised to write. Three years later, the lovers have lost contact and Germany is at war, with Herbert stationed at an air base near Hamburg, commanding air raids against Britain. His own mobilization parallels that of other Germans, and subplots follow the wartime escapades of four men from a Berlin apartment building. The movie thereby introduces the collective unity of Germans through their differentiations: the musical medleys of the *Wunschkonzert* from Mozart to Marika Rökk and the links in the chain of the people, from the gruff accents of the butcher and baker, who play their parts for laughs, to the quiet, self-sacrificing pianist.

Because the radio play *Wunschkonzert* has in fact created a national audience, the dedications read over the radio provide means to communicate that turn the plot, and so with Herbert's request for the "Olympiade Fanfare" Inge realizes he is still thinking of her. Inge goes to Goedecke, who plays himself in the movie, and he gives her Herbert's *Feldpost* address, an act that leads to a final reunion. What had been the separate paths of love and duty finally merge; a final shot of the lovers dissolves into the sounds of an air attack on England.

The congruence of love and duty is made even plainer in *Die grosse Liebe* (1942), the most popular film in the Third Reich, which incidentally makes a reference to *Wunschkonzert* in a way that confirms the program's cultural currency. In *Die grosse Liebe,* which casts Viktor Staal with Zarah Leander, the increasingly exacting demands of war over the course of 1941, from the battle for North Africa to the invasion of the Soviet Union, repeatedly separate the lovers but also offer grounds for reconciliation; just as in *Wunschkonzert,* the final scene takes place beneath the drone of bomber squadrons. Love in time of total war was thus closely calibrated with the conflict itself. (Since the lieutenant's injuries get worse, alert viewers might have wondered if love and duty, pitched higher and higher, would not lead to complete self-destruction.)

Both radio and film repeatedly reproduced the collective body of the German nation. In the film *Wunschkonzert,* reconciliation was the key theme: the monogamous, heterosexual love of Inge and Herbert alongside the renewal of comradely friendship of both with Helmut, Inge's erstwhile suitor and, it so happens, Herbert's subordinate. These ties were essential for the people's community to reproduce itself and mobilize for war. The film briefly contrasts the happy couple with Inge's aunt, whose love affair in World War I stumbled over the social prejudices that have disappeared in the Third Reich. The consciousness of national belonging is introduced as the difference between the wars. Both *Wunschkonzert* and *Die grosse Liebe* also gave considerable room to an old-fashioned generation of aunts, grandmothers, and Berliners with their famous "lip" *(Berliner Schnauze)*, who not only set off the modern, more capable young people but whose benevolent presence confirms the overall well-being of the Third Reich. Precisely the rounded-off nature of social relations revealed the contentment and self-sufficiency of German society. In a relatively lighthearted way, the film used the Volksgemeinschaft as the means to realize private happiness. More than twenty-six million filmgoers saw *Wunschkonzert,* the biggest hit in the Third Reich after *Die grosse Liebe,* confirming, at least to chief propagandist Goebbels, that art could "captivate the broad mass."[80]

That one of the requests in *Wunschkonzert* comes from ethnic Germans in "Rural District Warsaw" who donate their zloty to Germany's Winter Relief indicates one of the key purposes of popular entertainment in the Third Reich: the creation of a commonly shared culture to define Germans to one another and mark them off from others. Germans became properly German by consuming programs offered by the national media rather than the religious themes of rural folk culture. (Misunderstandings ensued, however, when Volhynian Germans from the Soviet Union found the films too racy.) To produce a common language of cultural belonging was worth considerable effort: the Nazis sent mobile cinemas to rural areas to advance *völkisch* literacy—hundreds of screenings took place every month in rural East Prussia alone.[81]

On the eve of the war, 5,500 cinemas offered Germans a total of 3.4 million seats. Although the number of feature films screened in Germany declined, the habit of going to the movies increased, so that a commonly held film repertoire was more likely. By 1936–37, with 6.8 annual cinema visits for every German, box-office attendance reached the highs of 1927–28 and more than doubled again before the end of the war (to 14.4), though it remained below British and American levels.[82] The shared excitement of hits and stars, the secondhand fare of advertising, request concerts, and fan magazines, as well as guest appearances on *Wunschkonzert* created a distinctively German popular culture. This more or less unregulated coordination was undoubtedly more important than the political coordination of the film industry under the censorious direction of Goebbels and his officials in the Propaganda Ministry. Films treated Nazi themes such as euthanasia, and the trio of antisemitic films produced in 1940–41, especially *Jud Süss,* added legitimacy to the Nazis' war against the Jews. But films made their greatest impact by reinforcing the effect of *unter uns.* Precisely because the Nazis believed that going to the movies molded and strengthened the people's community, and set the example for seeing the world in terms of heroic history, cinemas and film studios remained open even after cabarets and theaters were closed down in September 1944 as part of the measures of total war.

Unter uns was a media construction, the explicit aim of propaganda in the Third Reich. It was also the basis for the legitimacy of National Socialism, which created a broad-based feeling of contentment that encompassed most Germans on the eve of the war. Not all Germans joined in the national community, but the sheer force of the imagery and the busy schedules of national acclamation made dissent politically risky; but even more: dissent also appeared to be futile. The near total absence of opposition to the Third Reich after the assault on the socialist Left in 1933 was not the result of an absence of opponents or even the result of their terrorization. Rather, the opponents themselves accepted the evidence of national acclamation and saw no way to make inroads to organize political dissent, not after the first months of Nazi rule and not even in the last months of the war. Again and again, the Nazis drew strength from the public's acceptance of their own political premises: the permanence of the new time of the revolution, the complete break that had been made with Germany's political past, and finally the credibility of the people's community as a workable ideal in order to manage the opportunities and dangers of modern life. Indeed, consuming the images of acclamation became part of the experience of the Third Reich. Nazi propaganda found plenty of consumers willing to applaud the nationalization and heroicization of German history. From above and from below, camera-ready history favored the idea of the people's community, a consciousness of national belonging that overrode many of the social conflicts of everyday life. From the outside, from the perspective of German Jews, for example, the culture of national acclamation was very sensible and appeared to be quite uncoerced. From the inside, it appeared plausible, though incomplete.

2

Racial Grooming

Aryan Passports

"Heil Hitler!" was not enough. To belong to the people's community, Germans also needed to establish their racial bona fides. Anyone who wanted to enroll in a Nazi youth group, serve in the Wehrmacht, get married, or take a "Strength through Joy" vacation trip had to document Aryan identity. Germans had to show that they were "Aryans" to make a life for themselves in the Third Reich.[1] By 1936 almost all Germans—all who were not Jewish— had begun to prepare for themselves an *Ahnenpass*, or racial passport, which laid the foundation for the racial archives established in all German households. It was the exemplary artifact of the extraordinary ambition of the Nazis to recast Germans into a pure racial compact and to segregate out Jews and force them out of the country. The blank forms of the *Ahnenpass* could be purchased in any bookshop and notarized the births, marriages, and deaths of grandparents, parents, and children in order to certify the Aryan identity that was the basis of citizenship. The passport forced Germans to think about race.

The *Ahnenpass* enabled the Nazi regime to enforce the September 1935 Nuremberg racial laws, according to which people in the Third Reich belonged officially to one of four groups: Germans, with four Aryan grandparents; Jews, with three or more Jewish

grandparents; *Mischlinge,* or half-Jews, "first degree," with two
Jewish grandparents; and *Mischlinge* "second degree," with one.
Laws regulating the marriage of mixed Jews and others were complicated, but they forbade marriages between Germans and Jews. In
addition, the Nuremberg Laws no longer recognized Jews as citizens or afforded them equality under the law. Whereas an Aryan
identity opened the way for a future in the Third Reich, a Jewish
one closed it down.

Most people were familiar with "family trees," in which relatives
organized genealogies from the oldest known ancestors down several generations to the family clusters of the living generation. But
the table of ancestors Germans drew up to prepare their racial passports worked quite differently, from the contemporary individual
backward into time to include all blood relatives in an inverted pyr-
amid. "If the family tree is colorful and many-sided, depending on
the number of children and the structure of the family," one geneal-
ogist summarized, the table of ancestors was "characterized by
strict discrimination and mathematical uniformity." Beginning with
the individual in question, it traced "the direction of maternal and
paternal bloodlines" in order to certify the individual's blood purity
and thus her inclusion in the Volksgemeinschaft.[2] Significantly, the
state did not issue racial passports; Germans had to prepare them
personally. They thus attained for themselves their racial status as
Aryans. This task entailed considerable effort; individuals had to
get in touch with civil registries and the church rectories that recorded births and marriages before 1875 in order to gain the necessary validations for a nominal fee of ten to sixty pfennigs, usually
paid in postage stamps. In more difficult cases, Germans required
the "nose of an accomplished detective" in order to gather all the
data. "State archives and libraries have to be trawled . . . ranking
lists, muster roles, telephone books, bills of lading, guild records"
examined. They also made their way to "old cemeteries where tum-
ble-down graves might reveal yet another clue." Misled by a local

pastor, one prospective Aryan embarked on a quest that lasted one and a half years and cost over 150 marks before he located his Aryan grandparents.[3] Not surprisingly, the demand for professional genealogists boomed during the Third Reich.

Ahnenpässe invited Germans to conduct further research into their ancestors; in fact, genealogy became a popular hobby as people attempted to track down blood relatives all the way to 1800, sixty-two in all, just as soldiers in the SS were required to do. Even non-Nazis proudly unveiled their *Sippe*, kin, for show and tell. Enthusiasts went so far as to cultivate the genealogies of German dogs.[4] Jokes mocked the seriousness of the genealogical enterprise, but thereby made "Aryan" identities more homespun. "I am of agrarian origin," began the inquiry of one confused petitioner. Another insisted: "I looked up Aryans in the encyclopedia. They live in Asia. We don't have relatives there, we're from Prenzlau." However, all the humor about Jewishness in Germany, the fear of stumbling upon Jewish grandmothers and the relief when only a "Jewish great-grandmother," "who cannot hurt you anymore," turned up, did not dispel the suspicion that Jews *were* different.[5] Hence the increasingly authoritative semantic distinction between *Germans* and *Jews*. At the same time, what Christa Wolf referred to as "glitter words" such as "normal," "gene," and "alien," passed into everyday speech.[6] The Berlin diarist Franz Göll even undertook a "hereditary study" of his uncle's family:

This family produced seven children, of whom one, a girl, died in infancy. In their physical and mental constitution, three of the remaining children (Martin, Gertrud, Kurt) show the influence of the Amboss, who (Helmut and Margarete †) have a streak of Liskow in them, and one child (Rudolf) is a mixed type (physically = Liskow, mentally = Amboss).

The asthenic effect of the Ambosses is evident in the fact that Martin and Rudolf have made themselves economically independent (each renting or owning a tavern); Gertrud has made a magnificent match, considering (Mrs. Captain Matthes); and Kurt is trying hard to make something of himself professionally. The other two children clearly show that they have inherited the weak mental streak of the Liskows. Helmut, who as a child suffered in silence, trained as a baker but is still only an assistant, that is, a wage earner without the prospect of making himself independent anytime soon. Mentally too weak to effectively resist the reality of the ongoing demands of life, Margarete committed suicide. Her motive: a broken heart.[7]

Introducing Germans to their racial past, *Ahnenpässe* formed the foundation of personal archives. A cardboard box in Berlin's Landesarchiv contains old passports on preprinted pages that include lists of acceptable children's names in both Germanic (Adalbert to Wulf for boys and Ada to Wunhild for girls) and non-Germanic (Achim to Vinzent for boys, Agathe to Viktoria for girls) forms, as well as the "Law for the Protection of German Blood" of 15 September 1935, which prohibited Germans from marrying Jews. Private papers gathered inside the pages of the *Ahnenpass*: an old labor pass; a four-leaf clover; a restaurant bill; a marriage license; birth announcements of children; baptismal certificates; inoculation records; divorce papers; insurance cards; Winter Relief stamps; and also a father's correspondence with his son serving on the front; official confirmation of a soldier missing in action; a letter from a fallen man's comrade describing the whereabouts of the dead man's grave "in Aleksandrwoka (village center) . . . some sixteen kilometers south of Olenin, which is some sixty kilometers west of Rshew"; and, from the year 1945, a "welfare card for bomb victims" (on which was also handwritten "refugees from the East").[8] Family archives, racial categories, and individual identities became closely calibrated with one another over the course of the Third Reich.

For German Jews, the process of archiving ran in reverse. State laws required Jews and so-called racial Jews, who were converts to Protestantism or Catholicism but, in case of three or more Jewish grandparents, biologically Jewish in the eyes of the Nazis, to register themselves as Jews with local authorities and to carry identification papers that labeled them as such. But otherwise the paperwork Jews filled out served as a prelude to the confiscation of their property and finally to their murder. In Dresden, Victor Klemperer spent the morning of Wednesday, 29 June 1938, "filling out forms: Inventory of Assets of Jews." During the war Klemperer, like so many other Jews, was forced to move into the drastically smaller quarters of a "Jew house," which meant that he had to dispose of books and papers. "[I] am virtually ravaging my past," he wrote in his diary on 21 May 1941. "The principal activity" of the next day was "burning, burning, burning for hours on end: heaps of letters, manuscripts."[9] An inventory of "household assets" followed in December 1941.

Ahnenpässe were just the beginning of a much broader effort to get Germans to accept their racial responsibilities as Aryans. The Nazis considered two tasks to be of immediate importance. First, Germans needed to cultivate their genetic endowment by selecting healthy mates in love marriages designed to produce genetically fit children. Beginning on 1 May 1936, laws required state registry offices to present all newlyweds with a copy of Hitler's *Mein Kampf*. From then on, until the very end of the Reich in 1945, they handed out hundreds of thousands of copies of the eight-mark "people's edition" along with pamphlets providing advice on how to maintain good racial stock and prepare *Ahnenpässe*, "Germans, Heed Your Health and Your Children's Health," "A Handbook for German Families," and "Advice for Mothers." Newlyweds also received a coupon for a one-month trial subscription to a newspaper, preferably the Nazi daily, *Völkischer Beobachter*.[10] This prescriptive literature was designed to teach Germans how to document and comport themselves as Aryans.

Second, Germans needed to accept a new social ethic in which individuals were accountable to the collective. Nazi propaganda urged citizens to abandon Christian charitas and what it mocked as liberal *Humanitätsduselei*. In the new National Socialist order, "biology became destiny."[11] The state assumed responsibility for weeding unfit stock out of the population. As early as July 1933, the Ministry of the Interior drew up legislation that authorized the sterilization of allegedly genetically unfit citizens. A few years later the ministry prepared laws that required all prospective newlyweds to obtain certificates of genetic health from local public-health officials. The legislation was suspended in practice, but there is little doubt that it would eventually have been implemented. As it was, civil registrars had the power to require, on a case-by-case basis, couples to procure the certificates, which, in the event of a negative report, could and often did lead to sterilization. More than ten million Germans obtained a certificate of genetic health, which was necessary in order to claim entitlements such as marriage loans.[12] An *Ahnenpass* alone did not guarantee Germans a safe and prosperous future in the Third Reich.

The widespread circulation of *Ahnenpässe* and genetic certificates indicated the changing contours of everyday life in the Third Reich. The idea of normality had become racialized, so that entitlement to life and prosperity was limited to healthy Aryans, while newly identified ethnic aliens such as Jews and Gypsies, who before 1933 had been ordinary German citizens, and newly identified biological aliens such as genetically unfit individuals and so-called "asocials" were pushed outside the people's community and threatened with isolation, incarceration, and death. This regime of insiders and outsiders radically redefined what constituted a normal, ordinary life.

Richard Overy concludes that most Germans had little reason to think of the Third Reich as particularly sinister. "It was possible to live in Germany throughout the whole period of the dictatorship," he writes, "and perhaps witness an incidence of state repression on no more than two or three occasions in twelve years—an SA bully beating a worker in March 1933, a garrulous anti-Nazi neighbor taken off for an afternoon to the police station to be told to hold his tongue in November 1938, the town's Jewish dentist sent off for 'resettlement' in September 1942."[13] This observation is alert to the fact that National Socialism did not terrorize the German population into submission, and that the majority could "adjust," as Karl Dürkefälden had put it.

What Overy's summary overlooks, however, are the ways in which "ordinary" Germans came to see the world in racial terms. As parents, educators, volunteers, and soldiers, millions of Germans played new parts in cultivating Aryan identities and segregating out unworthy lives. They did not always do so willingly, and they certainly did not anticipate the final outcomes of total war and mass murder. At the same time, thousands of other Germans, who came from the most diverse backgrounds, suddenly found themselves regarded as racially Jewish, genetically inferior, or socially marginal and therefore ineligible to play a part in the newly constituted German polity. Race defined the new realities of the Third Reich for both beneficiaries and victims—it influenced how you consulted a doctor, whom you talked to, and where you shopped. After 1933 there were few people in Germany who had not confronted in unambiguous ways the racial and biological categories in which "normal" everyday life was cast.

Biology and the National Revolution

When Hitler came to power in 1933, National Socialists believed they stood at the very edge of history, poised to redirect the nation to fit the grooves of an envisioned Aryan future. The revolution had just begun. The whole previous itinerary of German history, in which citizens interacted as sovereign individuals, in which political parties and interest groups put forward public claims, and in which ethnic groups and religious communities commingled, came to an abrupt end. From the perspective of the Nazis, the year 1933 marked a sharp break. In place of the quarrels of party, the contests of interest, and the divisions of class, which they believed compromised the ability of the nation to act, the Nazis proposed to build a unified racial community guided by modern science. Such an endeavor would provide Germany with the "unity of action" necessary to survive and prosper in the dangerous conditions of the twentieth century. The task ahead was to make Aryans out of Germans. This endeavor rested on terror as the Nazis removed "unworthy lives" from the precincts of the people's community. It also remained incomplete, since Germans never fully abandoned traditional religious and ethical teachings on the sanctity of human life. Racial precepts were also misunderstood, and heredity and genetics mixed up with wilder ideas about blood contamination (not least because of Hitler's own confusion). Nonetheless, thousands of "ethnocrats" and other professionals mobilized to build the new biomedical structures of the Third Reich. They oriented their careers and ambitions toward the wide spaces that Nazi Germany's racial vision had opened up. And for many people, improving and rehabilitating what they took to be the injured, broken body of the German people was meaningful. Personal satisfaction was closely tied to realizing the social and political goals that the Nazis set for young people in the Hitler Youth and Reich Labor Service. The degree to which Germans accepted the Nazi worldview, recognized themselves as Aryans, and endeavored to racially groom themselves is startling given the limited period in which these developments took place. Germans did not become perfect Aryans anymore than they became full-fledged Nazis, but millions of people attempted to reorient themselves in accordance with Nazi Germany's racial future.

For the Nazis, biology was the key to the destiny of the German people. It offered a completely new understanding of human existence, rearranging what was necessary and possible, what was enduring and ephemeral, what was virtuous and dangerous. By thinking in biological terms, the Nazis recast politics in an exceptionally vivid way. In their view, Germany's biological substance was mortally threatened in the absence of emergency measures. The failure of democracy lay precisely in its inability to enact decisive preventive measures to protect the body of the people. At the same time, the Nazis believed that radical surgery and biological cleansing held out the prospect of rehabilitation that would insure Germany's survival in future wars. In other words, biology appeared to provide Germany with highly useful technologies of renovation. The Nazis regarded racism as a scientifically grounded, self-consciously modern form of political organization. The responsibility of government was to cultivate racial solidarity by overcoming social divisions, prohibiting racial mixing, and combating degenerative biological trends. As a result, National Socialist racial thinking was both pessimistic and optimistic. It drew up a long list of internal and external dangers that imperiled the nation. At the same time, it rested on extraordinary confidence in the ability of racial policy to transform social life. The dynamic of Nazism, which would lead to world war, mass murder, and ultimately the destruction of the racial state itself, derived from this combination of obsessive fear and utter confidence.

In their goal to remake Germany as a racial regime, the Nazis could rely on a generation of lawyers, administrators, physicians, and other university graduates who combined personal ambition with ideological radicalism. Strongly defined by World War I and the November Revolution, this was a middle-class cohort that despised democracy for having weakened the nation, and gravitated toward racial and biological thinking as a way to revitalize Germany. As Ulrich Herbert points out, their "radical, *völkisch*" perspective was not simply one political opinion among others. It amounted to a complete attitude toward life, a distinctive "categorical" certainty, a "martial spirit—battle-readiness, hardness, piti-lessness," which distinguished these radicals from their conservative parents. This "unconditional generation," which included Joseph Goebbels (born in 1897), the governor-general of occupied Poland Hans Frank (born in 1900), the film director Leni Riefenstahl (born in 1902), SS leaders Heinrich Himmler (born in 1900) and Reinhard Heydrich (born in 1904), the racial expert Walter Gross (born in 1904), Hitler's architect Albert Speer (born in 1905), and Adolf Eichmann, one of the leading architects of the "final solution" (born in 1906), emerged as the political elite of the racial state. The members of its cohort staffed much of the higher administration of the Reich Security Main Office, which after 1939 oversaw all aspects of security from ordinary criminal police work to the enforcement of racial legislation and the implementation of the "final solution." They really did constitute a "dictatorship of the young."[14]

Three primary tasks awaited Germany's racial warriors. First, it was necessary to increase the birthrate, which was taken to be an index of collective vigor. The Nazis offered tax incentives and interest-free loans to reward childbearing marriages, but they ran into an intractable problem: healthy and well-educated Germans tended to restrict the number of children in order to maximize their own quality of life, a typical trade-off in the modern world, while supposedly less healthy, less able Germans had higher birthrates. Although the Nazis promoted social services to help less fortunate families in the name of the Volksgemeinschaft, they also targeted allegedly genetically unfit citizens who continued to give birth to too many children and weakened the overall racial health of the nation. The second task of racial reclamation, then, was to weed out this unhealthy section of the population, primarily through sterilization. Although the state would assume the executive authority to mandate sterilizations, ordinary Germans needed to play their parts and recognize the necessity and morality of these drastic measures.

Finally, the third task was to eliminate foreign matter from the racial stock of the German people. Racial thinking presumed that only the essential sameness of the German ethnic community guaranteed biological strength. For the Nazis, the goal of racial purity meant excluding Jews, whom they imagined to be a racially alien people who had fomented revolution and civil strife and divided the German people. Within a few years, the Nazis resolved to shove Jews out of Germany altogether. For these racial policies to succeed, it was critical for Germans themselves to resist feelings of misplaced sympathy for neighbors and acquaintances who were actually dangerous racial enemies. Citizens had to be made into accomplices.

Both inside and outside the Nazi party, political activists and public-health professionals gathered with great excitement to promote one or the other of these eugenic measures. They understood themselves to be acting out of the highest idealism in the service of the German people. Even though Nazi biopoliticians believed they were following fundamental laws of history, the plans they drew up were audacious. The Nazis would later compare 30 January 1933 to 14 July 1789, the onset of the liberal era that the new racial epoch of the twentieth century had supposedly foreclosed.

The rapid rate at which the racial future crystallized in 1933 is astonishing. Even before the Nazis promulgated legislation, local activists had picked up the strands of racial policy. Local Nazi doctors in Dortmund greeted "the new era" with an April 1933 proposal to establish a municipal "race office" that on the basis of 80,000 files on schoolchildren would prepare a "racial archive of the entire population of greater Dortmund." In May 1933 physicians in Bremen called for comprehensive legislation to enable the state to sterilize genetically unfit people. "Let's Get to Work" was the watchword of these professionals.[15] Physicians, as well other party activists and even journalists, began to use a domestic-sounding vocabulary; a rhetoric of "cleaning," "sweeping clean," "housecleaning" strengthened the tendency to see politics in the drastic terms of friends and foes.[16]

Beginning in March 1933, local Nazis also targeted German Jews, boycotting Jewish businesses and attacking Jewish-looking pedestrians. Particularly on issues concerning Jews, thousands of Germans adjusted themselves with extraordinary speed. Universities proposed quotas on Jewish students proportionate to their numbers in the population, while corporations with less or more politeness asked Jewish board members to resign. Clubs and associations added statutes prohibiting the acceptance of Jewish members. At the same time, thousands of Protestants (such as Victor Klemperer), Catholics, nonbelievers, Zionists, Orthodox or Reform Jews, German nationalists, Communist partisans, and liberal intellectuals from diverse walks of life suddenly found themselves contained in the single monolithic category "the Jew." The journalist Sebastian Haffner noted that people in his circle in Berlin suddenly felt authorized to express an opinion on the "Jewish question," speaking fluently about quotas on Jews, percentages of Jews, and degrees of Jewish influence.[17] By no means was antisemitism the monopoly of Nazi party members.

The Nazi rulers in Berlin gave these local initiatives more permanent national form with two pieces of legislation that laid the basis for the racial state. On 7 April 1933 the government drew up the "Law for the Restoration of the Professional Civil Service," which forcibly retired all Jewish civil servants in addition to providing the legal means to dismiss political opponents of the regime. For the first time, the mob action of beatings and boycotts had been followed up with a legally sanctioned exclusion of citizens based on a formal definition of race, in this case the existence of a single Jewish grandparent. For a time the law made exceptions on the basis of seniority and for war service, and Nazis were themselves surprised when so many veterans (including Klemperer) received exceptions; these records of patriotic service were completely inconsistent with Nazi conceptions of Jews.

A few weeks later the minister of the interior, Wilhelm Frick, confirmed another aspect of racial policy: "We need to have the courage to structure the body of the people according to genetic value in order to place appropriate leaders at the disposal of the state." He made these remarks at the first meeting of a ministerial committee on "population and race," which met on 28 June 1933 to draft comprehensive racial legislation giving the state the right to sterilize citizens. New laws empowered local health offices to monitor the genetic health of citizens, to issue certificates of genetic health, and, if necessary, to order those found to be unfit sterilized. A wide range of public health-care professionals from doctors to nurses to social-welfare officers were enlisted in the effort to locate undesirables. A few days later Frick went on national radio to urge Germans to accept these measures and to abandon the "'outmoded' command to 'love thy neighbor.'"[18] The genetic reality of contemporary Germany, he claimed, was quite bleak, with at least 500,000 serious cases of genetic disability, and another 500,000 less serious ones, numbers that mortgaged the future of sixty-five million Germans. This dire situation was the premise for bold state action. Accompanying legislation promoted healthy births by offering interest-free "marriage loans" to newlyweds so long as both partners demonstrated their Aryan ancestry and provided certificates of racial fitness.

Hans Frank, a Nazi jurist and wartime governor of occupied Poland, later reflected that this legislation "represents most clearly National Socialism's worldview." Along with the civil service law, it demonstrated what the Nazi revolution was all about: the German population was being resorted according to supposed genetic values, a project that required all Germans to reexamine their relatives, friends, and neighbors. This radical intervention in the "right of the person" would not have been possible without the executive power assembled after a "turnaround such as that of 1933," admitted Arthur Gütt, a leading Nazi physician who drafted the sterilization law.[19] With 500,000 genetic failures in German households, and with more than a half-million Jews living in the country as racial aliens, and millions of healthy Germans only incompletely aware of their responsibilities as Aryans, the Nazis looked ahead to what seemed to be a long racial struggle.

Racial biology in Nazi Germany amounted to an extraordinary project of genetic reconstruction that mobilized thousands of activists. But it also made demands on ordinary Germans, who needed to visualize the Volk as a vital racial subject, to choose appropriate marriage partners, and to accept "limits to empathy." "It is not a party badge or a brown shirt that makes you a National Socialist, but rather your character and the conduct of your life," editors of the eugenic journal, *Neues Volk,* announced in July 1933. A "spiritual revolution" had to follow the accomplishments of the political revolution, insisted Walter Gross, the young director of the Office for Racial Politics in the Nazi party: it would "fundamentally remodel and reform." The biological revolution would overturn "even those things that today seem completely solid," he added ominously.[20] Gross put the emphasis on the efforts of genetically desirable Germans to practice what might be called racial grooming.

Some historians have taken the summer of 1933 to mark the end of the National Socialist revolution.[21] Across Germany, clubs and associations had been largely coordinated, the federal states mustered into the regime with the appointment of proconsuls answerable to Berlin, and all political parties except the National Socialist German Workers' Party banned. Hitler himself acknowledged in a speech in early July that "revolution is not a permanent condition and cannot be something that is carried out in perpetuity." He went on to say that "educating the people is the most important thing." Speaking little more than a week after the brutal massacre of workers arrested in the Berlin suburb of Köpenick, Hitler took the first steps toward curbing the SA, who continued to brutalize Communists and Social Democrats. A few months later he asked the paramilitaries "to extend a hand to former adversaries who demonstrate their loyalty" to the new state. To perpetually reenact the conflicts of the "period of struggle" before 1933 rather than focus on the conversions that had taken place since January inhibited the formation of the Volksgemeinschaft. The ideal was to "fill the entire Volk with a single ideal"—a task that, as Claudia Koonz points out, "meant making converts of their old enemies"; hence the stress on education.[22]

Hitler did not so much end the Nazi revolution as reconceptualize it. In his July 1933 remarks Hitler had added: "The new German state will be a complete fantasy if it does not develop the person."[23] This was the real revolutionary declaration: "a new German person" who would emerge through the application of the techniques of racial hygiene. The Nazis became increasingly preoccupied with assembling the racial compact, the finished form of the people's community. The scene of revolution shifted from raids on proletarian tenements to the staffing of public-health offices, and its primary warriors were not to be SA shock troops, whose numbers declined after Hitler's purge of its most rebellious leaders in June and July 1934, but educated, ideologically driven professionals who made up the higher ranks of the SS, which regarded itself as the racial vanguard of National Socialism. It was the modern, scientific world of "ethnocrats" and biomedical professionals, not the anticommunist Freikorps veterans of the SA, who devised Ahnenpässe and certificates of genetic health and evaluated the genetic worth of individuals.

Through 1933 Hitler returned repeatedly to the theme of fabricating a new people and creating a new political community. Germans just had to sit by the radio to catch snippets of the Führer's utopian fantasies. In November in Weimar, he promised that "if today there are still people in Germany who say: 'We are not going join your community, but stay just as we always have been,' then I say: 'You will die off, but after you there will a young generation that doesn't know anything else!'" A few days later he averred:

"When we have long gone, history will show that we left behind a Reich and a People."[24] With a panoramic vision of the future, a reliance on the verdict of history, and total confidence in the ability to travel from here to there, Hitler introduced Germans to the racial precepts of the Third Reich.

National Socialists were revolutionaries in their proclaimed objective of creating new men and new women who would acknowledge one another as racial comrades and recognize the dangers posed by racial undesirables. Doing this involved revisualizing the German population in a radically different way. A huge reeducation effort invited Germans to see race and to esteem racial value. It was also necessary to educate Germans to assume the physical and social responsibilities of racial comradeship and to acquire military skills. To this end, a vast network of *Gemeinschaftslager* or community camps was established across Germany; at one point or another, most Germans passed through them. Alongside concentration camps and killing camps, the training camps were fundamental parts of the Nazi racial project. Finally, Germany's racial stock had to be protected from racial undesirables, who were either incarcerated or sterilized, and from the broader political and moral threat represented by the alien presence of Germany's Jews. The years after 1933 constituted a period of learning how to sort and divide.

Seeing like an Aryan

In 1936 Heinrich Himmler, head of the SS and Germany's security services, and probably the most powerful man in the Third Reich after Hitler, noted with satisfaction that "the German people . . . have once again learned to see the body" and to judge on the basis of its "worth or unworthiness." A new visual regime repeatedly introduced the German body, most often in portraits of sunny athletes, large families, and marching soldiers, and sometimes by contrast in juxtaposed close-up shots of misshapen, degenerate individuals and formless heaps of people. In "The Camera," a well-received exhibit organized by the Nazi party in 1933, photographs bore such leading captions as "The Lines of the Hopeless," "How Do You Want Germany?" "Not like This Anymore!" and "Only like This!"[25] Photo essays in newspapers and magazines, and in the party's propaganda material, persistently used the technique of pairing good and bad, new and old, "genetically sick" and "genetically healthy," encouraging spectators to glance from one image to the other and to embark on the journey of refashioning the German people.

Nazi propagandists believed that these images were far more compelling than written texts. Increasingly ambitious exhibitions seen by millions of people followed. The most famous was the exhibit of "Degenerate Art," which over a four-year period beginning in the summer of 1937 toured thirteen cities and attracted over three million visitors who came to see specially selected examples of disproportionate, unnatural, and shocking forms of modern art. Over 400,000 people viewed the exhibit "The Eternal Jew" in Munich's Deutsches Museum from December 1937 through January 1938. Even a small town such as Rothenburg assembled a show on "Blood and Race," which was seen by 2,400 people, one-quarter of the town's population, in March 1937. These exhibitions encouraged the practice of looking. They allowed Germans to see contrasts, to make distinctions, to draw divisions. Precisely because Germans had begun to think in terms of *Feindbilder,* or "visions of the enemy," Goebbels regarded exhibitions such as these a "fantastic success."[26] The contrast "This or That?" *(So-oder-So?)* stressed the work of self-creation; the attainment of the ideal form depended on the eradication of old physical shapes. Not to make the effort would be to fall back into "the lines of the hopeless." "This or That?" was the show that the Nazis put on the road across Germany in the years after 1933.

The lead figure in the state's propaganda effort was Walter Gross, a young physician, only twenty-eight years old in 1933, who headed the Office for Racial Politics, a newly created bureau in the Nazi party that was answerable to Hitler's deputy Rudolf Hess. Gross considered himself a crusader for race consciousness, and it was through his efforts that citizens encountered the twinned images of newly self-conscious healthy Germans and degenerate, dangerous others. Already on 14 July 1933, the day the sterilization laws were promulgated and, tellingly, the anniversary of the French Revolution, Gross went on national radio to introduce Germans to the "new human beings" that National Socialism was determined to create and to urge listeners to embark on a spiritual and physical reformation of their selves. What was necessary, he insisted, was to "recognize yourself" ("Erkenne dich selbst"), which meant identifying with the idealized portraits of new Germans and following the tenets of hereditary biology to find a suitable partner for marriage, to marry only for love, and to provide the Volk with healthy children. And, with the portraits of degenerates in mind, it meant accepting "limits to empathy" as a revitalized Germany weeded out racial undesirables. Repeated references to the "false humanity" and "exaggerated pity" of the liberal era indicated exactly what was at stake: the need to prepare Germans to endorse what universal or Christian ethics would regard as criminal activity. "Of course people who have been peacefully living their lives, nestled in the peace and quiet of everyday life, will be shaken to their foundations," admitted Helmut Hübsch, one of Gross's colleagues, in January 1934; "the tragedy of their existence will reveal itself to them like an abyss. Decisions will have to made about the fate of individuals. Sacrifices on an unprecedented scale will have to be borne."[27]

The effort to inculcate a "Nazi conscience" swung into high gear in January 1934, when the sterilization law went into effect. Gross himself introduced the legislation in newsreels that juxtaposed "absorbing scenes" from a "mental asylum" with images of the "powerful figures of our Olympic hopefuls." Documentaries on all aspects of "population policy and racial hygiene," a blend, in Koonz's words, of "sentimental ethnic glorification and somber prophecy," followed in regular installments. An estimated twenty million people, one-third of the population, saw at least one of these films every year. By the middle of 1937 the Office of Racial Politics had trained over 2,000 "racial educators," who on the basis of an eight-week course in Berlin received a special speaker's certificate entitling them to address Germans on population and race policy. Certification was part of the effort to make German racism objective and scientific according to so-called laws of genetic inheritance and to keep out self-styled experts such as Julius Streicher, the party's Gauleiter in Nuremberg, known for his theories of blood contagion. Gross's educators fanned out across Germany, holding lectures for the general public, workshops for party members, and seminars for school classes. In 1938 an estimated 2.5 million people attended 25,130 events, taking away with them hundreds of thousands of pamphlets, calendars depicting the "new people" of Germany, and other propaganda material. A familiar item in doctors' waiting rooms and public-health offices, the illustrated magazine *Neues Volk* reached a circulation of over 300,000 in the last year before the war.[28] Filled with photographs, graphs, and tables, the propaganda of the Office for Racial Politics made the crucial distinction between quantity and quality—*Zahl und Güte*—easy to understand. Unlike Streicher's vulgar antisemitic newspaper, *Der Stürmer,* the *Neues Volk* appeared to be objective, a sobering statement of the difficult facts of life.

Yet it was lurid depictions of Jewish child murderers and sexual marauders that often made an impression and could be remembered long afterward. With a circulation of half a million, the newspaper was displayed in special "*Stürmer* boxes" that could be found all over Germany after 1933. On his automobile trips into the countryside, Victor Klemperer encountered them constantly: "the beautiful road to Oberkips is now called Adolf Hitler Strasse, and at the station *Der Stürmer* has its box." "At first, you read *Der Stürmer* only out of curiosity," noted one socialist informant, "but in the end, something sticks."[29] Passersby stopped to discuss the fantastic allegations. "Isn't that horrible," a bystander overhead two women in Fulda, "and it must be true; otherwise the Jews wouldn't stand for it!" The copy was so overwhelming that Klemperer half-expected "to find the body of a child" buried in his own garden. A few years later, it was with references to *Der Stürmer* that many invading soldiers described their impressions of the Soviet Union.[30]

Racial propaganda material littered German schools; even arithmetic problems multiplied the number of "idiots" in Germany. The Nazis opened hospitals and asylums to field trips so that schoolchildren could make the choice "This or That?" "We wandered through hundreds of corridors," reported Elisabeth Brasch about one 1935 excursion to a hospital in Kreuznach; "suddenly we were in a large room together with numerous girls, all of them half-crazy, crippled, deformed." On the walls, quotations from Hitler and Goebbels were interspersed with sayings from the Bible. This combination probably confirmed rather than contradicted the overall message of racial uplift.[31]

Pedagogues warned parents that children would come home from school with different ideas about morality. "Hans" and "Grete" should not be considered *gemütsroh,* heartless, one educator explained: "If, heeding the admonitions of parents, they no longer make fun of the unfortunate boy, then maternal upbringing has achieved a remarkable success. But to play with him? . . . Here children are following a primal instinct that rejects everything sick or weak or gross." As it was, back at the youth hostel after the outing to Kreuznach, Brasch remembered that "a lot of girls found each other's company, and in our discussions" about the sterilization law "we were completely opposed to the leader, who believed everything could be solved by radical means."[32]

There were certainly not "limits to empathy" when it came to the German body. From the "bleeding borders" torn apart by the Treaty of Versailles to the dangers posed by hostile air forces surrounding Germany, from the villages and towns overlooked by the route of the Autobahn to the luscious physiognomies of its people, which were staple items in illustrated magazines and picture books, right down to the "hands of mothers," the subject of a 1934 photo essay in *Neues Volk,* and finally, to the "hands of the Führer" himself, the German body was caressed over and over again, from morning until night, in countless school exercises and youth meetings and "Strength through Joy" trips.[33] Genealogies were prepared, bloodlines laid down, and the involvement of ordinary citizens in the nation's tumultuous history recounted in order to make everything a shining facet reflecting the well-being of the German people; even the people's radio was designated the VEB 301 to commemorate 30 January, when Hitler came to power. Yet for all the excursions that school classes and the Hitler Youth undertook in the countryside, for all the tents pitched, there was a striking lack of interest in the natural forms of the land, its wildlife, or geology. It was not the place called Germany, but the German people who inhabited it, a unity of blood and history, that received the lion's share of attention. This self-absorption made the exclusion of Germany's Jews, and other noncombatants in Germany's racial struggle, all the more complete.

The Camp

Thousands of community camps had the task of sculpting the new German person. Nazi pedagogues extolled *das Lager,* "the camp," as the privileged place where the "new generation was finding its form." When we think of camps in the Nazi period, we think of the network of death camps and satellite slave-labor camps that extended across the German empire in 1942 and 1943; or else we think of the concentration camps such as Dachau where the Nazis locked up their political opponents. A total of 100,000 people, mostly Social Democrats and Communists, spent time in concentration camps in 1933, so the threat of terror remained palpable. By the end of 1934, however, there were no more than 3,000 prisoners remaining in four main camps, Dachau, Sachsenhausen, Buchenwald, and Lichtenburg (a women's camp that was replaced by Ravensbrück in 1939). Until the war, Germany's "empire of the camps" was in fact filled mostly with "Aryans," either genetically unacceptable Germans who were removed from society in the years after 1935, so that the concentration camps filled up again to about 10,000, or, in much, much greater numbers, children, young people, and professionals training for their parts in the people's community.[34]

The "closed" community camp was the formative institution around which the Reich Labor Service was organized. The annual *Fahrt,* or outing, to an overnight camp was the most important event in the Hitler Youth calendar. And camps were the preferred sites for holding workshops to retrain professionals in racial science and other aspects of "national political" work. "When the sun sets," rhapsodized one observer, "camp crews all over Germany are standing at attention in flag parades." According to Adolf Mertens, who pioneered camp pedagogy, "a network of camps covers our country from the sea to the mountains, from the heaths and forests of the East to the industrial regions of the West." "There are camps in tents and in houses, camps for thirty and for several hundred, and even one thousand participants."[35] Most common were camps for party officials, for the SA and SS, and the Reich Labor Service. Two thousand summer camps accommodated over 600,000 boys and girls in the late 1930s; 3,200 military-style camps housed nearly 400,000 young people fulfilling their labor service on the eve of World War II; and 500,000 participants found shelter, mostly in tent camps, during the ten-day period of the Nuremberg party rally every September from 1933 to 1938.[36] Camps gathered up "lawyers, artists, doctors, civil servants, [and] corporate directors" for reeducation as well. Transit camps collected ethnic Germans prior to resettlement at the beginning of the war and German refugees fleeing the Soviet advance at the end. It is probable that most people in Germany were obliged to enroll in a camp at some point in the years 1933–1945.

The camp provided the institutional setting to take up Hitler's challenge that the task of the revolution was to educate people. Set apart from the familiar social contexts of family, work, and school, the closed camp was designed to break down identifications with social milieus and to promote *Entbürgerlichung* (purging bourgeois elements) and *Verkameradshaftung* (comradeship) as part of the process of *Volkwerdung,* "the making of the people," as the peculiar idiom of National Socialism put it.[37] Uniforms, the shared burdens of labor, and the egalitarian form of address—"thou" instead of "you," a significant gesture—were supposed to turn Germans into racial comrades. According to surveys at the time, the comradeship of the camps had real appeal, but the new social virtues demanded exacting discipline, especially for boys. Closed, militarized encampments, Germany's *Lager* resembled "total institutions" that made heavy demands on the mind and body. The Third Reich did not completely remake men and women, but to the extent that it succeeded, its success was in large part due to the camps.

For Hitler, youth was the guarantee of the future of the Third Reich. In what could just as easily have been the horrified words of a liberal opponent of Nazism, Hitler mused in 1938 on the ability of the regime to create Nazis out of Germans as they passed from one stage of life to another. "These boys and girls enter our organization with their ten years of age, and often for the first time get a little fresh air; after four years in the Young Folk they go on to the Hitler Youth, where we have them for another four years . . . And even if they are still not complete National Socialists, they go to

Labor Service and are smoothed out there for another six, seven months . . . And whatever class consciousness or social status might still be left"—Hitler did not think it would amount to much—"the Wehrmacht will take care of."[38] Enrollment for four years in the Hitler Youth and then six months in the Reich Labor Service was made mandatory for boys in 1936 and for girls three years later, providing Germany with a genuine *Staatsjugend*.

Alongside parents and school, the Hitler Youth came to be recognized as one of three institutions responsible for the socialization of children. Although it was heir to the legacy of Germany's youth movement at the beginning of the century, which had pioneered the idea that "youth leads youth," the Hitler Youth was much more militarized. The Hitler Youth did away with the traditional autonomy and cultivated rituals of youth groups, replacing them with the uniform standards of a single institution that enrolled hundreds of thousands of boys and girls. It also reduced social segregation. Both the Hitler Youth and the Reich Labor Service aimed to mix bourgeois and working-class youths in order to pull down social barriers to the formation of national race consciousness. This effort created opportunities for comradeship, something that many middle-class youth prized, but it also set the stage for bullying, which mostly middle-class youths endured.

With its long hours—Wednesday afternoons, all day Saturday—and relentless discipline, the Hitler Youth could not summon up the eager, selfless enthusiasm enjoyed by Weimar-era youth groups. Even overnight trips resembled military expeditions: "Everything was done in a totally military way, from reveille, first parade, raising the flag, morning sport and ablutions through breakfast to the 'scouting games,' lunch and so on to the evening . . . everything was done in terms of command obedience." "Marching in lockstep was the simple formula to train people to fall into order," notes Hans-Ulrich Thamer: "in lockstep—not as fast as you might want," went the Nazi-era marching song: "in lockstep—not as slow as you might want; in lockstep—you have to fall in with the whole; in lockstep—you can't think only about yourself; in lockstep—and the column stays together; in lockstep—and you will be unassailable." Boys chafed at the military-style discipline and rigid leadership structures imposed in the effort to prepare the next generation of German soldiers. Goebbels' own stepson, Harald Quandt, complained of "bad food, mistreatment, censored mail." Other children just found the service boring.[39]

However, the national sports competition organized by the Hitler Youth enrolled seven million boys and girls in 1939, twice as many as in 1935, and provided opportunities to achieve distinction. And the simple fact that young people had been assigned a role in rebuilding Germany gave the Hitler Youth legitimacy. It chipped away at the more parochial authority of parents and teachers. Despite being taunted in labor service for his glasses and his books, one middle-class adolescent assumed the bearing of the Hitler Youth, crossing his parents—"you old people need to be eradicated so that the new era can dawn!"—and revering the "unconditional loyalty to the group and the Führer principle"—like "all the others," added the Swiss journalist who provided the anecdote in 1944.[40] The consciousness of generation, and the assumption that old needed to be replaced with new, undoubtedly opened young minds to the tenets of racial hygiene, which were repeatedly parsed in workshops and lectures. Young people, who had been the most vulnerable group in the Great Depression, came to see themselves as the vanguard of a new society that promised to provide them with opportunities and experiences their parents lacked. More than a third of the 1938 graduating class of the Athenaeum Gymnasium in the north German city of Stade hoped to pursue a career as an officer in the Wehrmacht or a youth leader in the Hitler Youth.[41]

The six-month stint in the camps of the Reich Labor Service, to which the great majority of eighteen-year-olds reported, most clearly revealed the ambitions of the Nazis to remake young people. Under the motto "Work ennobles" or "Work sets you free," which was also on display at the concentration camps in Dachau, Sachsenhausen, and later Auschwitz, the camps organized their residents in military-style brigades to promote comradeship and discipline; young women had it easier, since they were usually sent to farms or households.

Unlike the work camps in the Weimar era, the settlements of the Reich Labor Service were closed; men could not leave the camp without permission, vacations were strictly limited, and reading matter restricted to National Socialist literature. *Arbeitsdienstmänner* (Labor Servicemen) toiled on public-works projects and received military training, in part to circumvent restrictions on the size of the German army. But the main point of the six-month service was to break down identifications with social milieus and thus to overcome the fragmentation of German society.

Every aspect of the labor service camps demanded that the young men step into line and find social acceptance. Arriving by train at a nearby railroad station, they marched in formation to the camp, where they traded their civilian clothes for the brown uniform of the Labor Service. In the first days, the men wrote short autobiographical statements, which became the basis for discussions about each person's ability to serve the community and become a good racial comrade. On the last evening, residents also wrote up evaluations identifying the individuals they considered qualified to assume leadership roles. These confessional exercises generated prescriptions for good conduct.

Arbeitsdienstmänner worked together as a unit, marched together, and relaxed together, an unending group existence designed to pull together the people's community. Strict order predominated during mealtimes: "none of the haphazard and random taking places and eating occurs here. That would be like running a restaurant," a fall backward into the individualizing tendencies of liberal society. The men were expected to set tables properly and to decorate them with flowers as part of National Socialist "table culture," since the labor camp was not a "tavern or a kitchen" either.[42] While men could form "affinity groups" after dinner, regulations stipulated that "convivial activities had to include everyone" at least twice a week.[43] As pedagogue Hellmut Petersen admonished, "your favorite booth in the bar is hardly the place to build a team." The entire organization of the labor camp was designed to create a new collective space to supplant the restaurants, taverns, and kitchens that upheld geographies of social origin and social status. Most camps consisted of standard wooden barracks built for 150 to 160 men, "rustic-military": "Military in its rigor, straight lines, and simplicity—lamp shade, motto, and bench, everything 'ship shape.'" The style was also rustic, "heavy and rooted to the soil."[44]

It was 50,000 *Arbeitsdienstmänner,* holding their trademark spades like rifles, who provided the stirring chorus at the beginning of Leni Riefenstahl's film *Triumph of the Will.* The next scenes cut to the folksy comradeship of the Hitler Youth encampment. The rally itself was the final culmination of a gigantic *Fahrt* in which as many as 3,000 extra trains transported 500,000 participants to temporary *Lager* in which they demonstrated their capacity to live as a collective. Year after year in the 1930s, a sizable share of Germany's young people, perhaps as many as one in five, took part in the ten-day extravaganza.

On film, the images of the Volksgemeinschaft looked compelling. But the camps themselves demanded hard work as participants struggled to prove their fitness as racial comrades. The physical labor was taxing; the work of fitting in was even harder. The egalitarian ethos encouraged working-class men to take down high-school graduates several notches. "Their long, one-sidedly intellectual education has made them unfamiliar with real life," explained Petersen; "they no longer remember the thinking and speech of simple, uneducated comrades." How to get them to think and act in a "simple, plain, straight-forward" manner? Petersen was frank: "by example, but also by rebuke, teasing, ribbing, name-calling, and even, though rarely, violence."[45]

Just how much comradeship the camps produced is hard to determine. Certainly it was middle-class youths who did the adjusting. Many got to know working-class fellows for the first time: "Guys with naked women tattooed on their arms, guys who spoke about their Marxist escapades before the seizure of power . . . guys who would kill you for the smallest insult to the group."[46] Elisabeth Brasch's brother, a high-school graduate, reported to a work camp in April 1937. In his letters home, he admitted that "life together" in the camp was "very difficult," because usually "the lower elements prevailed," but ultimately "people came together before they realized it." He took pride in fitting in and learning new things. His open-minded attitude, which acknowledged problems, probably applied to many other situations in the Third Reich: "We *have* to see the good parts . . . We have to go with the times, even if there are many, many things that we do not agree with. To swim against the current just makes matters worse." Brasch concluded that "despite all the difficulties, my brother was grateful for his labor service, which gave him rich insights into the diversity of human life." A year later, Elisabeth completed her own Reich Labor Service. Looking back in 1940 from exile in the United States, she wrote: "I did not collapse; on the contrary, after six months I left camp stronger and healthier than when I entered."[47]

Lager und Kolonne. According to Bernhard Rust, the minister of education, "camp and column" were the best means to make National Socialists out of young people; but adults who had been socialized in the Kaiserreich and the Weimar Republic needed a crash course.[48] The Ministry of Education authorized the National Socialist Teachers' League to organize retraining camps in order to "equip," as Rust put it, teachers with lesson plans in "heredity and race"; an estimated 215,000 of Germany's 300,000 teachers attended two-week retreats at fifty-six regional sites and two national centers that mixed athletics, military exercises, and instruction. The Office for Racial Politics also certified thousands of physicians in eight-day training sessions. For the physicians, judges, and lawyers who administered Germany's new sterilization courts, the Institute for Racial Biology in Hamburg provided specialized instruction. Before they were assigned to local public-health offices, social workers went off to camps housed in dormitories provided by the People's Welfare Service; "home evenings," hikes, and excursions interspersed the routine of racial and biological course work. Exactly how many adults took part in political retraining exercises is not clear, but Victor Klemperer's diaries mention a friend headed off to a "NSDAP-ordered pharmacists' 'coordination' day" in June 1933 as well as a professor of literature who had been sent to a camp in Königs Wusterhausen in 1937: "Teachers between forty and fifty. They slept six to a room, wore uniforms, did digging and sports, were given educative lectures. A headmaster talked about the character of the French; they were similar to the Jews, they did not love animals."[49]

Race thinking meant mobilizing citizens to shake Germans out of the "quiet of everyday life," as officials at the Office for Racial Politics had warned; it meant re-envisioning relatives as healthy Aryans who composed a uniform table of ancestors; and it meant creating new spaces to counteract exclusive loyalties to home or to the traditions associated with favorite booths in neighborhood bars. The Nazis designed *Fahrt, Lager,* and *Kolonne* to pull Germans out of social, political, and religious milieus. In this case, race could be strengthened by changing the environment. *Fahrt*—every year the offerings of the Reichsbahn expanded, services for group travel to transport Hitler Youth or "Strength through Joy" vacationers improved, bicycles were accommodated, and extra trains pressed into service to take visitors to the party rallies in Nuremberg. The number of "passenger kilometers" on the Reichsbahn increased steadily so that at the end of the 1930s it exceeded its pre-Depression levels by more than one-third. *Lager*—there are no comprehensive statistics, but the Nazis made use of thousands of training camps across the country. The number of annual overnight stays at German youth hostels, which were taken over by the Hitler Youth, nearly doubled, from 4.6 to 8.7 million, between 1933 and 1938.[50] *Kolonne*—more and more Germans had fallen into step with the Nazi regime.

Six prewar years was not a long time to create race consciousness or fashion a racial elite. Yet a new leadership of racial warriors had begun to assemble. With the massive expansion of the Hitler Youth to include girls as well as boys, more than 765,000 young people had the opportunity to serve in leadership roles. Many advanced in the ranks and received formal training and ideological instruction in national academies such as the Reich Leadership School in Potsdam. Twenty-one-year-old Melita Maschmann enrolled there in 1939 to prepare for her task resettling and educating ethnic Germans in the East. The Reich Labor Service also required thousands of camp commanders, political instructors, and work brigade leaders. Lore Walb had intense discussions about "race, belief, Charlemagne, blood, heredity" with her cousin Günther, who hoped to make a career in the Labor Service, despite his "bad experiences"—most likely hazing—and whose idealism she admired, "because he is a comrade."[51]

For boys, leadership experience in the Hitler Youth often led to the SS, the party's paramilitary and ideological vanguard. Under the command of Heinrich Himmler, the SS regarded itself as the core of an entirely new breed of men to lead the political and racial advancement of the nation. Ordinary members had to provide proof of their Aryan ancestry going back to the year 1800, senior officers back to the year 1750. As a self-conscious elite, the SS set for itself the task of breaking down religious affiliations as well as social prejudices and expunging principles of Christian love and mercy, which continued to sway most Germans. Moreover, the SS demanded that members adhere to more racially self-conscious codes of private behavior. It pressured unmarried SS men to find appropriate love matches, father children, and remain faithful to their wives once married. Prospective wives had to go to considerable lengths to document their own Aryan origins and demonstrate proper German comportment. The SS believed it was cultivating a thoroughly modern approach to life, which recognized that biological reproduction was linked to personal fulfillment as well as racial health. It spoke up for sexually happy relationships and defended wives who had careers of their own, urging husbands to help out at home. Modern, racially up-to-date, and lethally antisemitic, the ranks of the SS included nearly 800,000 German men, more than one percent of the population of "Greater Germany," between 1931 and 1945; over the same period, more than 240,000 women married SS men.[52]

Most citizens participated in the rituals of the racial community, in *Fahrt, Lager,* and *Kolonne,* but did they become racial comrades? The signs of belonging to the National Socialist community were plain to see: the "Heil Hitler!" greeting, Nazi flags, party badges. Racial vocabularies infiltrated everyday speech, though acts of kindness toward Jews did not disappear. The Reich Labor Service probably did create more social exchanges across class lines, but the experiences also left memories of humiliation. Social milieus unstratified as larger cohorts left for community camps, training exercises, and professional workshops. Nonetheless, traditional loyalties to the Protestant and Catholic churches persisted, and expanded during the war. Tantalizing hints about changing fashions suggest that clothes no longer indexed social origins as precisely as they once had. Nazi fashion arrived not so much in the form of blond braids and dirndls as in a sportier look that came with skin creams, smaller hats, and the navy-blue skirts and brown Alpine jackets of the League of German Girls. For her fourteenth birthday, at the end of May 1933, Lore Walb received "material for a brown Hitler jacket" and a jar of Nivea cream, presents that perfectly combined the homespun habits of economy and pretensions to worldliness, and the allure of both independence and belonging that characterized daily life in the Third Reich.[53] Schoolboys in elite secondary schools discontinued wearing their distinctive black caps; denoting status in this way had become unpopular. "A culture in which top hats, peaked caps, and school caps marked rigid social hierarchies" increasingly gave way to one in which men and even women from all classes wore the same hat, the fedora.[54]

Germans thought more about their racial heritage, and Lore discussed it with her cousin Günther, while Franz Göll offered up a full diagnosis of his family's health, but they were not more likely to marry and they did not "bestow upon the Führer," as the phrase went, more children. It is true that in the first year of the Third Reich, Germans were more likely to marry than they had been at any time in the 1920s. The trend continued in 1934, a year when some 11.1 marriages were recorded for every 1,000 inhabitants, up from 9.2 marriages in 1928 and 1929. The Nazis, who had created financial incentives for newlyweds, believed that the family values they celebrated had reversed the dangerous social trends that had discouraged marriage and limited family size. But in 1935 the marriage rate fell back to 9.7, and a few years later it was where it had been before the Great Depression. The temporary rise in the number of weddings was simply a reflection of the fact that couples had postponed marrying in economic hard times. Judged by their willingness to marry and have children, Germans were not so different in 1938 from what they had been in 1928; there was little the Nazis could do to reverse long-term trends that limited the number and size of families. Even SS families did not have proportionally more children. What changed was the nature of relations between men and women, which became more open, an indication that social milieu was less important and sex more available. The fun poked at alleged promiscuity in the League of German Girls suggests not only that "youth led by youth" had more sex but also that girls felt more independent. (The jokes are all based on the group's acronym, BdM, so that the Bund deutscher Mädel could become *Bund* deutscher Matratzen, "the League of German Mattresses," or *Bald deutscher Mütter,* "Soon to be German Mothers"; and they went on from there.)[55]

Germans also took on the roles of racial comrades when they accepted the inferior status of outsiders, "asocials," the genetically "unfit," and Jews. People repeatedly bumped into the divide between worthiness and unworthiness. Two by two, students at a medical institute took off their clothes and stood in front of the biology class in a demonstration of "racial characteristics." When her turn came, Gisela Otmar worried that the teachers would discover some unknown Jewish feature. As it was, she was told that she had an "eastern butt" and "slumped shoulders."[56] Did she try to stand straighter? Did she resent the bodies of other students? Did she sympathize a little bit with people who were not considered worthy? Perhaps so, because Gisela recalled the incident in postwar interviews; but other Germans continued to improve themselves by grooming themselves as Aryans, sitting up straighter, filling out the table of ancestors, and fitting in at the camps, which gave legitimacy to the selection process that had created Gisela's anxiety in the first place.

Unworthy Life

As community *Lager* filled up with young men, so did prisons. The Nazis responded to an intense desire for order in Germany in 1933. Fears of Communist revolutionaries mingled with more general anxieties about crime and delinquency. Since millions of Germans remained unemployed, however, it was difficult to distinguish the dangerous core of criminals or the larger group of what experts identified as "asocials," an underclass of delinquents, prostitutes, beggars, and the work shy, from the much greater numbers of destitute but virtuous citizens. Newspapers published lurid accounts of child molesters, serial murderers, and arsonists who walked city streets unseen. In a period when begging was common, uncertainty about who exactly was at the door, the "truly needy" or "delinquents" and "vagrants," made the public increasingly receptive to efforts to sort out the healthy from the unhealthy, the good from the bad. Germans would credit the Third Reich with getting rid of "the mischief of begging." The Nazi years were often remembered as a time of security when people could once again walk the streets unmolested or leave their bicycles unlocked. Attentive observers also noticed that itinerant musicians, typical big-city characters who, with their organ grinders, strolled from one tenement courtyard to another, diminished in number. The ragpicker's familiar cry, "iron, castoffs, paper," was not heard much anymore.[57]

Although the numbers of Communists and Social Democrats held in Germany's concentration camps dropped in 1934 and 1935, the number of German citizens caught up in large-scale police sweeps increased sharply. At the end of the summer of 1933, the police arrested tens of thousands of vagrants. As police shifted their attention from Communists to delinquents, they registered the Nazis' growing preoccupation with genetic and racial dangers. To cultivate the healthy body of Germans, the Nazi state designed positive measures such as marriage loans, improved access to public health care, and the foundations of a social security system. It also devised negative eugenic measures, which were less expensive, to weed out undesirable citizens whose alleged genetic disabilities left them unproductive or predisposed to criminal, delinquent, and other "asocial" behavior. "In the language used by both the Nazis and the scientists, this policy was called 'Aufartung durch Ausmerzung,'" improvement through exclusion.[58] Unlike the rehabilitative work carried out by millions of activists in the Hitler Youth, the League of German Girls, the Reich Labor Service, and the People's Welfare, smaller but powerful groups of biomedical professionals oversaw the identification and segregation of "asocials" and the sterilization of genetically "unfit" Germans. The German medical establishment regarded the national revolution in 1933 as the opportunity finally to abandon liberalism's misguided effort to care for the sovereign body of the individual; it worked closely with the Nazis to promote therapies to strengthen the collective body of the German people. Doing this meant making judgments about the value of the individuals and their ability to lead productive lives.

At first authorities worked inside the traditional justice system: Nazi-era defendants were charged with more serious offenses, those found guilty received longer sentences, and recidivists faced security confinements in state prisons. This was a tough, popular "law and order" approach. But given their ideas about genetics, the Nazis eventually moved in a completely different direction, shifting the emphasis away from punishment and deterrence and adopting a much broader demographic policy to remove racial "undesirables" from the community altogether. In the racial interpretation of crime, biology produced the criminal, making punishment and deterrence pointless. However, crime could be reduced by removing the dangerous body, either by isolating "asocials" in work camps or by sterilizing genetically "unworthy" individuals. In the Nazi legal system, genetics replaced milieu as the point of origin of crime, biomedical experts replaced social workers, and physical segregation replaced ameliorative social policy or detention therapy. Whereas community camps admitted the importance of social milieus by counteracting their effects, concentration camps denied the role of environmental forces altogether.

With the reorganization and centralization of Germany's police forces under the command of Heinrich Himmler in 1936, the security branch, which included both the secret state police, or Gestapo, and the Criminal Police, moved into position to combat "asocials" and "community aliens" as well as political enemies. Himmler and other SS ideologues developed an increasingly racialized theory of policing. They relied on criminologists, medical experts, and welfare officials who argued that heredity strongly influenced sociability, and rejected the nightwatchman concept to justify radical preemptive intervention. As Himmler explained, "the police have the responsibility to safeguard the organic unity of the German people, its vital energies, and its facilities from destruction and disintegration." This definition gave the police extremely wide latitude. Anything that did not fit the normative standards of the people's community or could be construed as an agent of social dissolution theoretically fell under the purview of the police. In many ways, Karl Dürkefälden's father had been right: in the Third Reich, there was no room for those who did not or would not fit in. But in practice, the security police left former socialists such as Karl, who had a family and a job, alone and concentrated on "asocials," who have not found a voice in German history. "The sheer number of descriptors," comments Ulrich Herbert"—'beggar,' 'vagabond,' 'work shy,' 'panderer,' as well as 'deadbeat,' 'freeloader,' 'troublemaker'—makes clear that what is at work here is a collective concept that encompasses all sorts of irritating or unnatural but not legally classifiable behavior."⁵⁹

Both regular police forces and the Gestapo began their sweeps through the ragged edges of town; between 1934 and 1937 the number of prisoners in concentration camps more than doubled, to 7,000; most inmates were "asocials." New camps added extra capacity to accommodate some 10,000 "asocials" arrested in the spring and summer of 1938 in two nationwide operations under the code name "Operation Work-shy." By the spring of 1938 an SS subsidiary, the German Earth- and Stoneworks Company, operated Flossenbürg in Bavaria and Mauthausen in newly annexed Austria. Thousands of other supposedly "asocial" or "work-shy" Germans were locked up in work camps. Gypsies often found themselves imprisoned in their own encampments, which police enclosed with barbed wire and placed under guard. Moreover, in the late 1930s, the criminal police began to arrest thousands of gay men for being "true" or genetically predisposed homosexuals (lesbianism was generally ignored or considered a fad, not a biological debility). Although male homosexuals could have been charged, convicted, and sentenced to state prison under existing antisodomy laws, many were simply pulled off the streets and thrown into concentration camps without court review. The camps also held hundreds of Jehovah's Witnesses, including the young *Arbeitsdienstmann* whom Günter Grass remembered. Over and over, the man simply insisted "Wedon'tdothat" until he was taken away: Germany's 30,000 Jehovah's Witnesses refused to swear an oath of loyalty to Hitler or to bear arms. Almost one-third were arrested at some point between 1933 and 1945.[60]

Run largely alongside the state justice and penal system, concentration camps became a dumping ground for *Gemeinschaftsfremde,* "enemies of the community," who were to spend the rest of their lives thrown away. Nazi propaganda had at first extolled the rehabilitative virtues of work and thus acknowledged the probability of release—"The Weakling Becomes a Man, the Disbeliever Finds a Life," wrote the *Hamburger Fremdenblatt* in one 1935 series about the work camp in nearby Rickling. Later, prisoners were not sentenced, but "thrown" into concentration camps permanently isolated from the community. National Socialism did not regard "asocial elements" as sufficiently "worthy" to enjoy the "public amenities of the Volksgemeinschaft." As a result, death rates soared, particularly among sick or alcoholic older men who made up the largest part of the "asocials." In Bautzen, a work camp near Kassel, the average age of the inmates in 1942 was fifty-nine.[61] These men usually fell to the bottom of the camp hierarchies that established themselves in the late 1930s. Inmates were identified by coded triangles sewn onto their clothing: red designated political prisoners, who were the best organized and, on the whole, the best treated, while black identified asocials, green professional criminals, pink homosexuals, and purple Jehovah's Witnesses. Before the roundup of Jewish men in November 1938, most Jews in concentration camps had been detained as political prisoners; nevertheless, the camp administration required them to distinguish themselves as Jews by sewing a yellow triangle beneath the inverted red triangle to form a Star of David.

The physical presence of the Gestapo in German life in the 1930s should not be exaggerated. In 1937 it employed only 7,000 people, including secretaries and other assistants, in a total population of some sixty million, in contrast to the Stasi's 90,000 regular employees in East Germany's population of seventeen million. Nonetheless, the Gestapo's aim, in collaboration with the criminal police, to sweep the streets of "worthless" Germans was visible enough. In Hamburg a train left the main railroad station every Thursday or Friday to transport inmates to the work camp in Rickling. The routine intervention of the police in the corners of daily life of German citizens explains why the Gestapo assumed the "almost mythical status as an all-seeing, all-knowing" creature that had placed its agents throughout the land to overhear conversations in order to enforce political conformity.[62] However, most of the people arrested by the Gestapo were "asocials," not jokesters or grumblers, who, when they did get in trouble, had been denounced by neighbors or acquaintances, usually for personal rather than political reasons. In fact, Nazi leaders regarded most denunciations as frivolous.[63] Nonetheless, stories and rumors abounded; the unlikelihood of denunciation or arrest did not undo the unpredictability of state surveillance. What is remarkable is that Germans remembered the Gestapo, not the people they arrested, a silent endorsement of operations against "asocials."

Whereas "asocials" could be relatively easily identified along the borders of respectability, the "genetically unfit," many of whom had children and spouses, were much harder to find. Nazi authorities were not even sure how many German citizens fitted their shifting definitions of biological degeneracy. Minister of the Interior Wilhelm Frick usually referred to a figure of about one million physically or mentally enfeebled Germans, which corresponded to the estimate of the renowned eugenicist Friedrich Lenz, though Frick also noted that other experts put the number as high as thirteen million out of a population of sixty-five million, a ratio of one in five. In a 1929 speech, Hitler himself had toyed with the possibility of culling four out of five German children; "the final result might even be an increase in strength."[64] As it was, the Nazis sterilized over 400,000 Germans, mostly in the prewar years 1934–1939. At least as many citizens faced the threat of sterilization, so that one million people and their families became entangled in this strand of the state's racial policies. These are extraordinarily high numbers, especially compared to the 45,000 individuals sterilized in the United States between 1907 and 1945 (German legal commentators reassured the German public by citing U.S. programs as precedents and quoting Oliver Wendell Holmes's 1927 opinion, "three generations of imbeciles are enough").

Unlike the "actions" against "asocials," sterilization proceedings reached deep into civil society. However, given the wide social net cast by this racial reclamation project, there was remarkably little opposition beyond the legal resistance of the defendants themselves. Most candidates for sterilization came from lower-class backgrounds, and since it was educated middle-class men who were making normative judgments about decent behavior, they were both more vulnerable to state action and less likely to arouse sympathy. The letters, diaries, and memoirs of German Jews, who were very alert to racism in the Third Reich, but also disproportionately middle-class, do not refer to racial legislation against non-Jewish Germans; the same goes for German resistance circles. The victims themselves, as well as their families, undoubtedly felt ashamed to be officially regarded as "unworthy." All of this indicates the extent to which Germans absorbed Nazi ideas about physical and mental normalcy. Even the *Volkssturm*, Germany's last-ditch line of defense in World War II, refrained from conscripting German men who had been sterilized; they were "unworthy of combat" (in the moral rather than physical sense).[65] Sterilization proceedings began almost immediately after the "Law for the Prevention of Genetically Damaged Offspring" went into effect in January 1934. Most candidates for sterilization were referred to one of Germany's 700-odd public-health offices by attending physicians in asylums and hospitals. Health officials also maintained systematic files on welfare recipients, schoolchildren, and convicted felons, and used these to identify potential candidates. In Berchtesgarden, in southern Germany, schoolteachers annotated the tables of ancestors prepared by schoolchildren and handed them over to public-health officials.[66] If local registrars became suspicious, simply the attempt to get married set sterilization proceedings in motion.

Once public-health offices received a referral, they assigned the case to a physician certified in racial biology. One young woman, accompanied by her fiancé, entered the doctor's office:

> The doctor read from my files and held it against me that my sisters had been in reform school and my mother had had a prior conviction, which I didn't know. I was very embarrassed. In the next room . . . everyone could hear my answers. The doctor kept going in and out of the room before he suddenly stopped in front of me and said something like, if one pound costs seven pfennigs, how much do seven pounds cost? Very timidly I said 1.05 Mark. What! screamed the doctor; if one-half pound costs fifteen pfennigs, how much do seven cost? Seventy pfennigs I said quietly. I was also asked about cities and rivers, almost all of which I could answer.

The objection to these sorts of intelligence tests was that they precluded a more general judgment about how people conducted their lives. In 1937 Gerhard Wagner, head of the Nazi Physicians' League, wrote a long memorandum urging that party branches rather than health offices oversee sterilization proceedings in order to prevent virtuous but uneducated comrades from falling into the clutches of zealous racial bureaucrats. Officials in the Ministry of the Interior, in turn, dismissed as "exceptions" the egregious cases Wagner enumerated. They argued for the scientific authority of hereditary biology and the necessity of its administration by public-health offices, a winning argument in line with the overall shift of power to biomedical professionals. Some intelligence tests, however, were put aside in favor of more general but equally arbitrary assessments of racial worthiness.[67]

Figures to measure the extent of genetic surveillance in the Third Reich are uneven but indicative: in the Prussian district of Düsseldorf, in western Germany, 1.0 percent of the population was evaluated in the years 1935–1941, and 40 percent of these were sterilized; in the state of Thüringen, 2.4 percent of the population was evaluated, and again 40 percent of these sterilized. In Berlin's Charlottenburg neighborhood, officials required one of every nine prospective newlyweds to procure a certificate of genetic health; 5 percent of these were barred from getting married.[68] (In Lippe, at least, thirty-eight of forty-two appeals to grant an exception to rejected marriage applications were successful, however.) There were hard lessons to be learned, as one young man, a dairy farm worker from Karlsruhe, insisted, when questioned by the Americans right after the war about his 1935 sterilization "(he cried bitterly here): 'I never filled out any applications or questionnaires or anything that had to do with the party since then.'"[69]

If the physician recommended sterilization, a three-person "sterilization court" issued a final, almost always concurring decision. Appeals could be made within an increasingly restricted period, but were seldom granted. Sterilization took place a few weeks later. In rare cases, however, determined individuals obtained court orders that postponed the operation for years. A twenty-year-old shopgirl, Flora S., had been a patient in a private sanatorium and then a state asylum for part of 1933. Her file found its way to the district physician in the public-health office of the Berlin district of Tempelhof, who diagnosed "manic depression" and recommended sterilization, particularly in light of the fact that Flora wanted to get married and her grandfather had committed suicide. Most sterilizations, however, rested on a diagnosis of congenital feeblemindedness or schizophrenia. Flora and her family responded with a long series of appeals and protests, winning several deferrals of the operation, which was initially scheduled for August 1939, rescheduled for May 1944, and finally set for June 1945, by which time the Nazis had been defeated; "for Flora S. the thousand-year Reich was a twelve-year effort to avoid sterilization." Flora was lucky; most appeals were not granted and most operations not postponed. In fact, the thinking was "better one too many than one too few." Almost one in ten candidates for sterilization had to be led to the clinics by police force.[70]

In her classic study of sterilization in the Third Reich, Gisela Bock points out that the sterilization proceedings put the voices of victims into the historical record, an unusual occurrence in Nazi Germany. Whether they were "pleading or imploring, beseeching or threatening, complaining or accusing, bitter or outraged, frightened or self-confident, resigned or enraged, oral or written, rhymed or unrhymed," the appeals were generally free of the "condescending" scientific language of biological racism. Observing that "this confrontation of two languages was also a confrontation of two different ways of thinking," Bock emphasizes how different the victims were from their Nazi tormentors. Faced with her own sterilization, the "schizophrenic" Emma P. objected: "Every person is also different like any other, and every case too."[71] There is no better antifascist statement.

During the war, the mobilization of physicians to the front and the progressive scarcity of medical supplies slowed the ability of public-health officials to sterilize "unworthy lives." Yet preparations for war had the effect of accelerating plans to murder "useless eaters" or "ballast existences" in Germany's asylums and mental institutions. The Nazis carried out involuntary euthanasia in order "to purge the handicapped from the national gene pool," but wartime conditions gave the program legitimacy and cover. Over the course of the war, more than 5,000 children were killed on-site by their caretakers, who typically increased the dosage of regular medicines so that the victims appeared to have died a "natural death." Adult patients, however, were murdered by poison gas in special institutions: gray buses delivered victims to Grafeneck in Württemberg, Bernburg near Dessau, and Hadamar in Hessen. As was the case with the children, victims included individuals who were physically or mentally handicapped, blind, or deaf and mute. Eventually the criminal charges that relatives threatened to bring against hospitals, the dismay of local townspeople who wondered why the patients "are never seen again"—"in one south German village, peasant women refused to sell cherries to nurses from the local state hospital"—and finally, in August 1941, the open denunciation of involuntary euthanasia by Clemens August von Galen, the Catholic bishop of Münster in Westphalia, prompted Hitler to order the special killing centers dismantled. Over 70,000 handicapped Germans had been murdered in an operation that, according to the grotesque statistics prepared by one official, promised to save the German state 885,439,980 marks and 13,492,440 kilograms of meat over a ten-year period.[72]

The euthanasia "actions" anticipated the Holocaust. Figuring out by trial and error the various stages of the killing process, from the identification of patients to the arrangement of special transports to the murder sites to the killings by gas in special chambers to the disposal of the bodies, and mobilizing medical experts who worked in secret with a variety of misleading euphemisms to conceal their work—the T-4 operation, a reference to the offices of the dummy corporations the Office of the Chancellor set up in Berlin's Tiergartenstrasse 4—the Nazis built important bureaucratic bridges that would lead to the extermination of Jews and Gypsies.

The subject of euthanasia provoked intense discussion among Germans. Galen's denunciatory words spread like wildfire in the summer of 1941. Released around the same time, *Ich klage an* ("I accuse"), a film that promoted the right to die voluntarily, left many of the eighteen million people who saw it asking nagging questions. Franz Göll in Berlin agreed that incurably sick people should be able to end their own lives, but he did not trust the Nazis to do it for them. "The fact is that it is totally possible," he carefully noted, "that the National Socialist state would use such a law to make it a duty for those without means and who are dependent on handouts from the state to more or less 'voluntarily' take their lives."[73] Soldiers on the front also took part in heated debates on sterilization and euthanasia. One of them was Heinrich Böll, who as an observant Catholic opposed both. "The arguments of our faith are just fantastically strong," he wrote his wife.[74] However, these arguments stand in contrast to general silence about the fate of German Jews, who were publicly marked and deported in these same months. Galen never once mentioned Jews in his public sermons or his private correspondence. Saul Friedländer points out that Galen's protest was the "only time in the history of the Third Reich that prominent representatives of the Christian churches in Germany voiced public condemnation of the crimes committed by the regime."[75] Debates on euthanasia revealed limits to the "limits on empathy," but they did so on an issue that might well have applied to almost anyone. In 1941 Germans could imagine living off a meager pension, or suffering incapacitating wounds in battle, or growing old and infirm. But they could not imagine being Jewish.

The Assault on German Jews

It was not always easy for Germans to follow Nazi guidelines regarding the Jews, but most people came to accept the basic premise that German life depended in some measure on solving the "Jewish problem." Friedländer describes Nazi antisemitism as "redemptive," part of a larger struggle to protect what so many Germans regarded as the wounded, bleeding body of the nation. As Koonz puts it succinctly, the Nazis promoted "self-love and other-hate" in equal measure and made each the premise of the other. This link between the "life" of Germany and the destruction of Jewish power lent an idealistic cast to the Nazis' anti-Jewish policies. Moreover, as Friedländer argues, the Nazis considered the Jewish threat to be "lethal" and active, a perspective that gave their assault on the Jews a sense of urgency and necessity that made German citizens more willing to go along.[76] During the war, Jews would be simply regarded as anti-German partisans. Of course, antisemitism had deep roots in Christian Europe. It was a familiar feature in everyday life in Wilhelmine and Weimar Germany; the largest nationalist associations, the Stahlhelm, the Jungdeutscher Orden, and the German National People's Party, all had "Aryan paragraphs," statutes that excluded Jews from membership and often defined Jews in racial terms so that conversions to Christianity did not efface Jewishness. But antisemitism remained limited by many other kinds of social interactions among neighbors or colleagues.

It was the strident antisemitism of newly charged National Socialists that created the primacy of "the Jews" in the intersections of social life: "the Jews" whose influence on German public life was endlessly debated after 1933, "the Jews" who still retained or had already lost their customers, "the Jews" who were the unfortunate victims of Nazi violence—in short, "the Jews" who, for whatever reason, had become a problem. All the different approaches toward neighbors collapsed almost overnight into the overriding distinction between Germans and Jews. The words "the Jews" obscured very different lives. But after 1933 use of the definite article became more accurate, since it described a social condition imposed on heterogeneous people.

Once actions against Jews were notionally linked to the betterment of Germany, the majority of Germans came to accept the validity not only of the collective category "Jews" but of the "Jewish question" and thus its resolution one way or the other. Antisemitism did not arrive on the scene as something completely new, but it acquired much greater symbolic value when people associated it with being German. The desire to embrace the project of national revival, to convert, to undo Versailles and 1918, helps explain why, often from one day to the next, both prominent and obscure Germans decided for themselves to become consistent in their relations with "the Jews." It was her "duty as a German" to see things from a racial point of view that impelled one acquaintance not long after the Nazis came to power to cut off contact with Victor Klemperer. Intellectuals such as the philosopher Martin Heidegger and the jurist Carl Schmitt did the same thing.[77] They simply refused to deal with Jews.

In exile in Grass Valley, California, north of Sacramento, Paula Tobias, a Jewish physician who had left her home in Bevern, south of Hanover, three years earlier, in 1938, gathered up old letters in which she had asked friends and colleagues why she no longer counted for German. The principal of the high school from which her son graduated admitted to her in 1934 that he had always felt Jews to be different from Germans. This alienation could hardly be explained "rationally," he admitted; it was really a matter of "blood and instinct." A close friend, who as a nurse had worked with Paula during World War I, also approved of anti-Jewish measures, which she considered to be in "the interest of the German people." It was important, Elisabeth Sextrohs wrote in September 1933, trying to be "as clear as possible," to push back the "preponderant influence of Jewry in all aspects of German life." True: it was "hard and tragic" for individuals to suffer. Elisabeth Gebensleben also weighed good and bad, but defended Jewish measures because they promised to restore German sovereignty. Antisemitism was tried on, and it often fitted.[78]

This deliberate stance, in which the antisemite ignored individuals and saw only the category, and did so for the sake of another abstraction, Germany, was the starting point for the violence against the Jews. "Redemptive" antisemitism could turn ferocious and cruel in a way that racial hygienic measures against "asocials" or the "feebleminded" did not, because actions against Jews were understood as purposeful, well-aimed attempts to ward off Germany's own condition of disunity and disarray. It was along this circuitry, in which Germans imagined themselves as the victims of Jews and other "back-stabbers," that "self-love" could turn into lethal "otherhate."

Everything changed for Germany's Jews in two months, March and April 1933. After the 5 March elections, a wave of violence descended upon Jews. As thousands of new converts joined the paramilitary units of the SA, whose numbers shot up ninefold from 500,000 in January 1933 to 4.5 million one year later, the scale of antisemitic actions expanded dramatically. Becoming a Nazi meant trying to become an antisemite as well. Nearly one in every four active adult men in Germany had turned himself into an *SA-Mann;* many other Germans stood in the ranks of the Hitler Youth or the Nazi party itself. No wonder visitors heard "the nonstop scuff of SA boots on the sidewalk" in the summer of 1933. On the Kurfürstendamm, Berlin's high-end shopping street, "Jews were beaten by the brown shirts until blood ran down their heads and faces," reported the *Manchester Guardian* on 10 March 1933.[79] Similar incidents took place in Braunschweig, Hamburg, Frankfurt, Kassel, and Wiesbaden. Nazis torched Königsberg's main synagogue. A crowd of 1,000 men, women, and children watched SA troops wrap the red-black-gold flag of the republic around the neck of Markus Bereisch, a prominent figure in Duisburg's Jewish community, and force him and two other Jews, who held the ends of the flag, to march through the streets—Charlottenstrasse, Universitätsstrasse, Königsstrasse—to the municipal theater. Nazis paraded Jewish shopkeepers around the streets of Göttingen in a cattle wagon; in Breslau, they dressed up one politically active Jew in a clown's costume before throwing him into concentration camp.[80] Public humiliations such as these depended on bystanders willing to take part in the spectacle. They accelerated the division of neighborhoods into "us" and "them."

Widely reported in the foreign press, the terrifying outbursts of violence set the stage for the national boycott of Jewish businesses in retaliation against defamatory anti-German propaganda circulating abroad. On Saturday, 1 April 1933, barely two months after Hitler had been named chancellor, SA men across Germany stood guard in front of Jewish shops, held up anti-Jewish placards, and generally intimidated pedestrians and shoppers. Though not particularly successful, the boycott confirmed to Jews that the threats they received on the street had the sanction of the government. Any doubts about the second-class status of Jews in Hitler's Germany were laid to rest with the "Law for the Restoration of the Professional Civil Service." It forced the retirement of civil servants who were Jewish, which the Ministry of the Interior defined in the most restrictive terms possible, on the basis of a single Jewish grandparent. What turned out to be temporary exceptions for veterans, the sons and fathers of veterans, and long government service exempted about half of all Jewish civil servants, but the precedent of drastically limiting the future of a group of citizens on the basis of an alleged racial identity was shocking. A few months after the Nazis' seizure of power, it was clear that race would be the principle around which the polity would be organized.

In uncoordinated fashion, local and state governments had already prohibited public contracts with Jewish firms in March 1933, so the boycott itself did not set in motion the economic bankruptcy of Germany's Jews, but it vastly accelerated the process. Private businesses across Germany followed the example of Karstadt, the big department store chain, which fired its Jewish employees on 1

April 1933 for no longer being "equal as coworkers" to non-Jews. At the same time, Jewish businessmen were asked to leave corporate boards, partly in the spirit of coordination, partly as a matter of "shared comprehension," and partly under pressure from competitors, who, for example, slandered Beiersdorf, one of Germany's largest pharmaceutical companies, for manufacturing "Jewish skin cream." By the middle of May Beiersdorf had "Aryanized" its board and its leading product, Nivea, which full-page advertisements in the *Illustrierter Beobachter* aggressively marketed as the means to achieve natural beauty.[81] (Nivea was therefore no longer "Jewish" when Lore Walb received a jar for her fourteenth birthday on 23 May.)[82] The startling events of the spring of 1933, when more and more Germans realized that they were not supposed to shop in Jewish stores and when German companies felt compelled to fire Jewish employees and remove Jewish businessmen from corporate boards, moved Germany quite some distance toward the ultimate goal of "Aryanizing" the German economy.

Face-to-face relations between Germans and Jews lost all their uninhibitedness as Germans adjusted their behavior to acknowledge the "Jewish question." "Within days" of Hitler's appointment as chancellor, regulars at the tavern or the café regrouped to exclude the card player who was Jewish; elsewhere, two gardeners, one of them Jewish, the other not, who for years had chatted as they worked, no longer spoke to each other; German children confided to their Jewish friends that they could not play or walk home with them anymore.[83] "Former friends provided the most painful evidence of a 'new era,'" remarks Marion Kaplan. Averted glances, hostile stares, and sudden hushes in conversations greeted Germany's Jews wherever they went. It was as if Jews had interrupted something to which they did not belong. "Suddenly we discovered that we were different," remembered one Jewish observer. This racial coordination of social life occurred almost entirely voluntarily, so that one observer, writing at the end of May 1933, expressed the hope that this "Aryan fad" would soon pass. "Not every gymnastic group and skat club has to be made up only of 'Aryans.'"[84]

New in all of this was not antisemitism per se, but the termination of ambiguous, indeterminate social relations among neighbors. For many non-Jewish Germans, this rested on an extraordinarily conscientious public bearing; for Jewish Germans, it meant "social death." Even when individuals mustered the "civil courage" to shop *beim Juden*, they did so with the same categories in their heads as those who boycotted Jews. Neighbors in Wedding who remarked that "the Jews haven't done anything to us" despised antisemitism but upheld the separation between "us" and "them" at which it aimed.[85] Custom and habit gave way to self-conscious and inhibited interactions structured by the unambiguous knowledge of race. From one moment to the next, Jews tumbled into a "cold pogrom" that was as extensive as the German nation itself, an extraordinary event in the structures of feeling in modern European society.[86]

Germany's Jews were no longer nonchristian, but non-German, a distinction that lingered well after 1945. When Victor Klemperer was asked, "Do you have a *German* wife?" the question was posed in a way that assumed that Klemperer could not be German. This sense of mutual exclusion encouraged people to accept the racial definition of "Jew" and thus of "German" or "Aryan" as well. The categories also promoted the use of the collective singular "Jew" instead of words that recognized that there were many sorts of Germans, including many sorts of Jews. "There is no difference between Jews and Jews," Goebbels would later insist.[87]

The acknowledgment that there was a fundamental difference between Germans and Jews revived much older superstitions holding that physical contact with Jews was harmful or that Jewish men defiled German women. This attention to the physical nature of Jewish difference explains why the manufacturers of Nivea skin cream went out of their way to remarket their product and why municipalities first put swimming pools and only later other amenities off-limits to Jews. Swimming bans were imposed in Munich and Nuremberg at the beginning of the summer season in 1933; prohibitions were in place in Berlin as in most places by 1935, though in Hamburg not until 1937. Schools also pulled Jewish students out of swimming lessons. It was awkward at first to make neighbors aware of the new antisemitic regulations. "The children were told right away, but in a friendly fashion, about the sign regarding non-Aryans at the South End pool," reported the non-Jewish stepfather of two Jewish girls who had been given the choice of trying to pass as non-Jews: "They are still very undecided, but it preoccupies them a great deal. Reni will probably no longer go, but the pool doesn't mean as much to her as it does to Brigitte."[88] Eventually both Germans and Jews avoided renegotiating race at every juncture and simply adjusted to the new rules.

Jews also avoided contact with Germans. They could not help but suspect that basically all their neighbors—a few good friends excepted—had become Nazis. Sixty thousand Jews, more than 10 percent of the total number living in Germany, emigrated in 1933 and 1934. They included Anne Frank, born in 1929 into a family of Frankfurt Jews who moved to Amsterdam, established a successful business, and then found themselves surrounded by Nazis for a second time when Germany invaded the Netherlands on 10 May 1940.

However, leaving was not easy. Aside from the difficulties of finding employment, learning a new language, and obtaining visas, most Jews did not want to abandon Germany. While interest in Jewish heritage and theology grew after 1933, and Zionism became more appealing, identification with German cultural traditions remained strong. "I have truly always felt a German," wrote Victor Klemperer at the end of March 1933; it was Nazis who were "un-German," he added two years later. "We were so German," "we were so assimilated," "we were so middle class"—Kaplan aptly notes both shock at developments in Germany and misplaced hope that the country would come to its senses.[89] Indeed, for many people, the bizarre nature of Nazi ideas seemed to be a guarantee that the whole edifice would eventually topple under its own weight. Conditions had to get better because they could not get worse—Jewish friends invited for coffee at the Klemperers' in Dresden debated endlessly how much support Hitler had, how sturdy the regime was, how trustworthy German culture might be. Sometimes Germans seemed to be all of one voice, antisemitic, racist, self-absorbed with their people's community; at other times they appeared to go about their business without much interest in Nazism, its strident speechmaking, or its collective zeal. Here, old acquaintances no longer spoke to each other, but over there, neighborhood women continued to shop for clothes in the stores they had always patronized, as if textiles circulated according to older, more enduring habits of sociability. This uncertainty, which German Jews shared with other observers of Nazism, sustained a "wait-and-see" attitude.

Not a day passed when somewhere in Germany Nazi hooligans did not shove bricks through the windowpanes of shops owned by Jews or sing wildly antisemitic songs as they walked by Jewish homes or synagogues. An example was "When Jewish Blood Spurts from My Knife." "I froze on the sidewalk," Valentin Senger remembered when he heard the song for the first time in Frankfurt. "An image rose up in front of me: Mama and Papa and me with knives in our bellies and throats, the blood spurting from our wounds." As it was, "the marchers turned off toward the station," but "I was to hear that song on many different occasions."[90] During the summer of 1935 local Nazis revved up anti-Jewish campaigns. In Ballenstedt, Quedlinburg, and Harzigerode, Hitler Youth fanned out across local business districts to hand out red leaflets, "Eat Jewish food, and you'll die," "The Jews are our misfortune," "Never patronize the Jews." *Stürmer* boxes went up. It became increasingly difficult to avoid the boycotts or not to put up the sign on the shop window "Jews are not welcome." "What am I going to do?" wondered Richard Tesch, an owner of a bakery in Ballendstedt's marketplace: "Israel has been buying goods from me for a long time. Am I supposed to no longer sell to him? And if I do it anyway, then I've lost the other customers."[91]

The racial basis of Nazi antisemitism had a radicalizing effect because it posed the question: If Jews represented an alien, dangerous presence in German society, did it not make sense to banish them completely? As it was, all the attention to the "Jewish question" revealed just how intertwined Germans and Jews had become. The growing incidence of intermarriage in recent decades, particularly in the cities, had resulted in an estimated 70,000 "half-Jews" and nearly twice as many "quarter Jews." For the Nazis, intermarriage represented a double danger: it imperiled both the purity of Aryan racial stock and the ability to make reliable distinctions between Germans and Jews. Did Jewishness lurk inside Germans who had a Jewish grandparent or great-grandparent? If so, how far back in time did Jewishness extend? Lingering questions about the Jewishness of converts to Christianity or the Germanness of blond, blue-eyed Jews persisted as well. The "Jewish question" made finding a workable definition of Jews and Jewishness more necessary.

Announced at the Nuremberg party rally in September 1935, the Nuremberg Laws acknowledged the second-class status of Jews by stripping them of their citizenship as "Germans" and by prohibiting marriage and sexual contact between Germans and Jews. They also aimed to sort out who was and was not a Jew in more ambiguous cases. A Jew was defined biologically as anyone with three or more Jewish grandparents, whose own Jewishness had been determined by religious affiliation at birth and not, as the Nazis themselves admitted, by scientific or biological criteria. "Aryans" who married Jews and practiced Judaism were regarded as Jews, although Jews who had converted to Christianity remained Jews. The cases of *Mischlinge* revealed both the intentions of the regime and internal disagreements about racial policy. For those Nazis such as Streicher, the publisher of *Der Stürmer*, who believed that the blood of Jews represented a contagious threat, any sexual contact between Jews and Germans defiled Germans and polluted Aryan stock. Accordingly, Germans needed to be physically protected from Jews—a line of reasoning that explains the prohibitions against Jews entering swimming pools and Jewish physicians attending German patients. The Nuremberg Laws reflected these pernicious ideas by making it illegal for Jewish households to employ servants under the age of forty-five. As the last example shows, it was usually Jewish men who were imagined to prey on German women: the gender of the Jewish peril was male, while Aryan vulnerability was female. Following the logic of the argument that Jewish blood was contagious, half-Jews and quarter-Jews were just as Jewish as full Jews in their capacity to pollute the German body. There was no such thing as a "half-stain." A great deal of emotional power had built up behind this argument, which was never relinquished. As a virulent antisemite, Hitler himself was drawn to this view.

On the other side of the question were biopoliticians such as Walter Gross who considered themselves to be adherents of a modern, scientific worldview in which genes determined and passed on Jewish characteristics. From this perspective, half-Jews and quarter-Jews carried both good and bad genes and therefore could not be regarded as completely Jewish. Gross and others argued that mixed Jews would eventually be absorbed into the Aryan race if they were prohibited from marrying each other. Although Jewish characteristics could persist and mutate just as easily as they could disappear—Hitler came to believe that mixed Jews continued "flirting" with Judaism until the seventh generation, when the "purity of Aryan blood" was restored—there was also a compelling practical side to sorting mixed Jews as Germans. Thousands of "pure" Germans were related by blood or marriage to people with Jewish grandparents, and their exclusion from the racial community would arouse public disapproval. Moreover, *Mischlinge* would be lost to the Wehrmacht. The genetic basis of racial categories also squared with other Nazi policies such as sterilization and euthanasia. In the end, Hitler accepted Gross's argument, although he sought from him explicit reassurances that the offspring of a German woman who once had had sexual relations with a Jew would be pure.[92] The tangle of prohibitions and permissions was duly published in the newspapers. According to security reports, most Germans welcomed legislation clarifying the position of Jews and hoped it would bring to an end the graffiti and broken windows of anti-Jewish hooliganism. Social Democratic informants registered more critical voices, but conceded that antisemitic propaganda was taking effect; people generally agreed there was a "Jewish problem" in Germany that needed to be resolved.[93]

In theory, the Nuremberg Laws established two different races, one with full political rights, the other with the status of a "guest" population. Appropriate passports and identity papers followed. This amounted to an extraordinary rearrangement of political and human rights in an effort to exclude a group of former citizens. Yehuda Bauer rightly calls these actions a "total rebellion" against the conventions of the modern world. For Germany's Jews, the laws erased any doubts that they had been completely excluded from the reconstituted German polity. Some chose to wait Hitler out, but the status quo left them without a meaningful future. A final push also shoved Jews out of the German economy. With nearly full employment by 1936, it was much easier to "Aryanize" Jewish businesses, which fell into eager Christian hands, or simply to liquidate corner shops to reduce competition. There was no synchronization of the policy of "Aryanization," but it was largely accomplished by 1938. "Of the approximately 50,000 Jewish small businesses operating at the end of 1932," writes Kaplan, "only 9,000 still existed by July 1938," that is, before the November pogrom.[94]

Aryanization was accompanied by a barrage of loud anti-Jewish, anticommunist propaganda. News reports, documentary films, exhibitions, and textbooks disseminated the latest "scholarly findings" on the "Jewish question." Exhibits on "Degenerate Art," Bolshevism ("World Enemy No. 1"), and "The Eternal Jew" traveled from city to city in 1937. In the context of the Spanish Civil War, which broke out in July 1936, the Moscow "show trials" against old Bolsheviks in August 1936, and the November 1936 anti-Comintern pact between Germany and Japan, the Nazis persistently linked Germany's Jews to the Communist threat. "Bolshevik terror" figured as one of the centerpieces of the 1937 Nuremberg rally, at which Goebbels demonized Jews as the primary enemy of the Western world: "look, this is the enemy of the world, the destroyer of cultures, the parasite among the nations, the son of chaos, the incarnation of evil, the ferment of decomposition, the visible demon of the decay of humanity." "Never since the rise of Christianity, the spread of Islam, and the Reformation has the world been in such turmoil," echoed Hitler, who identified the culprit as "Jewish Bolshevism in Moscow."[95] This campaign resonated with deep-seated fears of Communism that should not be underestimated, fears based on recollections of the general strikes in 1919 and 1920 and gruesome stories about atrocities in the Russian civil war. It also fortified the image of the Jew as an intractable, immediate danger. Even observers who explicitly rejected the "deification of blood and race" "agreed completely with all the insights into the terrible dangers of Bolshevism."[96]

The requirement that Jews add "Sarah" or "Israel" to their legal names in January 1938 made even more clear the aim of the Nazis to register Jews as a prelude to physical expulsion. ("Aryans" also changed their names in the Third Reich, although they did so voluntarily, as in the case of the young SS recruit who Germanized Günter to Günther or the priest in Günter Grass's novel *Cat and Mouse*, who turned Gusewski into Gusewing.)[97] "Where Should the Jews Go?" screamed the headline of *Das Schwarze Korps*. In February 1938, the answer was "Out!"[98]

In the three years after the Nuremberg Laws, more than one-third of Germany's Jews emigrated. They sold their property, divided personal belongings, and secured visas with the help of the *Philo-Atlas*, a guide to places of refuge around the world, "a genuine Baedeker of flight" that was the Jewish counterpart to the railway timetables by which other Germans organized their "Strength through Joy" vacations and Hitler Youth trips.[99] At railway stations across Germany, the two lines crossed each other, with Jews making their way to new, uncertain lives, usually in Palestine, Britain, and the United States, and their German neighbors on energetic missions to rebuild and strengthen the Volksgemeinschaft.

The Anschluss with Austria in March 1938 vastly accelerated the project of racial cleansing. It added proportionally more Jews to the expanded German Reich and occasioned both delirious celebrations of the Führer's success in putting the German body back together and vicious scenes of mob terror against Austria's Jews, who, outside their plundered shops and homes, were forced to clean streets on hands and knees and otherwise delight onlookers. "We're doing soooo well, we love the Führer soo much and sooo unanimously," Klemperer mocked this self-love in summer 1938. Austrian Nazis outstripped their German counterparts in promulgating racial legislation down to the nasty details: 100 days after the Anschluss, laws prohibited Austrian Jews from entering public parks, from walking on beaches, from dressing in traditional *Tracht*.[100] When police summarily arrested 2,000 prominent Jews and sent them to Dachau, the concentration camps began to fill up with people incarcerated simply for being Jews. By the end of 1938, most Jewish property in Vienna had been "Aryanized." The racial bureaucrats in the security service who were assigned to Austria, notably Adolf Eichmann, a young second lieutenant in the SS, speeded up Jewish emigration, which had become the explicit goal of the Third Reich. The SS did this by centralizing emigration procedures, standardizing the process of fleecing Jews before their departure, and requiring wealthy Jews to subvent the exit of impoverished Jews. Within six months, more than one-quarter of all Austrian Jews had fled, something that had taken the *Altreich* the previous five years to accomplish. Events in Austria indicated the usefulness of state-sponsored terror.

The vernacular tag, at least in Berlin, of *Reichskristallnacht*, or "night of shattered glass," to designate what should be considered a nationwide pogrom against more than 300,000 Germans Jews in November 1938, was inflected with sardonic humor, which mocked the pretentiousness of Nazi vocabulary in which *Reich*-this and *Reich*-that puffed up the historical moment of the regime.[101] But since the reference was to the shattered windowpanes of shops and not to the scores of victims killed or hundreds of synagogues torched or thousands of Jewish men hauled off to concentration camps for weeks and months, the term *Reichskristallnacht* does not adequately indicate the horror of what took place in the early morning hours of 9–10 November 1938. And explicitly regarded as a matter of the Reich, it overlooks the role played by ordinary German on the streets of towns and cities. The pogrom confirmed that Jews in Germany were not simply a persecuted minority but a racial enemy whom the Nazis were willing to murder as "free game" if Jews did not or could not emigrate on their own. What the pogrom demonstrated as well was that the Nazis could carry out the most extreme policies with the help of police, town officials, and other citizens. In one of the largest police operations in German history, local police, party leaders, and SS officials cooperated to arrest one in every five male Jews, about 25,000 in all. Finally, the pogrom heightened the belief that the Jews were "different," that they had "bad karma," that it would be better if they left.[102] The ninth of November has proved to be a loaded day in German history: it marks the outbreak of the 1918 Revolution, Hitler's failed putsch in 1923, the pogrom against Jews in 1938, and, more than fifty years later, the fall of the Berlin Wall in 1989.

The pogrom was not the spontaneous response of outraged Nazis and other Germans to the assassination of Ernst vom Rath, a minor German diplomat in Paris, by seventeen-year-old Herschel Grynszpan. Hitler and Goebbels ordered the destruction of synagogues and the arrest of thousands of Jewish men as soon as they learned that Rath had died. The orders were relayed to party and SA offices over the night of 9–10 November. But the rapid and uniform responses by local Nazis indicated a basic readiness and desire to carry out anti-Jewish actions. The content of the orders did not shock those who received them. Indeed, to read the accounts of the pogroms in town after town is to gain the impression that all uniformed Nazis knew what to do not because they read the same marching orders but because they shared the same images of Jews. Well-appointed homes were ransacked and formerly prominent citizens tormented because Jews were regarded as profiteers whose wealth and social standing mocked the probity of the Volksgemeinschaft; children and the elderly were terrorized because they were "the Jew" whose very existence threatened Germany's moral, political, and economic revival; the most intimate household objects were destroyed in order to send the message that Jews had no place in the Third Reich.

Sometime after midnight, in the early hours of Thursday, 10 November 1938, local party, SS, and SA offices received orders to burn down synagogues and destroy (but not loot) Jewish homes and businesses. Instructions cautioned police and firefighters not to intervene unless German life or property was endangered, which meant that freestanding synagogues such as the one on Berlin's Fasanenstrasse burned, while those enclosed by apartment blocks as in Rykestrasse did not. In addition, they ordered party officers to arrest a quota of preferably prominent and wealthy Jewish men. Officials at the concentration camps in Dachau, Sachsenhausen, and Buchenwald had been alerted to prepare for 10,000 additional prisoners each. Almost everywhere the assault on the Jewish community began with the synagogues, 267 of which were destroyed across Germany. Throughout the night, Goebbels received updates about the pogrom as he watched the "blood-red [glare] in the sky" from his Munich hotel room: "the synagogue burns." "From all over the Reich information is now flowing in: fifty, then seventy synagogues are burning . . . In Berlin, five, then fifteen synagogues burn down." SA men and party members then moved through the streets, "going for a stroll" as they warned the police in one community, to ransack Jewish stores. Nearly all Jewish business still operating in Germany in November 1938 were wrecked. "As I am driven to the hotel," noted Goebbels, "windowpanes shatter. Bravo! Bravo!"[103] Later in the day, the sites of terror were plain for all to see. One Berliner "watched his fellow passengers as he traveled past the burning Fasenenstrasse synagogue between the S-Bahn stations Savignyplatz and Zoologischer Garten the next morning: 'only a few looked up to see out the window, shrugged their shoulders, and went back to their paper. No astonishment, no one asked any questions.'"[104]

By five or six in the morning, the SA men turned their attention to the homes and apartments of their Jewish neighbors. Synagogues had been set on fire before, and businesses trashed, though never on this extraordinary scale; but the invasion of homes to terrorize families and destroy their possessions was without precedent. "Organized parties moved through Cologne from one Jewish apartment to another," wrote the Swiss consul a few days after the events had taken place. "The families were either ordered to leave the apartment or they had to stand in a corner of a room while its contents were hurled from the windows. Gramophones, sewing machines, and typewriters tumbled down into the streets . . . One can still see bedding hanging from trees and bushes." Not far away, in the small town of "Sonderburg," when neighbors saw "the furniture and possessions of a Jewish family being tossed from a second-floor window—watching in horror as the feathers from the down quilts floated in the air—they tightened their shutters, secured their doors, drew their curtains, and trembled for themselves." After "five young fellows" arrived at six in the morning with an ax to chop up one girl's home, schoolchildren followed to throw stones; the result was that "my father had a heart attack in the kitchen." In the small Franconian town of Treuchtlingen, which Michael Wildt has examined, the businessman Moritz Mayer recalled that eight to ten SA men broke into his house between four and five in the morning: "In the kitchen, the dishes were smashed down to the last piece; in the cellar . . . the women were themselves forced to smash wine bottles and canning jars. After the SA came the plebs, then the school youths; each party continued destroying and stealing." The Jews fled the small town, leaving behind their belongings and running to the train station "through a cordon formed by the mob, accompanied by its derisive laughter."[105] Elsewhere elderly Jews were punched, thrown down staircases, and bloodied by young and adolescent Hitlerites.[106]

Whenever the SA threw Jews out of their apartments, incidents grew more ugly because the enemies of the Jews turned the streets into stages for rituals of degradation and humiliation. In front of burning synagogues, Nazi toughs forced Jews to destroy the Torah or to sing and dance. The American consul in Leipzig left a gruesome account of men, women, and children pushed onto the banks of a small stream that flowed through the Zoological Park where passersby taunted the victims and spat on them.[107] Across Germany, ninety-one Jews were killed during the rampage; many more were driven to commit suicide or died of heart attacks or perished in the custody of Nazi guards.

In every town, Germans knew the main tormentors and could identify the children who followed in their wake. They witnessed shocking acts of plunder, humiliation, and arrest. Neighbors talked

for weeks about horrible incidents such as the death of Dora Stern—
"Stern's Dora from Dog's Alley"—which may or may not have
been due to the fact that an SA man threw her out the window of
her house. But the inhabitants of Arheiligen, a small town outside
Darmstadt, did know that Dora's father hanged himself beside her
deathbed.[108] Clearly, without the orders from above, the pogrom
would never have happened; but once it was set in motion, it became a public event in which bystanders were forced to be witnesses. How did witnesses explain to themselves what they had
seen? Most Germans were ashamed of the pogroms that had taken
place in their neighborhoods. Criticism of the disruption of public
order was widespread, but should not be taken completely at face
value. It undoubtedly veiled deeper moral objections that were otherwise difficult to articulate in Nazi Germany. "Decent people are
usually asleep between two and five," observed one secretary in
Berlin about Nazi claims that the anti-Jewish action expressed popular outrage: "You can't set fire to churches before you get up."[109]
Karl Dürkefälden, long the single holdout in a Nazi family in the
Lower Saxon town of Peine, reported on the shock. His sister
Emma had become deeply troubled by the destruction of houses of
God, no longer believed in Hitler's professions of peace, and simply couldn't stand to hear his acid tongue. Long swayed by the regime's pronouncements, his mother-in-law also wondered whether
the Nazis would torch Christian churches next. That the gossip
among neighbors passed along atrocity stories such as the one about
"Sterne-Dora" certainly indicated outrage at the brutality of the
Nazis but also astonishing unawareness of the generally depress-
ing conditions in which Jews lived in the Third Reich. Gossipers
were basically passive, telling about but not intervening in dramatic
events. Karl's father, in any case, brought up the point about the
bottle of blood allegedly found in the ruins of Peine's synagogue.[110]
He represented the large number of citizens who regarded Ger-

many's Jews as aliens who did not deserve sympathy. According to Fritz Stern, the failure of Germany's Protestant and Catholic churches to say a word about "the destruction of sacred places" expressed "a total, almost unbelievable moral bankruptcy."[111] About one of every five Jewish men living in Germany was arrested on 10 November and spent weeks in harrowing conditions in the concentration camps of Dachau, Buchenwald, and Sachsenhausen. The men were humiliated in ways that distinguished Nazi violence against Jews from Nazi violence against Social Democrats or "asocials." In Saarbrücken, men were torn from their homes still in their pajamas, herded together, and sprayed with water from a municipal street sprinkler. In Kiel they were marched two by two through the streets and forced to shout: "We are the murderers." Upon reaching a local gymnasium, Erfurt's Jewish men were put into custody and tormented and forced to do calisthenics for the amusement of the guards until buses finally arrived for the journey to Buchenwald.[112] Once in the camps, prisoners endured long hours standing in formation without sufficient food or water, extreme deprivation that gave way after several days to a routine of harsh physical labor. Guards mercilessly terrorized Jews who once had been their fellow citizens but who were now addressed as "you dirtbags, you Jewish pigs, you pathetic pigs, you lowdown riffraff."[113] In concentration camps in which there had been an average of three or four deaths every month, hundreds died in November and December 1938; all told, perhaps more than 1,000 Jewish inmates perished.[114] It was two or three months before the men returned to their wrecked homes and businesses.

Since the aim of the pogrom was to force the emigration of Germany's Jews while expropriating their property, the aftermath of the physical assault was not an uneasy peace but a ferocious legal and financial campaign. First, Germany's Jews were held responsible for the public disorder that had followed the death of Rath. On the day of the pogrom, Goebbels came up with the idea of a

Sühneleistung, or "atonement fine," which a ministerial conference set at one billion marks. Jewish taxpayers were required to hand over 20 percent of their total assets in four installments ending in August 1939. This windfall increased the state's annual revenues for 1939 by 6 percent. In addition, the government confiscated 225 million marks in insurance payments.[115] All Jewish businesses were Aryanized or liquidated. Finally, a Central Jewish Emigration Office, established as a branch of the state security apparatus, facilitated emigration, though not before fleecing Jews, whose assets, cash, and jewelry had been seized and deposited in blocked accounts. Since destitute Jews were less able to emigrate, SS planners admitted that they would be left with what they imagined would be an impoverished underclass of criminals. In fact the SS newspaper, *Das Schwarze Korps,* rushed into print what looked like a policeman's "perp book": "a small selection" of photographs featured photographs of the imprisoned physicians, lawyers, and other professionals whose newly shaven heads created the "eternal semblances" by which Jews dissolved into criminals.[116] "When we get to that stage of development," announced *Das Schwarze Korps* under the headline "Jews, What Now?," "we would stand before the hard necessity to exterminate the Jewish underworld as we exterminate all criminals in our law-abiding state: with fire and sword! The result would be the actual and final end to Jewry in Germany, its complete destruction."[117]

Called together by Hermann Göring in his Aviation Ministry on 12 November, Nazi officials quickly followed up the pogrom with legislation that would clear German national space of Jews. The discussion was conducted with sadistic flair. Once the terms of the financial robbery of Germany's Jews had been hammered out, Goebbels turned the meeting to proposals he had been promoting for months: German Jews would be banned from theaters, cinemas, cabarets, and museums. A few weeks later, fully drafted legislation banned Jews from amusement parks, circuses, and skating rinks.

Goebbels attempted to segregate the railroads, clearing Jews out of German compartments and forcing them into specially designated Jewish ones. He also asked for legal measures that would keep Jewish travelers from sitting down until all Germans had found their places. This point Göring debated: "Should a case such as you mention arise and the train be overcrowded, believe me, we won't need a law. We will kick him out and he will have to sit all alone in the toilet all the way!" Göring and Goebbels were not far apart on the issue of seating; in the end, Jews were banned from sleeping and dining cars. Göring went on to expel Jews from Germany's parks, though he considered leaving them a few parcels populated by Jewish-looking animals: "the elk has a crooked nose like theirs." The amused statesmen continued down the list, expelling Jewish children from German schools and empowering local police to extend bans on the physical presence of Jews as they saw fit. Jews were eventually banned from the main streets of Berlin's government district, Wilhelmstrasse and Unter den Linden. Newspapers published the new legislation "right away," as Göring insisted, "this week, slam-bam, the Jews should have their ears slapped, one slap after the other."[118] Although neither Göring and Goebbels imagined mass murder at the meeting, the excessive nature of their comments and their facility in dehumanizing people pointed them in that direction.

In April 1939 new federal legislation withdrew the protection of rent-control laws from Jews. Now landlords could evict their Jewish tenants if municipalities guaranteed another form of housing. In order to isolate Jews and free up apartments, local Nazis contemplated "Jew houses" and other detention centers. Although most "Jew houses" were not established until the war, officials forced Detmold's 100 Jews into six Jew houses, on Sachsenstrasse 4 and 25, Paulinenstrasse 6 and 10, Hornsche Strasse 33, and Gartenstrasse 6, as early as April 1939.[119]

The six months of legislation that followed the pogroms prepared the physical destruction of the infrastructure of Jewish communities. It placed Germany completely outside the orbit of European politics. As far as the Nazis were concerned, Germany's Jews had become utterly disposable, and their physical elimination could be contemplated: this was the revolutionary consequence of the pogroms of November 1938. Less than three months after the November events, on the occasion of the anniversary of the seizure of power on 30 January 1939, Hitler prophesied "the annihilation of the Jewish race in Europe" in the event that "international finance Jewry" succeeded in "plunging the nations once more into a world war."[120] These genocidal words should not be confused with Hitler's actual decision to proceed with murder, which was probably not made until the fall of 1941, or with its implementation in the spring of 1942, but the record conveys clearly that Hitler stated his intention to kill the Jews in the event of a world war.

"Gradually they're all coming back," wrote Ruth Andreas-Friedrich in her Berlin diary in January 1939: "the ones from Buchenwald and the ones from Sachsenhausen, with shaven skulls and eyes overfull of suffering." This return was a prelude to emigration and final departure. Friends took out the *Philo-Atlas*: "Where's La Paz? Oh, yes, in Bolivia . . . The globe is shrinking: Brazil seems a stone's throw, London like an afternoon's excursion to Wannsee." But it wasn't like a trip to the Wannsee. Emigrants were stripped of their assets and compelled to liquidate their households and to leave behind their belongings except for the few worldly things permitted refugees. "We break up households, we auction off dishes and peddle libraries. Seven sets of Heine. Nine copies of *The Magic Mountain*. Eleven of *All Quiet on the Western Front*, and twelve Bibles."[121] Emigration meant the dispersion of the archive of Jewish life in Germany, scattering the traces of ancestors and the signs of collective history. While German "Aryans" were driving their ancestries deep into Germany's past, German Jews were cutting loose from their heritage.

In January 1939 Hans Winterfeldt's little sister enrolled in a *Hachschara*, a camp that trained young people for the strenuous life of Palestine's *kibbutzim*. Those who "made it" received visas in Berlin a few weeks later. "The exact date was determined by the Palestine Office at 10 Meineckestrasse. In the meantime, the Chaverim and Chaverot, which is how the future kibbutz inhabitants called each other, invited each other to their homes for small celebrations. Only Hebrew songs were sung . . . and the hora was danced in a big circle." Zionism offered an appealing cultural and historical destination to many of Germany's Jews, and every day in Berlin, Frankfurt, and Breslau more Hebrew words replaced German ones, *bevakasha* instead of *bitte*, or "please," and *boker tov* instead of *guten Morgen*. These were new words too, alongside the Nazis' "glitter words." Younger Jews had an easier time, and families split off in different directions as teenage Zionists such as Winterfeldt left for Palestine, or as adult men emigrated ahead to Britain or the United States in order to secure employment, or as children—more than four out of five by the end of 1939—were packed off to live with uncles and aunts abroad, so that "children turned into letters."[122] Hans's sister left from Berlin's Anhalter Station at ten at night on 9 March 1939. He remembered the departure: "With barely a lurch the train began to move. You almost were not aware of it because all the people walked alongside . . . in order to maintain contact with the departing children for as long as possible. They waved, first with, then without handkerchiefs." When his mother lost sight of the train, "she emitted a cry like a wild animal . . . this scream was the expression of powerlessness . . . at the same time, it was a spontaneous reaction to the feeling that she would never see her child again. I heard this scream in my ears for a long time."[123] It was a long time before most other people, in Germany or anywhere else, heard it.

3

Empire of Destruction

Writing Letters

In Elsa Morante's novel *History*, Ida Ramundo, the schoolteacher whom Morante uses to tell about wartime Rome, walked through the ghetto after the Germans had begun to deport the Jews of Rome, Italy, in the middle of October 1943. It "had been totally stripped of all its Jewish flesh, and only its skeleton was left." She then approached the nearby freight yards around Rome's Tiburtina train station. "A horrible humming sound" drew her closer. It sounded like the din of "kindergartens, hospitals, prisons," this time, however, "all jumbled together, like shards thrown into the same machine." The noise came from voices in cattle cars, locked, but filled with men, women, and children. The wagons were windowless except for a grilled opening at one end, where Ida, half-Jewish herself, could see hands poking out between the bars. One of the prisoners threw a piece of paper down to her. When Ida stooped down to pick it up, she saw that "scattered on the ground along the cars . . . were other similar crumpled notes among the rubbish and garbage." She did not have "the strength to stay and collect any."[1]

Less than two years earlier, a policeman noted in his summary report on the "transport" of German Jews from Düsseldorf to Riga in December 1941 that whenever the train stopped prisoners would call out to travelers waiting in the train stations, asking them to

143

post letters. These letters were final transcriptions of life before Jewish deportees were pushed into ghettos when they arrived at their destination a few days later. Among the items most frequently confiscated from German Jews as they boarded deportation trains were blank postcards and postage stamps; authorities in Würzburg collected 358 six-pfennig postcards, 142 six-pfennig stamps, and 273 twelve-pfennig stamps before sending deportees on their way on 24 March 1942.[2]

A photograph taken at the edge of the ghetto in Lodz, Poland, probably from the year 1942, shows a young woman bending down to write what must have been her last letter before she was forced onto a train that would take her to her death in the killing center in Chelmno. Very few of these last letters ever arrived. As late as August 1944, in his perilous existence in Dresden, Victor Klemperer could not figure out "*who* among the people in Theresienstadt is allowed to correspond with whom." Nonetheless, news of the Hirschels had "reached one or other person, and we heard of the death of Jon Neumann." With smuggled letters, private diaries, and secret archives, Jewish victims made enormous efforts to leave behind accounts of the atrocities the Nazis were committing. Klemperer himself was able to write furtively in the pages of his diary, which Eva, his non-Jewish wife, smuggled out to a friend in the countryside for safekeeping. Jewish resistance fighters in Warsaw and Jewish inmates in Auschwitz established valuable archives in hidden places.[3] Secret writings have come to light in Berlin as well as in the main areas of extermination, in Poland, Russia, and Ukraine, but most texts have not been found. These writings hold the voices of the victims.

The note handed to Ida in the train station hinted at the violence of expulsion. Yet it also revealed still unsevered connections to the ghetto. "If you see Efrate Pacificho tell him we're all in good health," Ida read the piece of paper in her hand: "Irma Reggina Romolo and everybody going to Germany hole family all-right the

bill pay Lazarino another hundred and twenty lire debt becau."
"becau"—writers were often interrupted. Writing was not easy,
and the chance to post letters unpredictable. Millions of other letters were never written; in the ghettos, authorities prohibited correspondence or banned letters in favor of preprinted postcards.
Moreover, the victims who survived selection in the death camps
in Germany and Poland in the years after 1942 did not have paper
or pencils. A non-Jew, Ruth Andreas-Friedrich saw her friends in
Berlin deported one by one over the years 1941, 1942, and 1943,
and she never heard from them again. And the letters the victims
pushed through the cracks of cattle cars, or passed on in stolen moments at train stations, rarely got to Efrate Pacificho or anyone else.
They littered the railroad tracks of German history for a few hours
and then drifted away.[4]

However, non-Jewish Germans wrote letters and posted and read
and saved them. In time of war and separation, the letters to and
from soldiers serving on the front lines were precious signs of life.
They were avowals of love and longings for home. They described
the battlefield and conditions of military occupation and eventually
provided historians with crucial documents about popular attitudes
toward the war and knowledge about the Holocaust. It was the dis-
locations of war that set people to express their thoughts about life
and death in the 1940s. "Never before had so many workers, artisans, and farmers committed themselves to regular private correspondence" or to comment on historical events; one middle-aged
baker wrote more than 350 letters before his death in the summer
of 1945.[5]

In Germany, forty billion pieces of mail went back and forth between the home front, which contributed the lion's share, and the
battle front in the years 1939–1945—about the same volume of
correspondence as in World War I; 12,000 people worked for Germany's military postal service during World War II. In May 1942 a
single division in Belorussia received 2,192 sacks of mail and sent

off another 1,004. Given that three out of four Germans were displaced from their homes at one point during the war, most correspondence has not survived. Letters from the home front, which were not usually kept by soldiers, who were on the move and almost half of whom died, are more rare. Even so, Germans wrote millions of letters every day, and despite air raids and evacuations, families, historical societies, and state archives managed to preserve thousands of war letters. Germans lost the war, but they saved much of the testimony of their exertions and sacrifices.[6]

Fighting on the eastern front, Albert Neuhaus, owner of a delicatessen in Münster, cherished the army's regular mail delivery: "You are just great! Mail yesterday evening, mail this morning, and mail again this evening," he wrote his wife Agnes in September 1941. In turn, he promised to be a faithful correspondent, asking his young wife for writing paper, envelopes, and film, entrusting comrades departing for Germany for leave with letters to post, and sending back home the mail he had received for safekeeping: "I'm including the mail that came about eight days ago; please save it!"[7] In time of war, families frequently established archives in order to document their role in national history.

Thus, by the time the Nazis began to deport German Jews in the fall of 1941, the simple act of writing or mailing a letter distinguished Germans from Jews. The distinction affected the ability of people in the war to bear witness, to send news, and to make sense of extraordinary events. It indicated the destruction of one community of remembrance and the survival of another. Although Germans made poignant statements about combat and death, they usually did so from the perspective of bystanders, soldiers, and perpetrators, not victims. Compounding the horror of genocide in World War II, then, is the destruction of testimony and thus the difficulty—though not the impossibility—of finding non-Nazi voices in the records that historians must use to tentatively explain the murders and the murderers. The fact of German empire both enabled and disabled the production of vernacular texts, which had the effect of breaking and distorting lines of sight both then and now.

During the big offensive campaigns in Poland in September and October 1939, in the West in the spring of 1940, and again in the Soviet Union a year later, Germans could not tear themselves away from the radio. "The events are so unbelievably big," confirmed one man from Görlitz at the end of June 1940: "it's the same with us; we don't turn off the radio all day long." "Everyone stands around the radio," noted a diarist on 24 June 1941, just after Operation Barbarossa against the Soviet Union had begun. Millions of soldiers composed their excited letters home in the aural space of the radio and imagined their loved ones in a similar placement. "You can't but hear," concludes one historian, "the extent to which soldiers oriented and pumped themselves up according to Hitler's speeches. In the letters, it is clear that he does not just influence them as a propagandist would, but, on closer examination, serves as their mouthpiece."[8] Radio broadcasts facilitated a sense of connection to the historical epic of National Socialism; "listening to the radio, you have a better sense of events because you get the big picture."[9]

After listening to Hitler's announcement to soldiers on 1 October 1941—"well, my comrades"—in which he pronounced the "beginning of the last great deciding battle of the war," Albert Neuhaus wrote an explicitly documentary letter to his wife intending "to provide a bit of insight into our experience." In this way, the "affection and enthusiasm" with which Hitler's orders were taken were relayed back to the home front. Albert also left his wife detailed instructions on keeping mementos of the war. "Dear Agnes! I am sending you six rolls of film to develop. I don't have to tell you how important these pictures are to me. Let me ask you to develop these pictures with *total care* in a 6 x 9 format. Preferably, silk smooth matte finish." Albert later requested bigger, 12 x 18 centimeter enlargements to provide "an ornament for our apartment."[10] Letters and photographs, and the effort to archive them, indicated the extent to which soldiers deliberately placed themselves in world history and adopted for themselves the heroicizing vantage of the Third Reich.

In the flush of victory, soldiers' letters home conveyed the new experiences of victorious armies on the march in foreign countries, enhancing page by page National Socialism's "collective experience." There was a heady excitement of seeing new places; sometimes soldiers compared the campaign in France to a "big Strength through Joy trip."[11] It was with an uncomplicated sense of superiority that even ordinary *Landser* (as German soldiers called themselves) regarded themselves in the first two years of the war. They described the fine wares they stole in France or the impoverished conditions of the eastern lands they occupied, confidently knowing "which town is German and which one is Polack." In World War II as in World War I, soldiers classified friends and foes in terms of relative cleanliness, but in this conflict they were much more apt to make sweeping judgments about the population and to rank people according to rigid biological hierarchies. Even the ordinary infantryman adopted a racialized point of view, so that "the Russians" the Germans had fought in 1914–1918 were transformed into an undifferentiated peril, "the Russian," regarded as "dull," "dumb," "stupid," or "depraved" and "barely humanlike." These words make "the vocabulary of the First World War seems almost harmless."[12]

War letters provided the Nazis with valuable confirmations of their own propaganda. Soldiers ridiculed the pretensions of Communism, the "so-called 'workers' paradise,'" and swore to the accuracy of the most vicious antisemitic stereotypes: "you read the *Stürmer* in Germany and look at the pictures," relayed one noncommissioned officer serving in Russia in July 1941, "and you will get only a small picture of what we see here and what atrocities the

Jews have committed."[13] From the perspective of the regime, letters from the front served to justify the war and to bind together the nation in a common purpose. Military officials underscored the importance of writing home; letters from the battle front supplied "a kind of spiritual vitamin" for the home front and reinforced its "attitude and nerves."[14]

If war letters conjured up the enemy with the stock imagery of National Socialism, they also revealed limits to ideological mobilization. Already in December 1941, with the end of the blitzkrieg, Goebbels acknowledged that letters from the field no longer corresponded to the regime's propaganda campaign in Berlin: "Actually the impact of letters from the front, which had been regarded as extraordinarily important, has to be considered more than harmful today," he noted: "soldiers are pretty blunt when they describe the great problems they are fighting under, the lack of winter gear . . . insufficient food and ammunition." Unit commanders subsequently distributed instructions on "The Art of Writing a Letter," urging soldiers to write "manly, hard and clear letters." Many impressions were "best locked deep in the heart because they concern only soldiers at the front . . . Anyone who complains and bellyaches is no true soldier."[15]

By February and March 1942, with the belated arrival of Christmas packages, letters were more optimistic. Even so, soldiers wrote about the enormous work they put into hardening themselves physically and emotionally. A few weeks after the fierce winter battles around Moscow, Hans Olte admitted to his parents that "I have already cried and I have tried violently to suppress my fears. It is terrible . . . So far, I have made it and I will continue to cope." Along similar lines, Albert Neuhaus confided to his wife: "to be quite honest, once in a while I get a little homesick. These are moments of inner trial, a struggle between desire and duty. But I have to endure." Soldiers tried hard to follow Wehrmacht instructions, but they really wanted to come home. After receiving a commemorative medal honoring his service during the "Winter Battle" of 1941–42, Albert noted that he would have preferred to be transferred back home. In October 1943 Agnes sent him "crackers, soap, razor blades, toothpaste, and pudding mix," but she did not add rolls of film, and Albert himself no longer referred to photography in his letters.[16] Albert Neuhaus was killed in Russia in March 1944.

"The beginning and end of Olte's transformation," comments Klaus Latzel, "can be best illustrated by two letters from his correspondence home: 'Oh I'd love to be out there with the soldiers,' in May 1940, and 'When will this endless murdering be over?' from May 1944."[17] Soldiers such as Albert Neuhaus and Hans Olte continued to fight and to kill, mostly out of a sense of duty and a desire to protect Germany itself, but they no longer thought of themselves as vanguards of National Socialism.

The ability to fight a race war did not come easily. Hannes Heer stresses the moment of "shock" and the subsequent process of "renormalization," which occurred repeatedly over the course of the war. "The tale told by the letters written by the majority of soldiers who invaded the Soviet Union in summer 1941," he explains, is of the "experience having turned them 'into a different person,'" of a process of 'inner change' having occurred, of being forced to 'completely readjust,' and also of having to 'throw overboard several principles.'" Heer recognizes that for a minority of men this "adjustment" was a harrowing process of "'split consciousness' which ended either in their resigned withdrawal" or in defiant solitude; but most soldiers adapted: "they became 'hard,' 'indifferent,' and 'heartless.'" A "New Man" became recognizable in these conditions. According to Kleo Pleyer, a reporter on the eastern front, "the battle-gray German was spared nothing in the Soviet Union. He did not just go through a triumphant offensive attack, as in France; he also had to keep his head amidst enemy artillery that lasted hours, days, weeks. He has seen one comrade after another fall bloodied to the ground, he has seen the shredded corpse of a friend. For months

he lived in hell . . . But for all this he only became stronger, harder."
What emerged on the eastern front was a new kind of brutal hero-
ism that had been incubated ideologically in the 1920s but put into
practice only in the 1940s; the combat soldier increasingly assumed
the virtues of unsparing and ruthless strength. "Here war is pursued
in its pure form," reflected one soldier in July 1941; "any sign
of humanity seems to have disappeared from deeds, hearts, and
minds." Another soldier concluded in November 1943: "With the
senses of a predator we recognize how the rest of the world will be
ground between the millstones of this war."[18]

When the first leaves were extended to the Wehrmacht in Russia
in spring and summer 1942, Goebbels warned civilians that homecoming soldiers might resemble strangers. This was so because combatants were participating "in a gigantic struggle of worldviews."
"It is understandable" that "uncompromising thinking about the
war, and its causes, consequences, and aims" would produce "points
of friction" with "life at home." It was necessary for families to
"live up" to the brutal "face of the war."[19] Goebbels was preparing
Germans for what soldiers on leave would tell them about the murder of innocent Jews.

It is precisely because soldiers accepted the remorseless terms of
racial war as simple facts that they could pass on news to their families about the conduct of the war and the destruction of Jews in
such unselfconscious registers. The most shocking records are the
photographs that soldiers took. Among the photographs that Albert Neuhaus sent and Agnes developed in the summer and fall of
1941 was one ("roll XII, 7") depicting a "Russian spy" hanged
"because he stole Lieutenant Gödecke's exercise pants." Since spies
do not steal pants, Neuhaus had completely internalized the disproportionate measures of the war, a "point of friction" with Agnes,
perhaps, who, after the war, corrected the subsequent typescript of
the letters by crossing out "spy" and writing "boy." On his way for
home for leave in June 1942, Albert snapped a picture ("roll XIII,
16") of Jewish women working under armed guard in a railway

yard in Stolpce: "it is a unique picture."[20] Most of these prisoners would be murdered one month later. Albert raised no questions about how this photograph came to be or his involvement in it. Photographs taken by other soldiers depicted partisans hanged in market squares and Jewish civilians shot on the edges of town. That many of the photographs of massacres showed soldiers holding cameras indicates the keen interest in documenting their part in the war. The camera facilitated a cool, distanced relationship to events and thereby provided emotional armor to the witnesses. Yet photographs remained basically commemorative: photographs of the Holocaust exist for the most part because German soldiers took them and saw to it that they were developed and preserved in private archives. Indeed, the fine grain to German atrocities became apparent when the Polish underground infiltrated Foto-Rys, a Warsaw photo shop frequented by Wehrmacht soldiers, and delivered the shocking prints to the Allies.[21]

Letters involved more explanation than photographs, but they provided clear statements about the complicity of the German army in killing civilians. "Ludwig B," a private stationed in or near Kiev, passed on news about the massacre of Jewish civilians at Babi Yar in September 1941: "The mines that have been laid still make it dangerous. In Kiev, for example, there was one explosion after another. For eight days the city has been burning—it is all the work of the Jews. As a result, Jewish men between the ages of fourteen and sixty were shot, and women too; otherwise there'll never be an end to it."[22] Ludwig framed the murders tactically and ideologically, linking them at once to explosions set by partisans in Kiev and to the broader recognition that women had to be killed in order to destroy the Jews as a people for the sake of the future. The soldier adopted the dual roles of victim in the midst of urban terrorism and of perpetrator, who accepted the difficult responsibilities of history.

The news of the shooting of Jewish civilians in the Soviet Union spread quickly by letters in autumn 1941. It was known to most

Germans who cared to know. Just to take one example of the open talk along the home front: the city employee who came to read Anna Haag's water meter in a Stuttgart suburb at the end of November 1941 "told about a relative, a SS man, who reported that he had had to shoot down 500 Jews, including women and children, in Poland, that many were not dead, but others were just thrown on top, and that he could not take it anymore."[23]

Events left other soldiers shocked and speechless; many admitted that they had seen terrible, unprecedented things, but insisted on withholding details until they returned home. Letters also contained expressions of terrible desperation and unbearable sadness. Soldiers wrote home as "Bocky," "Pitt," and "Kurdelbumbum."[24] It was in a combination of horror, reportage, and sentimentality that news of the war, including references to the mass shootings of Jews, reached the home front.

In whatever register, the letters and the conversations they generated back home indicated one more thing. Most Germans held on to their ability to witness and narrate their experiences, in the first years, as part of a new, greater German empire that would be reflected in war stories passed on by veterans and battlefield photographs adorning living rooms, and later, as part of a suffering, dutiful nation in arms against overwhelming odds. The victims of the Nazis, by contrast, found themselves engulfed in a disaster that was difficult to comprehend. The annihilation of Jewish communities was accompanied by the destruction of photographs, letters, and diaries—the private papers of deportees fueled a constant fire in Austerlitz, a satellite camp of Drancy (near Paris) where Jewish prisoners sorted through stolen goods—and thus the destruction of evidence of adjustment, attempts to escape or to resist the invaders, of the documentation of crimes, and of the comfort offered to friends and family.[25] This asymmetry in historical records persisted in accounts written after the war. A triumphant history of the Third Reich could not be written, of course, but admiring accounts of the Wehrmacht, which was carefully distinguished from Nazi leaders who had allegedly misled and betrayed it, were published and remained authoritative for many decades. Historical research into the Holocaust lagged well behind scholarly investigations into the military history of World War II. Even today it is hard to imagine what a full account of the Shoah might be, since the destruction of the accounts of the victims is so vast. The exceptional fact of the murder of the majority of Jews in Europe created silences that are difficult to gauge. The disparity in the ability to bear witness—this, too, was part of the German empire.

The Imperial Project

Much as Germans hated the Treaty of Versailles and placed it at the center of their postwar histories, Hitler did not aim at a revision of the political settlement of World War I. In the months of preparation before the September 1939 invasion of Poland, Hitler quite frankly admitted that the war was not about Danzig, which had been a "free city" under the mandate of the League of Nations since 1919, or the "Polish Corridor," which divided East Prussia from the rest of Germany after World War I; these were pretexts, sentimental, effective in the court of public and world opinion, but ultimately sideshows to his larger purpose. The war was fought to secure German living space in the East. In the mid-1920s Hitler had shifted his focus from France and Versailles to Poland, the Soviet Union, and the German empire that might be established there. "Russia is our Africa," Hitler later said. Hitler confirmed his ambitions to senior generals of the Reichswehr just three days after he came to power in 1933: the reconstruction of Germany's armed forces and the acquisition of living space. Hitler thought in explicitly racial terms; he and leaders in the SS envisioned a future in which hundreds of millions of Germans, liberated from the cramped, urban confines of the "Old Reich," established colonies across eastern Europe, harvested immense but underutilized wealth, and acquired for themselves security and prosperity. Nazis linked this "new, utopian vision of an Aryan-dominated Europe" to the destruction of indigenous, Slavic peoples, whose survivors would be reduced to undifferentiated workers and slaves, and to the demolition of Jewish communities, whose inhabitants would be shunted into faraway reservations or killed. The most extreme outcomes of four centuries of European imperialism, the disappearance of entire nations, the bondage of others, the Nazis made their immediate goal.[26]

In 1941 Hitler insisted that "the Germans," and "this is essential," he emphasized, "will have to constitute amongst themselves a closed society, like a fortress." The fortress was his guiding idea. Even when Germans were at the height of their power, Hitler rejected any attempt to forge alliances with subordinate powers. Unlike other Nazi leaders, Hitler was uninterested in restructuring western Europe in ways that might hold out a measure of independence to Vichy France. He rejected meaningful collaboration with other fascist movements on the continent; the only exception was his alliance with Italy. In the East, there was never any question of building anticommunist alliances with the Baltic states or Ukraine. The SS mobilized contingents of foreign fighters, but this strategy did not signal a rehabilitation of traditional imperial networks. Hitler's model was not Britain's India and limited self-rule. It was the United States, where, in Hitler's view, European settlers had conquered the continent, killed the natives, and established a new society on top of them on the basis of racial superiority.

War was the genesis and aim of Nazi actions. It was the glimpse of a unified Volksgemeinschaft at the beginning of World War I that provided National Socialism with the social model at the core of its ideology. As the "August Days" of 1914 had supposedly welded the German people together, war in the 1940s would realize the racial utopia of the Germans and affirm their superior status as a people able to make history and determine its destiny. At the same time, only the single-mindedness of a militarized people's community would enable Germany to wage successfully the dangerous wars it saw ahead in the twentieth century. In this regard, what the Nazis considered to be the lessons of collapse in 1918 determined how the legacy of 1914 was to be used. To Hitler and the postwar generation of activists who shaped the National Socialist movement, Germany could triumph in a future war. This was the crucial insight that conciliated a country deeply troubled by its defeat. But Germany could do so only by managing the people's community according to racial principles. Concretely this meant the destruction of the economic and political power of Jews; the implementation of both positive and negative eugenic measures, including sterilization and euthanasia, in order to strengthen the *Volkskörper;* and the relentless exploitation of newly conquered territories in eastern Europe. In addition, both propaganda and social policy were required to tie German workers emotionally to the collective whole. The Nazis refought the existential drama of World War I, but in reverse, moving to eliminate the dangers represented by 1918 in order to arrive at the unity of 1914.

The Nazis had no master plan to acquire the living space they believed Germany needed in order to survive. What seems clear is that the Nazis planned for a major conflict in western Europe in order to break the power of the status quo before launching a dynamic war for empire in eastern Europe. Once Germany had acquired Austria and Czechoslovakia in 1939, the order in which Hitler's wars would be fought put France and Britain first, Poland and the Soviet Union second. Yet with the Czechoslovak "crisis" solved, Hitler lacked the trigger for war. When strategic negotiations with Poland over other issues broke down in the spring of 1939, war against Poland moved into focus. It was Poland that provided the excuse for a general war against France and Great Britain. Nazi Germany's Non-Aggression Pact with the Soviet Union in August 1939 secured Germany's eastern flank but did not alter Hitler's intention to conquer the lands of the old Russian empire after victory in the West. However, after the fall of France, at the end of summer 1940, Hitler postponed the invasion of England and prepared instead for his June 1941 invasion of the Soviet Union. What Hitler and his military strategists had assumed would be a difficult, even protracted war on the western front succeeded brilliantly, though it failed to knock Britain out of the war. Hitler was both extremely confident in the ability of German power and more cautious on the question of Britain. A new strategic framework subsequently fell into place in which Germany would vanquish the "easy" target of the Soviet Union before invading Britain. The thinking was that Germany's summer victory in 1941 would destroy one of Britain's two potential allies, encourage Japan to concentrate its offensive capacity against the United States, and ultimately undermine Britain's only other ally. In the meantime Germany would secure living space and acquire the resources it needed to defeat Britain and take possession of the old colonial empires in 1941 and 1942. The confidence of Germany's leaders, and particularly Hitler, in the summer of 1940 is dizzying. However, this overall record of improvisation in 1938–1941 does not mean that Hitler was a sheer opportunist, the mistaken assumption of the British historian A. J. P. Taylor; the long-range goal of a greater German empire organized along racial lines remained in place at all times.[27]

Since no precise plan for German empire existed, there was also no preconceived resting or end point for German ambitions, no boundaries for the empire. Thus in 1939–40 the eastern borderlands of occupied Poland appeared as a mighty barrier between the Germans and Soviets; a year later these peripheral territories were the center of German colonization efforts, which had advanced into the Soviet Union and pushed the borders of German-dominated Europe far to the east, toward the Urals, and to the south, toward the Caucasus. Some strategies anticipated conquering the entire globe.[28]

Finally, the pace of the war influenced imperial policy. The prevailing assumption in 1939–1941 that the war the Germans were fighting would be quick and would come to an end, "next" year at the latest, allowed Nazi strategists to postpone comprehensive solutions to the "Jewish problem." Successive victories also had the effect of enlarging and radicalizing the proposed solution, which advanced from a "reservation" in 1939–40, in which German and Polish Jews would rot someplace in occupied Poland, to a plan in the spring of 1940 to dump all of Europe's Jews onto the French island of Madagascar, and finally, in the summer of 1941, to the removal of all Jews in Europe into the "East" of the vanquished Soviet Union. The anticipation of a final victory justified postponing these ever-larger schemes to the near future. The reverse also held true: setbacks had the effect of drawing the "final solution" closer into the present. Thus by the time the Nazis realized that the war with the Soviet Union would drag on, sometime in the late summer or early fall of 1941, the "Jewish problem," as the Nazis saw it, had expanded to encompass all European and Soviet Jews, and the "final solution" they proposed had shifted from a territorial one, in which Jews would be shipped out beyond the empire, to an exterminatory one, in which Jews would be moved around only to be killed within the borders of the empire. Hitler and his inner circle probably discussed the deportation of all Jewish men, women, and children in Europe from Crete to Norway in the summer of 1941, largely agreed to carry out such a campaign in the early fall, and reconfirmed it to party leaders in mid-December, but the Nazis implemented the "final solution" on a comprehensive scale only when rolling stock and extermination camps became available in the spring of 1942. However, the origins of the Holocaust lie in Germany's determination to fight a race war in Poland in September 1939.

The Germans invaded Poland on 1 September 1939 without any clear idea of what precisely to do with the conquered territories. A week before the invasion, Hitler made clear that he anticipated a ruthless campaign that would be carried out with "the greatest brutality and without mercy." The aim, he told his generals on 22 August, was the "destruction of Poland" and "its living forces" in order to secure the rights of "the strongest" power, eighty million Germans (including Austrians). Not even the outbreak of fighting on the western front with France should deter the German invaders from their purpose in the East, Hitler reiterated. At the time, Hitler probably confirmed the role that SS units would play behind military lines. Their task was to destroy the "living forces" of Poland by incarcerating or killing Poland's intellectual leadership, the nobility, teachers, civil servants, and the clergy.[29] This division of labor between conventional and political military forces became standard for Nazi operations, but it does not mean that the Wehrmacht fought "conventionally" or remained "clean" while the SS did the "dirty work," as postwar myths suggested. The Wehrmacht was an integral part of the racial war the Nazis waged. Its treatment of Polish civilians and prisoners of war was vicious, its collaboration with SS shooting parties routine.

The German invasion of Poland was brutal and quick. Alexander Rossino has examined the "murderous march" of the XII Corps of the Eighth Army as it advanced from Silesia northeast toward Lodz in September 1939. Soldiers shot bystanders at random, burned houses and barns, and turned their guns on terrified Poles when they tried to flee. From the outset, German troops fought a number of heavy battles and met with resistance from armed civilians after regular Polish forces withdrew, prompting the Wehrmacht and SS regiments to carry out harsh reprisals in which townspeople, whom the Germans were already disposed to see as dangerous and shrewd, were rounded up, beaten, and shot. When German soldiers came under attack, loud bursts of machine-gun fire cleared the area: one soldier attempted to reproduce the sounds of his assault: "Tak tak tak s s s s sühhhsühhhh tak taktak f f f f tak tak tak." Though considered too slow by the SS, court-martial proceedings held in the rear by the Wehrmacht to prosecute suspected guerrilla fighters handed down as many as 200 execution orders every day. The Wehrmacht also executed thousands of captured Polish soldiers and deported Polish Jews into eastern Poland, which the Soviets occupied on 17 September.[30]

In western Poland, where thousands of ethnic Germans and Poles lived side by side, the treatment of unarmed Polish and Jewish civilians was particularly harsh. Ethnic Germans mobilized into auxiliary paramilitary units known as *Selbstschutz* and worked closely with the SS to identify Poles who had fought against the Germans in partisan uprisings after World War I and to arrest and execute Polish leaders. In the short interval between the retreat of Polish troops and the advance of German units, Poles also committed atrocities against ethnic German civilians. Several hundred Germans, for example, were killed in Bydgoszcz, formerly the Prussian town of Bromberg, on 3 September. In the accounts of Nazi propagandists, the number of German victims killed in Bromberg increased by many thousands; Hitler himself set the total number of German victims in Poland at 60,000, although the Wehrmacht initially set the figure (high) at 5,000. Once the gruesome exaggerations of the ethnic German "passion" on "Bloody Sunday" were in place, Einsatzgruppen, the mobile killing units of the SS, and the *Selbstschutz* conducted vicious reprisals that over a ten-day period resulted in the murder of 1,200 people, including the city's leading citizens and its entire Jewish population (Victor Klemperer's father had served Bromberg as rabbi in the 1880s). That Jews paid with their own lives for the deaths of German civilians was clear to anyone reading Goebbels' Berlin paper, *Der Angriff,* which reported at the end of October 1939 that Bromberg was "judenfrei."[31]

"Bloody Sunday," later infamously memorialized by Edwin Erich Dwinger in his bestselling novel *Death in Poland,* served as a justification for the war itself. "At the outbreak of the war I was utterly convinced of our superior moral position," remembered Melita Maschmann, at the time a twenty-one-year-old Hitler Youth leader;

"The news of the 'Bloody Sunday' . . . thoroughly justified a war against Poland in my eyes." It also fitted well into established stereotypes, which cast Poles as inferior but mortal threats to the well-being of the German people; turning history around, the 1941 hit movie *Heimkehr* depicted Polish assailants and defenseless Germans. The conviction that Germany was at war in order to regain sovereignty and freedom lost in World War I was widespread. One lieutenant in southern Poland mentioned to his company that "my father fell here on the San, I don't know where, perhaps here . . . When on the next day," the regimental report continued, "another man in the company found a large, rusted, German steel helmet, every reservist held it long in his hands looking at it in silence. It became very clear to all of us that this was sacred ground, sacred because it had already drunk the blood of a generation before us."[32]

At the same time, the speed of the German victory confirmed notions of German superiority. In the East, Germans strutted. "You are the master race now," SS General Ludolf von Alvensleben informed his ethnic German recruits; "don't be soft—be merciless." Authorities hammered in the importance of treating the Poles as inferior people to all representatives of the German occupation from senior civil servants down to the Hitler Youth. "Every German who goes East is in the first instance 'the master' in relation to the 'alien,'" read the instructions of the National Socialist Women's Organization, which sent volunteers to Poland. For Polish Jews, the consequence was especially cruel and humiliating treatment. In Zamosc a local physician, Zygmunt Klukowski, observed German rulers settle in. On 14 October he noted in his diary: "the Germans required that all Jews work at cleaning the streets, even though it is a Jewish holy day. The Germans are treating the Jews very brutally. They cut their beards; sometimes they pull the hair out." On the next day: "They order the Jews to take at least a half-hour of exhaustive gymnastics before any work." And the next: "The Germans are beating the Jews without any reason, just for fun."[33]

German "freedom" was based on the unfreedom of Poles and especially Polish Jews. The Germans set about "cleaning house," as one general put it in September 1939, in order to destroy the Polish nation, its "living forces" and its cultural identity. In the months that followed, Einsatzgruppen rounded up and shot or imprisoned thousands of teachers, intellectuals, officers, and priests. One thousand seven hundred Polish priests were sent to Dachau; half of them died before the end of the war. The SS also endeavored to kill off the Polish nobility; Alvensleben even shot his own relatives, telling them that "if he did not shoot them he would have to face them in the next war." Fifty thousand Polish civilians were killed by the end of 1939 alone.[34]

The Nazis drew up more far-ranging plans for Poland in October 1939. In contrast to the protectorate status of Bohemia and Moravia and the semi-independent client state of Slovakia, which had been carved out of Czechoslovakia in March 1939, Poland was to disappear as an administrative and cultural entity. In Himmler's view, it was just "ethnic mush."[35] While the Soviet Union incorporated eastern Poland, Germany annexed Poland's western territories, creating two new *Reichsgau*, or centrally administered subdivisions: Danzig–West Prussia and Wartheland, which became part of the German Reich. The rest of Poland, including the districts of Warsaw, Lublin, and Cracow, was dissolved into a German imperial entity, the General Gouvernement, administered by a governor-general, the thirty-nine-year-old Hans Frank, a leading Nazi jurist. Although Poland was to disappear, Poles did not, and millions found themselves living inside the new borders of the German Reich. Their fate would be decided by audacious plans for eastern Europe that Hitler outlined with references to a "new order in ethnic relationships," the "resettlement of national groups," and the "arrangement of the Jewish problem" in his victory speech to the Reichstag on 6 October 1939. He appointed Himmler "Reich Commissioner for the Strengthening of Germandom" and left his ideological militants to fill in the details.

Himmler pursued three interrelated goals to lay the foundations for an eternal German Reich. First, the commission proposed to trawl the Polish population in the annexed territories for racially valuable individuals who could be Germanized, while the majority would be deported to the General Gouvernement. There they would form a "labor reservoir" for the Reich. Second, German administrators needed to resettle ethnic Germans whose return from the Soviet Union and the Baltic states the Nazis had negotiated in October 1939. And finally, SS planners envisioned a Jewish "reservation" around Lublin to which German and Polish Jews would be deported. This far-reaching demographic plan foresaw the displacement of millions of people, including eight million Poles in the annexed territories of Wartheland and West Prussia. The scale of planning in a few weeks in the autumn of 1939 was breathtaking. The territories became an exemplary "field of experimentation" for "the capacities for imperial restructuring."[36] While the precise content and the scale of plans changed, two goals did not: the prospect of far-reaching Germanization and the "final solution" to the "Jewish problem."

A series of talking points guided the construction of German empire:

1. In place of the right to self-determination, the right to exist
2. In place of arbitrary sovereignties, natural hierarchies
3. In place of states and state borders, ethnicities and ethnic borders
4. In place of zones of friction in east-central Europe, a nationally and socially aligned order

This was a task "not for one, but for all coming generations." In this regard, the war was epoch-making. It offered the movement its "second great chance for 'National Socialist self-realization.'"[37]

Although historians have scoured archives around the world to piece together the racial policies of the Nazi empire, the overall design was clear and its promise celebrated and publicized by leading German writers. The novelist Hanns Johst accompanied Himmler on two inspections of occupied Poland in order to write a modern-day saga depicting Germany's rise to power. In *Call of the Empire, Echo of the People,* he described his second journey, which took him to all the main stations of the empire. He set out at the end of January 1940 from the train station Berlin-Friedrichstrasse, traveling in Himmler's private railroad car, "which was hooked onto the regularly scheduled express to Cracow." The empire builders arrived in Przemysl, on the new German-Soviet border, in time to welcome thousands of ethnic Germans from Volhynia. "They heard the voice of the fatherland, the voice of their blood, the voice of their fathers," wrote Johst as he experimented with epic style. Like "big children," he continued, switching registers, "they are well-behaved . . . under the eyes of their Führer." Himmler's party returned across Poland, "through a sunken, antediluvian time," to Cracow: "locomotives whistle and howl, screech and gnash. The sentries' steps tramp back and forth beneath the window of the compartment . . . back and forth, the pendulum swing of Germany's new time in this world." The next day Johst accompanied Himmler on a visit to the barracks of SS Einsatzgruppen, whom the SS leader urged: "Never become soft . . . never become brutal!" "I love the pioneers of this new state, who so obviously demonstrate the binding qualities of our race," Johst added. At a farewell meal, the author sat between Hans Frank, the governor-general, and Friedrich Schmidt, district chief in Lublin, "in whose domain the Jews of the Reich will be gathered to receive their first territorial reservation in Europe." A colonial master at home as well in literature, Johst received as his reward a steady supply of domestic servants from Germany's concentration camps; when the Polish girl didn't work out, he was sent a young Jehovah's Witness from Ravensbrück.[38]

However, in 1939 and 1940 the Germans lacked the physical capacity to move millions of people or to improve the "new provinces." While the opportunities of war promoted ambitious long-range planning, the demands of the war forced Germans to adopt more modest approaches. The arrival in late 1939 and early 1940 of tens of thousands of ethnic Germans from the Soviet Union, Latvia, and Estonia reshuffled operational priorities. Moreover, labor shortages in Germany interfered with plans to deport Poles, many of whom were transported west into the *Altreich* as slave laborers instead of being pushed east into the General Gouvernement as castoffs. Circumstances also repeatedly postponed deportations of Jews to Lublin, while Governor-General Frank strenuously opposed everyone else's efforts to dump their "refuse" into what he wanted to develop as a "model territory."[39] Germany's racial administrators picked at one or another strand of Germany's imperial policy, reclaiming German bloodlines, resettling ethnic Germans, deporting Poles, or searching for a "final solution" to the "Jewish problem." They made only slow progress, without, however, losing sight of the all-embracing ethnic struggle in which they believed Germany found itself.

From October 1939 through February 1940, some 190,000 ethnic Germans arrived in Germany in two great waves of immigration from territories that the Soviet Union had occupied in September 1939 and would annex a year later. About one-third of this number, mostly middle-class Germans, came from Latvia and Estonia; the rest, nearly 130,000 peasants and artisans, had made their homes in Galicia and Volhynia in what had been eastern Poland. In the fall of 1940 another 30,000 ethnic Germans were repatriated from the General Gouvernement. At the same time, a third wave of 137,000 immigrants from the Soviet regions of northern Bukovina and Bessarabia, near the Romanian border, and 77,000 Romanian Germans from Dobrudsha and Bukovina entered the German empire. By the end of 1940 German authorities had registered 500,000 ethnic Germans, most of whom they expected to settle in the annexed territories. In the winter of 1941 another 48,000 ethnic Germans arrived from Lithuania. After the invasion of the Soviet Union in June 1941, the Germans expanded their efforts, searching for Germans among the indigenous populations of Galicia, Belorussia, and Ukraine. By the end of 1944 a total of over one million ethnic Germans had been identified.

The arrival of so many ethnic Germans placed real limits on how extensively German colonizers would be able to restructure eastern Europe. Himmler's demographic planners intended at first to deport the majority of the eight million Poles from the annexed territories as soon as possible. But it very quickly became clear to racial administrators shuttling between Berlin, Cracow, and Lodz that extraordinary population transfers on this magnitude were not feasible in time of war. Trains could transport only about 1,000 people at a time, and railroad cars were required to move troops for the planned invasion of France in the winter of 1940 and then again for the strike against the Soviet Union in the spring of 1941. The expulsion of Jewish and non-Jewish Poles from the annexed territories was therefore calibrated increasingly closely to the inescapable requirement to resettle ethnic Germans. Thus an unwieldy sequence of increasingly ambitious long-range plans coexisted alongside a series of short-range maneuvers, which were executed to make room for ethnic Germans.

Four short-range plans resulted in the deportation of 260,000 Poles from the Wartheland between December 1939 and January 1941. By the end of December 1939 the German authorities had deported more than 87,000 Poles eastward into the General Gouvernement, where they were left to fend for themselves. A winter action in February and March 1940 pushed another 40,000 out. In order not to interrupt farm production or disrupt the food supply, further deportations were postponed until after the harvest in 1940. In the meantime, repatriated ethnic Germans languished in temporary camps; German authorities could not supply enough Polish "homes" to keep up with the growing number of new German immigrants. The intention to remove 600,000 additional Poles from the Wartheland over the course of 1940 resulted in the expulsion of only 133,000 people. Further slowing these deportations was the decision to identify and reclaim Poles with Germanic blood and to select out able-bodied Poles to work in Germany. As Karl Schlögel remarks, German racial politics was well on the way to turning eastern Europe into a "switching yard for entire nations and ethnic groups."[40]

Nazi policy toward the Jews shifted as the problem of resettling ethnic Germans came into focus. The intention to fundamentally reorganize the population of eastern Europe by establishing new German colonies in the annexed territories and reducing the Polish nation to a "forced labor regime" invited the Nazis to conceive of a "final solution" to the Jewish problem. The East provided the space into which the Nazis could expel Jews, whose numbers under German control had increased dramatically. Moreover, the wide-scale expropriation of the property of Polish Jews in the annexed territories in October 1939 destroyed their economic independence and confirmed their disposability in German eyes. German administrators conscripted Jews in their jurisdiction as forced laborers, and robbed them of their property whenever the need arose, but they worked on the assumption that the Jews would disappear into the General Gouvernement in the very near future. The will to deprive the Jews of the means of existence was there, even if the resources to fully implement deportation plans were not. Scattered deportations of several thousand Jewish families from the Wartheland took place at the end of October, but no comprehensive deportation of Polish Jews occurred in the fall of 1939 or the winter of 1940 despite all the talk about a Jewish "reservation." In this way, the war inflated German ambitions by repeatedly offering the period after the war as the moment when the grand designs could take shape. Notions of "after the war" and "the East" complemented each other to provide the time and place for the realization of increasingly ambitious imperial plans.

The business of deporting Poles fell to Himmler's newly created

Reich Commission for the Strengthening of Germandom, which established resettlement centers *(Umwandererzentralstelle)* responsible for evaluating and expelling Poles and immigration centers *(Einwanderungszentralstelle)* to admit ethnic Germans. Agronomists and student volunteers assigned to the resettlement centers prepared village maps and farm inventories in order to determine which Polish homesteads to expropriate and how many to assign to ethnic German families; usually each German householder received two Polish farms in deference to his racial superiority. In order to protect the livestock and to keep Poles from making off with their belongings, the police arrived without warning before dawn. From one dark moment to the next, Poles lost both their homes and their livelihoods. Every deportee was allowed to quickly pack personal belongings weighing no more than twenty-five to thirty kilograms, but otherwise everything was left behind, "so that the Volhynian Germans who follow can carry on the household and the farm without any problems." By eight or nine in the morning, the dispossessed families were assembled at local "holding camps," and by midafternoon they had been transported to "evacuation camps" in Lodz, or Litzmannstadt, as the Germans renamed the city. At the same time, German volunteers readied the farmsteads, which were assigned to ethnic Germans, who arrived by buses from nearby "transit camps" around noon. Colonists subsequently made their new homes with the furniture, dishes, and linens of deported Polish families.[41]

In Lodz the unfortunate Poles found themselves incarcerated in "evacuation camps" in order to undergo racial and medical examination. Unless they were judged to be potentially eligible to be reclaimed as Germans, the Polish families were bundled into "assembly camps," their third station since being expelled from home. There they waited for trains to transport them to the General Gouvernement. From May 1940 through January 1941, ninety-two trains hauled whole communities away. Once in the General Gouvernement, these luckless people were sometimes assigned to farmers or they made their way to relatives or simply starved on the streets. Meanwhile German "ethnocrats" identified a minority of Poles as suitable for Germanization and placed them in "selection camps." Poles judged to be "capable of becoming German again" were deployed to Germany as workers, whether they wanted to go or not, although they were not subject to the harsh restrictions later imposed on "pure" Polish workers in Germany. To meet a growing demand in wartime Germany, thousands of Polish girls categorized as racially assimilable ended up in Germany working as maids and farm hands with no control over their future.[42]

The commission also screened ethnic Germans already living in the annexed territories. They ended up in one of four categories on a comprehensive *Deutsche Volksliste,* or German Ethnic Registry. While racial criteria determined whether an individual would be placed on the registry as a German and thus protected from expulsion, political loyalties and cultural affiliations determined in which category of the registry he or she would be classified. "Asocials" and other "genetically inferior" Germans were identified beforehand and handed over to the SS to be put into concentration camps. Category 1 was reserved for Germans who had actively promoted the German cause in Poland in 1939, while Category 2 encompassed individuals who spoke German and felt themselves to be German. Anyone in Categories 1 and 2 automatically received German citizenship. Categories 3 and 4 granted "German citizenship on probation" to individuals who were regarded to be racially German but spoke Polish at home and sent their children to Polish schools. "Probation" often meant a labor assignment in Germany as a way to complete "Germanization." Since Poles in the annexed territories lacked legal rights and stood to lose their property, there were considerable advantages to applying for membership on the *Volksliste;* even so, many eligible Poles refused. After 1945, other people found themselves inside German racial categories that had lost their usefulness.[43]

With the invasion of the Soviet Union in June 1941, the center of

German empire moved farther and farther eastward. Working under the rubric of the "Generalplan Ost," Germany's racial planners prepared to build colonies in 1942 and 1943 in the very same places where they had retrieved ethnic Germans and dumped Poles in 1939 and 1940. Frank envisioned making the General Gouvernement "as German as the Rhineland" and accelerated policies of Germanization. A monument to fallen German soldiers was even planned for Warsaw. "Our Last Days in Stanislau," an account of the trek westward written by one young ethnic German in 1939, were no longer "last days" once Stanislau and the rest of Galicia (and Ukraine and Crimea) reappeared on Germany's imperial map a few years later.[44]

Operating in a much larger territory after 1941, the Reich Commission for the Strengthening of Germandom installed mobile immigration centers on special trains in order to find Germans or Germanic types—over time the definitions became less strict—eligible for racial reclamation and thus conscription into the military or the Reich Labor Service. Since the purpose of racial reclamation in 1942 and 1943 was not to bring Germans back "home," but to seize anyone who was racially acceptable in order strengthen the beleaguered *Volkskörper,* administrators fished out many individuals who did not consider themselves ethnic Germans and threw back into the pool older and less productive Germans; individuals over the age of forty-five were generally not eligible for Germanization. As far as the Reich Commission was concerned, "'creaming-off' of so-called 'superior' elements" weakened non-German ethnic groups while fortifying the master race. "All Germanic blood to us—or be wiped out," Himmler summarized. In fact, while Poles and Ukrainians not selected for Germanization could be deployed to Germany to work, their former neighbors, colonists in newly organized "German villages," the remote outposts of German empire, found themselves besieged by partisan warfare waged by those who had nothing to lose thanks to this harsh system.[45]

Finally, the ethnic Germans arriving from Latvia, Estonia, and the Soviet Union, who had been greeted with such fanfare as parts of "the biggest migration of modern times," quickly scattered into an archipelago of far-flung relocation camps stretching across the German empire. In the annexed territories, 10,000 Polish residents in asylums for the mentally ill or the infirm were murdered in order to make room for incoming Germans. Camp administrators often subjected the ethnic Germans to a militarized regimen, separating them by sex and treating the newcomers as children, if not prisoners. Immigrants recounted their handlers' brusque and threatening words, which carried echoes of the fate meted out to the former inhabitants of the very buildings the ethnic Germans now occupied. Once the Baltic Germans were evaluated according to physical attributes, social and cultural skills, and professional capacities, they were divided one of two categories, with the great majority assigned as "O," which assured their integration as new German colonists into the service, retailing, and artisanal economy of the annexed eastern territories (hence the *Ost* designation), or the much less favorable "A," which meant a labor assignment in the old Reich (hence the *Alt* designation). Even so, the undeveloped German economy in the Wartheland left thousands of people without meaningful employment and, for those who were in their forties or fifties, the prospect of permanent institutionalization in old-age homes.[46]

Rural peasants, the Volhynian and Galician Germans were, in principle, easier to settle, but only as long as German resettlement authorities expropriated enough Polish farms and did so according to a plan that created cohesive villages that would form the infrastructure of new German colonies. Successive waves of migration into the German empire in 1939–1941, as well as transportation shortages and difficulties carrying out the desired expropriations, ended up stranding hundreds of thousands of ethnic Germans in more than 1,500 "observation" camps, where they languished for years. As in the case of the Baltic Germans, Volhynian and Galician

Germans and later Bessarabian and Romanian Germans were divided by authorities from the immigration centers into "O" and
"A" cases; when Polish farms were available, "O" settlers were
shipped to "transit" camps in the Wartheland and, on the morn-
ings when German police had successfully evacuated Polish villages, transported to their new farms in "Strength through Joy"
buses.[47] By the end of 1940, 71,000 ethnic German colonists had
been resettled in the Warthegau. Nonetheless, in 1941 more than
250,000 ethnic Germans, most of them assigned to the privileged
"O" category, remained in "observation" camps waiting for assignments in the East; in 1942 the number was still 130,000. Despite
the swastika-emblazoned flags and Hitler portraits that camp authorities ordered by the truckload, reports indicated that ethnic
Germans in the camps had grown depressed. Many were ready to
return to their old homes. Although the Ethnic German Liaison
Office generally rejected petitions by ethnic Germans to go back
home, it allowed applicants who "are worthless to us" and whom
"we have an interest in deporting"—that is, the old, the very young,
the unproductive—to return, in this case to Romania.[48]

The actual work of colonization in the annexed territories began once ethnic Germans received homesteads. Thousands of volunteers streamed toward the new frontiers of the empire to help
Germanize the new settlers. "The aim was not," Elizabeth Harvey
points out, to assimilate the Poles, as had been the case in imperial
projects carried out by the British or French, "but to eradicate
'Polishness' and ultimately eliminate the Polish population from
'German soil.'" Arthur Greiser, the Gauleiter of the Wartheland,
addressed one group of student volunteers: "We must give the land
a new face. The lack of culture must vanish . . . Step by step, farm
by farm, village by village, town by town, the foreigner must be
pushed back, until only Germans remain." Young women assigned
to the East as part of their Hitler Youth or Reich Labor service
played crucial roles in tidying up what Germans contemptuously

referred to as the "Polish economy." They were the ones who readied expropriated Polish homes for the new settlers who arrived later in the day. According to reports prepared by the Reich Commission for the Strengthening of Germandom, volunteers "cleaned the farm and the house of the often atrocious filth, decorated the table with flowers to welcome the settlers, and cooked a meal so that the settlers would quickly feel at ease in their new home."[49] References to decorations and flowers indicate the importance authorities put on creating a distinctive German lifestyle, as had been the case in the Reich Labor Service camps.

"Far from being a private matter, remote from the affairs of state and nation, the German home was elevated into the site where the nation was generated and reproduced," argues Harvey. Hitler Youth *Mädel* paid regular visits to the homes of ethnic Germans to make sure that they looked properly German, replacing the paper flowers they regarded as kitschy with fir twigs and substituting Hitler portraits for the images of saints; "one can really call that progress," the students beamed. German women also warned their families not to strike up friendships with Poles, to eat with local farm hands, or to let their children play with Polish kids. Beginning in 1940, the "Christmas action" brought hundreds of volunteers to the annexed territories for a few weeks to teach ethnic Germans how to make Christmas presents and ornaments and to sing Christmas songs and thereby to construct German culture. Other recruits staffed schools and kindergartens; the National Socialist Welfare Service ran 495 year-round and 393 summer kindergartens in the Wartheland alone. Older children enrolled in local branches of the Hitler Youth and the League of German Girls. In this context, Germanization was indistinguishable from Nazification. Of course, there were limits: housewives resented nosy volunteers, German farmers continued to work with Polish neighbors, and newcomers often felt unsettled, first, when German fortunes in the East soared with the invasion of the Soviet Union, because they thought they would get better land farther east, and then, after the Battle of Stalingrad, because they assumed they would eventually have to be moved to safety somewhere in the west.[50] Nazi colonial planners envisioned an infrastructure of towns and cities and highways that would complete the Germanization of the new territories. Most of this was not built unless it directly contributed to the German war effort. Lodz, which in 1939 was annexed to the German Reich, became the administrative capital of the Wartheland, attracting civilian administrators, SS racial teams, businessmen, and student volunteers. They moved into apartments whose Jewish residents had been evicted: "Two thousand keys are waiting for Germans to come and open the doors to their new homes," explained one newspaper.[51] Auschwitz, formerly Oświęcim, was also expanded as an administrative center linked to the concentration camp and the industrial plants such as I. G. Farben that opened there after 1941. Katowice also became an increasingly important industrial city in the Reich economy. Although work began on an Autobahn to connect Berlin, Breslau, and Cracow, for which Jewish slave workers supplied much of the labor, German colonization was a goal more anticipated than achieved along streets renamed Glueckaufstrasse, Wikinger Strasse, and Kurfürstenstrasse, but otherwise not well traveled by German settlers.

At least in the early days of 1940 and 1941, a frontier spirit prevailed; volunteers from the Reich were keen to make a contribution to the German cause and exulted in the initiatives they were allowed to take. For German pioneers in the Wartheland, this effort often involved commandeering "our hard-working Jews" to undertake repairs or establish gardens and selecting furniture and other goods from among the items stolen from Jewish households: "You just have to pick out what you want. It was so much fun." Did rooms seized from Jews or Poles need to be cleaned up?— "already several strong-looking Jewish rascals have been picked up and shipped to us . . . who else will do all the work around here?"[52]

"Everywhere Jewish gangs are at work," reported the author of a popular book on the war. Volunteers and administrators shared a "can-do" mentality that "took it for granted that the non-German population could be exploited and removed to make way for Germans."[53]

The frontier also beckoned visitors to see the sights of the nascent German empire, the most terrifying and fascinating of which were the remnants of Jewish communities. The newly established Jewish ghetto in Lodz, "in which the members of this crooked-nose race have been assembled," was a popular stop for German visitors from the *Altreich*.[54] A main road divided the ghetto and thereby offered visitors easy access. "Feeling themselves to be venturing on to the 'front line' of the struggle for Germandom," Elizabeth Harvey comments, "they were gripped by the spectacle of 'real' Jews." And "having seen what films, books, and Party training courses conditioned them to see, they then reproduced the stereotypes exactly in their reports." One young student jotted down her impressions in October 1940: "The most shocking sight in this town . . . is the ghetto, an enormous district fenced off with barbed wire, where the streets and squares swarm with Jews roaming around, many of them truly criminal types. Just what are we to do with this rabble?"[55] Even after the Jews were deported and murdered, the deserted streets of Jewish neighborhoods exerted a powerful attraction. In the summer of 1943, a field trip sponsored by a "Children's Rural Evacuation" camp in the General Gouvernement toured the town of Gorlice. "We were on our way right after we finished the potato soup," wrote one of the teachers, a twenty-three-year-old woman from Hamburg; "afterward we walked through town a bit and took a look at the 'former Jew alley.'" The guard who accompanied the group "made sure no one else was listening" and then in his broken German told the adults that "all the Jews without exception were shot eight months ago." (In fact the massacre occurred in August 1942.) Although only the adults got the inside story, everyone trooped through the "Jew alley." A week later, teachers and children undertook an expedition to Biecz. On the way there, they stumbled onto the remains of an abandoned Jewish labor camp: "Hundreds are buried here!" reported a Polish gendarme. Biecz itself was almost completely deserted: "If you looked carefully you could make out the names of the former owners above the doors: Isaac, Moses, Sarah . . . In this desolation, the immense Gothic church appeared completely unreal." Nonetheless, "Erika sat at the organ and played for us. The children sat totally quietly on the pews, listened to the music, and gazed reverentially into the church."[56] A Baedecker for the region described resuscitated German towns such as Cracow and Lublin, adding the matter-of-fact parenthetical "(now Jew-free)" as if the location had been recently upgraded. Whatever became German was also no longer to be Jewish, an equation that was broadly accepted; accordingly, one Nazi functionary simply added "Jews are not seen anymore" to her report on Cracow, where "so many Germans are walking around this German cityscape that it feels just like home."[57]

As Nazi colonizers themselves admitted, many Germans continued to regard the East as *unheimlich,* sinister—an understandable response given the territories' Jewish deportees and vengeful Poles. Most Germans needed to be lured there with salary bonuses, improved rations, and tax incentives. Yet this was a time and place when a twenty-nine-year-old teacher from Thüringen could take satisfaction in the work she had done in "her realm" in Galicia; ride out under a bright moonlit sky with "Staff sergeant L." on the night of the Allied invasion of France; see "in the distance [that] a Polish village was burning and a great cloud of smoke hung in the sky"; and comment in her diary before going to bed that "one could really forget all one's worries—yes, cares?—in this paradise with flowers and horses." By this time, however, the empire was crumbling. Already at the end of 1943 the German colonies or "settlement pearls" that had been established a year earlier in Ukraine had to be evacuated; as a result thousands of ethnic Germans entered the Warthegau and added yet another circle to the rings of camps in the Third Reich.[58] In February and March 1945, during the final Russian offensive, they would join the long treks westward, prompting Goebbels to comment: "What is coming into the Reich under the brand name 'German' is not exactly impressive. There are more Germans fighting their way into the Reich from the West than peacefully entering from the East."[59]

The Expansion of the German Empire

At first, the audacity of the Nazis in seeking to enrich themselves at the expense of the rest of Europe was matched by dramatic success. The invasion of Norway, which followed the unhindered occupation of Denmark in April 1940, gave Germany access to Swedish iron ore and a base for air and sea operations against Great Britain. A month later Germany invaded the neutral nations of Holland, Belgium, and Luxembourg and assaulted France, which capitulated on 22 June 1940. In a mere six weeks the Germans had conquered western Europe and destroyed the military capacity of their historic foe, France. Although the military operations were not conducted with the ferocity of the war against Poland, the Germans deliberately targeted civilians, first by launching a series of propaganda films about the Wehrmacht and Luftwaffe campaign in Poland to "shock and awe" Europeans, then by making good on the threat, destroying the Dutch port of Rotterdam in bomber raids on 14 May, for example, and thereby demoralizing the population into an uneasy collaboration with the new empire. To its enemies, Nazi Germany appeared to be a colossal power.

For Goebbels, the defeat of France wiped away the last vestiges of German paralysis and helplessness. "One feels newly born," he commented on the day of France's surrender. The shame of Versailles had finally been "amortized." Nazi leaders spoke dramatically of a *neue Gründerzeit,* a "new beginning," in which, spurred on by Italy's late entry into the war effort, "nationalist Europe is on the march, while the liberal world is on the verge of collapse."[60] Victory appeared to confirm the credibility of National Socialism's racial ideas. And German leaders began to fashion a new register of active verbs to reorder the political and social universe. They promised their citizens an age of unprecedented economic prosperity. Robert Ley of the German Labor Front outlined a "Social Security System for the German People" that would provide universal health care, regulate wages and offer professional training on a national scale, and renovate Germany's housing stock. Thanks to Germany's victory, "the time has come to liberate the Germans from heavy labor," asserted another social planner. In the future, Goebbels explained, the German people would take on "a kind of supervisory role. They have earned this right as the master race."[61] Of course, Germans never saw the good times their leaders promised, but until the end of the war they took advantage of the fruits of Nazi tyranny, enjoying markedly better food rations than other Europeans thanks to agricultural goods seized from Ukraine, Holland, and Denmark, and gaining the benefits of the coerced labor of nearly eight million foreign workers.

The prospect of empire dazzled the Nazis. Goebbels conferred with officials in the Chancellery to scrap Germany's antique script in order to make German a "real world language," ambitious civil servants contemplated appointments as colonial administrators in Africa, the editor of Münster's newspaper excitedly reported on plans to integrate the Low Countries and Scandinavia into the German Reich, while ordinary soldiers dreamed of assignments along the edges of empire: "We're guessing and betting: the south of France? Holland or Poland? over Italy to Africa? home—home? No one believes that," recalled Hans Hoeschen: "What would we be doing home?"[62] This confidence in German power was not a passing phenomenon. It struck deep into the self-conceptions of soldiers and civilians. Until the very end, one sixty-two-year-old construction worker in Detmold believed in Germany's final victory. "I could not believe that Germany would lose the war until I saw a tank in front of my door." Why not? "In the last war, Verdun was defended for months. In this war, it fell within two days. Poland fell in 18 days, France collapsed after 4 weeks," he explained; "I can just shake my head in amazement about such a war." "Seen psychologically," comments Norbert Frei, "it was during this period that expectations were set without which the conduct, or rather the endurance, of the Germans in the second half of the war cannot be adequately explained."[63]

The rapid conquest of France made a "final solution" to the "Jewish problem" more likely. For the first time, in the spring and summer of 1940, Germany's political leadership conceived of an overall project to deport all the Jews in German-occupied Europe and thus eliminate what the Nazis took to be the single greatest threat to Germany's security on the continent. While the initial plan to resettle the Jews on the French island of Madagascar eluded the Nazis since the British retained control of the high seas, the intention to "solve" the "Jewish question" on a continental scale remained in place.

Finally, the quick victory over France revised Germany's timetable for war against the Soviet Union. "I am convinced that our attack will sweep over them like a hailstorm," Hitler reassured nervous generals in January 1941. Therefore he reversed the stages in his thinking and ordered the Wehrmacht to "crush the Soviet Union in a rapid campaign" before "ending the war against England."[64] But as planning advanced for the invasion, code-named "Operation Barbarossa" in honor of the emperor who led the Third Crusade to liberate Jerusalem at the end of the twelfth century, Hitler and other leading Nazis increasingly saw the Soviet Union as the key to Germany's strategic, economic, and ideological ambitions. By the spring of 1941, the ideological objectives of the war, the final destruction of Bolshevism and the security of living space, had become paramount. Hitler regarded the war as an all-or-nothing confrontation with his greatest ideological opponent.

The escalation of the war on the Jews needs to be understood in terms of the anticipation of this final imminent victory. Both utter confidence in German victory and in the realization of grandiose imperial plans in the postwar period *and* the increasingly desperate mobilization against what became a worldwide coalition of enemies in December 1941 shaped German policy. Euphoria encouraged the formation of increasingly radical anti-Jewish measures, while the prospect of defeat consolidated their murderous implementation. It is also important to realize that the Nazis genuinely regarded the Jews as a dangerous political entity. Later in the war, Hitler believed he possessed a crucial strategic advantage because he had physically eliminated the Jews whereas the Allies had not.[65] Whereas German victories made it possible to envision comprehensive solutions to the "Jewish problem," German setbacks made the destruction of European Jewry appear more necessary. Since National Socialism was premised on the notion that Germany had been the singular victim of world history, the resistance that German armies met after 1941–42 tended to reaffirm rather than undermine the racial and ideological message of the Nazis and to strengthen rather than unravel—at least until the very end—Germans' identification with Nazism.

Soldiers in the Polish campaign often crossed the lines where their fathers had fought in World War I and believed they were recovering long-established German interests, but the armies assembled to invade the Soviet Union mobilized to reconfigure the continent in an utterly new way. The Nazis envisioned nothing less than the destruction of the Russian people, the wholesale exploitation of the agricultural regions or "surplus zones" in the south, and the destitution of industrial and urban areas, the "deficit zone" in the north. This monumental act of triage, known as the "Hunger

Plan," was to provide the Wehrmacht with the resources it needed, since the German economy itself could not feed the invading army, and secure agricultural imports for the Reich. Eventually the former Soviet Union would be resettled with German colonists who would establish a new frontier for "Aryan" civilization. Military planners reckoned with the deaths of twenty to thirty million Russians: "Without a doubt, umpteen million people will starve if we take what we need out of the country," concluded economic experts in May 1941.[66]

Hitler set the tone early on. In a two-and-a-half-hour speech to his generals on 30 March 1941, he declared the war to be a "war of destruction," in which the aim was to demolish the social foundations of Communism. Soldiers needed to act accordingly: "A Communist is no comrade before or after battle," insisted Hitler.[67] Subsequent "Guidelines to the Troops" referred to Germany's "deadly enemy" and demanded "ruthless and energetic measures against Bolshevik agitators, partisans, saboteurs, Jews, and complete eradication of any active or passive resistance." They plainly licensed soldiers to fight a race war against civilians. Political commissars and Communist leaders were to be killed outright. "The executive machinery of the Russian empire must be smashed," ordered Hitler, with "utmost brutality." Hitler specifically authorized the SS to carry out the "special tasks" required in the conflict between "two opposed political systems," vastly expanding the field of operations behind forward lines.[68] Although the association of Bolsheviks and Jews was clear enough, it was not until some weeks after the invasion that Hitler and SS leaders decided to systematically annihilate Jewish communities in the Soviet Union.

"The invasion begins at 3:30 A.M. A total of 160 divisions. An offensive line 3,000 km long." With over three million men assembled along a front that stretched from Finland in the north to the Black Sea in the south—a distance of about 1,000 kilometers, not 3,000—the invasion force on 22 June 1941 was the largest ever seen in history. That night, Goebbels had invited guests to watch David Selznick's *Gone with the Wind*, a film not yet released in Germany, but which Goebbels admired for its depiction of a morally strong-armed Confederacy. After the screening, he noted in his diary: "You can hear history breathing." Since Germany and the Soviet Union had signed a non-aggression pact, the invasion surprised many Germans, despite rumors throughout the spring, as it did the entire Soviet military establishment right up to Stalin. After the war, the day 22 June 1941 was often taken to be the moment when Germans began to realize that the policies of the Nazi leadership conflicted with the interests of the nation. "Too many dogs, and you have a dead rabbit," they remembered themselves thinking about Hitler's wars.[69]

Germans reported on their anxiety at the time. "War with Russia—Why? How Come?" asked the writer Grete Dölker-Rehder in her diary. In Münster, Agnes Neuhaus wrote to her husband, searching for just the right image to convey her shock: "I can tell you, I was chilled to the bone, I ran around like a chicken with its head cut off. I just didn't know what to think, I couldn't do a thing." But Germans also made efforts to understand the invasion and to align themselves with the new ideological horizon. Dölker-Rehder continued writing to herself: "This is how I figure it . . . We need Ukraine, as the Führer maintained in *Mein Kampf* . . . Moreover, we need Russia to get to Iraq . . . That is politics." She came to the conclusion: "This much is clear: no one has serious concerns about the outcome of the war." "At first I was at a total loss for words," confirmed another diarist in Porta, but soon enough "I came to really appreciate just how grand his diplomacy really is."[70] Over the course of a single day, Germans worked to calibrate themselves to the new aims of National Socialism. As Hitler himself realized, never again would civilians and soldiers have so much confidence in Germany's military might. By the end of that Sunday, as Victor and Eva Klemperer walked home along Dresden's Südhöhe, they saw "dancing in the Toll House, cheerful faces everywhere . . . the Russian war is a source of new pride for people, their grumbling of yesterday is forgotten."[71]

Propaganda promoted the feeling of invincibility. In Berlin, Ruth Andreas-Friedrich marveled at Goebbels' showmanship, although this particular display was actually thought up by Otto Dietrichs, press secretary in the chancellor's office: "On the principle of seven days' scrimping for one day of plenty, he's been gathering victories for a week, to pour them out upon the people now as if from a watering can." On 29 June, "every fifteen minutes a blast of trumpets; a few beats of a Lizst prelude; special bulletin: Brest-Litovsk. Special bulletin: Bialystok, Grodno, Minsk. Special bulletin . . . special bulletin . . . Special bulletin. We put our hands over our ears. We don't want to hear any more. It's abominable taste to dress up the bleeding and dying of uncounted men for a Sunday treat. History speeded up by the camera? But no matter where we go, the radio screeches, Special bulletin—special bulletin."[72]

At first, the war first appeared to follow the pace of a "continual special news bulletin" that pulled Germans together into a "community of experience."[73] The three army groups very nearly followed the timetable outlined by Hitler, who believed the war would be won in four months—"I estimate less time than that," added Goebbels; "Bolshevism will collapse like a house of cards"—which meant that the Wehrmacht did not need to be provisioned with winter gear, a deliberate decision. Army Group North raced across the Baltic to seize the major sea ports and threaten Leningrad, while Army Group Middle, following roughly the route of Napoleon's invasion force, moved to conquer Minsk and Smolensk on its way to Moscow. Moving more slowly, Army Group South had encircled Kiev by mid-September and taken over 600,000 prisoners. Stalin's armies "simply disappeared from the face of the earth," observed the CBS correspondent in Berlin, Howard K. Smith.[74] From the beginning of operations in the Soviet Union, the Wehrmacht deliberately conducted a war of annihilation that resulted in the death of millions of Soviet prisoners of war. Thousands of soldiers were shot outright on the battlefield, as had been the case with prisoners in Poland, but the vast majority died in overcrowded holding camps, where they were exposed to the elements and left to starve. The advance of German armies, which encircled entire Soviet divisions, was so dramatic that German soldiers, who undoubtedly shared the anti-Slavic and anti-Bolshevik prejudices of their society, slipped easily into the roles of racial superiors that the Nazis offered them. By the time Nazi leaders exerted themselves in the late fall of 1941 to improve conditions in the prisoner-of-war camps so that they could use the Soviet inmates as slave laborers, most of the three million men who had been captured in 1941 were dead. The Wehrmacht's treatment of "Asiatic" and "subhuman" Soviet prisoners of war, in contrast to the 1.2 million prisoners it was able to take care of in the West in 1940, was its singular contribution to Germany's race war.

SS Einsatzgruppen following the armies also targeted unarmed Jewish men as enemy combatants, in effect opening up another front in the war. It was in Operation Barbarossa, in the summer of 1941, that all the rhetoric about destroying the Jewish enemy became reality. By August and September, Einsatzgruppen had begun to kill entire households and whole neighborhoods and counted the number of Jews they murdered every day not in hundreds, but in thousands.

However, German casualties were also high, with over 100,000 soldiers killed in the first three months of the war, more than double the combined losses in Poland and France. At home, fiery young Nazis such as Lore Walb were taken aback by the sacrifices the war demanded. One of her cousins had fallen on the first day of the campaign: "What an example of a man died with him!" "The losses are hard, if on the whole light," she added. A month later Walb lost another cousin, her comrade Günther. She began to feel more brutal toward the Russians and more concerned for the Germans: "Even if we destroy the Russians, these subhumans, a terror to all civilized nations—just look at the newsreels—we will also end up bleeding to death. It is the bravest, the most audacious, the most courageous, it is the best who have to die." Early in August 1941 the *Völkischer Beobachter* conceded what Walb had learned for herself: "Every German citizen now knows that the fight has been bloody and bitter. We have recognized that we are dealing with the most difficult enemy we have met so far." At the front, the chief of the General Staff of the army, Franz Halder, realized that extraordinary Soviet casualties had to be balanced against the size of the manpower reserve of "the Russian colossus": "at the start of the war we reckoned with about 200 enemy divisions. Now we have already counted 360." Only a few weeks into the invasion observers began to wonder if "we are beating ourselves to death," a colloquialism that stuck.[75]

Divisions between the political and military leadership emerged in August as well, with Hitler demanding that Germany concentrate its energies southward toward Ukraine while his generals argued to no effect for continuing the assault against Moscow. In October, however, a military victory appeared close at hand. In a publicly broadcast speech on 3 October, Hitler referred to an "already broken" enemy that would "never rise again." Visitors in Berlin noticed Russian dictionaries in bookstores and overheard excited conversations about Germany's "new, rich colony."[76] Indeed, one Wehrmacht soldier stationed in Cologne, Heinrich Böll, the future novelist, had been taking Russian lessons since early July. In the first days of October, headlines in the Nazi party newspaper, *Völkischer Beobachter*, raised expectations higher and higher, "one long howl of triumph," in Victor Klemperer's words, culminating in the large-type assurance that "The Hour of Reckoning Has Struck: Campaign in the East Decided!" on 10 October 1941. A week later, however, headlines had shrunk back to reporting on continuing operations.[77]

Germany's offensive operations stalled in November, and a devastating Soviet counteroffensive against Army Group Middle gained momentum in December. "At the end of November the Russians finally began to fight back," noted Lili Hahn, a half-Jew living in Frankfurt, with satisfaction. The effects of extreme cold, insufficient supplies, and costly casualties took a harsh toll on German divisions. At the end of December, dire circumstances forced Goebbels to appeal to the public for donations: "warm wool items, socks, stockings, vests, overshirts or pullovers, and warm woolen underwear, undershirts, underpants, suspenders, warmers, headgear, earmuffs, wrist and knee guards, furs of any kind . . . thick, warm gloves . . . woolen scarves of all sorts." The detailed list conceded a great deal.[78] Soviet losses were catastrophic as well; by the end of the year 1941, over 460,000 soldiers had been killed in combat and 3.3 million men taken prisoner, two-thirds of whom, according to the Wehrmacht's own figures, died before the end of the year. More than 600,000 soldiers were executed outright as political enemies or inferior "Asiatics." In the same period, German SS and Wehrmacht units, operating in the occupied territories of the Soviet Union, murdered 500,000 Jewish civilians. In the first six months of Operation Barbarossa, German forces wiped out one in every five hundred people on the planet.

Final Solutions to the "Jewish Problem"

War with the Soviet Union put the goal of empire within the grasp of German invaders. National Socialism was on the verge of establishing a vast German-occupied zone in which the nations of eastern Europe would be destroyed and their people ruthlessly exploited or annihilated. Furthermore, German colonies in the former Soviet Union would provide the greater German Reich with the necessary military and economic platform to undertake further global conquests. Empire also enabled the Nazis to achieve the goal of removing the Jews whose existence in Europe they believed was incompatible with Germany's revival. However, the nature of the war on the Jews changed over 1940–41 as territorial solutions—ambitious, unprecedented, and deadly though they were—gave way to comprehensive exterminatory solutions and as the Nazis reached beyond German and Polish borders to seize and murder all Jews in Europe. "In the final analysis," the minister of aviation and chief of the Luftwaffe, Hermann Göring, explained to thousands of true believers in a speech in October 1942, the war "is about whether the German and Aryan prevails here, or whether the Jew rules the world, and that is what we are fighting for out there." With the campaign in the Soviet Union, the Nazis picked up the last remaining piece of their racial project, the final solution to the "Jewish problem," which had languished since the end of the war against Poland nearly two years earlier.[79]

The war against Poland in the fall of 1939 ended with the determination to deport Jews living in Germany, the newly annexed territories, and the General Gouvernement into a special reservation to be carved out around Lublin. The proposed timetable was a year, but the Reich Security Main Office, the central SS office in which the regular and security police forces had been organized, pushed for immediate deportations from Austria and the Protectorate of Bohemia and Moravia in October and from Germany in November 1939. Two trains actually left Vienna for Lubin in October before the transports were suspended because of "technical difficulties" and then canceled altogether. However, the SS planners continued to regard Lublin as the future site of a Jewish reservation. They did so over the growing objections of Governor-General Hans Frank, who opposed "precipitous and unplanned" deportations; he already had to cope with thousands of Poles, both Jews and non-Jews, pushed into his territory to make room for German settlers in the Wartheland. Hitler overruled Frank, who returned to Cracow at the end of February 1940 and reported to associates a few days later with angry sarcasm: "We don't have enough Jews here, we can still fit in many more, it's just the beginning. Actually what we're suffering from is a lack of Jews. We will be able to fit in at least 400,000 to 600,000. Then we can start to talk about what will happen to them."[80]

The systematic deportation of German Jews may well have been planned to begin in February 1940, when the SS deported more than 1,000 German Jews from Stettin and Schneidemühl to villages around Lublin. Elsewhere local Gestapo offices received instructions to begin assembling Jews in selected larger cities. Himmler confirmed to Nazi Gauleiter on 29 February 1940 that although his offices would continue to encourage Jews to emigrate, the General Gouvernement would have to accept the majority who remained. However, impending military action in western Europe disrupted deportation plans; in mid-March 1940 Gestapo offices suspended further preparations. After October 1939, powerful but unrealistic expectations and conflicting goals repeatedly revised, suspended, and revived the efforts to deport Germany's Jews to Lublin in what for the Nazis was a frustrating "chronology of failure."[81] A few months later, however, the defeat of France opened new possibilities, raising expectations for a comprehensive "final solution."

The rapid success of Germany's armies in the invasion of western Europe brought hundreds of thousands more Jews under German control but also emboldened Germany's racial planners. At the end of May 1940, Himmler presented Hitler with a comprehensive memorandum, "The Treatment of Alien Populations in the East," which recommended "screening and sifting" for racially valuable elements to be Germanized and educating the "mush" that remained only to levels needed to perform slave labor. On the question of Jews, Himmler proposed "to completely erase the concept of Jews through the possibility of a great emigration of all Jews to a colony in Africa or elsewhere." This was the origin of the Madagascar Plan. Fanatical antisemites in Germany and elsewhere had mentioned the French colony off the coast of East Africa before, but suddenly in the spring and summer of 1940 the idea "spread like wildfire."[82] Germany imagined it would be able to deport all of the millions of Jews in German-occupied Europe, for which neither the policy of emigration nor the Lublin reservation, the intended destination in 1939–40 for some 2.3 million German, Austrian, and Polish Jews, was suitable. The plan also appealed to Hans Frank, who opposed the deportation of more Jews into his district, and it satisfied the Gauleiter across Germany and Austria who, in the face of Frank's opposition, could now deport their unwanted Jews somewhere else. Moreover, Madagascar was big enough that Nazi planners could add into their calculations the Jews of western Europe, southeast Europe, and the French colonies in North Africa. In no time state security officials were working with an estimated total of 5.5 million Jews, who in 1940 constituted the "Jewish problem" for which a "final solution" had perhaps been found.

Hitler and his foreign minister, Joachim von Ribbentrop, pitched the Madagascar proposal to their Italian counterparts, Mussolini and Galeazzo Ciano, in bilateral discussions held on 18 June in Munich to discuss the future of the French empire. Soon thereafter the German Foreign Ministry prepared more detailed plans. According to experts' reports, Madagascar did not possess valuable resources, a fact that made it expendable, and yet, with a great leap of imagination, was sufficiently large and fertile to support a Jewish colony. Flipping through *Meyer's Lexicon*, Franz Rademacher, the desk officer for Jewish affairs in the Foreign Ministry, noted that Madagascar's highlands offered respite from the sultry coastal areas, which were "very unhealthy for Europeans." He gave the project his full support: "The desirable solution is: All Jews out of Europe."[83] Even before Rademacher delivered his initial findings, the Gestapo informed the Reich Organization of Jews in Germany that the war would be over shortly and a "colonial reservation" would be made available.[84] Rumors of deportations to Madagascar even reached Victor Klemperer in Dresden.

As it was, the Madagascar Plan was dropped almost as quickly as it had been taken up. Not only would it require, according to one estimate, 120 ships to transport one million Jews a year, a five-year undertaking that did not provide the quick solution policymakers desired, but the British retained control of the sea routes. Nonetheless the plan marked an important stage in Nazi thinking. In the first place, it amounted to genocide because it envisioned the destruction of long-established Jewish communities throughout Europe and the starvation of survivors in a virtual penal colony. Second, it permanently established the continental parameters to the "final solution," which in the Madagascar Plan included all Jews in German-occupied Europe. And finally, it revealed the great interest German authorities had in ridding their territories of the Jews. The Madagascar Plan consolidated political investment in a comprehensive final solution that would rid Europe of Jews.

As preparations for the invasion of the Soviet Union took shape during the fall of 1940 and winter of 1941, the formal properties of the Madagascar Plan were adopted by Adolf Eichmann, a ranking SS expert on Jewish affairs, in a report he submitted to Himmler and which Himmler outlined to the annual Gauleiter conference in Berlin on 10 December 1940. Eichmann referred to the need to resettle 5.8 European Jews to "a territory yet to be determined." It was clear that this destination would not be Lublin or anywhere else in the General Gouvernement, since Eichmann's counts included the 1.5 million Jews there. He could only have meant the conquered territories of the Soviet Union, which stretched out indistinctly in the Nazi imagination. The gigantic proportions of Hitler's design for the Soviet Union, once they became clear, pushed what lay on the other side of the frontiers of the German empire far beyond the Urals, into "the East" and "the North." It was into this beyond that Eichmann proposed deporting European Jews immediately after the war with the Soviet Union had been won. Eichmann also pointedly mentioned Jews "in the European economic sphere of the German Volk" in allied countries such as Romania, Slovakia, and Hungary that German troops did not occupy.[85]

Since German military planners reckoned on the deaths of many millions of Russians, it is possible that Eichmann's unidentified territory was simply a euphemism for mass murder. Although the four SS Einsatzgruppen that Hitler and Himmler had charged to carry out the "administrative" as opposed to military side of the new order did not enter the Soviet Union with precise orders to slaughter Jews, the "political commissars," "plunderers," and "partisans" they reported killing were, for the most part, Jews. In just a few weeks it became clear that the main administrative task of the Einsatzgruppen, each of which was initially composed of 700–1,000 men, was the complete eradication of Jewish life in the occupied Soviet territories.

From the first days of the invasion, Einsatzgruppen attempted to destroy Jewish communities in the occupied territories by organizing local non-Jewish proxies to instigate pogroms such as the one examined by Jan Gross in his important book, *Neighbors*. On 10 July 1941, one-half of the town of Jedwabne in eastern Poland set upon the other half; local Poles hacked Jewish men and women to death on the streets, shot them in front of newly dug graves, and finally shut the survivors in a barn and burned them to death. Similar horrifying scenes played themselves out for several days at the end of June 1941, when German troops entered Kovno (Kaunas), Lithuania, where 3,800 Jews were brutally murdered by civilian gangs eager to exact their revenge on a group they held responsible for collaborating with the Soviet Union when it had occupied Lithuania a year earlier. As many as sixty similar pogroms took place in eastern Poland, which the Soviets had annexed in September 1939 and the German troops occupied in June and July 1941. The ranks of Communist leaders did include disproportionate numbers of Jews, but the Soviets had also expropriated Jewish property and deported wealthy and educated Jews to Siberia; since Jews in the towns were more apt to be middle-class, they were more likely to be targets of the Communists. In any case, whatever resentments Lithuanians harbored against Jews, the Germans did not find it easy—"surprisingly," as Walther Stahlecker, the commander of Einsatzgruppe A, added—to instigate local pogroms. In eastern Poland, Einsatzgruppe C had the same experiences: "Unfortunately the attempts undertaken at that time to carefully inspire Jewish pogroms did not show the anticipated results." The fact was that "a notable antisemitism on racial or idealist grounds is not understood." Showing locals the antisemitic propaganda film *Der ewige Jude* did not help either.[86]

What the pogroms did reveal was the ultimate aim of the SS Einsatzgruppen, which was the destruction of Jewish life. It was not long before the twenty, thirty, or fifty Jewish men killed by SS shooters for being partisans, "intelligentsia," or "leadership" gave way to hundreds shot in retaliation for massacres such as the one in Lwow at the very end of June, when the Soviets had massacred thousands of Ukrainian nationalists before retreating. Once the Germans discovered the scale of destruction in Lwow (or Lemberg in what had been the Austrian-Hungarian empire), the SS shot 7,000 Jewish men in a two-day killing spree on 2–3 July 1941. German propaganda made the most of the atrocities perpetrated by Stalin's secret police, for which they held "the Jews" publicly responsible. Like Bromberg in the Polish campaign, Lemberg served as a license for the war that was already under way. It provided the gruesome imagery of the massacres that the Nazis maintained the Communists and Jews would have undertaken against German civilians had Hitler not attacked preemptively. In the weeks that followed, Einsatzgruppe C reported regularly on its "deliberate measures of retaliation against plunderers and Jews," actions against scores and then hundreds of Jewish men, Peter Longerich comments, that were "schematically independent of the situation on the ground."[87] In August the SS began killing women and children.

It is not likely that dynamics on the periphery propelled events forward or that Hitler was only vaguely aware of the unfolding genocidal policy in the field. Hitler had always taken an active role in setting Germany's policy on the Jews. He authorized the precise definition of who was a Jew in 1935, gave his assent to the pogrom in November 1938, and both postponed and set in motion the first deportations of Jews from German cities in the autumn of 1941. It seems probable that he authorized the killing of entire Jewish communities in order to clear the ground for colonization. To be sure, SS leaders such as Himmler, Kurt Daluege, head of the Order Police, and district commanders Friedrich Jeckeln and Erich von dem Bach–Zelewski traveled extensively in the field and pushed their subordinates to undertake more extensive operations. "Make decisions in the field!" Himmler exhorted his officers in 1942: "I do not make decisions in Berlin, rather I drive to Lublin, Lemberg, Reval, etc. and at those places in the evening, then, eight, ten, twelve major decisions are made on the spot." Well adjusted to the command structure of the SS, but also sharing the ideological zeal of the military elite, unit commanders showed remarkable ability to carry out coded or implicit orders. Workshops, directives, and mandated progress reports fine-tuned their "anticipatory obedience." SS officers did not mindlessly carry out orders from Berlin, as they often suggested in postwar criminal trials. Hitler and Himmler played central roles in sanctioning murder, but they relied on a broader consensus to get the job done.[88]

Throughout July 1941, Hitler followed the advance of his invasion armies with a growing sense of euphoria in which the leader virtually took possession of the conquered lands. His language lost all obfuscation: he anticipated that Leningrad and Moscow would be "rubbed out," as he put it in a conversation with Goebbels on 9 July, and envisioned new provinces in Crimea, "our Riviera." Highways would connect the Reich to its newly won empire; as Hitler imagined it late at night on 5 July 1941, Germans would drive their

Volkswagens to see and colonize the lands they had fought for. The great mistake of imperial policy up until now, Hitler commented, had been to restrict the spoils to the rich. By contrast, Nazi imperialism would serve the German people. A few days later, on 16 July 1941, Hitler outlined his intentions to party leaders in Berlin. He promised never to abandon the territories Germany had seized; they would be transformed into a "Garden of Eden"—a striking contrast to how imperial territories had been viewed two years earlier, when the General Gouvernement had been described as a "labor reservoir" and used as a dumping ground. In 1941 Hitler showed much greater determination to remove the indigenous inhabitants from the occupied territories. "All necessary measures—shootings, evacuations" were permissible in order to take possession of the new colonies.[89] Himmler, whom Hitler made responsible for security in the new territories on 17 July, vastly accelerated the conquest of Hitler's "garden," increasing the strength of the Einsatzgruppen elevenfold during the summer of 1941, deploying more police battalions, and authorizing the formation of auxiliary police units made up of foreign nationals from Ukraine, Belorussia, and Lithuania.

Himmler inspected the units regularly, and on a 14–15 August visit to Minsk he witnessed a killing action and passed down verbal orders from Hitler directing the Einsatzgruppen to shoot all Jews. Two days later, on 17 August, Himmler briefed Hitler, most likely to confirm the feasibility of large-scale shootings; a day later Hitler assured Goebbels that German Jews would be deported to the East soon after the expected victory.[90] Orders that all Jews in the Soviet Union were to be killed made their way down to the field commanders. When August Rosenbauer arrived to take charge of Police Battalion 45 in southern Russia in early September 1941, he was briefed by his superiors. According to his postwar testimony, "Jeckeln said, we have the order of SS Reichsführer Himmler whereby the Jewish question must be solved. Born to be serfs, the

Ukrainians will work for us. But we have no interest in seeing the numbers of Jews increase; for that reason the Jewish population must be exterminated."[91] Moreover, Berlin demanded regular updates about the progress of the killing: SS-Brigadeführer Heinrich Müller, head of the Gestapo, informed the commanders of the four Einsatzgruppen on 1 August 1941 that "the Führer is to receive reports from here regularly about the work of the Einsatzgruppen in the East." Hitler requested "especially interesting visual material" such as "photographs, placards, leaflets, and other documents" about SS operations as quickly as possible.[92]

In August 1941 the scale of the killing widened dramatically. Up to mid-August, the four Einsatzgruppen had murdered about 50,000 Jews. This was a massive increase over the killing undertaken in Poland two years earlier, yet it represented only one-tenth of the number of Jews the SS units would kill in the next four months. Operating in Lithuania, Einsatzgruppe A's commando 3 "shot 115 women among 4,239 Jews 'executed' during July," but murdered 26,243 women and 15,112 children in the total of 56,459 Jews killed in September.[93] There was now a new expectation that *all* Jews should be killed. The ongoing murder of Jews, the anticipation of a complete victory over the Soviet Union, and the heady prospect of new, clean colonies in the East were closely intertwined. "Jewish deaths," Sybille Steinbacher argues, had become "a numerical value calculated into plans to 'create space for Germans.'"[94] In the Soviet Union, genocide was the product of German ambition, not a symptom of the "barbarization" of warfare. In fact in 1941 German forces killed more Jewish civilians behind the front lines than Soviet soldiers in combat. By the end of the war, nearly two million Jews had perished in the Baltic territories and the Soviet Union, most of them shot in 1941 and 1942 not far from their homes by German Einsatzkommandos.[95]

"Village by village" and "town by town," as the Nazis put it, the "big campaigns" of fall 1941 cleared entire regions of the western

Soviet Union of Jews: Smolowicze, then Mogilev; Borisov, Bobruisk, Vitebsk, then Gomel. "Ukraine without Jews"—this is how Vasily Grossman, author of the postwar novel *Life and Fate,* summarized it when he returned to the devastated area of his birth three years later.[96] In those same places, SS Einsatzgruppen received Himmler and other dignitaries, sent regular reports to Berlin about their progress, and achieved by themselves what the pogroms they had attempted to instigate had not. At the end of September 1941, the German Sixth Army entered Kiev, the capital of the Ukrainian Soviet Socialist Republic. The city had been besieged for weeks, and much of the population, including two-thirds of Kiev's 220,000 Jews, had fled for their lives. Nonetheless, partisans continued to operate underground, and on 24–26 September they blew up a number of large buildings, including the Hotel Continental, headquarters of the Wehrmacht, killing several hundred German soldiers and leaving the city center in ruins. Wehrmacht and SS leaders met with the city commandant, Major General Kurt Eberhard, on 26 September and resolved to shoot "at least 50,000 Jews" in retaliation.[97] In the thinking of the day, "Wherever there is partisan, there is a Jew, and wherever there is a Jew, there is a partisan."[98]

It was a matter of routine for the SS to assume command of the killing operation, but Colonel Paul Blobel and his Sonderkommando 4a relied on the assistance of the Sixth Army, with whom Blobel had worked efficiently in his murderous march through Ukraine. The Wehrmacht printed the posters ordering Kiev's Jewish population to assemble at a public place on the morning of 29 September and guarded the route to the suburban ravine where the Jews were murdered. Most Jews believed the deception that they would be resettled, since they could hardly be mistaken for combatants; more than 30,000 mostly old or very young and disproportionately female members of Jewish community gathered at eight in the morning. However, they were not led to the train station, but toward the Jewish cemetery and to the ravine at Babi Yar. "I still remember today the horror that struck the Jews when they reached the edge of the ravine and got their first sight of the bodies below," testified Kurt Werner, an SS shooter: "Many of them started screaming with fright. You can't imagine what strong nerves it took to go on with that filthy job there."[99] Guards ordered the Jews to "different places, where they first had to put down their luggage, then their coats, shoes, and their outer garments, and finally their underwear."[100] After a few minutes the victims were naked. They were then pushed by Ukrainian policemen to the edge of the ravine. In his postwar testimony, Werner recounted: "They had to lie down with their faces to the ground. In the gully there were three groups of soldiers, with about twelve men in each. New groups of Jews were being sent down constantly. The new arrivals had to lie down on top of the corpses of the Jews who had just been shot." "The faces of young people fell ashen before my eyes," recalled another witness, Dina Proniceva, in 1967. Pistol shots and machine-gun fire could be heard throughout the day. The log of Sonderkommando 4a subsequently reported the massacre: "In collaboration with Einsatzgruppe HQ and two commandos of police regiment South, Sonderkommando 4a executed 33,771 Jews on September 29 and 30."[101]

The scale of the attempt by the Wehrmacht and the SS Einsatzgruppen to kill an entire city of Jews in two days, the effort to wipe away the evidence by digging up the bodies and burning them two years later, and the large number of participants that such an operation required and of witnesses who could see what was going on made Babi Yar stand out. News about Babi Yar spread quickly through the Army High Command; in Breslau, Willy Cohn, a Jewish high-school teacher, heard about a "big bloodbath" in Kiev as early as 11 October. Soldiers mentioned it in their letters or when they were on leave at home. Karl Dürkefälden's brother-in-law, Walter Kassler, wrote his parents from Kiev on the last day of the year that "there are no Jews here anymore; I will have to tell you myself what happened to them." At home in Celle on leave in June 1942 he finally provided the details as he knew them: "50,000 Jews were rounded up in a pit and blown up so that they were immediately buried." In Dresden in April 1942, Eva Klemperer bumped into the carpenter who had built her garage back in 1936. Now wearing a corporal's uniform, he told her over beer stories about his time in Russia, including "the mass of bodies buried under the exploding earth" in Kiev. Postwar trials clarified details, generated testimony such as that offered by Werner, and ended with the conviction and execution of the main SS leaders, including Paul Blodel. "Just as the name 'Auschwitz' has become a symbol for the mass killing of Jews by poison gas in quasi-industrial procedures," writes Wolfram Wette, "so 'Babi Yar' stands for the mass executions carried out by mobile SS units in the first two years of the war against the Soviet Union."[102]

There were thousands of Babi Yars across the Soviet Union, and each detonated against a community of innocents and against a particular understanding of the world. The Jews of Kiev could not imagine that women and children and the elderly would be held responsible for the bombing of the Hotel Continental. Like so many Jews in German-occupied Europe, they assumed that the Germans would not lose the opportunity to make use of their skills and their labor during the war. It is not comprehensible to walk alongside Kiev's Jews and to imagine the fright, the noise, and the worry over children and parents who faltered as guards pushed them along roads and, without regard to sex or age, ordered them to undress and forced them to run to the edge of the ravine. Because the shooters killed an entire community, the victims cannot speak for themselves; their records have been dispersed, their memories crushed. Babi Yar remains a ravine.

Historians are often asked about the composure of Jewish victims as they faced their deaths. On trial in the 1950s and 1960s, German shooters remarked on the passivity or the dignity of the victims, as though the comportment of the weak might relieve the guilt of the strong. But witnesses such as Kazimierz Sakowicz in Ponary, Lithuania, left behind a different account. Sakowicz's house in the country was located a few hundred meters from a killing field. In the diary fragments he hid in lemonade bottles that he buried in the ground before his own death in 1944, Sakowicz recorded the words of innocents who exclaimed: "What are you doing?" or "I am not a Communist!" He heard Jews scream at German guards, he saw people spit at soldiers; he witnessed someone who "stuck a knife in the head of a German." From his window, Sakowicz could see that many Jews tried to escape, and when they ran through fields and forests, German or Lithuanian soldiers ran to catch them.[103] We know that victims tried to batter their way out of deportation trains, breaking through the boards nailed to imprison them. They also ran out of the lines of march. And it is important to realize that most people did not die alone. They tried to hide the horror of the anticipation of death from the children for whom they were responsible.

The massacre in Kiev illustrated the procedures the SS Einsatzgruppen had routinized: the deceptive posters; the undisclosed location; the different piles for items of value and for clothing, which made it easier to pick goods up and donate them to the Red Cross or People's Welfare; the delegation of certain tasks to auxiliary Ukrainian police units; and the cooperation with the Wehrmacht. The role of the Wehrmacht in the killing process at Babi Yar is important to keep in mind because after the war it was common in Germany and the United States to distinguish between fanatical antisemites in the SS and basically honorable soldiers and officers in the Wehrmacht. However, this distinction is not tenable, and so the question of the extent to which the army of eighteen million men and thus German society at large shared the ideological goals of the National Socialists must be posed. We know that the Wehrmacht did much more than print up posters or guard the forested routes to killing sites. The diary of the Wehrmacht private Richard Heydenreich, which fell into Soviet hands and excerpts of which were already published in 1943, detailed the role of the Wehrmacht in murdering Jewish civilians. As early as July 1941, with the capture of Minsk, "our battalion was assigned the mission of . . . shooting all the Jews in the city."[104] Many regiments had standing orders to kill all Jews they encountered in areas in which they advanced. Security divisions of the Wehrmacht were also charged with clearing out partisans in the rear, which amounted to hunting down Jews and killing them in the field or handing them over to the Einsatzgruppen. As was the case in Serbia, where the Wehrmacht killed almost all adult male Jews in retaliation for ongoing partisan attacks in the summer and fall of 1941, Jews were collectively identified as the "mortal enemies" of the German army and the German people.

Many Wehrmacht soldiers felt drawn to the killing operations of the Einsatzgruppen, standing around as spectators, taking photographs, and volunteering to be shooters. By August 1941 the command of the Sixth Army felt it necessary to issue orders prohibiting individual soldiers from participating in SS executions unless required to do so by superiors. Nonetheless, the stage management of killing actions by amateur photographers, the commentary in letters back home on the dirty and dilapidated "paradise of the workers," and general contempt for the "subhuman" Soviet soldiers, at least in the early months of the war, when millions of weak, unshaven prisoners confirmed popular racial stereotypes, left "no doubt that racism was a fact of everyday troop life." In one army unit, stationed in Pinsk, "lively discussions" about the day's events revealed that most Wehrmacht soldiers endorsed the killing of male Jewish civilians, something that had just taken place.[105]

It would be wrong to counter the argument that the Wehrmacht was "clean," whereas party institutions were not, with the opposite claim that Wehrmacht and SS soldiers were basically the same or that soldiers everywhere, in whatever uniform, assumed the role of killers. Jürgen Matthäus and Christopher Browning have carefully examined the dynamics of the killing units. There were always "a few committed, full-time killers" as well as "a sufficient supply" of executioners to got "the job done," a fact that in turn "allowed a small minority to consistently abstain without facing serious repercussions."[106] Richard Heydenreich volunteered—"of course"—when his Wehrmacht lieutenant asked for "15 men with strong nerves." Other soldiers took pleasure in the Jew hunts that the army conducted: "there are always some wild goings-on here . . . just your kind of thing," wrote one company commander to his brother back in Germany in October 1941. But, as Browning has argued in his classic study, *Ordinary Men,* in the case of the majority of men, small-group dynamics, the desire not to appear to be a coward, and a feeling of responsibility to cooperate in the completion of unpleasant tasks explain the behavior of the shooters more than ideological commitment. "Always take part"—*immer mitmachen*—constituted the ethic of comradeship.[107]

However, Browning's sample may have led him to underestimate the role of ideology. Whereas the middle-aged men of Reserve Police Battalion 101 seemed to be pulled across occupied Poland by events they did not fully comprehend, the Einsatzgruppen and auxiliary police battalions that took part in the killing of civilians in the Soviet Union recruited younger and more ideologically attuned volunteers. They were led mostly by ambitious, racially schooled police professionals, not by commanders like pliable "Papa Trapp."[108] Most of the men in the Einsatzgruppen shared a worldview in which Jews endangered Germany and in which Germans had reentered the stage of history as superior warriors to finally establish a new order. Without a sense of morality "mass murder could not have been implemented," concludes Harald Welzer.[109]

Identification with Nazism and its goals for the German people did not mean that killing came easily. "Sometimes you just have to weep. It is not easy if you are such a lover of children, as I am," complained Fritz Jacob, a police inspector, to his SS superior in Hamburg. But soldiers got tougher, they overcame the initial shock, and they adapted themselves to the new conditions. A few weeks later, Jacob wrote back: "I am grateful for your admonition. You are right. We men of the new Germany have to be hard on ourselves." Of course, it was extraordinary "to exterminate a whole family when only the father is the perpetrator," Jacob faltered again in midsentence. He even recognized that "this would not be possible according to the regular course of legal action." However, he picked himself up again by appealing to the necessity of history: "We will clear the way without pangs of conscience, and then," he added, "the world will be at peace."[110] SS shooters on trial in 1958 also remembered appealing to history as they encouraged one another to accept their obligations: "Man alive! Damn it again," is the sort of thing they had said on the killing ground; "this is what our generation has to endure so our children will have a better future."[111] It was an ongoing struggle to assume the role of killer, since "regular" moral and legal concepts continued to conflict with National Socialist ideology.

The Deportation of German Jews

The resolve in late July 1941 to clear Jews from Soviet territory by killing them in order to prepare for the arrival of German colonists did not take the form of a comprehensive order to destroy all the Jews in Europe. Not until fall did these two parts of Nazi policy, the destruction of the so-called Jewish-Bolshevik threat in the Soviet Union and the "final solution" to the "Jewish problem" in German-occupied Europe, come together to form a single exterminatory policy. Meeting in Berlin in mid-August, Hitler's chief ideologues confirmed that the Führer had once again rejected any proposal for the deportation of German Jews until end of the war, which was expected to come very soon. Reinhard Heydrich, chief of the Reich Security Main Office, gained the impression that some evacuations might be permitted soon, but the overall message was to wait until after the war. This was hardly a reprieve for Jews; Hitler had already ordered the mass killings of Soviet Jews in the very place he intended to send the rest of Europe's Jews. In discussions with Goebbels on 18 August 1941, he repeated the words of his Reichstag prophecy in which he predicted the "annihilation" of the Jews in the event of a world war. "It is coming true in these weeks and months," summarized Goebbels. Hitler and Goebbels began to let events in the Soviet Union shape their idea of what would happen to the Jews more generally: "In the East the Jews are paying the price, in Germany they have already paid in part and will have to pay still more in the future," explained Goebbels.[112] A month later, however, Hitler ordered the immediate evacuation of 60,000 Jews from Germany, Austria, and the Protectorate of Bohemia and Moravia. On 18 September 1941, records show Himmler busy at work, setting the deportation process in motion before the end of the war. What had changed?

There are two possible explanations. One emphasizes concessions to new circumstances. In August it was increasingly clear that the war was costing Germany considerable casualties and would not be won in 1941. What is more, with the Anglo-American commitment to achieve "the final destruction of the Nazi tyranny" in the Atlantic Charter on 14 August 1941, the German leadership accepted the fact that the United States would enter the war one way or another, exposing, in Hitler's mind, the international power of Jewish capital to control events, thereby polarizing the world into an all-out struggle between Jews and Aryans for survival, and thus confirming his Reichstag prophecy of January 1939. Following the logic of Nazi antisemitism, the Jews had in fact succeeded in instigating a world war, and each Jew in Europe was consequently more dangerous than ever, which is why giving German Jews the opportunity to emigrate, as was still theoretically the case, or allowing a hardened minority to survive the rigors of labor camps appeared to be counterproductive. The weeks in late August and early September therefore strengthened arguments for a preemptive strike against German and European Jews. It made the Nazis more willing to commence a cumbersome two-stage process of deporting Jews to "eastern territories" in the fall of 1941 before deporting them "farther eastward" the following spring.[113]

On the other hand, the timing of the deportation orders in September is consistent with the argument that "a second peak of victory euphoria" emboldened Hitler to proceed with deportations, just as the first peak in July had led to an escalation in SS operations in the Soviet Union. In contrast to the cautious mood in August, the Germans appeared to be on the brink of victory after their seizure of Kiev in mid-September.[114] But perhaps more important than month-to-month variations in the mood, which are difficult to gauge, was the fact that Hitler and Himmler had tied the establishment of German colonies ever more closely to the mass murder of Jewish civilians. The utopian vision of a "Garden of Eden" precluded the improvised structures of the General Gouvernement with its labor reservoirs and ghettos. As a result, the offensive against the Jews escalated rapidly after June 1941. The Einsatzgruppen focused their activities almost entirely on killing Jews; the SS expanded the definition of plunderers and partisans to encompass all Jewish men, and finally targeted whole Jewish communities. With every week, the war on the Jews more nearly realized Hitler's prophecy. In this context, a postponement of the "final solution" until after the war was quickly becoming unnecessary. Both the rising tally of Jewish dead in August and September 1941 and the realization in October and November 1941 that the war would not be over by the end of the year combined to bring push anti-Jewish policy closer and closer to implementation "during" the war and eventually into the present. This acceleration increased the plausibility of an exterminatory rather than territorial solution.

From September 1941 on, events moved very quickly. A fundamental radicalization of Germany's war against the Jews can be observed in the late summer of 1941, although the decision to immediately seize and exterminate all European Jews had not yet been made. On 17 September Hitler conferred with Ribbentrop and then Himmler and most likely made the decision to begin what he had postponed just a month earlier: the deportation of German Jews. On 18 September Himmler informed Arthur Greiser, Gauleiter in the Warthegau, that "the Führer wishes that the Old Reich and Protectorate be emptied and freed of Jews from west to east as quickly as possible." Himmler originally intended to begin with the resettlement of 60,000 German Jews into the ghetto in Lodz, but facing the opposition of local officials, whom he lectured about "the interest of the Reich" and "the will of the Führer," he scaled back the number of people the ghetto was expected to take to 20,000 Jews and 5,000 Gypsies and made alternative plans to send 25,000 Jews to Minsk in Belorussia, 20,000 to Riga in Latvia, and 5,000 to Kovno in Lithuania.[115] Since local authorities in the new deportation sites were surprised by the orders and had insufficient time to prepare for the arrival of thousands of Jews, it is clear that the center was directing the course of events. Reich authorities also promulgated supplementary legislation that legalized the seizure of abandoned property and finally prohibited the emigration of German Jews in October 1941: the gates were now closed, the procedures sorted out. "The Jews were supposed to leave, the Jews didn't want to leave," had described the case before 1938; in 1941 the case was now: "the Jews were not allowed to leave, the Jews wanted to leave."[116]

With the decision to kill Soviet Jews and to deport German Jews, the Nazis recalibrated the spatial and temporal coordinates of the "final solution" so that it steadily moved from something that would take place "over there" in the near future to an event "here and now." Since 1939, every "final solution" that the Nazis had envisioned, from the establishment of a Jewish reservation near

Lublin, to the resettlement of a Jewish colony in Madagascar, to expulsions "farther east" in the Soviet Union, had been premised on achieving the absence of the Jews "here." As long as the overall goal to bring about the "absence" of Jews remained in place, then the abandonment of a territorial solution "over there" implied the adoption of an exterminatory solution "here." The autumn of 1941 marks the point when the aim of getting Europe rid of the Jews became getting rid of Europe's Jews. The change did not come all at once. It is unlikely that the September order to deport German Jews, which was implemented beginning in mid-October 1941, was accompanied by an explicit decision to physically destroy all Jews in Europe. Although German Jews transported to Kovno were killed upon their arrival, the majority of other deportees were not. They endured terrible conditions in ghettos where, the German Jews learned to their horror, the original inhabitants had been murdered to make room for the new arrivals: 11,500 in Minsk on 7 November, and 25,000 in Riga in two separate actions, on 30 November and 8 December 1941.[117] Both the Reich Security Main Office and local authorities were still making distinctions between German Jews and eastern Jews. The SS largely completed the first wave of deportations by the new year; 53,000 German and Austrian Jews had been expelled from their homes and transported across the German Empire to a grim, uncertain fate.

The process of switching from "over there" in the near future to "here and now" created a host of new problems. As soon as the deportations began, party and government officials received a flurry of petitions appealing individual expulsions and complaining that mixed Jews, Aryan partners of Jews, decorated war veterans, and other important Jews had been arbitrarily included in the transports. These were the "A-one" Jews, the exceptions to the rule, whom even some Nazi loyalists tried to save, that Himmler contemptuously recalled to party and SS leaders in his notorious Posen speeches in October 1943. The petitions soon became a major headache for party leaders and threatened to open anti-Jewish policy to semipublic scrutiny and case-by-case negotiation. These concerns probably led Himmler to order local authorities in Riga to hold onto 1,000 Jews from Berlin on 30 November 1941. He was too late; they had been shot. Yet the note he jotted down after a telephone conversation with Heydrich—"Jewish transport from Berlin: no liquidation"—suggests how routine the possibility of mass killing had become to planners in the Reich Security Main Office. Moreover, the different responses of SS authorities in Lodz, Kovno, and Riga, as well as questions raised by the Wehrmacht after the massacre in Riga, pointed to the need, as Browning argues, "to accustom the German bureaucracy to the idea of systematic mass murder."[118] The main purpose of the Wannsee Conference, initially scheduled for 9 December 1941 but postponed on 8 December, after Japan's attack on the United States, to 20 January 1942, was to provide notice that the SS, under the leadership of Reinhard Heydrich and Heinrich Himmler, intended to organize deportations on a European-wide scale. The meeting ironed out the definition of Jews who would be deported and outlined the use of slave labor in the East. Concerns about a breed of super-Jews, "the hardiest," who would somehow survive confinement in labor camps or deportation across the Urals, indicated that a territorial solution was giving way to an exterminatory one; but the shift was not complete at the time of the Wannsee Conference.[119]

At the same time, in November 1941, Heydrich authorized the use of the walled garrison town of Theresienstadt in the Protectorate of Bohemia and Moravia as a concentration camp for elderly German Jews, invalided or decorated Jewish war veterans, and "doubtful cases." Once they could point to Theresienstadt, German authorities had an acceptable answer to the countless inquiries about whether "an eighty-seven-year-old Jew had to be deported, or whether some other octogenarian could not be left alone." It allowed the Nazis to "save face with the outside world," conceded Adolf Eichmann.[120] Later on the Security Service sent Theresienstadt residents to the death camps without public fuss. Deportations to Auschwitz began in January 1943; the last transport left Theresienstadt on 30 October 1944. "Transports arrived, transports left, the beds emptied out and filled up again," recalled Ruth Kluger, who passed through the camp in 1942–43. Thus, Theresienstadt was not an *Endlager* after all, but "the stable that supplied the slaughterhouse."[121]

The shift in the overall tone in the autumn of 1941 is unmistakable. The Russian campaign had cost the lives of over 100,000 German soldiers, and the United States had clearly signaled its intention to enter the war. In this context, Hitler returned repeatedly to his 1939 Reichstag prophecy. He placed it closer and closer to the present: "We are getting rid of the destructive Jews entirely," he assured associates on 17 October 1941; "I proceed with these matters ice-cold. I feel myself to be only the executor of a will of history." The great historical purpose that justified final decisions and final solutions surfaced again in Hitler's discussions with Heydrich and Himmler a week later, on 25 October, when he indicated that the Germans were "writing history anew, from the racial standpoint."[122]

Hitler used the same apocalyptic vocabulary in his meeting with the Nazi Gauleiter on 12 December 1941, a day after he declared war on the United States. It is likely that it was at this meeting that Hitler confirmed his intention to deport and kill all the Jews in Germany and the rest of Europe. There is no transcript of what Hitler said, but accounts left behind by both Goebbels and Frank agree on the key points.

"Concerning the Jewish question," Goebbels wrote the next day, "the Führer is determined to make a clean sweep. He prophesied to the Jews that if they were once again to cause a world war, the result would be their own destruction. That was no figure of speech. The world war is here; the destruction of the Jews must be the inevitable consequence. This question is to be viewed without sentimentality." A few days after the gathering on 12 December, Hans Frank returned to the General Gouvernement and informed his associates in Cracow that "we must put an end to the Jews, that I want to say quite openly." Again, Frank echoed Hitler's insistence that "we want to have compassion only for the German people," for we have "sacrificed our best blood" for the future of Europe. None of this would be easy, Frank reminded his subordinates: "In Berlin, we were told: why all this trouble; we cannot use them . . . liquidate them yourselves!" Frank followed this acknowledgment with an exhortation: "Gentlemen, I must ask you, arm yourselves against any thoughts of compassion," and fortify resolve to "destroy the Jews, wherever we encounter them and wherever it is possible, in order to preserve the entire structure of the Reich."[123] This is the evidence of Hitler's order to murder the Jews.

The planners of mass murder repeatedly invoked the need for frankness and hardness—once the decision to deport the Jews had been taken, party activists required steeled nerves. After weeks of wavering, in which the SS and the party leadership had answered Wehrmacht inquiries and fielded appeals on behalf of individual Jews, Hitler had set for the party the goal of the extermination of the Jews. With "the clean sweep," the "ice-cold" commitment, the harsh economy of sentiment and compassion, he appealed to the work ethic of political revolutionaries.

The National Socialists' struggle over compassion is a useful reminder of how seriously the party imagined the difficulties ordinary Germans or even Nazi loyalists might have in accepting the deportation of Jews. Even at the highest levels, Nazis constantly struggled to uphold the moral righteousness of their murderous activity and to stamp out any qualms or reservations. This work of fortification demanded a campaign that vilified the Jews as enemies of Germany and accordingly threatened them with "extermination," but withheld specific details about their deportation or fate in the East.

The stridency of anti-Jewish propaganda increased with the introduction of the Jewish star in September 1941. Goebbels intended to put the marked enemy in front of Germans, whose lives were touched more directly by the expanding war against the Soviet Union. Forced to work in a factory in Berlin, Elisabeth Freund reported on the material that "a horrible wave of antisemitic propaganda" had left behind: "Along the whole Kurfürstendamm signs hang in almost every shop," Freund noted: "'No Entry for Jews' or 'Jews Not Served.' If you walk along the street you see 'Jew,' 'Jew,' 'Jew' on every house, on every windowpane, in every store. It is difficult to explain why the Nazis, these devourers of Jews, want to paste this word all over their city." Nazi words spread into buildings and mailboxes: "Early in the morning leaflets lying in the stairwell call openly for a pogrom. The notices that report that a soldier has fallen in action blame the Jews for his death!" According to Howard K. Smith, "the leaflet was jet-black, with a bright yellow star on the cover and under it the words: 'Racial Comrades! When you see this emblem, you see your Death enemy!'"[124] "There is no difference between Jews and Jews," reminded Goebbels in a ferocious article in *Das Reich* in November: "the Jews are Guilty."[125] Jews would pay for the death of every German soldier, he promised. The article did not mention deportations, but the party's declarations did not hide the regime's intention to attack Jews as the collective enemy of the German people.

Goebbels was not sure whether the introduction of the Jewish star benefited the regime. He admitted that intellectuals in Berlin had not learned to judge from a racial point of view, and he polemicized against "false sentimentalism and pity."[126] Nazi activists had been trying to expunge this ordinary, slender sense of decency since 1933. Most Germans recognized a "Jewish problem," but it was hard to blame impoverished, persecuted neighbors. Local party leaders acknowledged this difficulty when they reminded party members of their duties as racial comrades and offered suggestions on how to subdue feelings of pity. "An effective means to curb false pity and false feelings of humanity is my habit of long standing not even to see the Jew, to see right through him as if he were made of glass, or rather as if he were thin air," wrote one obliging party member to his Stuttgart newspaper.[127]

If one person refused to see, another looked away, and a third saw only what he wanted to. On 25 September 1941, Paulheinz Wantzen, the editor of Münster's newspaper, encountered for the first time a Jew marked with the star: "The man wears it on the left side of his coat; he hugs the side of the houses with great timidity." The description indicated a flicker of pity, but soon enough Jews were, in Wantzen's renditions, accomplices to their own fate. In Berlin, he observed, Jews were "still remarkably well dressed," a muddle of words around the derivative root "mark" which unconsciously transformed the star into a suit. Jews did not give the impression "that they are walking around in a funk." Once Wantzen knew Jews to be wearing the star in a "very blithe, almost ostentatious" fashion, he had completely succeeded in purging himself of sympathy. "Gentlemen" might make negative remarks about vulgar Nazi policies, but the "voice of the people" played along. "You hear," Wantzen continued, passing on gossip from the street, that "Jews now have a penchant for holding their attaché cases or purses under the left arm so that the star is as hidden from view as possible." And "besides," added Ursel, a young wife in Berlin who commented on the Jewish star in a letter to her sweetheart on the eastern front, "you hear that the Germans in America have to wear a swastika on the front and back." (The bit about the front and back she got right, but it applied to Jews in the Lodz ghetto and in the rest of the annexed Warthegau, an indication of the convoluted transmission of political knowledge in Nazi Germany.)[128] Jews were obviously being talked about in the diffuse but authoritative way in which strangers were brought up in the in-and-out categories of the people's community, but conversations quickly turned back to the

Germans themselves, to the burdens they had been forced to bear, and to the course of the war generally. Goebbels tried to choreograph on an international scale the small-scale trial that he wanted to stage whenever a German met a Jew on the street. Evidence indicates that far from concealing the war on the Jews, German officials intended to conduct "a large, well-organized" trial of Herschel Grynszpan, whose assassination of a German embassy official in Paris had provided the Nazis with the pretext for the November 1938 pogrom and whom the Germans had illegally seized from France in July 1940. What else would such a trial have justified other than the deportations of Jews from their homes? Goebbels himself took charge of the preparations at the end of January 1942 (after the Wannsee Conference), venting his frustration over Grynszpan's claim that he had had a homosexual affair with the German diplomat, but otherwise planning for a trial that would be at least in part be public, though he indicated that Hitler would have the final say. (Hitler evidently remained attentive to anti-Jewish policy.) In February 1942 Goebbels' special deputy, Wolfgang Diewerge, returned from Paris, where he had interviewed the former French foreign minister, Georges Bonnet, who, Goebbels claimed, agreed to testify that in light of "the Grynszpan affair" Jews had pressured French statesmen to declare war on Germany in 1939. In the end, of course, there was no trial, and Grynszpan died (and almost certainly was killed) in German custody; but the reasons for abandoning it are not clear. The nagging issue of homosexuality probably got in the way, and Bonnet's statements seemed less than adequate. In April 1942 the Nazis dismantled the world stage on which they had intended to announce the "final solution."[129] Even without the trial, however, Hitler's "epochal judgment" on the Jews, his January 1939 prophecy, was showcased in party propaganda and broadcast in public statements. The deportation of the Jews in German-occupied Europe to death camps did not occur in silence, but in the din of what Hitler praised as "effective antisemitic propaganda."[130]

The Holocaust

Nazi Germany murdered Europe's Jews in order to realize its utopian project of reorganizing the continent along racial lines. The Nazis did not simply consider the Jews racially different or inferior but feared them as agents of social decomposition who threatened the moral, political, and economic health of the nation and its empire. According to the Nazis, Jews would not be allowed to compromise Germany's ability to fight a war, as had allegedly been the case in 1914–1918. Jews were also understood to be the main basis of support for Bolshevism and for international finance capitalism, a contradictory position that was no less firmly held for being illogical. This made Jews across Europe nothing less than enemy combatants to be seized and eliminated. It is important to realize that Hitler genuinely believed that Jews in Germany and everywhere else in Europe presented a direct danger to the new Reich. Without "the extermination of the Jewish people," Himmler admitted in 1943, "we would most likely be where we were in 1916–17."[131]

As Germany began to lose the war, the Nazis tirelessly extended their murderous reach and spread the knowledge of the murder of the Jews so that Germans and their allies would realize that they had burned the bridges behind them. In other words, Nazi propaganda reframed the crime in conventional moral terms and suggested to perpetrators how the Allies perceived them in order to fuel the determination to fight to the bitter end. As a result, the Nazis spared no effort in the spring of 1944 to kill hundreds of thousands of Hungarian Jews who had survived the war until then. Over the course of the war, the murder of the Jews became an increasingly desperate policy in which the "final solution" would not follow a final victory, but rather final victory depended on the "final solution." In the summer of 1941, it was the megalomania of Nazi imperialism which encouraged Hitler and Himmler to abandon the idea that the "final solution" had to wait until the end of the war and to implement it in the Soviet Union immediately. Soon thereafter, the realization that the world war would not be over "next spring" and that German authorities would not be able to deport the Jews whom they had impoverished and ghettoized pushed planners to contemplate killing the Jews under their control. As the war entered its third year and expanded into a world conflict, the Nazis believed that the immediate destruction of European Jews was necessary if Germany was to emerge victorious. And finally, in 1943 and 1944 the "final solution" was regarded as the only way for Germany to hold onto its crumbling position of strength. The logic of the Nazis' antisemitism led them to the ultrarevolutionary "position from which there is no escape."[132]

Once Nazi Germany had survived the military crisis of the winter of 1941–42 and resumed forward operations against the Soviet Union in the spring, the deportations of Jews resumed. Now SS administrators deported German Jews to the ghettos in Izbica, Piaski, and Zamosc around Lublin, although when the trains stopped in Lublin they selected small numbers of men to send to the labor camp at Majdanek. The General Gouvernement had been reinserted into the process because killing camps had been built in Belzec and Sobibor as guarantees that the territory would eventually be "Jew free," not a dumping ground. The Nazis began to clear scores of ghettos in the General Gouvernement with terrifying brutality, even as they continued to add more deportees. In March and April 1942 they transported 30,000 Jews from Lublin's ghetto to Belzec's gas chambers. At the same time, in the spring and summer of 1942, they deported 70,000 Jews from the ghetto in Lodz to Chelmno, a railhead fifty kilometers away, where victims were forced into mobile gas vans and murdered. In the first comprehensive attempt to deport foreign Jews, the Nazis began to transport thousands of Slovakian Jews to Lublin. At a time when authorities were still figuring out rail capacity and selection procedures in the death camps, the periodic emptying and restocking of the ghettos was standard operating procedure. But very quickly, less than four weeks after the new wave of deportations had begun, sometime in April 1942, Hitler seems to have made the decision to send the transports directly to death camps in Belzec and Sobibor and later Treblinka or to extermination facilities in Auschwitz (in the Wartheland). At the end of July 1943, grateful SS officials thanked railway officials for untangling transportation knots in the General Gouvernement, making it possible for trains with 5,000 "representatives of the chosen people" to arrive in Treblinka every day.[133]

With the seizure of Jews from across Europe and the aim to kill immediately all but a small fraction of "work Jews," "the Final Solution as we now understand it was fully underway." The "machinery of murder was disconnected from the schema 'evacuation–resettlement–labor conscription,'" which survived only as a vocabulary of camouflage and deception. Throughout 1942 the fundamental exterminatory aim of the "final solution" became more clear, but also more unfathomable, especially to victims, who could not believe that there was no utilitarian or economic logic behind the Nazis' policies and that nothing qualified their "political" intention to find and murder all Jews under their control, men, women, and children. Victims went to Auschwitz expecting the worst, but "not the unthinkable," wrote Charlotte Delbo, a non-Jewish inmate.[134]

By the time a trainload of Slovakian Jews arrived at the Birkenau complex in Auschwitz on 4 July 1942, the camp had refined the process of killing. At the railway siding, SS officers divided new arrivals, selecting small groups of "work Jews," who were registered as inmates with numbers tattooed on their left forearms and, for a few months before their deaths in circumstances the Nazis called "destruction through work," labored under miserable conditions in the factories German companies established in Auschwitz. During the war Auschwitz came to be a huge construction site, a boomtown in which tens of thousands of foreign laborers as well as captured Jews worked. But the majority of Jews transported to Birkenau were not selected as workers. Nor were they registered.

Disproportionately old or very young, and most of them women, who constituted 60 percent of the victims in the death camps, they entered the camp to be murdered. Children were killed by the trainload. Through trial and error, SS personnel worked out the entire process: camouflaging the operation with instructions about showers; robbing Jews of their last clothes and personal belongings, which were sorted and stored; sending naked victims to their deaths in gas chambers; and retrieving and disposing of the bodies in fire pits. Specially built crematoriums were installed later. On 17 July 1942, almost exactly eleven months after he observed SS shooters in Minsk, Himmler visited Auschwitz. He inspected the various stages, from the arrival of 2,000 Jews from Holland—they composed the first transport of Dutch Jews who had been rounded up in Amsterdam and deported from the transit camp at Westerbork two days earlier—to the selection of 1,531 workers on the ramp—an unusually high proportion—to the murder of the remaining 449 Jews in the gas chamber in Bunker 2, and the burning of the corpses. After viewing the operation, Himmler ordered the "resettlement" of more than one million Jews in the General Gouvernement by the end of the year 1942. That same night the SS, aided by the Paris police, completed raids in which 12,884 Jews were seized; two days later the first of ten transports left the holding camp in the velodrome at suburban Drancy for Auschwitz, a frightening, arduous journey that would take more than three days.[135] The Nazi extermination of the Jews of Europe had shifted into high gear.

Himmler made sure that ethnic Germans received the warehoused clothes of murdered Jews. For Christmas 1942 each German "is to be outfitted with one dress or suit, a coat and a hat, and, as long as supplies last, three shirts and appropriate underwear." After railway lines were laid directly into the camp and the gas chambers expanded and crematoriums built, over 10,000 people a day could be killed in the Auschwitz-Birkenau camp, with the result that massive amounts of clothes and other goods were stockpiled.

In the warehouses, which inmates called "Canada" for the riches they supposedly held, "liberators found about 370,000 men's suits, 837,000 women's coats and dresses, huge amounts of children's clothing, about 44,000 pairs of shoes, 14,000 carpets, and prostheses, toothbrushes," and other belongings from the families who had been murdered. At one point German authorities freighted away the baby carriages they had confiscated; according to one witness, "it took more than an hour for a column of carriages, five abreast, to pass."[136]

Auschwitz was not the only death camp. Most Polish Jews were murdered in Sobibor, Belzec, and Treblinka, where 250,000 Jews, mostly from the Warsaw Ghetto, had been gassed by the end of September 1942. Whereas the Germans dismantled these camps in 1943 once the ghettos in the General Gouvernement had been cleared and their inhabitants killed, Auschwitz operated until January 1945 and claimed more victims than any other camp, about one million Jews, 74,000 non-Jewish Poles, 23,000 Gypsies, 15,000 Soviet prisoners of war, and 25,000 other civilians. These numbers are hard to fathom, yet Auschwitz was a definite place. It lay within the borders of the newly annexed Wartheland and thus within the borders of the German Reich. It was at the center of huge plans to industrialize and Germanize the eastern frontier. What had been known before the war as little "Jerusalem," with Jews constituting 8,000 out of some 14,000 inhabitants in 1939, Oświęcim was renamed Auschwitz by German occupation authorities and largely rebuilt as a model industrial city, with single-family homes and garages and a growing German colony made up of industrialists, white-collar employees, and SS officers and their wives and children. Stores, schools, and doctors' and dentists' offices opened to cater to the Germans. The settlement had its own soccer field and swimming pool. A barkeeper from Wuppertal operated Gasthaus Ratshof in Auschwitz's marketplace while the Baedecker recommended the Hotel Zator to overnight visitors. "It is noteworthy," writes Sybille Steinbacher, "that Auschwitz became a German city precisely at the moment when the murder of Jews in the camp took on a systematic dimension."[137] There is no doubt that residents in Auschwitz knew exactly what was happening in the camp. Toward the end of his speech, in which he greeted newcomers, Auschwitz's German mayor brought up the concentration camp: "over there behind the meadows," he pointed. *"Every week more prisoners arrive, but the total always remains the same!"* he felt it necessary to explain. He repeated himself one more time so that everyone could do the math and figure out that "more prisoners" must have been subtracted each week.[138]

About half of the Jews who were murdered by the Nazis and foreign auxiliaries in the years 1939–1945 died in 1942, the most calamitous year of the "final solution," which was implemented quickly and thoroughly in a period when German armies continued to hold the offensive. More than one million mostly Soviet Jews had been killed in 1941, and more than 2.6 million German, Polish, Slovakian, French, Dutch, and Belgian Jews followed in 1942. "We will certainly complete the migration of the Jews within one year; then there will be no more migrations," affirmed Himmler in July 1942[139]

By comparison, the years 1943 and 1944 were mopping-up operations, characterized by the increasing frustration of the Nazis when their own allies, sensing the new direction to the war, withheld Jews, and by ruthless deportations when Germany's armies occupied former client states, as was the case with Italy in September 1943, Hungary in March 1944, and Slovakia in August 1944, or marched into areas formerly occupied by the Italians; thus in the late spring and early summer of 1944 German troops spared no effort to hunt down Jews on the Greek islands of Rhodes, Corfu, and Crete, the far-flung territories of the Nazi empire. Jewish uprisings in the Warsaw Ghetto in April and in Sobibor in October 1943, along with a surge of partisan activity in the rear, hastened German efforts to complete the destruction of Polish Jewry and to begin dismantling the camps; Sobibor and Treblinka were closed in the fall of 1943; Belzec had already been dismantled at the end of 1942. One and one-half million Polish Jews were murdered by gas in these three places in about eighteen months. In the last two years of the war, the SS also deliberately killed Jews who had survived in Poland or Ukraine as slave laborers. In June 1944 Germans deported the last "work Jews" in the Lodz ghetto. The last major operation in the "final solution" was the seizure of more than 437,000 Hungarian Jews in the spring and summer of 1944—just about the same time as the Allies landed in Normandy. Only the late intervention of Hungary's government on 6 July 1944, in the face of Allied air raids, saved Budapest's 200,000 Jews. The Nazis murdered about three-quarters of the Jews they deported from Hungary upon their arrival at Auschwitz; the rest, mostly young adults, they deployed as slave laborers (a direct telephone hotline connected the war ministries in Berlin to the selection ramp in Auschwitz), more than half of whom survived the war.[140]

In Hungary, as elsewhere, whole communities of Jews were destroyed in a single blow. SS murderers and local collaborators destroyed villages and neighborhoods; they destroyed graduating classes, youth cohorts, and extended families; they destroyed soccer teams, cliques, movie audiences, choirs, orchestras, and synagogue congregations; they destroyed "kindergartens, hospitals, prisons" and all the other assemblies of interest and inclination that made up collective life. In eastern Europe, the seven million speakers of Yiddish in the 1920s had been reduced twenty years later to less than 700,000; a language and culture that had once been as robust as Czech or Greek was now smaller than Estonian or Basque.[141] Among Jewish survivors on the continent it was hard to find the elderly or the young. In this exterminatory aim of the war the Nazis very nearly won.

The "final solution" had almost been realized before Germany's defeat at Stalingrad at the end of January 1943. The Holocaust was implemented not by beleaguered German armies, but by victorious SS forces who believed they were carrying out the judgment of history. Moreover, since the deportation of German and Austrian Jews was more or less finished when the war really hit the German home front, in the spring of 1943, German memories of the war focused on the aerial bombardment, the flight of Germans from the East, and the destruction of Germany's military power, but almost entirely omitted the Jews. Whereas the advance of German armies in the years 1939–1942 was accompanied by the extraordinary biopolitical design that resulted in the resettlement, deportation, and murder of millions of civilians, the long retreat of the Germans and their engagement with Soviet and Anglo-American forces in the years 1943–1945 was more conventional, so that even the Allies never quite understood the nature of the race war that the Germans had unleashed at the outset. For a long time, World War II ended up obscuring the Holocaust, which only in the last thirty years has become central to an understanding of modern history.

It should be clear that the doctrines of race war guided German policies from the start. Nazi Germany was determined to establish an empire to secure German power and sovereignty. Perpetrators repeatedly justified the destruction of nations and the murder of civilians in terms of German freedom. The tasks of protecting the German body from outside dangers, supplying it with sufficient resources, and conquering an empire were paramount. Less than four weeks after the invasion of Poland, Hitler, Himmler, and the rest of the Nazi leadership set out to realize a bold future in which the greater German Reich would be transformed into a continental empire based not on the administration of "lands and peoples" but on the ruthless subjugation of "spaces and races," as Vegas Gabriel Liulevicius has put it.[142] At first the Nazis dedicated their immediate efforts to resettling and denationalizing Poles and to colonizing the newly annexed territories with ethnic Germans. Polish Jews always received the worst, most arbitrary treatment, but a comprehensive policy to resolve the "Jewish problem" on a European scale took shape only with the war in the west and the Madagascar Plan in 1940. From then on the implementation of the "final solution" grew in importance, as did the stakes associated with it. With the invasion of the Soviet Union in June 1941, the destruction of the Jews as the most perilous enemy and the greatest obstacle to Germany's colonial dreams in the East became a top priority and consumed valuable military and operational resources. Germany's war aims cannot be separated from the Nazis' racial goals. This inextricable entanglement is what makes World War II fundamentally different from World War I and explains the terrible scale of civilian deaths. Nearly 60 percent of the casualties in World War II were civilians; in World War I the figure was 5 percent. The war was first and foremost about the life and death of civilians in the German empire.

The destruction of "lands and peoples" devastated Europe. The Germans smashed society in Poland, the central field of demographic and racial experimentation: more than five million Poles, including three million Jews, perished, about 16 percent of the prewar population. In World War II Poland lost proportionately more people than any other nation. In addition, 12.5 million Soviet citizens, including one million Jews, one-half the prewar Jewish population, died, a total that along with horrific military casualties added up to more than 13 percent of the prewar population. Lithuania and Latvia lost more than 10 percent of their citizens and almost all Jewish inhabitants. Military operations in southeastern Europe ruined Yugoslavia and Greece. Across Europe, civilians suffered the extreme political and economic privations of German occupation, which was deliberately organized to exploit the defeated nations in order to provide for the well-being of German civilians. No other war had killed so many people in so short a time: between thirty-five and forty million Europeans in the years 1939–1945.

Nazi Germany could rely on local collaborators, sometimes with more, sometimes with less success. This was so for the simple reason that until 1943 the German-dominated new order appeared to be permanent and German power invincible; antisemitism and fascist sympathies were contributing but secondary factors. In this context the Nazis implemented the "final solution" and found partners willing enough to cooperate in the vast effort to deport the Jews, particularly in 1942. Without the collaboration of local police and civilian authorities, who were not ideological confederates, the Nazis would not have been able to round up more than 100,000 Dutch Jews; over 70 percent of the "racial" Jews in the Netherlands, 107,000 out of 140,000, were transported mostly to Auschwitz and Sobibor and murdered; 5,000 returned home after the war. The French police assisted in the roundup of Jews in France, two-thirds of them foreign-born, among them many refugees from Germany and Austria who had already suffered assaults by the Nazis; 75,000 Jews in France were deported and murdered. The Germans seized a lower proportion of Jews in Belgium not least because the police were less efficient and less compliant: a total of about 25,000 mostly foreign-born Jews, or 43 percent of the Jews in the country. The Italians proved to be inhospitable to the Nazis' racial ideas. As a consequence, the SS managed in 1943 and 1944 to deport fewer than 8,000 Italian Jews out of a total Jewish population of 43,000, though most of these were murdered. Local collaborators also delivered hundreds of thousands of Hungarian Jews to the Germans; about 380,000 people, constituting one-half of Hungary's Jewish population, were murdered, for the most part in Auschwitz in the spring and summer of 1944. It would take many decades for Europeans to begin to examine their own roles in the Holocaust or to consider the Holocaust as a central, defining event in European rather than just German history.[143]

What was the balance of the "final solution" across the rest of Europe? More than five-sixths of the 71,000 Jews in Greece were deported and killed, a figure that included the ancient Jewish community in Salonika. Of the 82,000 Jews in Yugoslavia before the war, no more than 20,000 survived killings carried out mostly in Serbia and Croatia by German authorities as well as their Croat clients. Three-quarters of the Jews in the German protectorate of Bohemia and Moravia were murdered, as were two-thirds of the Jews in Slovakia; no less than 145,000 people in all. Only 1,700 of the 49,000 Jews deported from Austria survived, although two out of every three Austrian Jews had fled the country before the war. The vast majority of Jews who still lived in Germany when deportations began in 1941 were murdered, about one-third of the pre-1933 population of 500,000 people. Jews along the edge of the German empire, on the island of Rhodes, in Denmark, and in Norway, fell victim to the "final solution" as well. The Nazis murdered just under six million Jews in Europe between 1939 and 1945.[144]

The Germans were not the only perpetrators, and the drastic dimensions of the Holocaust often obscure murderous actions by Romanians, Poles, Ukrainians, and Hungarians; but copycat murder was a phenomenon of German-occupied and German-dominated Europe. Circumstances turned much worse for the Jews of Europe whenever the Nazis turned up. It was not a dangerous dynamic of war, collaboration, and revenge that explains the scope and magnitude of the Holocaust, but the Nazis' determination to wage war on the Jews and to fully realize a new racial order based on the total moral and political sovereignty of the German people, an objective that was very nearly accomplished in the year 1942. German history invaded the histories of the European nations, broke apart those societies in lethal ways, and changed their political destinies for the rest of the twentieth century. In Germany itself, the "final solution" was not imposed by foreign troops or opportunistic collaborators or political outsiders and social marginals but by the Germans themselves, by the SS, Nazi party members, professional university-trained cadres in party and state organizations, and countless civilians in large administrative bureaucracies. Berliners could walk as easily down Grosse Hamburger Strasse to the Jewish Home for the Aged, which served as an assembly point for Jews to be deported in 1943, as they can today. The S-Bahn stop back then was called Börse; today it is Hackescher Markt. The final chapter will explore what German citizens knew about the killings and how Germans and Jews responded to the knowledge of the catastrophe of deportation and murder.

4

Intimate Knowledge

Train Station

"Once again, on the train, and the difficult lives of all these people around me! The couple evacuated from Cologne with kids, the husband on leave from Africa waiting on the platform in Kassel. Next to him, a blinded soldier, on his way to the School for the Blind in Marburg, greedily smoking the cigarette that his companion has stuck in his mouth. Then a big, fat soldier on crutches, without shoes, his feet wrapped in bandages, the frozen toes amputated. Next to him, two soldiers from around Vjazma; they have been on the road for seven days, their homes in Cologne are burned out, their families don't have a roof over their heads. Children from cities in the west evacuated to the countryside. Hitler Youth, called up to a military training camp, pore over guidebooks on the proper use of a submachine gun. An SS officer dozing next to his very beloved bride. A Ukrainian who has been traveling for twelve days to locate relatives in his homeland but is unable to get there—field operations, partisan warfare. He is completely exhausted, enervated, starved, works in a munitions factory."[1]

Lisa de Boor, a journalist, sketched just one scene from the mobilized landscape she saw all around her. From the vantage point of a local train pulling into the town of Marburg in March 1943, the war had plainly chased people from one place to another across the empire. In and out of train stations, conscripts in the Hitler Youth and Reich Labor Service deployed to training camps. Soldiers shuttled back and forth to the front to take advantage of military leaves. It was a long journey, because Germany had become so big. When Willy Reese returned to the front—"Lodz, Warsaw, Orsha, Smolensk"— he was rarely sober: "I drank day and night: brandy, vodka, gin." Along the way, the young man passed ambulance trains returning to the West. As the war ground on, civilians crossed paths with wounded soldiers more and more frequently. The damage caused by the war just a month after Germany's defeat at Stalingrad was also plain to see in the movement of refugees, in this case, families displaced from Cologne, which had been the target of Britain's first thousand-bomber raid in May 1942 and continued to be a primary target, although the biggest air raids on German cities were still to come. While some people struggled to get back to their homes to locate family, the Nazi party organization sent thousands of children from their homes into the safety of the countryside. The vast majority of Germans resettled at some point during the war years in what Goebbels described as a "colossal turnover of the German population."[2]

At the same time, Nazi Germany needed more and more foreign workers, who by the middle of 1944 totaled over 7.6 million people, most of them captured in Poland and the Soviet Union and railroaded in to toil as slave laborers in the empire's industrial plants and agricultural fields. The majority of these laborers, constituting about one-quarter of the total workforce in wartime Germany, worked in terrible conditions, often under armed guard and sustained by meager rations. They unsettled observers, who did not always perceive their bondage. Many workers had a day off on Sunday, when they milled around train stations and taverns. "Frenchmen, Poles, Ukrainians, girls too, heaped together in front of the main train station. Dirty, shivering, most without coats, the girls in summer dresses and headscarves," wrote de Boor: "An unending sense of gloom hangs about these people so far away from home."[3]

Back and forth. In many ways, the railway station, connecting people to the camps and to the front, and the point of arrival and departure for thousands of Jewish and Polish deportees, prisoners, foreign workers, and German resettlers, expressed the new mobilized social organization at which the Nazis aimed. The German Reichsbahn hauled over three million Jews to their deaths. Trains represented the point of departure from the familiar to the unknown. "At the beginning of the memory sequence," recalled Primo Levi, "stands the train."[4] Trains and train stations offered both Germans and their victims frightening glimpses into the different spheres of life and death in the Third Reich.

At the beginning of the war, in January 1940, the SS "bard" Hanns Johst walked around Bahnhof Friedrichstrasse in Berlin on his way to the outposts of the German empire and portrayed "Scenes of the War" in triumphant verse.

Trains come in from the west front. . .
Trains roll toward the East. . .
Trains roll toward the West. . .
Trains come from Poland. . .
Uninterrupted . . . day and night. . .
A steely pulse pulls train after train into this thundering shed. . .
Pushes train after train out to the fronts. . .
to the front of yesterday . . . To the front of tomorrow. . .
Soldiers climb out . . . climb in. . .[5]

Since then, however, railway stations had begun to fall apart under the strain of war. The demands of wartime mobilization ripped up schedules, so that civilians waited longer for more crowded trains. "Three hours waiting" in Kassel left travelers "dull, gray, depressed." Even local trains were filled to the last seat; luggage cluttered the corridors. "The compartments are filthy, the seat cushions tattered, the windows rusted," summarized one Swiss visitor to "secret Germany," as he entitled his wartime reportage. René Schindler also noted the uneasy encounters that took place in train stations: "you can hear all German dialects, and also quite a lot of Italian and French, even the Balkans are well represented." Conversations among strangers, even with foreign workers such as the Ukrainian on the train to Marburg, centered upon the war. "People fall into conversation with each other everywhere, in the streets, in the shops, in the train station," wrote Lisa de Boor, "talking about how it can no longer go on 'like this.'" But the war did go on just "like this." "Casualty reports, bomb attacks, mortal fear, flight from the cities into the countryside, the dread for tomorrow and the day after, these are the topics of conversation."[6]

However, at this point, in the spring of 1943, fewer and fewer people discussed German Jews, let alone encountered them in train stations. Indeed, had Germany's war not gone so poorly after Stalingrad, the victims in the death camps would have remained out of sight forever. As it was, the hardships of the war brought non-Jewish prisoners as well as foreign laborers into the open as they worked for the crumbling German Reich. Air raids pulled the satellite camps of the main concentration camps directly into German cities, where brigades of prisoners worked under guard as glaziers, roofers, and menial laborers in order to repair bomb damage. The concentration camp at Sachsenhausen provided Düsseldorf with a brigade of 600 workers and Duisburg with 400; Neuengamme sent 750 men to Bremen and 250 to Osnabrück, while Buchenwald supplied Cologne with 1,000 workers. Prisoners of war or political prisoners, the men worked twelve-hour days, seven days a week, and slept in temporary prisons often established in the middle of neighborhoods in sight of apartment buildings and schools. German civilians were wary of these uniformed prisoners, whom they took to be criminals. They reserved their greetings for the SS men who guarded them, while it was Belgian and French workers who passed candy or cigarettes to the prisoners. In the city of Munich alone there were 120 labor camps for prisoners of war and another 268 for foreign workers; in Düsseldorf there were a total of 155; in Berlin there were at least 666.[7] Charlotte Delbo, a French political prisoner in Auschwitz, recounted her January 1944 journey through the train stations of wartime Germany. A non-Jew with a scientific background, she was fortunate enough to be transferred from Auschwitz to Ravensbrück in order to work in an agricultural research station. Since there were only a few dozen prisoners to be transferred, the group traveled under guard by regular train. In the towns they passed, Delbo saw brigades of foreign workers deployed around train stations, and as she approached Berlin she saw ruins in the city. "We felt the very same satisfaction we experienced in Auschwitz when we used to watch interminably long ambulance trains, their white roofs painted with a large red cross, returning from the east with their load of wounded soldiers." It was necessary to change trains in Berlin, so the SS guards directed them into the subway, where they saw a sign for toilets. The women asked permission and went in— an extraordinary passage from Auschwitz to the ladies' room at the Schlesischer Bahnhof: "The attendant in charge, an old woman, saw us enter her mosaic-decorated palace, which smelled of disinfectant, without registering any surprise. Obviously, one saw all kinds of things in Berlin at that time, and the old woman's worn face no longer reflected any amazement. 'Poor kids!' she said, however, in a voice as worn as her features, and she unlocked for us the coin-operated cabins." On the subway, however, commuters kept their distance from the prisoners, who stood out in their stripped uniforms and wooden clogs; they, in turn, whispered to frightened passersby, "We're French political prisoners; we're not criminals." Several stops later, they arrived at what must have been Bahnhof Zoo. Outside the station, the group once again saw foreign workers clearing rubble. "They turned out to be Italians, skinny, so skinny!"

reported Delbo: "not as thin, however, as deportees."⁸ These collisions between Germany's prisoners and German civilians belonged to everyday life, although they usually took place without much contact or communication.

But Jews had largely disappeared, and had they not lost the war, the Germans in the Third Reich would never have seen Jews again. Over the course of 1942, German soldiers fighting in the Soviet Union stopped mentioning Jews, who for the most part had been murdered or managed to escape across Russian lines. In the first stages of the deportations, German officers stationed in Poland still would have heard the familiar sounds of south German *schwäbisch* or a "Berliner's snout" in ghettos, since thousands of German Jews were first "evacuated" to villages around Lublin or to Lodz without being killed. But after the spring of 1942, once deportation meant extermination, encounters became less frequent. Uniformed personnel occasionally talked to German Jews, since the Security Service deployed reserve police battalions to deport and kill Jews in the General Gouvernement in the summer and fall of 1942, when the extermination camps were not always fully operational. So it was possible, on 13 July 1942 in the Polish village of Jozefow, for one policeman from Hamburg to fall into a conversation with a mother and her daughter from Kassel or for another to escort a decorated World War I veteran from Bremen into the forest before shooting him. In Komarowka, in September 1942, a policeman moving Jews to the "transit ghetto" in Miedzyrzec, a place the German policemen called *Menschenschreck,* human horror, before victims were shipped to the death camp in Treblinka, even recognized the woman who used to run the Millertor-Kino, a movie theater in Hamburg. And until the end of 1942, the deportations of Jews from Germany were visible, even public affairs that prompted a variety of responses, from shock to satisfaction. By the middle of 1943, however, Germany was more or less *judenrein.* At this time the "public notices prohibiting Jews from using park benches, tele-

phone booths, swimming pools, restaurants" had become unnecessary and were "gradually removed."[9]

In the last two years of the war, the Jews appeared only as an abstraction, a power conjured up to explain fierce Allied bombing attacks on German cities. Thus Jewish neighbors disappeared at the
very moment when the hardships of the war began to take their toll,
when German memories became more dense, and when civilians
were more apt to see themselves as victims rather than victors. For
the Germans, the horrors of the war did not encompass the suffering of the Jews. When the war came home to Germany after Stalingrad in early 1943, the Jews were no longer there.

Imprisoned in a German work camp, Lilli Jahn tried desperately
to see her children. A tip by a neighbor had led to her arrest for fail-
ing to properly identify herself on the calling card she had stuck to
the door of her apartment: it should have read "Lilli Sara Jahn,"
not "Dr. med. Lilli Jahn." She was arrested late in August 1943 and
incarcerated in a work camp in Breitenau, near Kassel, although
she was already extremely vulnerable, since her husband had divorced her a year earlier and thus left her without the legal protection of a Jew in a "privileged marriage." Her arrest left her five children alone. The eldest daughter, fifteen-year-old Ilse, worked to
maintain the household and wrote to her mother as often as possible. It was Ilse who passed on news of the massive bombing raid
that devastated Kassel on 22 October 1943:

And so we went along: Bahnhofstrasse, Kurfürstenstrasse, Stände-
platz, Hohenzollernstrasse, Kronprinzenstrasse, Motzstrasse, Miets-
kaserne, Luisenstrasse, Hindenburgplatz, Stadthalle, Harleshäuser
train station and back home. Not a single store exists any more.
Kassel is just not there. Really, I'm not exaggerating. All the side
streets are piles of rubble as well . . . Tens of thousands of people
have sadly, sadly perished. Mom, you don't even know where you
are in the middle of these ruins.

Lilli Jahn was allowed to post only one letter every month, but she smuggled more out. It was the firestorm in Kassel, the arrival of the war on the home front, that provided the opportunity for a possible meeting between the imprisoned mother and her children. She explained in a letter on 14 November 1943:

> Now pay attention, dear children, but keep absolutely quiet. Since the bomb attack we don't have a separate wagon for us, and so we sit with the other people in the compartments. If we do this right, we could meet one time . . . but you have to be very careful on the station platforms so you don't give yourself and me away. Once on the train, we can talk with each other.

It is unlikely that this encounter ever took place; further correspondence makes no mention of it. Lilli Jahn was deported from Breitenau to Auschwitz on 17 March 1944 and died there three months later at the age of forty-four.[10]

What is remarkable about the exchange between Lilli, a Jew, and her daughter, a *Mischling,* is the radical difference in perspective. Ilse is chatty, walks around, and attentively maps the extent of destruction and sympathizes ("sadly, sadly") with bombed-out Germans, while Lilli only accidentally finds herself placed among non-Jewish Germans, from whom she is otherwise cut off, is circumspect, and emphasizes the ever-present danger in German public places. The shocks of the war are evident in both accounts, but Ilse's anticipates the sentimentalized, beleaguered, and self-absorbed stories that Germans told one another, which Lilli's tries to pierce: "Now pay attention, dear children." The two streams of narrative were drifting apart, although we would not know of Ilse's and Lilli's heartbreaking contacts in the fall of 1943 if an unnamed German guard at the camp had not smuggled out all of the children's letters to Lilli before her deportation to Auschwitz and returned them to the family, which rediscovered the correspondence in 1998. That the letters existed forgotten for so many years is an indication of how forcefully one set of traumatic memories can displace another and how completely people are enveloped by particular narratives.[11]

At the very end of the war, the destruction of Germany even allowed a few Jews to escape their captivity and to pass as Germans who had lost their papers in bombing raids or evacuations from the East. Victor Klemperer, who on the day before the Allied bombing of Dresden on 13 February 1945 had received summons to report to a work brigade there, could, after the bombing had wrecked the city and destroyed the identification papers and ration cards of thousands of survivors, leave on his own accord for the countryside, where he registered as "Victor Klemperer and nothing else." "I sat in restaurants, I traveled by train and tram—as a Jew in the Third Reich, all of it punishable by death." The arrival of thousands of refugees, who had fled eastern Germany during the final Soviet offensive and milled around the roads into Berlin in the late winter of 1945, allowed Inge Deutschkron and her mother to come out of hiding in Berlin, blend into the crowds, and pass as "Aryans."[12]

In similar fashion, Ruth Kluger, her mother, and another companion slipped out of a forced march of Jewish prisoners and a while later managed to slip in with groups of refugees: "We were overtaken by your own stream of refugees," she wrote to a German audience many years later, "and followed the homeless, who were choking on their own misfortune and no longer asked full of suspicion where this or that stranger came from." It was the death marches that gave Germans one last chance to glimpse concentration-camp inmates who had been forced to travel roads to new, desperately overcrowded assembly points in the middle of Germany at Buchenwald and Bergen-Belsen. At one point, some weeks before the end of the war, Kluger went into the Bavarian town of Sträubing to run some errands and there caught sight of a column of prisoners guarded by SS soldiers. It is not clear whether these were Jewish prisoners—they could have been Jews in transit from Auschwitz to Dachau—but, Kluger notes, "I had never seen 'us' from the outside. What separated me from them were just a few weeks, after we had been together for years." Kluger could also watch the victims being watched by the Germans, as she recounted in her 1992 memoir:

> They walked right through the middle of town, in broad daylight, and there were townspeople to my right and my left who looked away. Or closed their faces so that nothing could penetrate. We have our own troubles, kindly spare us yours. We waited on the sidewalk until the train of "subhumans" had passed. When a few weeks later the Americans occupied the city of Straubing, none of its citizens had seen anything. And in a sense no one had. For you haven't seen what you haven't perceived and absorbed. In that sense, only I had seen them.[13]

Jews returned after Germany lost the war, not, except in rare instances, as former neighbors and deportees, but as parts of the history of the war that was fundamentally different from German memories of the war, a difficult history that Germans over the next decades would have to try to comprehend. By 1943, however, the stories that Germans told about the Jews had petered out, overlaid by far more voluminous stories about themselves, about Stalingrad, the bombing of German cities, the huge fears of the catastrophe of defeat and national collapse, and the desperate evacuation from the East. In 1945 these could not make room for revelations about the Holocaust.

The ability of Jews to report on their fate had vanished almost completely with the deportations to the death camps, while Germans continued to witness and write about their fate and sing songs about miracles. The two catastrophes, the one Germans heaped upon the Jews and the one they brought upon themselves, were obviously related to each other, but they were also incommensurate and asymmetrical, and each shaped the memories and narratives of postwar contemporaries in fundamental and, at first, mutually incomprehensible ways.

Jewish Witnesses

The requirement to identify themselves with a Jewish star as of 19 September 1941 came as a terrible shock to German Jews. The star was, as Klemperer reported, "black on yellow cloth, at the center in Hebrew-like lettering 'Jew,' to be worn on the left breast, large as the palm of a hand." "I myself feel shattered, cannot compose myself." For a few days Klemperer did not go out at all, despite "glorious weather." "Yesterday," Klemperer wrote on Tuesday, 23 September, "I really did go through the middle of town on the front platform" of the streetcar, making "purchases at Heckert's, Paschky's and Güntzel's." Still, "the most wretched, bitter feeling." His companions in the "Jew house" tried to console themselves: "this was the final act—I too believe it is the fifth act. But some plays . . . have *six* acts." As many Jews who left eyewitness accounts indicated, German passersby looked on sympathetically. Some even sought out marked Jews in order to criticize the regime: "Not so bad, your sign, at least you know who you're talking to, who you've got in front of you, you can speak your mind for once," remarked one streetcar conductor.[14] Yet gossip also featured Jews who avoided showing the star or else displayed it ostentatiously. A story told to Elisabeth Freund about an encounter on Berlin's elevated split German responses right down the middle: "A mother saw that her little girl had sat down next to a Jew; 'Lieschen, sit over here, you don't have to sit next to a Jew.' Suddenly an Aryan worker stood up: 'And me, I don't have to sit next to Lieschen.'"[15] Within a month, on 15 October 1941, the Nazis had begun to deport German Jews, carrying out Hitler's decision not to postpone any longer a "resettlement" to the East until after the end of the war. It was at this point that most congregations turned their backs on Protestants and Catholics who wore the star; the seizure of church bells aroused more opposition than the seizure of church members. Identified by the star, Germany's Jews were most visible just before they disappeared.

The official line was that Jews were being deported to labor camps in Poland and elsewhere in the "East," accomplishing the long-held political goal of making Germany "free of Jews" and providing the economic benefits of Jewish labor during the war. Of course, Nazi leaders had no intention of providing deported Jews a spare, if sustainable, existence, even when, for the period October 1941 to June 1942, they did not generally kill German Jews on arrival. Goebbels described the destination he imagined for deported Jews in August 1941: "They will be worked over by the harsh climate there."[16] However, the ruse of deportation at least in the years 1941 and 1942 made it easier to extract Jews from non-Jewish neighbors, who themselves were reassured by the idea of resettlement. It made it easier to transport the victims, who still hoped to survive; made it easier as well to get Jewish authorities to cooperate; and made it easier, finally, to rob the victims, who had put their affairs in order. These were duplicitous maneuvers perfected by the SS, but what did Germans Jews themselves, and their German neighbors, know about the conditions that awaited the deportees in the East?

Jewish households usually received letters from the police or the Jewish community announcing their "evacuation transport to the East."[17] "The alarm is unbelievable," reported Elisabeth Freund about the impending deportations demanded by the Nazis in October 1941: "What is going to happen to these people? Are they going into the countryside, into barracks, or to Poland?" Klemperer also tried to make some sort of sense out of the news of deportations in order to guess what was going to happen at the end of the journey: "Every day news from many cities, departure of large transports, postponements, then departures again, with sixty-year-olds, without sixty-year-olds—everything seems arbitrary. Munich, Berlin, Hanover, Rhineland . . . the army needs the trains, the army has released trains."[18] Jews to be deported also received notification informing them that all their goods and possessions had been expropriated and instructing them to keep their households clean and their former property in good order until the time of departure. A list specified what personal items, clothes, and tools Jews were authorized to take along with them, but it was short: spoons "(no knives or forks!)," a pot or a pail, and perhaps a ladle, some clothes; not much more.[19] The last hours before leaving home were difficult to bear. Hamburg's Ingrid Wecker remembered: "People have to bring all these things. And then to stuff everything into the suitcases—it was all so terrible. What do you bring? Photographs of relatives? Later, you think, no, pull them out. Better to take a warm coat or a scarf."[20] In the morning, deportees shut off the gas and electricity, locked the front door, and mailed their house keys to local authorities or handed them over to police at assembly points.

In Berlin, Inge Deutschkron actually saw her aunt and uncle, formerly a businessman in Spandau, picked up early one morning. Her aunt came out of the building first, "with a much too big rucksack on her back, in a rush, quickly, as if she just wanted to get it over with. My uncle tottered out afterward. They did not glance back, not once, as the men closed the back of the van." Jews believed (and were led to believe) that they were to be deported to self-sustaining labor camps. Photographs depict Jews arriving at assembly camps with extra clothing, tightly packed rucksacks, and even mattresses. "We assumed that we would have to perform heavy labor under difficult circumstances," recalled one survivor from Kassel, but we had no "evidence that the aim of our journey was to be our physical destruction."[21]

Sometimes Jews spent days in assembly camps where they were vulnerable to the torments of their SS guards, as had been the case with the men arrested after the pogrom in November 1938.

Selected Jews in Nuremberg awaited deportation in the stadium where until 1938 the Nazis had celebrated their party rallies; the guards had taken care to remove straw sacks so that the unfortunate deportees had to sleep on bare ground. In the morning, SS men forced Jews to do humiliating exercises, *Frühsport,* calisthenics, which cameramen filmed. Often enough the SS, which was in charge of loading the trains, forced Jews to part with their luggage in order to make more room in the railway cars, or they uncoupled the baggage car in the back before the train departed, but such actions were probably not the rule in 1941, when the idea of some sort of life on the German frontier was not yet simply a camouflage for murder. Enough possessions entered Lodz or the ghettos around Lublin for expropriated Polish Jews there to resent, even in the horribly meager conditions that prevailed, the relative wealth of the German Jews who had joined them.[22]

In the meantime, the humiliations heaped upon German Jews who remained in their apartments or, as was increasingly the case, in the cramped rooms of "Jew houses," became more terrifying. Although more Jews were drafted into factories or deployed as beasts of burden, they were forbidden to use public transportation except, as instructions drawn up by the Ministry of the Interior detailed, when workers had more than one hour or seven kilometers to walk to work or schoolchildren had more than one hour or five kilometers to walk to school. Jewish schools were closed at the end of June 1942 in any case.[23] To get to her work detail in Berlin, "Nanny has to walk five and a half kilometers in the morning and in the evening, that is, one and a half hours there, one and a half hours back—isn't that terrible," reported her mother Selma; "you wake up one hour earlier, around five, and get home an hour later, around seven or half-past seven, if you're lucky." Bureaucrats exerted themselves to eliminate small conveniences; thus Jewish commuters were not permitted to "buy twelve-journey tickets or transfer tickets, but only the expensive single-journey tickets."[24]

Since the police were now able to identify starred Jews, they enforced the nine o'clock evening curfew (eight o'clock in winter) that had been imposed on all Jews since the beginning of the war. Authorities banned Jews from public spaces altogether over the Christmas holidays in 1941. From 24 December to 1 January they were allowed on the streets only between the hours of three and four in the afternoon in order to shop. Beginning in 1942, Jews were no longer allowed to keep pets; since the animals in question were "Jewish," they had to be killed even if their owners found non-Jewish friends to care for them. On 19 May 1942 the Klemperers brought their tomcat Muschel to the vet's office on Dresden's Grunaer Strasse, where Eva watched it be put to sleep with an anesthetic: "The animal did not suffer. But *she* suffers."[25]

The worst was the lack of news from the East. "Seven more transports in January," noted Selma Fleischer in December 1941, "and the first haven't even written yet." "Still nothing from our loved ones," she confirmed almost one year after the deportations from Berlin had begun; "is everyone still alive? We begin to doubt it." No mail was an ominous sign in this mail-mad country. "They've vanished from the face of the earth."[26] A few postcards did arrive from the ghettos around Lublin, where thousands of Germans Jews had been transported in the first wave of deportations in the winter of 1941–42. When the ban on correspondence was lifted briefly in Lodz in December 1941, residents bought over 20,000 postcards. Although their messages revealed little, they represented signs of life. The ban on mail was reimposed on 5 January 1942. No mail at all was allowed out of the ghetto in Minsk. Most deportees simply left Germany without a trace. The silence afterward forced Jews who remained behind to contemplate the desperate conclusion that the transports out of Germany ended in death. Moreover, when the second wave of deportations began in March 1942, German authorities paid much less attention to treating the deportees as future colonists: more brutal police interrogations took place; fewer tools could be taken along on the journey; luggage accompanied the transports less frequently. It was not unusual for authorities to strip Jews of the last material bits of their legal identities by confiscating wedding rings and personal papers.[27]

At the same time, the SS invaded "Jew houses." Klemperer's diaries leave a detailed record of SS soldiers plundering households, destroying precious foodstocks, spitting in the faces of residents, and forcing elderly Jews to humiliate themselves. (These visits stopped after 1942, when the deportations had largely been completed.) Gradually residents understood that they had become completely disposable. Klemperer was certainly not the only one to imagine "death sneaking up," an anguished realization that there were fewer Jews left to round up in 1942, leaving him more vulnerable, and also growing clarity that what deportation meant was death.[28]

Knowledge about the "final solution" remained fragmentary until the very end of the war. Klemperer was unusually well informed: he heard rumors about the Madagascar Plan in 1940 and about the massacre at Babi Yar and the shooting of Berlin Jews in Riga a year later. But it was not until after his liberation that Klemperer learned that most deportations after 1941 had led Jews straight to death camps. Even as he sorted out the evidence of mass murder during the war, he continued to think of his neighbors who had been deported from Dresden as alive. He harbored frightening suspicions, but remained uncertain enough to sustain hope. This was possible primarily because Klemperer, like most observers, tied the calamity of Jews to specific events: "the murders in Kiev . . . And, and, and," as he wrote in January 1944. Momentous events or atrocities structured the way he considered the Jewish catastrophe. "Now, of all times," Klemperer commented after Germany's defeat at Stalingrad, "one can no longer assume that any Jews will return from Poland alive. They will be killed before the retreat. Besides, people have long been saying, that many of the evacuees don't even arrive in Poland alive. They were being gassed in cattle trucks during the journey."[29] To his mind, most Jews, many Jews, might well have been still alive; their death was contemplated in the future tense.

As the defeat of Nazi Germany became more apparent, surviving Jews asked themselves again and again, "How many Jews are still alive in Poland?" Klemperer himself was pessimistic, although he still tied the murder of millions of Jews, "shot and gassed," to retaliatory actions unleashed by beleaguered German armies. "Who is still alive?" was accompanied by the more open-ended question "Who will survive?"[30] During the war, Klemperer did not imagine the deliberate and systematic murder of Jews in industrial facilities. He could not comprehend the horrible outcome without some sort of short-term cause such as defeat, even as he understood the European-wide scale to the "resettlement" effort. The timing of the circulation of increasingly authoritative reports about genocide in the fall of 1944—leached by Klemperer's circle of associates from comments by German soldiers, from Swiss newspapers, and from the BBC—warped Klemperer's understanding of the murder of the Jews, which in his view had occurred in immediate, present time in response to Germany's desperate military situation and not largely, as was the case, in 1942 and 1943 in the attempt to build a German empire along racial lines.

The cruelty of German authorities and the relentless pace of deportations in the spring and summer of 1942 did not add up to secure knowledge about mass murder. Many Jews in these terrible years also suppressed their worst fears in order not to make the days while they remained in Germany intolerable. "Out of consideration for my parents, I avoided talking about conditions in Poland as long as I was around them," remembered one young man in Berlin who planned to go underground. Last letters to family members outside Germany tended to comfort rather than inform, although in one extraordinary case Erich Frey left behind detailed information in the event that his daughters in the United States would seek, after the war, restitution for the murder of their father, who anticipated his own death—and Hitler's too.[31] Outside the largest cities, mostly elderly Jews were isolated, prohibited from listening to the radio or purchasing a newspaper. They knew even less.

Most Jews in Germany in 1942 contemplated the future in a combination of "not-knowing, knowing, not-wanting-to-believe." But it is also likely that at some point "knowledge full of foreboding about the mortal threat" became concrete.[32] A startling increase in suicides in the Jewish community indicated widespread determination to avoid being murdered by the Nazis. As a result of persecution, the aggregate suicide rate among Germany's Jews after 1933 was already disproportionately high, one for every 100 people, but during the period of the deportations it doubled. In Berlin, where most Jews still occupied their own apartments, the rate in 1942 and 1943 was even higher. As many as one in ten Württemberg Jews who received a deportation order in 1941 and 1942 committed suicide, mostly by taking the barbiturate Veronal—Klemperer dubbed Veronal "Jewish drops." The last 450 Wiesbaden Jews were deported on 1 September 1942; in the preceding five days 30 others had taken their own lives.[33] Walter Schindler, a Berlin lawyer, described the depressed mood at the beginning of the year 1942: "About forty people lived in the Pension Bernhard, of whom about fifteen took their own lives over the course of six weeks. They said their goodbyes after dinner as if they going on a trip, went up to their rooms, and the next morning we heard the ambulance drive up and take away forever the lifeless bodies." According to Raul Hilberg, "the 'perpetual question' among Jewish acquaintances was: 'Will you take your life or let yourself be evacuated?'"[34] One of those who took Veronal was Martha Liebermann, the eighty-five-year-old wife of the Expressionist painter Max Liebermann, who from her apartment on Pariser Platz could see the SS coming with a stretcher to get her in March 1943.

Suicide was easier for people living alone or for elderly couples, but involved anguished discussions when households included children or parents. Jochen Klepper, who was not Jewish, and his Jewish wife, Hanni, and her grown-up Jewish daughter from an earlier marriage, Renate, began talking about suicide in October 1941, just days after the first deported Jews left Berlin. Jochen, the author of a well-received 1937 novel about Frederick the Great, had a melancholic streak and had earlier contemplated taking his own life; he persistently spoke in favor of suicide. Hanni was not so sure; however, she did say she would commit suicide if the Nazis forced her to divorce her husband and sent her "out of the country." In contrast, nineteen-year-old Reni wanted to live, and was clearly unsettled by the morbid thoughts of her stepfather, who had informed her that in the event that she wanted to commit suicide, he and her mother would die with her. Renate, in turn, replied that her parents should not continue to live for "her sake," even if she was deported. Evidently this was not the last word. Even so Klepper reported that "Renerle is more and more resolved in her decision to commit suicide if she cannot emigrate and cannot escape deportation, even though she still hopes." What made the conversations particularly vexed was the knowledge that neither the parents nor the daughter had been able to part from one another when Renate had had the opportunity to accompany her older sister to England in May 1939. All three ended their lives on the night of 10 December 1942 after Klepper's personal appeal to Adolf Eichmann to allow Renate to emigrate to Sweden failed.[35] In this case, suicide was an ambiguous pact to remain together.

Other German Jews considered living underground, and about 15,000 tried to do so. However, without ration cards or identity papers this was an extremely difficult course of action. It demanded that "submarines," as they were called, abandon their relatives, whose fate they would see from the outside, cut off as Deutschkron was when she watched her aunt and uncle marched off. In a city like Berlin, where Jews had resources and contacts and could move about more easily, there was considerable resistance to the deportations. Some 5,000 to 7,000 Berlin Jews went underground as "submarines," about one in twelve Jews who were left in the city in 1943, of whom at least 1,500 survived the end of the war. It should be clear that anyone who lived in the underground did so thanks to the courageous efforts of individual Germans. No longer marking themselves with the star, a few "submarines" "made forbidden visits to bars, theaters, and the like" and pieced together news of the mass murders taking place in the East. Kurt Lindenberg recalled: "I occasionally bumped into soldiers or civilians who, without knowing whom they were talking to, reported on what they had seen in their trips to the occupied territories, how deported Jews were murdered in sometimes brutal, sometimes elaborate ways. I heard these reports more and more frequently."[36]

Over 50,000 Jews were deported from Germany in the first wave of deportations, which ended in January 1942 (in addition to two transports in February). By the end of 1942 the Nazis had deported another 50,000 men, women, and children, this time mostly to Theresienstadt, leaving about 40,000 Jews living in Germany. Despite terrible mortality rates as a result of disease, Theresienstadt was not a death camp. It was a walled garrison town, a ghetto. Beginning in September 1942, Jews imprisoned there were even allowed to write monthly postcards, so guardedly good news slowly trickled back to Germany. These signs of life conflicted with rumors of mass murder. However, Theresienstadt was not what the Nazis euphemistically called an *Endlager*, or "final destination." Beginning in January 1943 and continuing through October 1944, the vast majority of Jews who were brought to Theresienstadt were deported to Auschwitz and murdered.[37]

Over the course of 1943, the Nazis deported Jews who remained in Germany. In "factory actions" in January and February the Gestapo rounded up thousands of Jewish workers in essential war industries. Suddenly one morning, "You could see police vans hurtling through the streets of Berlin," remembered Deutschkron. "When they stopped in front of a building, uniformed and civilian officers barged out, ran inside, led someone out, put him in the van, and sped on to the next house . . . They picked them up as they were—in pajamas, in overalls, without coats." In Berlin 7,000 individuals were simply hauled off factory floors, packed into "green Minnas," the patrol wagons of the police—counterparts to the feared "black Marias" in the Soviet Union—and sent directly to Auschwitz. "No more counterpressure to Gestapo," concluded Klemperer, who recorded the arrest after many delays of Jewish workers at Zeiss-Ikon, the famous optics manufacturer in Dresden.[38]

Mishandled at every step in the deportation process, so much so that German secretaries working in the transit camp the SS had installed in the Clou theater on Berlin's Zimmerstrasse (where Hitler had made his first Berlin appearance in 1927) blanched with horror, Jewish prisoners had little reason to think they would survive.[39] Goebbels, who for years had fought to override Wehrmacht objections to deporting skilled workers, gloated. "I am convinced that by liberating Berlin of the Jews I have accomplished one of my greatest political tasks," he reflected in his diary in April 1943; "When I consider how Berlin looked in 1926 when I came here, and how it looks now in 1943 when the Jews are being evacuated completely, I realize just what has been achieved in this sector." In June the last employees of the Reich Organization of Jews in Germany received deportation orders. Nearly all the 15,000 Jews still alive in Germany in 1944 lived in "privileged marriages," many of them confined like the Klemperers in "Jew houses" and assigned menial labor. Life remained dangerous for surviving Jews, since local authorities tried, with some success, to deport them at the very end of the war. "Privileges" also ended with the death of Aryan partners. In the case of "Aryan cancer" and the "Jewish star," a story related by Klemperer, physicians recommended that the Jewish wife of an Aryan man slowly dying of cancer try to alleviate his suffering, although any effort she made would hasten the moment when she, as a Jewish widow, would be forced to place herself on the lists of potential deportees.[40] Since 1939, 134,000 Germans had been deported because they were legally defined as "racial Jews" according to the Nuremberg Laws; about 7,000 survived the Nazi assault.

Across Europe, the transit camps, where the Gestapo assembled Jews before deporting them to death camps, provided witnesses a special platform to collect knowledge about what was happening, as Klemperer himself was doing from his "Jew house." Once the deportations took place, however, the collection of evidence ended. As Philip Mechanicus, who "week after week" had seen "how thousands of Jews were rounded up like in cattle cars and taken to an unknown destination," pointed out from Westerbork, in Holland: "And not a single Jew has come back to give us a report." Incomplete reports did exist from Theresienstadt in 1942 and 1943 and even from some of the ghettos in the General Gouvernement.[41] On the whole, however, deported friends and family simply disappeared into a territory that rumor and suspicion made frightening but the absence of certain knowledge kept vague and undefined. It was from this *Vorhof zur Hölle,* or "Hell's Kitchen," as Westerbork was called by inmates, from other transit camps or Theresienstadt, from ghettos such as Lodz and Warsaw, or from the precarious safety of a "privileged marriage" that it was possible to witness and document the catastrophe that was engulfing Jews in Europe. In these perilous places, thousands of Jews took on the roles of diarist, chronicler, archivist, or historian. Chaim Kaplan described his "sacred task" as a diarist in the Warsaw Ghetto as a "flame imprisoned in my bones, burning inside me, screaming: Write!"[42]

Eyewitness accounts described many of the same things, as Sandra Ziegler notes:

> arrival in the camp, number, barbed wire, roll call, selection, transport, delousing, showers, soup, bread, illness, heaven, hell, heart,

eyes, ships, trees, clouds, SS uniforms, helmets, boots, guns, dogs, cars, marches, yelled orders, cups, spoons, gas chambers and crematoriums, lilies, sand, railroads, "train on the wrong track," final destination, children, laughter, hunger pains, shaven heads, barracks, sport, camp boulevard, lists, Jewish police, soup, bread, suitcases, labor detail, transport, postponement, Berlin, Den Haag, Amsterdam, America, England, Allies, fate, ordeal, final solution, God.[43]

It was from this terrible place in European history that Jews discussed the course of the war, in which now both the Soviet Union and the United States were fighting against Nazi Germany. Some people were optimistic about the course of the war; others were pessimistic about either the moral fiber of the Allied nations or their ability to beat the Germans in time to save Jews. In the Warsaw Ghetto, at least until the "Great Deportation" in the summer of 1942, Chaim Kaplan "described how people were able to build feasts of hope from the smallest morsels."[44] Jewish diarists attempted to calculate German intentions and to make sense of the extreme conditions in which they found themselves. It was in assembly points across the German Reich that prisoners debated whether they would be able to return home or forgive Germans. For the most part, until 1942, people awaiting deportation could not believe that the Nazis intended to kill all Jews, even when the BBC reported on the murder of an estimated 700,000 Jews as of June 1942.

Reading and writing depended on certain resources: paper and pen, of course, and a place to store personal items, and also a zone of privacy and security beyond the reach of Nazi jailers. These existed in transit camps and "Jew houses," but once chroniclers were deported in freight cars to death camps it was nearly impossible to write. It was at the moment of deportation that the diaries written by Philip Mechanicus and Elly Hillesum in Westerbork come to an end and when diarists left behind their diaries to live days in the death camps that, to use Alexandra Garbarini's formulation, were numbered but not recorded. The inability to report on the mass murder of Jews, Gypsies, and prisoners of war and thereby to establish foundations of postwar memory was almost complete. The most detailed records such as the diary kept by Victor Klemperer in order to "bear witness, precise witness" could not witness the horrifying outcome of the Nazis' intentions to kill all Jews in Europe. "Whoever writes, lives," summarized Ruth Kluger in her harsh assessment of autobiographical texts such as her own: "The report, initially undertaken in order to bear witness to hopelessness, slips out of the author's hand to blossom into an 'escape story.'"[45]

Outside the death camps themselves, the Jews who probably acquired the clearest knowledge of the Holocaust were the inhabitants of the ghettos in Poland. During the forty-six days of the "Great Deportation," when the Germans transported five out of six of the 300,000 inhabitants of the Warsaw Ghetto to the death camp at Treblinka between 22 July and 12 September 1942, when 2,000 to 10,000 deportees assembled on the Umschlagplatz on the ghetto's edge every day, it became plain to survivors that in killing able-bodied workers the Germans intended to kill all Jews. "God! Are we really to be exterminated down to the very last of us?" asked Abraham Lewin on 28 August 1942. "We know that whole communities have been wiped off the face of the earth," and he made the bitter estimation in light of this new knowledge: "we can say that of the two million Jews of the *gubernia*," or General Gouvernement, "about 10 percent are left . . . Polish Jewry is finished, it exists no more." At the same time, Lewin learned that western European Jews were being killed in the death camps as well. The large numbers of Jews who remained in the ghetto in Lodz until their final deportation in summer 1944 also acquired knowledge about the Holocaust; many inhabitants recognized the clothes of deported residents when these were recycled for reuse in the ghetto. Writing from Warsaw or Lodz, or from hiding outside the camps in 1942, "one diarist after another had reached the conclusion that no segment of the Jewish population would be spared when the Germans began to deport Jews in that year regardless of their designation as workers." For the Jews, "the war is already lost," realized Margarete Holländer.[46]

That these diaries exist at all is remarkable. Some were saved by non-Jewish friends, others were smuggled out of the camps or hidden in attics; one was found with pages ripped out on top of a stove in a house in Lodz, another by the side of the road along which the Jews of Stanislawow had been marched before they were shot in an outlying cemetery. This is the same "Stanislau" from where ethnic Germans had been repatriated into the Reich in 1939 and to where they were resettled in new colonies in 1942. The diary entries that can be read today are shards of the evidence that, as Garbarini points out, "annihilation is incomplete when memory is preserved."[47] This evidence is telling, since the Nazis tried to silence Jews and to speak in their name as victorious racial overlords. But the texts of persecuted Jews also mark off silence that the deportations finally imposed. Between the time when Irène Némirovsky wrote notes for her novel about Germany's war on France ("reread Tolstoy," she reminded herself in June 1942) or smuggled letters to her children from the holding camp in Pithiviers, near Orléans, after her arrest by the French police in July 1942, and the time when her daughters made a sign with their names on it and went each day to wait for their mother at Paris' Gare de l'Est, where survivors from the camps were beginning to arrive in the late spring of 1945, there is a great deal that is unknown. (Némirovsky was deported to Auschwitz on 17 July 1943; she was murdered there on 17 August.) Diaries and novels were written on the edges of calamity, where knowledge was incomplete, precision impossible, the end not known. But the bitterness and sadness that Denise and Elisabeth shared when they turned around and left the Gare de l'Est for the last time they also shared with thousands of Jews and Gypsies who had been transported from places like Pithiviers to places like Auschwitz, a journey for which Tolstoy was not a guide.[48]

German Witnesses

German "Aryans" talked furtively but frankly about the mass shootings in the Soviet Union in the fall of 1941. The letters soldiers sent home from the front and later the reports they delivered when they returned on leave spread the news to German households. The startling facts that women and children were included in the killing operations, that victims had been forced to undress before being shot, and that Jews fell into open graves left such strong, frightening impressions on the minds of Germans that these images absorbed almost all the information about the deportation of Jewish neighbors and their fate in the East until the very end of the war. What Ruth Andreas-Friedrich wrote in her diary in 1944 were the stories from 1941 and 1942: "'They make them dig their own graves,' people are whispering. 'They take their clothes away—shoes, shirt. They send them to their death naked.'"[49] By contrast, knowledge about the industrialized killing process, in which Jews from across Germany and Europe were sent either directly or indirectly via assembly camps such as Theresienstadt to facilities with chambers into which gas was pumped until everyone who had been shut inside was asphyxiated, was much more imprecise. Rumors circulated about victims gassed in trains or in tunnels, which Klemperer had heard, but there was little concrete knowledge about Auschwitz, a town inside the expanded borders of Germany in which over one million Jews were murdered between 1942 and 1945. Mass shootings, ditches, self-dug graves remained the dominant images. As long as the deportations were linked with the shootings in the Soviet Union rather than with systematic gassing in the city of Auschwitz, connected as it was to the German telephone network with the area code 2258, then the fate of the Jews was more easily pushed into another faraway, less knowable universe. "They went away, went into a dim darkness," wrote one sympathetic observer.[50] Incarcerated Jews in Westerbork or Lodz themselves used a corrupt, proliferating vocabulary of evacuation and resettlement.

The news of gassings was filtered, first by the euphemisms of the racial administrators, who, once a territorial solution to the "Jewish problem" gave way to extermination, retained the cynical vocabulary of "deportation," "resettlement," "migration," and "work service"; and second by the brutal but still obfuscatory language of the SS itself, which referred to "working through" *(verarbeiten)* "arrivals," "pieces," and "cargo."[51] It is also likely that the Nazis came to believe that the German people were not ready for the knowledge of the systematic murder of European Jews. Nazis and other Germans constantly monitored themselves for their feelings of humanity or *Gefühlsduselei* (cheap sentimentality) and armored themselves with arguments about the righteousness of Germany's actions in the wake of all that its people had suffered, but they never completely freed themselves from previously authoritative moral judgments about the sanctity of life. This ambivalence inhibited open talk about extermination. Auschwitz remained shocking in the Third Reich. Even when Himmler spoke openly about the murder of Jews, as he did to party leaders in his infamous speech in Posen on 6 October 1943, he did not mention gas chambers. For Germans and Jews alike, during the war and for many decades thereafter, the facts of Auschwitz were extremely difficult to apprehend: the truth of the matter "exceeds our worst fears," wrote Ursula von Kardorff on 27 December 1944, and it continues to do so in ways that we cannot know.[52]

Knowledge about the "final solution" was also shaped by the growing costs of the war. Deportations took place just as Germans began to comprehend the war as a more protracted struggle of survival between themselves and the Russians and to concentrate on their own dire problems. Hitler had authorized the mass murder of

Soviet Jews in July and agreed to commence deportations of German Jews in September 1941, when he still contemplated total victory, but Germans themselves saw the deportation process unfold in November and December 1941, when the German offensive had been pushed back. Moreover, the aerial bombardment of German cities, which grew more serious in the second half of 1941 and intensified dramatically in 1942 and especially 1943, was frequently regarded as commensurate with or punishment for the murder of the Jews, a settling of accounts. Yet as it became clear that the Third Reich was losing the war, in the months after Stalingrad, Germans, out of a mixture of fear, guilt, and shame, sought to avoid entanglement in the "Jewish question" altogether. Toward the end of the war, many people deliberately screened out information about the Jews, the camps, and the murders. Topics that had featured in conversations in 1941 and 1942 no longer did so in 1943 and 1944. Thus, in an effort not to become accomplices to the murder of Jews, Germans became accomplices to the dismemberment of the knowledge about murder. The course of the war strongly regulated how Germans stored, picked up, and passed on knowledge of the Holocaust.

It is difficult to get at the voices of ordinary Germans in the war years. Police and Gestapo reports were filtered at various levels and were designed as much to convey unanimity as to evaluate dissent. But two unofficial reports, both from the west German city of Münster, provide clues about the conversations German civilians had about the deportations of German Jews. In an unpublished "chronicle of the war," an unidentified historian left this report of December 1941:

> Today I belonged to those who check out two more taverns and mix with the guests at the bar. In the second place in the Aegidistrasse, as I stand among midlevel civil servants, artisans, and businessmen, I hear that all the Jews will have to leave Münster by the thirteenth of the month. This news is followed up with an animated discussion.

Most of the drinkers at the bar completely support this measure. The Jews will be put in large labor camps in the East so that they can work there and also they will free up urgently needed apartments in Münster. That's right, that's right, echoes the chorus of approval from bystanders who now know that the housing shortage will be alleviated . . . In town even women take an active interest in the rumors about the transport of the Jews.[53]

The chronicle indicates that the deportations were the stuff of daily conversations both among men in taverns and among women on the street. Although this Nazi loyalist portrayed the various elements of German society, "civil servants, artisans, and businessmen," to be "very satisfied," the discussions were nonetheless "animated" and therefore possibly contentious. Moreover, the deportations were linked to housing, which, in west German cities that had been bombed by the British since 1940, was scarce. The housing shortage served as a pretext for the deportations in Hamburg, where in the summer of 1941 Gauleiter Karl Kaufmann repeatedly urged authorities in Berlin to remove Jews in order to provide rooms for Germans.[54] As the bombing grew worse, Germans began to speak as victims, and they contemplated the fate of the Jews in proportion to their own suffering. And finally there is the fact of the city chronicle itself. There were repeated attempts to preserve the deportation of the Jews in the archive of what was to be a triumphant history of the Third Reich. In Berlin, Goebbels hoped to film deportations, and in Stuttgart and Nuremberg authorities in fact filmed the assembly and entraining of Jews in November 1941. In Bad Neustadt local Nazis photographed elderly, malnourished Jews on 22 April 1942 as they stood before the fountain in the marketplace and even arranged group shots before marching their neighbors to the train station for deportation. They later enlarged the photographs and hung them in picture windows in the center of town to document the successful action.[55]

Paulheinz Wantzen, the Münster newspaper editor, left a similar account in his diary. In early November 1941 he noted the rumors about impending deportations; a few weeks later he jotted down a reminder "to get material and details after the fact," since he had been in Berlin when the first of Münster's Jews had been deported. Moreover, he, too, linked the deportations to the reallocation of apartments to bombed-out Germans. Wantzen went on to assert that the new rigors of war with the Soviet Union required the deportations, although he never spelled out his logic: "the German people, who until recently still had a completely humanitarian sense of sympathy, have finally, in the shadow of events in the East, abandoned it. We are cured forever." The diary also recorded the deportation of the last of Münster's Jews on 30 July 1942. They would have been mostly elderly Jews, since the first deportations in Münster had been restricted to people under the age of sixty-five. It turned out that a former university professor "struggled with his hands and feet against his deportation, while the others went willingly and gave generous tips to several men from the Security Service who helped them with their heavy suitcases, since some of these Jews were already just too flabby. One SD man is said to have made ninety marks."[56] Like his diary entry of what "you hear" about marking Jews with the Star of David, Wantzen's writing passed along gossip circulating at the time. The account was framed in a way that would limit empathy, which Wantzen described as a sickness from which he found himself to be "cured." Gossip introduced the misbehaved professor and flabby, suckered Jews. Not everyone responded as Wantzen did, but the evidence suggests that the daily traffic in shared news included the plight of Jews but worked against any identification with them.

The deportations were not always visible, since many Jews in Germany were already confined in assembly camps on the edge of cities. But in Berlin and Münster, neighbors monitored the departure of Jews—"'the one on the second floor? The Jewess, you mean,' says the concierge. 'They came and took her away. Day before yesterday. Oh, along about six'"—and watched as they were marched off. Inge Deutschkron recalled the pedestrians walking about during Berlin's "factory actions" in February 1943: "people on the street stand still, whispering to each other. Then they quickly go on their way, back into the security of their homes." Germans might have felt good reason to do nothing more than turn away; in his widely read (and rebroadcast) November 1941 article that accompanied the deportations, "The Jews are Guilty!" Goebbels threatened Germans who associated with "the Jew": "Anyone who continues to uphold personal contacts with him," he wrote, "belongs to him and must be regarded and treated as a Jew." Around the same time, Klemperer himself found it "courageous" that a non-Jewish acquaintance talked to him in the streetcar, since the radio "is said to have explicitly warned against any association with Jews."[57] After the fall of 1941, Germans who had a friendly word or brought food to a Jewish neighbor exercised more caution. Thus it was mostly in silence that Germans, wherever Jews lived, watched the police deport their neighbors.

Here and there, however, crowds gathered to scold the SS and to debate the deportations, as a secret police report from Detmold in July 1942 revealed:

> It could be observed that a large number of older people's comrades generally criticized the measure to transport the Jews out of Germany. All sorts of justifications were made more or less openly taking a stand against the transport. It was said that the Jews in Germany were condemned to die out as it was . . . Even those comrades who had proven their National Socialist convictions, even when it had not been in their interest, stood up for the Jews. From among those loyal to the church came the warning: "that the German people will one day await God's judgment." National Socialist loyalists tried to make it clear to those who thought differently that the action was completely justified and urgently necessary. They were contra-

dicted with the argument that the old Jews can't do us any harm anymore, since they wouldn't "hurt a fly."[58]

In this case, it seems clear that most onlookers opposed the second round of deportations, which was made up of mostly elderly Jews, and that some people in the crowd tried to persuade others by using morally principled arguments, which prompted the informant to think of them as religious, sentimental, and somewhat old-fashioned, or that they advanced more utilitarian arguments about the elderly Jews' dying out, which might have made more sense to Nazi loyalists.

There must have been enough disconcerting opposition to the anti-Jewish actions for security forces to falsify reports, as they did in Bielefeld, where they turned the population's "apprehension" into "appreciation."[59] But other reports indicated that applause greeted columns of Jews on the way to train stations. Children heckled—Klemperer reported that Hitler Youths were his worst tormentors—but adults also sent Jews off with horrible adieus: "Just look at those cheeky Jews!" "Now they're marching into the ghetto"; "Just a bunch of useless eaters!" These dirty phrases complemented the ice-cold cynicism of German authorities who had rounded up "you Saras and Israels," laughed at the fate of the "chosen people," and sent them off as human cargo. Frank Bajohr argues that the deportations were extraordinary events in locally bound histories, something that allowed residents to transgress normal rules of social interaction.[60] But antisemitic feelings ran deeper than that; race baiting had always drawn a crowd in the Third Reich, from the humiliation of Jews in the first weeks of the regime, to the punishments meted out to German women accused of sleeping with Poles and other alleged racial inferiors during the war, to the heckling of deportees. Even after the war, when the extent of the Holocaust was well known, many Germans interviewed by the Americans stuck to their old positions. Although the murder of

Jews was a *Kulturschande,* a scandal, one medical student from Munich explained, "I do think that during the war it would have been all right to have German Jews *interned*—otherwise, from the treatment they received before the war, they would naturally have hindered the war effort." In other words, the persecution of Jews before 1941 justified their deportation after 1941. "Most Jews, as you know," insisted a former Red Cross nurse in Kempten, "fought against National Socialism, and in time of war that cannot be tolerated."[61]

Germans were not merely spectators. As Christopher Browning notes, "at the highest level the Finance Ministry, Foreign Office, and Transportation Ministry had all been eager participants. At the local level, small-town mayors ensured that their handful of Jews were included, cleaning ladies collected overtime pay to conduct strip searches of the female deportees," and the German Red Cross provided food and hot drinks for the SS guards who accompanied the transports.[62] The Gestapo, their secretaries, and the cleaning ladies gathered together for a party after successfully deporting the first 1,000 Nuremberg Jews on 29 November 1941. While a local tavernkeeper served drinks, the group snacked on food pilfered from the evacuated Jews, raffled off items found in their stolen bags, and danced the polka to accordion music.[63] Eleven Jews from this transport survived the Holocaust. In Detmold, civil servants updated files by recording the forwarding addresses of former Jewish residents: "departed to an unknown location," "departed to the East." The file of one debtor was closed in July 1942 because the case worker assumed "that Steinweg will never return to Detmold."[64]

Even more astonishing were the public auctions that distributed the expropriated property of Germany's Jews. Knowledge about these auctions was so completely suppressed in the postwar years that historians have only in the last ten years or so become aware of their extent. Since the property of Jews who crossed the German

border belonged to the state, according to timely legislation promulgated in November 1941, local and federal officials wrote back
and forth about which goods of deported residents to requisition
for their purposes. Civil servants in Württemberg, for example,
contemplated the rich booty suddenly available in the town of Baisingen: "Dr. Schmal's easy chair is probably not right for the main
office; I suggest instead that we take Wolff's plush chair as well as
Ebert's chaise longue, since it is particularly nice." After the first-
rate furniture belonging to Schmal, Wolff, and Ebert had been stolen, ordinary Germans received an opportunity to plunder what remained. Some residents even attempted to reserve in advance desirable property before deportations took place. German Jews still
lived in Baisingen when on 11 May 1942 finance officials held a
public auction directly outside one of the large shuttered houses to
offer up all sorts of household goods for cash. Since the property of
Jews was generally regarded to be of high quality, and Germans
had money but not much to spend it on, there were many interested parties about town. Other Baisingers were appalled by the
proceedings. Many years later one woman remembered asking her
mother to take a look at the fine bed linens for sale: "No, no, she
couldn't use none of it," the daughter recalled forty years later;
"she couldn't sleep in them, she'd not get her rest anymore."[65]

Still crowds gathered around the stuff. "We have to keep our
rooms locked," reported Victor Klemperer at Christmastime 1942,
"because the place is crowded with people inspecting the goods."
These were the possessions of the Jacobys, who had just been deported from the "Jew house" in which the Klemperers also lived.
The art and antiques of the Jacobys in Dresden were just a fraction
of the goods that German officials stole. It took 30,000 freight cars
to haul into Germany the requisitioned goods of west European
Jews. Most of this was destined for cities that had been bombed. A
notice in the *Oldenburger Staatszeitung* advertised a sale at Strang-
mann's tavern on Sunday, 25 July 1943: "Porcelain, enamel goods,

beds, and linens for sale." Bombed-out residents had first pick at four in the afternoon, followed by "large families and newlyweds" at half-past four, and everybody else at five. Since much of the loot came from Holland, Oldenburgers referred to the goods as "Dutch furniture."[66] How many people participated in the auctions? Frank Bajohr estimates that 30,000 Jewish households in Germany and western Europe were broken up into 100,000 Aryan homes in Hamburg alone.[67] Certainly not most Germans, but considerable numbers relaxed in chairs and slept in sheets that had once belonged to their Jewish neighbors.

The terrible destruction wreaked by Allied bombings made it easier to justify disposing of Jewish property, since the Jews were held partially responsible for the attacks. Auctions offered an unexpected opportunity to acquire hard-to-get high-quality items in an increasingly spartan war economy, but they also expressed the sense of entitlement that Germans came to feel vis-à-vis Jews, who, they half believed, had just bombed them out. However, even as Germans spun out these fantasies and reduced Jews to the crude racial stereotype of international conspirators, they indicated that they knew about the deportations and the killings for which the Jews, in this convoluted scenario, were now seeking revenge.

The association between Jews and Allied air raids needs to be unpacked. The relatively light destruction of the first British bomber runs in 1941 had in some west German cities served as a premise for demands to deport Jews. By the middle of 1942, when more than half of Germany's Jews had already been deported and when the first major air raids against Hamburg and Cologne had taken place, the argument was reversed, and Jews were blamed for the bombing, which then served as an argument or justification for their dispossession and deportation. What is interesting, however, is that while regime propaganda simply put the blame on international Jewry, talk on the street went further and blamed the Jews who, from their powerful positions abroad, were taking revenge on

Germany for the cruel treatment they had suffered. Or else, the Allies were punishing Germany, or Germany was being punished in some sort of divine reckoning, for persecuting the Jews. With this idea of retaliation, public opinion established a link between what had happened to Jews and what was happening to Germans. Rumors even circulated that cities such as Würzburg had not been bombed because the synagogue there had been spared in 1938 (which was not true: all seven had been destroyed or damaged in the pogrom) or that the city had suddenly become vulnerable once it had deported its last Jew, who was said to have told the townspeople as much upon his departure.[68] These urban legends could and did imply fundamental criticism of the deportations. Even as the air raids grew worse, the German crime with which they were implicitly linked remained large enough to sustain the equivalency all the way to the end of the war. In these wild scenarios, no one ever said that Jews went overboard in the destruction they meted out. But if popular reactions to the air raids revealed guilty knowledge about the treatment of the Jews, the association between persecution and bombing also enabled Germans to relieve themselves of guilt, since they had become victims, too. When it came to the Jews, many Germans let themselves be bombed into a clear conscience.

In other versions, Germans blamed Jews for directly working against them, making Jews out to be so powerful that they were nothing less than Nazi caricatures of the Jewish world conspiracy. In their "exit interviews" from the Third Reich, German informants repeatedly brought up the power of Jewish capital. "The reason why Germany lost the war," argued one thirty-eight-year-old housewife from Hamburg whom American interviewers coded as "anti-Nazi," "is because she persecuted the Jews . . . and the Jews have the Capital. Everybody knows that."[69] The last three words were a creation of the Third Reich. "We could not win this war," insisted a carpenter in Munich, and he began his long list. First "there was the persecution of the Jews which brought all the Jews in the world against us." According to one housekeeper, a self-professed Nazi, the party had made a tactical mistake: "Do you think that the Americans, who have always stuck together with the Jews, would have bombed our cities if they had known that there were Jews living there?"[70] She implied that the Germans should have kept Jews in cities as hostages, a notion that circulated throughout the war. But for all their blunders, the Nazis had obviously taught their racial lessons well, since, in the minds of countless civilians, German Jews loomed as a powerful international, almost Americanized force. Jewish neighbors had become a dangerous, terrifying abstraction, "the Jew"; such a perception had been the Nazi aim all along. Among all these hundreds of interviews stored in College Park, Maryland, the closest an informant comes to talking about a particular Jew is a man named Rothschild, who admitted his sympathy for Jews since he was constantly being mistaken for one: "in this way, I came to sympathize with the plight of the Jews more than I would otherwise perhaps have done."[71]

Once German Jews had been deported and their goods auctioned off, they were largely forgotten except perhaps as the bogeymen of the air war. After 1943 the regime's antisemitic propaganda was curtailed because the "Jewish problem" had in the main been resolved. Only a few people attempted to imagine or pin down the fate of their neighbors as Ruth Andreas-Friedrich did in Berlin. Her honest desire to humanize the fate of friends translated into an honest inability to understand the extent of the crime the Nazis had committed. "This horror is so inconceivable that imagination rebels at grasping it as a reality," she wrote in February 1944:

Some sort of contact is broken here; some conclusion is simply not drawn. It isn't Heinrich Muehsam that they're sending to the gas chamber. It can't be Anna Lehmann, Margot Rosenthal, or Peter Tarnowsky digging a grave in some remote desolation under the whiplash of the SS. And certainly not little Evelyne, who was so proud of having once eaten a pear in her four years of life. No, Evelyne Jakob died differently from those tormented ones; she died more humanly, more comprehensibly, more imaginably.[72]

With its "No" that must be there, but is not, this diary entry is as clear as any non-Jewish German text about what the "final solution" meant while it was taking place. Andreas-Friedrich referred directly to gas chambers, not to the gas vans or tunnels. But she also kept this specific knowledge tied to gravedigging and thus to mass shootings in fields and forests. News from the eastern front in the summer and fall of 1941 and rumors about the killings of Berlin Jews in Riga in November 1941 structured what most Germans knew about the Holocaust before 1945. They imagined Babi Yar, but not Auschwitz, despite direct references to the death camps on BBC broadcasts in June 1942 and again in June 1944. (Karl Duerkefälden was an exception: given what his brother-in-law had passed on about the massacres in Russia in 1941 and what Hitler himself had said about the "extermination" of the Jews in 1942, he believed BBC reports about gassing.)[73] This template of knowledge kept anti-Jewish actions tied to specific events or massacres, not to an ongoing centralized process of extermination.

Even such an informed journalist as Ursula von Kardorff, alert to the crimes of the regime and connected to resistance circles, had not heard of Auschwitz until she finally learned of the enormity of the mass murder from the *Journal de Genève* in December 1944. She locked herself in a toilet and pronounced the unfamiliar name: "The camp is said to be in a place called Auschwitz." Sifting the evidence, she noted that "the article seemed serious, didn't sound like atrocity propaganda." What she had read was a secondhand report based on the testimony of two Czech Jews, Rudolf Vrba and Alfred Wetzler, who in April 1944 escaped from Auschwitz with intimate details of the extermination process and a label from a can of

Zyklon B gas. Although inmates in Auschwitz actually anticipated Allied help during the spring and summer of 1944 ("almost a month had passed since the flight"), which would have been confirmation that Vrba and Wetzler had accomplished their task, the report did not even reach the World Jewish Congress and the International Red Cross in Switzerland until June. The Swiss newspaper that Kardorff read in Berlin six months later provided details (the BBC had broadcast a summary at the end of June 1944): "Apparently the Jews are being systematically gassed there. They are led into a large washing room, allegedly to shower, then gas is pumped in through invisible pipes. Until everyone is dead. The corpses are burned." Kardorff then wrote in her diary: "Have I now to believe this terrible report?"[74] Her comment is both strange and character- istic of her compatriots. Kardorff seems to stop to consider what the knowledge about Auschwitz will do to her, presumably as a German. Even for this anti-Nazi, it was frightening to contemplate the ways in which she would have to rethink her autobiography, the military service of her brothers, and the history of her prominent family and the country in general. (This difficulty would eventually prompt the observation that the Germans will never forgive the Jews for Auschwitz.)

René Schindler, traveling through Germany in the fall of 1944, detected a growing sense of shame, which he attributed not only to Germany's military defeats but to foreign broadcasts about the fate of European Jews. The color of shame was washed out by defensive maneuvers, however. "Again and again in discussions about this topic emphasis is put on the leading role of the party," commented Schindler; "SS and security service, Gestapo . . . stand in clear con- trast to the Wehrmacht, for example."[75] Even before the war had ended, questions about complicity were answered with untenable but conscience-easing distinctions between the Wehrmacht and the party, between good Germans and bad Nazis, between virtuous patriotic efforts and secretive actions taken in "night and fog."

Knowledge about the Holocaust was perceived as a direct assault on German identity.

In sum, there was general knowledge about the deportations as a result of firsthand reports about widespread shootings of unarmed civilians in the Soviet Union. As a result, the Holocaust was largely contained by the knowledge of mass murder on the military front. In the early 1940s many Germans knew brutal facts: the inclusion of women and children in the ranks of innocent murdered Jews, the procedures that left victims naked at the edge of pits, and also the scale of massacres such as Babi Yar. They also understood the entanglement of "ordinary Germans" serving in the Wehrmacht in the murders. But without specific knowledge of Auschwitz, the killings could be regarded as events and episodes, pogromlike detonations in a brutal war which did not have the character of systematic or patterned extermination and which could conceivably leave many deported Jews alive. Outside Poland, Jewish observers at the time also tended to see the murders as pogroms, which, as the historical record of centuries of persecution demonstrated, had destroyed communities but not extinguished a civilization. Even Victor Klemperer never reached the definitive conclusion that the main point of deporting Jews from Dresden was to kill them. Rumors about gas were too vague to dislodge the dominant image of shootings in the faroff terrain of the East.

A second point: most Germans probably objected to the deportations of their Jewish neighbors, but that opposition was overlaid by the emergence of the abstract image of the Jew as a monolithic, dangerous force precisely at the moment when military setbacks and bombing raids began to preoccupy German thoughts. The effect was growing indifference to the fate of Jews. The difficult course of the war after 1941 also made it easier for civilians to participate in the auctions of Jewish household goods, since they saw themselves as victims in a war in which Jews might well be playing some sort of nefarious role. Opinions on the Jews most likely shifted during the war, so that Germans who opposed the seizure of Jewish neighbors down the street in 1941 may well have come to accept crude racial stereotypes and even endorsed the transfer of the Jewish population when the air war began to inflict serious damage after 1943. After the war, surveys confirmed that a large segment of the German people had come to agree with the basic premises underlying Nazi policies on the Jews.[76]

When Walter Kassler came home to Celle on leave from the Soviet Union in June 1942 he expressed a hodgepodge of contradictory views about the genocidal actions he had witnessed there. "Walter emphasized repeatedly, 'We can be happy that we are not Jews.'" This was the swaggering, victorious warrior speaking, but Kassler was now at home with his sister and brother-in-law and probably needed to provide a little more in the way of moral justification. "At first I didn't understand," he explained, "but now I know; it is a matter of existence or nonexistence." Still, his brother-in-law Karl Dürkefälden, the old Social Democrat, pressed the point: "But that's murder." Certainly the rest of the world would consider the shooting of civilians murder, a realization that made Kassler briefly evaluate the actions of the Germans from the perspective of the enemy. He replied to Karl: "Certainly it has gone so far that they will do to us as we have done to them, if we should lose the war."[77] The perpetrator realized his crime at the moment he contemplated his own defeat and had to commit himself to the achievement of victory so that the crime would not be exposed and punishment would not follow.

It was partly on this commitment that the extraordinary tenacity of German soldiers was based in the last, terrible years of the war. Goebbels came to the same conclusion after Stalingrad. The murder of so many Jews meant that there was no going back: "And that is a good thing. Experience shows that a movement and a people who have burned the bridges behind them fight with much greater determination than those who are still able to retreat."[78] In other words, the crimes against the Jews provided the Germans with the will to victory in what British propagandists aptly described, in a play on the "Strength through Joy" movement, as "Strength through Fear." Knowledge of the Holocaust was buttressed by the Nazis' attempt to make the German population understand that the bridges had been burned and that there was no choice but to fight on.

Perpetrators and Victims

"What sort of fate do we and Germany face??? Do we have to be completely beaten down again? Can heaven permit our destruction??? Such a faithful, courageous people cannot be *allowed* to go under—even if maybe mistakes were made, but the others also made mistakes . . . There has never been a people who have undertaken such great accomplishments; we can't just be annihilated. We have the same right to live as any other people. Why should we alone be subjugated?"[79] Lore Walb, now twenty-three years old, confided her despair to her diary at the end of November 1942, after German troops had given up Tobruk in North Africa and found themselves besieged in Stalingrad. The downfall she feared was not the physical destruction that threatened Jewish deportees, who also asked themselves why they were condemned to die and why they could not live. It was the prospect of the downfall of the nation that overwhelmed her. Walb retraced the narrative of Germany's redemption from the disaster that she believed had befallen it in 1918, when, as the Nazis saw it, the home front had buckled, along the path to rebirth, which Germans had achieved thanks to National Socialism. Germany was both a beleaguered victim, in 1942 as in 1918, and the redeemed subject of its own history, which it mastered through faith and courage. In the shock of defeat, Walb and millions of other Germans desperately attempted to ward off a repetition of the catastrophe of 1918, which loomed as a persistent, proximate danger.

Stationed in France, the soldier Heinrich Böll, who in ten years would emerge as a gifted novelist, had come to similar conclusions. Without mentioning Stalingrad, he wrote to his wife, Annemarie, in the shadow cast by the battle in December 1942: "The war is steadily taking on a gray, pitiless form, no longer so victorious . . . or exhilarating as in the beginning; it has become hard and bitter." Like many other soldiers, he went on to contemplate defeat. "God willing," he hoped, "everything will turn out alright. It would be terrible if everything once again is for nothing . . . if in a pure political sense it is all in vain for our people. We have already had at least twenty bitter poor and unhappy years since Versailles." Böll was not a Nazi, but he loved Germany and could not imagine losing "the freedom" the Nazis had gained for it: "freedom we have come to know . . . but peace, peace we don't know yet." After Stalingrad, he had the frightening impression of being seen by the French once again as one of the vanquished; he contemplated his own disintegration. "The French have come up with a dirty new trick," he recounted, "which, when I saw it for the first time, hit me like a ton of bricks! Really the effect is amazing; they simply write 1918 on the walls, just the combination of numbers without commentary, just an oppressive little number": 1918.[80]

In these formulations, Nazis and Germans were not the same, but the Nazis were the ones who had made possible the recovery of the nation, a recovery that remained the object of attention and desire. The resulting contrast between the collapse produced in 1918 and the present situation signaled the basic legitimacy of the national revolution of 1933 and of the "new time" it had inaugurated. Soldiers wanted an end to the war, just as civilians expressed dismay with many aspects of Nazi rule, but neither soldiers nor civilians could imagine losing the Germany they believed they had recovered. The year 1918 represented not just military defeat, but complete political and moral chaos, the end of collective national life. The year 1933, by contrast, represented the recovery of national life through the virtues of discipline, unity, and authority. Put another way, after years of war, the pre-1939 years may have come to be seen as prosperous, normal, and so deeply German that it was possible in 1942 to love the Third Reich but to despise the Nazis. In this way, the idea of Germany had been covertly Nazified as well as Aryanized. The majority of Germans preferred to win the war and keep the Nazis than to lose both the war and the Nazis. Very few hoped for Germany's defeat. (A salty Berlin tailor, Hugo B, was one exception: "Every day the same shit. Nothing to eat, nothing proper to drink, no schnapps, no cigars, no pleasure, no variety. And the war just goes on and on . . . The necessary millions will first have to be slaughtered before this stupid human race comes to its senses. This is exactly the way it was in the first world war. So slaughter yourselves. And you can just kiss my ass!" The theologian Dietrich Bonhoeffer was another: "I pray for the defeat of my country," he wrote in 1944.)[81]

In her lament, Lore Walb refers to "mistakes." In a diary that never mentions the word "Jew," it is not clear what she is referring to, but it is difficult to believe that the mistakes mean anything other than the deportation of German Jews or the treatment of occupied populations more generally. The "mistakes" are introduced when she exclaims that the German nation "just can't" go under. Walb conjures up a divine court of history in which the Germans should not go under despite their mistakes. In other words, she embraces both the nation and the guilty knowledge it produced. In the last years of the war, many Germans came to realize that Germany had committed a great crime—and they were more clear about it than Walb—and they worried that if Germany went under it would do so because of this crime. Insofar as Germans did not want to see the defeat of Germany, and very few did, they chose to live with Germany and with the knowledge of its crime. Walb was by no means alone: in the Third Reich, in what Susanne zur Nieden refers to as an "autobiographical pact" with National Socialism, diarists generally avoided the topic of the Jews.[82] If the term collective responsibility is apt at all, and I think we shy away from it too quickly, it is apt not because all or most Germans were perpetrators but because, in the shock of defeat, Germans proved willing to bury knowledge of crimes against Poles, Russians, Jews, and Gypsies so that Nazi Germany might live. Shame trumped guilt.

The shock of defeat was not the fact of military defeat itself, something that was absolute and unconditional in May 1945, but the realization, after the blitzkrieg victories ended in the fall of 1941, that Germany might lose the war and fall to ruin. Just when this shock was experienced varied from person to person. Walb grew concerned as early as December 1941, when the Germans stalled in front of Moscow. "I still believe in victory; victory will be ours because it has to be ours, for we want to live, after all!"[83] For most Germans, the shock came with the Battle of Stalingrad, where the German Sixth Army was destroyed and 90,000 soldiers were taken prisoner in the winter of 1943. It was at this time that Germans began to contemplate defeat and question their loyalties to Hitler. Some people thought that Hitler was no longer mentally fit. In the summer of 1943, things were slipping: the Allies had landed in Sicily, Mussolini had been overthrown, and Anglo-American bombing raids struck relentlessly at German cities. It was no longer possible to contain wild stories about "Goebbels' suicide" or "Göring's fall" that circulated throughout the empire.[84] By the autumn of 1944, when Soviet troops had reached the eastern borders of the German empire and British and American forces approached the western borders, the German people had become deeply pessimistic. Confidence in Germany's survival eroded rapidly and completely after the final Soviet offensive on 12 January 1945. Yet, in face of all this trouble, there was almost no political opposition to the regime right until the end of the war. The basic legitimacy of the Third Reich remained intact because Germans could not envision a desirable alternative to National Socialism. The shaky, unmistakable fluctuations of pessimism and optimism after Stalingrad recorded the mood, but did not derail the alignment of most people with the war effort. What is more, a majority of Germans became ever more enmeshed in the system once they accepted the fierce dictates of total war. They cast their lot with the survival of Nazi Germany, buried the knowledge of murder, and burned their moral and intellectual bridges.

The commitment to fight on rather than lose the war finally withered in the winter and spring of 1945, when fanatical Nazis exhorted the German people to fight to the death so that the idea of an unbowed German nation might live on in history. But short of this redemptive, suicidal self-sacrifice, Germans, taken as a whole, demonstrated remarkable commitment to National Socialism in the war. Not even evidence of discontent at the highest military levels, plain to see with the failed attempt to assassinate Hitler on 20 July 1944, cracked the legitimacy of the regime. Indeed, the plot benefited the regime more than it hurt it. The two collectives, Germans and Nazis, were so thoroughly enmeshed that ordinary people after the war never extended proper honor to the assassins; nor did they purge their neighborhoods of pernicious local Nazi officials. Instead, most Germans amnestied themselves. Their awareness that "the murderers are *unter uns*" at all levels of society explains why the Bundestag overwhelming voted in favor of judicial amnesty in the early 1950s and why this legislation found such broad support among the German public. After all, what was the family going to do after 1945 with the repatriated father who had written to his children during the war: "You can trust your Daddy. He thinks about you all the time and is not shooting immoderately"?[85] Veterans returned home with scary, toxic knowledge that resurfaced in the postwar rush to amnesty everyone except a small band of Nazi criminals at the very top.

When Germans did finally cut themselves off from Hitler, the Nazis, and the Third Reich, they did so not out of a sober assessment of the impossibility of victory, which would have been quite clear to most people in 1944. They cut themselves off largely out of a feeling of having been betrayed. In the "exit interviews" that the Americans conducted in the spring and summer of 1945, German informants generally described their relationship to the Nazis in two ways. Opponents of the regime, particularly older workers and Catholics, stressed their blunt ideological differences with National Socialism, which were no doubt harder in 1945 than in 1940. They often sounded ironic and had clearly thought about the issues that had troubled them for some time. "Instead of the six million unemployed there are now approximately fifteen million dead," wrote a clear-sighted Franz Göll.[86] Otherwise, the subjects the Americans questioned complained that they had been betrayed by Nazi leaders and misled by propaganda of lies and deception. These are the vague, melodramatic, almost hysterical voices of former Nazi loyalists who made up the majority of the German population. Their sense of betrayal rested on a strong identification with the Third Reich right up to the moment of abandonment, when the inability of the Nazis to stabilize the fronts and defend the country, to avenge Allied air attacks with super weaponry, and to rely on anything new in the final stage of the war but a ragtag army of young boys and old men mobilized into the *Volkssturm,* defensive units formed under command of the SS, was exposed. Anger at the Nazis for insisting on the invincibility of the German cause at the cost of thousands of lives helps explain why so many Germans could support the system for so long and then, from one moment to the next, sometime in March, April, May 1945, reject the Nazi leadership. As a result, Germans came to perceive themselves as the victims of a cruel history, in which a series of catastrophes, from Stalingrad to the air raids on German cities to the displacement of millions of people from eastern Germany to the occupation of the country by foreign troops, combined into something that smashed into everyday existence.

Their sense of betrayal, the perception that they had been completely deceived and manipulated, made it difficult for Germans later to examine their own histories in the years 1918–1945. It was hard for the deceived to see themselves as collaborators. They directed their criticism at relatively small numbers of "criminal" high-level Nazis, the puppeteers, in a way that cleared themselves, the puppets. Feelings of betrayal also explain why postwar affirmation of the accomplishments of Nazism, from Autobahns to "Strength through Joy," held longer than loyalties to individual Nazi leaders, Goebbels, Göring, Himmler, the whole bunch who, with the possible exception of Hitler, held very little interest to Germans (as opposed to American or British history buffs) after the war. "Damn them," sixteen-year-old Lieselotte was swearing at the Nazi pack, "these war criminals and Jew murderers," in April 1945, but disbelieving that it was all for naught; it could not be "Germany's end, even if it is ours." Like so many others, she blamed the Nazis for destroying Nazism. As one American intelligence officer explained, "Hitler is blamed for losing the war, not for starting it."[87] In the end, even when people felt released from Hitler's charisma, they still mourned the National Socialism they had helped establish in their deeds and desires. To examine the transformation of German victors into German victims, it is necessary to return one last time to the eastern front at the end of 1941.

Imagining the End of the War

Hitler believed that the 1941 military campaign against the Soviet Union would be over in four months. Because the Nazis did not contemplate a long conflict, military strategists did not plan on or prepare for an operation that extended into winter. These failures in foresight leveled a double blow upon German soldiers, who in the winter of 1941–42 found themselves stuck at the front without proper equipment in unexpectedly harsh conditions, facing increasingly tenacious Soviet troops. By November, Germany's final push to Moscow had been stopped. "The Russians didn't give an inch."[88] Large casualty rates ripped up the chain of command. The war diary of Lieutenant Gerhardt Linke, staff officer in the 185th Infantry Regiment, described "our men," who "are in an extremely dejected mood. Many of them are unfit for action, both from wounds and from sickness, and there is nobody to fill the gaps. Every day our fighting strength diminishes. Two weeks ago there were 70 men in the company, today there are only 40 and tomorrow there will be only 35 . . . Newly appointed unit commanders are poorly trained and unable to cope with the difficult tasks imposed upon them." Then in early December 1941, the Soviets launched their first counteroffensive, relying on reserves the Germans could not match. Not until January 1945 would German divisions be as depleted and at risk as they were in December 1941.[89]

It gradually dawned on German soldiers that they were not fighting inferior men. One man in the infantry raised this question in November 1941: "Why do the Russians fight until the bitter end? That is what we ask ourselves. Why are there so many martyrs for the Bolshevik idea, which must have enormous power?"[90] A German Wehrmacht interrogator who sent unknown numbers of Russian partisans to their deaths also wondered. "What is it, anyhow," he asked himself, "that makes them so? Love of country? Or Communism that has entered their blood and suffused the whole system? It really must be so if some of them, particularly the girls, do not shed a tear when they are beaten and do not flinch when they are led to execution." Obviously the racial and gender categories with which German commanders approached the waging of war had been misleading, if not imprisoning. Well after Stalingrad, almost two years after the first Russian counteroffensive, Goebbels could not understand why, if "every single soldier who comes back from the eastern front personally feels himself to be heads and shoulders above the Bolshevik soldiers," the Germans were "retreating and retreating."[91] In the end, he estimated that the Russians might possess the better Nazis. Soviet generals, he conceded, "are convinced Bolsheviks, extraordinarily energetic figures . . . you can tell from their faces that they are cut from good stock. For the most part these are the sons of workers, cobblers, farmers," the very classes in which Goebbels believed Nazism was rooted. "Well then," he concluded, "we have to come to the painful conclusion that the Soviet military leadership comes from a better class than our own."[92]

Given the problems, the only answer inside this racial scheme was to produce better Germans to fight a ruthless total war. "There is not so much talk about the end of the war anymore," admitted Goebbels about the mood in Berlin at the end of 1941, "because everyone knows that it lies far in the future." But at the same time the long war with Russia squared with Nazi ideas in which national existence was a matter of constant struggle and racial superiority was defined by the willingness to persevere and sacrifice. War came to be "regarded both as the 'highest expression of the life' of a people and as a nation's only chance for survival."[93] Since the very existence of the nation was at stake, it followed that total war would be waged by all necessary means. The only guarantee for the security of the homeland was the extermination of the enemy and the occupation of its living space. Total war was nothing less than the complete operationalization of National Socialism.

In December 1941 and January 1942, German military commanders demanded the utmost of soldiers, ordering them to hold their lines at all cost. To this end, they imposed harsh military discipline. Willy Reese, a twenty-one-year-old bank employee from Duisburg, reported on the despair among frontline troops in early 1942. "One sentry who collapsed in a haystack and carried on sleeping was court-martialed and shot. Another man was unable to find his way" in the dark. The result: "sentenced to death for cowardice in the face of the enemy." No fewer than 15,000 German soldiers were actually executed during the war, most of them in 1944 and 1945. This version of military justice kept soldiers in line; in point of fact it was not so different across Soviet lines. Reese himself felt completely "lost" under these circumstances. He never found the way back to his old self, a separation he continued to track remorsefully until his death in June 1944. Yet he came to accept an awesome, frightening new identity as warrior: "We are war," he wrote, "because we are soldiers."[94] And the war the Germans brought with them wherever they went grew worse and worse. Partisan attacks on the Germans picked up substantially during 1942, especially in Belorussia, where by October fully three-quarters of forest land was held by partisan bands. Goebbels described their activity as "breathtaking." Terrified German soldiers saw "partisan hideouts, partisan camps, partisan bunkers" across the territories they traversed and tried in vain to regain control with a ruthless scorched-earth policy. By the end of 1944 the Wehrmacht had destroyed over 5,000 villages and killed 2.2 million civilians, almost a quarter of the Belorussian population.[95]

In 1943 Willy Reese wrote a poem, "Carnival," admitting what he had done and who he had become. It began with the terrible deed that so many soldiers must have carried out or witnessed:

> Murdered the Jews,
> marched into Russia
> as a roaring horde,
> tyrannized the people,
> hacked them in blood,
> led by a clown,
> raging in blood,
> everyone knows
> what we bring.

Reese was appalled, but he had become a soldier. "I have quit fighting against the unavoidable," he wrote home in 1943.[96] Other soldiers were equally direct about the new men who inhabited their old bodies. As Walter Kassler had come to realize, "now I know, it is a matter of existence or nonexistence." Private Alfred G. used the same expression of intransigence in March 1942: "It is about the struggle of two worldviews: it's either us or the Jews." There was no escaping the new necessities of life on the battle front. "You must wait, sit, devise, and do the worst things," reflected Harry Mielert in March 1943, "act mechanical and hard, look and see the inhuman without batting an eyelid."[97] The majority of soldiers struggled to fit the harsh new type that total, existential war imposed on them even as they longed for their home leaves to come up.

The private spaces of diaries reveal the degree to which Germans tried to be equal to this challenge, accepting the harsh realities of the war and warding off misgivings about its conduct or doubts about final victory. Even as writing allowed individuals to ventilate their uncertainty about National Socialism, it provided them with opportunities to strengthen their resolve and to bolster their loyalties to the nation and the Führer. Lore Walb, for example, used her diary to monitor herself and to fortify her morale ("!!!"). Other observers set for themselves the example of brothers, sons, and fathers: "The front experiences of men frequently became the point of orientation for the behavior of women."[98]

Total war released enormous energies. The Winter Relief campaign for 1941–42 went into high gear to aid the soldiers fighting in the "East." In his appeal, Goebbels requested Germans donate basic items such as gloves, sweaters, and socks; such details made it quite clear to the public how seriously the military effort had faltered. By the middle of January over sixty-seven million items had been collected by two million volunteers across the country.[99] The campaign the next year, in the shadow of Stalingrad, was even bigger. In the spring of 1942, Goebbels' Propaganda Ministry organized a large exhibition to show what the Germans were supposedly up against. Opened on 8 May 1942 in Berlin's Lustgarten, in the center of the city, "the Soviet Paradise" displayed large blown-up photographs depicting the poverty of the Soviet Union and the political terror of the Communists in grisly detail. In the first month, over 750,000 people had seen it, about one in five Berliners. A few people must have wondered why the Germans were having difficulty defeating such an incompetent, self-destructive regime, but most probably went to see for themselves what the struggle was about: "friend" or "foe," "me" or "you." For opponents of the Nazis, on the other hand, total war was the first sign of Nazi weakness. Lili Hahn, alert to German racism because her mother was Jewish, could not contain her sarcasm when she heard the new tone to speeches: "Threatened with extermination? Us? Those were new words out of the mouth of the Führer! Did he breathe something about either/or? Didn't he maintain up to now that Germany was the strongest country in the world, triumphant and unassailable?" By the end of the war the "either/or" would be expressed as "Friss, oder du wirst gefressen!" (Devour them, or you will be devoured!).[100]

The Nazis themselves were not quite sure how far they could push German civilians. The specter of 1918, when Germany had been allegedly "stabbed in the back" by Jews and socialists, hung over all major political decisions. "One could not be cautious enough," Hitler warned. All in all, the Nazis kept Germans buttered up with more plentiful rations than the populations in the Allied nations they were fighting received. Low wartime taxes on the middle classes and none on the working class, and generous allowances to soldiers and their families, kept home-front families relatively content. There was none of the corrosive political grumbling that women and children had passed along while standing in line outside shops during World War I. U.S. military interviews conducted immediately after the war indicated that most people found the rationing system to have been fair. Ordinary Germans fully realized that they had avoided the bitter wartime conditions of 1916 and 1917 because the Reich had forced exactly those conditions on everyone else in Europe in 1943 and 1944. A business manager from Münden put it succinctly in July 1945: "food, stolen from other countries, was plentiful."[101]

Observers from across the political spectrum repeatedly checked the body of the people for signs of discontent, that is, for the symptoms of 1918. It is difficult to pierce the seeming unanimity that the government tried so hard to create. In public, people may have acted in one way but thought in another, a discrepancy that also accompanied the "Heil Hitler!" greeting. Nonetheless, the tendency to pat the people's body down for signs of unrest is telling because it reveals the long-term impact of Germany's defeat in World War I. Like many Germans at the time, Klemperer closely studied the patriotic vocabulary of death notices in newspapers. During the Russian campaign he noted the "decreasing use of the formula 'For Führer and Fatherland.'" Its use was not "infrequent, no, only less frequent, by no means unusual," he corrected himself in March 1942. In Münster, editor Paulheinz Wantzen noticed the same trend and reported that his readers regarded religiously phrased notices or simply the phrase "for *Volk* and Fatherland" as signs of discontent with regime policies. After large air raids, Nazis made it a point to study the mood in working-class neighborhoods. Wantzen wondered whether the Ruhr, badly hit by the Allied bombing since the beginning of the war, would hold; and in Berlin, Goebbels traveled to proletarian Wedding to bolster morale, which he invariably found to be good.[102] The crack in morale was always anticipated, but initial anxiety was usually relieved by demonstrations of national solidarity—to the satisfaction of Goebbels and Wantzen, to the despair of Victor Klemperer and Lili Hahn.

Stalingrad turned World War II. After the defeat of the Sixth Army in the beginning of February 1943, German forces never recovered the strategic offensive. Arrayed against the world, Germany would not have won World War II under any circumstances, but the certainty of an Allied victory became clearer only after Stalingrad. Even so, the war did not end for more than two years because German armies fought with extraordinary tenacity. Although the Germans covered a great deal of territory in their summer 1942 advance into the Caucasus, supply lines and troops were stretched thin along hundreds of kilometers. After punishing battles for control of Stalingrad, the Russians deployed reserve forces who were able to outflank, isolate, and trap the Sixth Army in what was called a *Kessel*, cauldron, at the end of November 1942. At once confident after having emerged from the winter crisis the year before and anxious to demonstrate to his allies that Germany could win the war, Hitler repeatedly reaffirmed his no-retreat order, sealing the fate of the army in Stalingrad, which fought in ever more degraded conditions until it surrendered in broken pieces between 30 January and 2 February 1943.

The defeat at Stalingrad was followed by the lost battle for Tunisia ("Tunisgrad," with 250,000 German prisoners, which Polish patriots celebrated with homemade vodka named "Tunisowka" for the occasion) and the Allied invasion of Sicily. "We just can't get out of these crises anymore," admitted Goebbels. At the end of 1943, "we look back . . . and really see only defeats." Stalingrad, which soldiers fighting there knew as *Stalingrab*, or "Stalin-grave," ended in the deaths of nearly 150,000 German troops, with 90,000 taken prisoner. The Red Army lost nearly 500,000 soldiers there in the seventy-two days of fighting. A German victory would have been even more catastrophic, since Hitler intended to annihilate the civilian population of the city.[103] Even so, given the large number of German dead, the entire texture of the war in Germany began to change. Both soldiers and civilians increasingly saw themselves as defenders of Germany against Russia and as defenders of European culture against Communist tyranny, rather than as the vanguard of a greater German empire. The German aggressor placed himself more frequently in the position of underdog, the victim of a titanic disaster that was robbing the German nation of its historical destiny. As a result, Germans tended to use the passive tense to describe the catastrophe overtaking them. Their private tragedies were magnified by the potential destruction of collective national life and embroidered by networks of memory that gave meaning to the dead. Thus while Stalingrad corroded morale and raised questions about German leadership, it also strengthened feelings of national solidarity in a "community of fate."

Torrents of words followed the defeat at Stalingrad even though the regime had been circumspect while the battle was still raging. National Socialists tried hard to recast the dire situation as an epic drama in which the bitter struggle of Wehrmacht soldiers represented the enduring life of the German nation. Hitler and Goebbels understood exactly what was occurring in Stalingrad. "The troops have nothing to eat, nothing to fire, nothing to shoot with," Goebbels summarized his meeting with a young major who had been flown out of the cauldron. Goebbels then stepped back: "A scene of genuine, classical greatness." This was also precisely the image Göring composed in the first major public response to Stalingrad, which he gave in a speech on 30 January 1943, the tenth anniversary of the Nazi seizure of power. In what the men in Stalingrad actually heard as their own "funeral oratory," Göring compared the Germans on the Volga to the Spartans at Thermopylae, whose sacrifice ensured Sparta's place in history. As Michael Geyer argues, "Stalingrad would be remembered because of the grandeur of defeat, which inscribed the defeated into history. A battle to the death—which is why Nazi propaganda wanted the soldiers in Stalingrad dead and why Göring publicly declared them dead on the eve of the surrender—would make those who fought in Stalingrad immortal."[104] "They died so that Germany might live" announced the headline in the *Völkischer Beobachter*. As many as 100,000 soldiers surrendered, but the regime never acknowledged their existence, preferring to broadcast the epic version of the battle in which soldiers had fought "to the last round." In the coming months, mail from the prisoners would be intercepted lest news of their survival disrupt the myth of their heroic death (though news did leak out). Goebbels was contemptuous of General Paulus, whom Hitler had promoted to field marshal at the last minute in a clear signal to him to continue to fight or take his own life: he had had the choice "either to live fifteen or twenty more years or to immediately acquire an eternal life of fame for many thousands of years."[105] Friedrich Paulus ended up a policeman in East Germany and died in 1957.

The myth of Stalingrad came close to acknowledging that Germany could not win the war but also implied that the example of its struggle would guarantee the future of the nation, unlike the armistice in 1918. Goebbels cast the challenge of fighting the war in epic terms even at the very end, in an extraordinary address in April 1945. "Gentlemen," he addressed officials in his Propaganda Ministry in the wreck of Berlin,

> in a hundred years' time, they will be showing another fine color film describing the terrible days we are living through. Don't you want to play a part in this film, to be brought back to life in a hundred years' time? Everybody now has the chance to choose the part which he will play in the film a hundred years hence . . . Hold out now, so that, a hundred years hence, the audience does not hoot and whistle when you appear on the screen.[106]

In order to rescue German history as the Nazis saw it, and to avoid the stain of defeat as in World War I, Hitler did not contemplate negotiations with the Soviet Union, as some of his advisors counseled him to do, and instead ordered Germany's armies to fight on. "What we found so disheartening," remembered Paul Fussell, a British soldier who was wounded in Germany in March 1945, "was the terrible necessity of the Germans' pedantically, literally *enacting* their defeat."[107]

The cost of this drama was the lives of millions of soldiers and civilians. Most Germans did not enroll in the epic sketched out by Hitler and Goebbels. When all was lost, they did not sacrifice themselves, but surrendered, although thousands of loyal Nazis killed themselves and their families in April and May 1945 in order to avoid facing Germany's defeat.[108] Still, before the final break with the regime, Germans waged an intense struggle to remain true to the cause, something that demanded accepting the continued sacrifice of the lives of German soldiers. Regime loyalists were hit hard psychologically and physically by the news of Stalingrad and other disasters such as the air raid against Hamburg in July 1943: they became physically ill, lost the ability to concentrate, and even committed suicide.[109] In the demoralized fall of 1943, the fifteen-year-old Berlin schoolgirl Lieselotte G. wondered whether a final victory was impossible. If so, she confided to her diary, "then maybe it would be better—before more thousands die, before more misfortune settles over Germany, wouldn't it be better—but no, that cannot and must not ever happen. I see all the fallen before me. And if we should all go under, at least there will not be another 1918. Adolf Hitler, I believe in you and in Germany's victory." Lieselotte initiated but then could not actually finish the thought of Germany's surrender, and like thousands of others she chose, at least at this moment, to continue the war against the world rather than risk the total oblivion of Germany's fallen in two world wars.[110] Stalingrad posed a difficult struggle of faith.

Long after 1945 Stalingrad served to rehabilitate the nation, in this case by illuminating the basically virtuous army of ordinary, wounded, suffering German soldiers. It humanized and sanctified them. Postwar memory transformed the army "from culprit to savior, from an object of hatred and fear to one of sympathy and pity, from victimizer to victim."[111] Knowledge about the murderous march of the Sixth Army into the Soviet Union in the summer and fall of 1941 and its presence in Kiev during the massacre at Babi

Yar in September 1941 was completely overridden by the disaster narrative that unfolded at Stalingrad eighteen months later. It would be a long time before history asked how and why the army found itself in Stalingrad.[112]

More convincing to most Germans than the call to total sacrifice in epic battle was the declaration of total war that Goebbels announced on 18 February 1943 in his famous Sportpalast speech. In front of 10,000 Berlin party loyalists, which film crews panned to pick out prominent figures such as the actor Heinrich George for the newsreels, Goebbels sought to calibrate the war effort to the new hard circumstances that emerged after Stalingrad. The premise of total war was the possibility of defeat, which Goebbels described in a way that projected exactly what the Germans had already done to Jewish, Polish, and Soviet civilians onto the Germans themselves: "the liquidation of our educated and political elite," "forced labor battalions in the Siberian tundra," and "Jewish liquidation commandos." This fate could be avoided only by sheer force of will and the complete mobilization of society. Since Germans wanted victory, they also needed to adjust to a more "spartan way of life" and accept the enlistment of "millions of the best German women" in war industries. With effective populist rhetoric, Goebbels attacked privileged elites and unresponsive bureaucrats in the name of the "people's community." He pulled the people, clear-eyed, modest, willing to sacrifice, closer and closer together in his speech, addressing his audience directly, intimately: "We are all children of our people, forged together." He repeatedly asked: "Do you agree?" "Are you prepared?" Loud, deafening shouts of acclamation in favor of total war provided the answer.

A barrage of "appeals, instructions, decrees, speeches, conferences, and publications" followed the speech. Fourteen million copies of "Do You Want Total War?" were distributed to party offices.[113] Audiovisual space registered the hard conditions as well. The Swiss journalist Konrad Warner described the images in public places in the fall of 1943: "Jews in top hats and bags of money peer out from behind the Hammer and Sickle, the Union Jack, and the Stars and Stripes across a landscape of wrecked cathedrals, orphaned children, and the butchery of the front lines." His colleague René Schindler reported on the same scenes: "'Victory or Bolshevik Chaos!' proclaimed placards on the walls of every German city."[114] "Special bulletins" and victory fanfares on the radio had been replaced by the endlessly repeated formula "A tough war, tough spirits!"

With rounds of choruses and songs and uninterrupted applause coming from the audience, Goebbels' "total war" speech has often been regarded as pure spectacle. Loyal party members did make up the audience, but the basic premises of Goebbels' speech resonated with the German public: the horror of military defeat, which would bring about social and political collapse more terrible than in 1918; the direct occupation of the country by the Allies and the "bolshevization" of society; therefore, the need to continue fighting at all costs despite reversals of fortune; and finally, support for policies that would more equally distribute the costs of war. Criticisms about the conduct of the war remained intense. Local Germans despised Nazi officials for not serving on the front, and they remained troubled by the number of non-Germans recruited and conscripted to work in the Reich. Even so, most indictments of Nazi policy were made in the name of the people's community and did not question the legitimacy of the regime or the soundness of its aims.

The conduct of total war brutalized German society. Hundreds of air raids bludgeoned civilians and destroyed their homes, while Nazi authorities enforced ruthless discipline in the factories and punished defeatist talk with death sentences, which had been rare in civilian courts before 1939. But the harsh work of the Nazi institution, the People's Tribunal, especially in 1944 and 1945, rested on the willingness of citizens to denounce their neighbors for buying and selling goods on the black market, listening to foreign radio broadcasts, or breaking laws against racial mixing. More and more people expressed their fears and thirst for revenge in the racist vocabulary of National Socialism. Even Germans critical of the regime blamed the air raids on Anglo-American "plutocrats" and powerful if undefined Jewish "capital" and hoped for the deployment of the weaponry of revenge and retaliation. Civilians also heaped anger on foreign laborers, whose harsh working conditions were compounded by the fear and loathing that surrounded them. Nicholas Stargardt points out that "although the regime aimed at transforming the values of its citizens, it was not its successes, but its failures, that played the decisive role in this process."[115]

It was in the conditions of total war that Nazi words came to correspond to reality as more and more Germans understood the war to be an apocalyptic struggle in which Germany would either survive or be annihilated. What made the dichotomy "us or them" or "all or nothing" so compelling, however, was not simply that events seemed to confirm the general proposition that war came down to a fundamental struggle for existence. It was also the specific recognition that Germany had committed a great crime. The Nazi ideologue Alfred Rosenberg traveled to party offices to explain the situation to local leaders. Münster's editor Paulheinz Wantzen attended one of these meetings in Trier on 8 May 1943. The talk was very frank. Liberating Europe from "Jewish leprosy," as Rosenberg put it, was "not brutality, but rather clean, biological humanitarianism. Better that eight million Jews disappeared than eighty million Germans. The bridges have been broken behind us, and there is no way back anymore."[116] When Himmler addressed SS officers and party leaders in separate meetings in Posen in early October 1943, the purpose was not to keep a secret, despite his references to the "unwritten and never to be written page of glory in our history," but to leave no doubt about the facts of extermination: "Now you know," he concluded. In other words, "Himmler wanted to rob the Gauleiter of 'any excuse.'"[117] In November 1943 Goebbels made the image of burned bridges public: "As for us," he wrote in *Das Reich*, with a circulation of 1.4 million, "we've burned our bridges behind us. We can't go back, and we don't want to anymore. We will either go down in history as the greatest statesmen of all time, or as the greatest criminals," he concluded.[118]

By portraying National Socialists as criminals, the Nazis aimed to fortify the German people with the knowledge of murder; they produced the intimacy of complicity, not the distance of ignorance. It becomes clear that the Nazis wanted to manage, but not entirely conceal, the facts of the Holocaust. And whereas they had appealed to a specifically "Nazi conscience" to motivate killers and justify killing in 1941 and 1942, they now appealed to traditional moral concepts to make Germans see themselves as the Allies did. To assemble "Strength through Fear," Nazi propaganda relied on the ability of Germans to recognize the criminal nature of the regime and to resolve to fight on in order to avoid a final moral reckoning.

By the summer of 1943, after massive Allied air raids on Cologne and Hamburg, the war had come home to German civilians. Yet British and American strategists were wrong to assume that the unrestricted bombing of German cities would bring the economy to a halt or break German morale. In fact, the air war confirmed Nazi assertions that the Allies intended to destroy the German nation and for a time strengthened rather than weakened Germany's resolve. Nearly 100,000 British and American airmen lost their lives, most of them at the beginning of the campaign, while more than 600,000 German civilians, mostly women and children, were killed, most of them at the end—a poor ratio for the Allies. As the U.S. Strategic Bombing Survey discovered after the war, German morale held up, and the Nazis even won credit for providing efficient social services in the immediate aftermath of air raids. Hitler came to believe that the destruction on the home front tied Germans more closely to the regime, which in many ways was true.[119] Ultimately, however, bombing did break the back of the war economy and convince Germans that they had indeed lost the war. These outcomes served as the air war's most persuasive justification, but bombs did not foment internal rebellion. Although, in view of the ruined cities, opponents of the Nazis contemptuously recalled Hitler's famous election promise in 1933 that in "four years' time, you will not recognize Germany," a reference that got a few people in trouble with the Gestapo, other jokes indicated reserves of resilience. Berlin's bombed-out district of Charlottenburg was nicknamed "Klamottenburg" (dud city), for example, and Steglitz "Steht-Nichts" (nothing left standing). In the Third Reich there were professional comedians who made a living making fun of the air war until they themselves were bombed out and lost their gags.[120] Were these funny men victims or loyalists?

Civilians talked endlessly about the bombing, which for residents of urban areas had become the dominant experience of the war by 1942. Recollections of the war returned repeatedly, obsessively to the air war and to the suffering of German civilians, as any oral historian will know. A great many Germans came to remember the war as if they had spent it in an air-raid shelter. But what was significant was not simply the frightening hours sweating out the bombing but the sense of "belonging together" that developed when people shared gossip and feelings of fear, relief, and the renewed anticipation of attack. Geyer refers to the "tyranny of young virtue" when considering how young soldiers, air-raid wardens, municipal workers, and other civilians "maintained the infrastructure of bureaucracy and everyday life in bombed-out cities." Wartime films, including *Die grosse Liebe*, prized the community of fate that had been tugged together in air-raid shelters; subplots took care to contrast the general spirit of cooperation among common folks with the persnickety attitude of a few bourgeois grumblers. Germans were all in the "same boat," with each air-raid shelter forming a "cellar people" with its own jokes, taboos, and tricks. The baker, the young wife with a husband missing in action, the refugee girl from Königsberg, the elderly drapist, the booksellers from down the street, the state councillor and his one-legged demobbed son, the chemist, and finally the concierge and his two daughters and orphaned grandson—in diverse groups such as this one in a Berlin apartment building, Germans managed the best they could. They followed the directives of air-raid wardens, relied on the People's Welfare, and, whether they were for or against the Nazis, used the propaganda term "air terror" or "terror attack" to describe what was happening.[121] By contrast, Jews in the underground hardly mentioned the bombing that they also endured; they did not feel part of a beleaguered German community.[122] It was the rare individual, like the doorman whom Americans stumbled upon after the war in the ruins of Kassel, a member of the Nazi party, as it turned out, who recalled that he "had saved a picture the paper published some years before of bombed London. I showed it to my friends when we were bombed and when they talked of how terrible the Allies were." He was not "too bright," the interviewer added, but possessed "that literal objectivity that sets limits to self-deception."[123] Most (bright) Germans, by contrast, thought of themselves as innocent victims of Allied air attacks.

They also assumed the role of combatants. As their letters and diaries reveal, soldiers and civilians put considerable stock in the "retaliation rockets" the regime promised to fire into civilian populations in Great Britain and both literally and figuratively watched with anticipation as they flew overhead. The German public and Hitler himself put great faith in the reach and efficacy of the weapons, as became clear during 1944, when people took measure of Germany's difficult position yet believed that a final offensive could avoid defeat. However, the capacity for "retaliation appears to be greatly exaggerated among the broad masses of people," admitted Goebbels already in January 1944.[124] One consequence of the Nazis' failure to retaliate against Britain was the widespread conviction in 1945 that the Nazis had completely misled the Germans.

Nonetheless, the soup kitchens of the People's Welfare; the jokes about Charlottenburg; the hit parade, from the sad notes of Lale Andersen's "Lili Marleen" to the consoling registers of Zarah Leander's "I know one day a miracle will happen" or "It's not the end of the world," favorites from the 1942 record-breaking movie *Die grosse Liebe,* to the spunky air-raid tune "Berlin, Berlin, I love you even in the dark"; the desire for revenge, the hope for miracles; the storyline of victimization; and propaganda prattle that careened between escapism, encouragement, and endurance—all this revealed that the people's community continued to function. The war generated popular culture; the Shoah did not.

Two Swiss journalists, Konrad Warner and René Schindler, traveled back and forth across Germany in the years 1943 and 1944. Their conversations confirmed that people generally accepted the difficult premises of total war. At a table of regulars in Berlin, Wehrmacht officers, scientists, and engineers "gleefully" criticized the party. But ultimately they checked themselves; such talk was "unproductive" because "no one knew . . . a way that would lead to something better." To surrender unconditionally, as the Allies demanded, was inconceivable. "What is it that will happen to us," the discussants contemplated, "when the Russians march in? Better to lose everything than to back down now . . . The terrible sacrifices of our soldiers should not be in vain. We have to win!" A "thousand-year Reich" was just a "propaganda phrase," confided one businessman. Nonetheless, "it has become clear that England will not concede us a thing. And as events on the eastern front have proven, the Russian danger must be vanquished. There is no choice for us; our single aim must be victory." In his view, war had been forced on Germany. A soldier on leave spoke up: the choice was either victory or deportation to Russia, and "new inflation, new starvation" at home, which the armistice had brought after World War I. "There will not and must not be a repeat of 1918!" insisted another informant. As Geyer explains, a majority of Germans "wanted nothing more than an end of war," but "another majority . . . could not see themselves living in defeat," and it was this second majority that fought on in the last years of the war. The general mood was well captured in the rueful joke retailed countless times in 1944 and 1945: "Kids, enjoy the war! Who knows what peace will look like!"[125] ("Kids" reproduces the *unter uns* effect.)

Reactions to the failed plot to assassinate Hitler on 20 July 1944 confirmed the public's identification with the regime and its determination to continue fighting the war. The plot was widely interpreted in terms of the collapse of 1918, as an intended "stab in the back," this time by reactionary officers rather than revolutionary workers. Waves of demonstrations in support of Hitler swept across Germany, recalling the plebiscitary mood of 1933. In Vienna, 350,000 people assembled in Schwarzenberg Square the night after the assassination attempt. Spontaneous outdoor rallies also took place in Hamburg, Stuttgart, Kassel, Weimar, Breslau, Münster, and Frankfurt; many of these cities had been heavily bombed. In Paderborn, 20 percent of the population reportedly gathered to show support. "In many regards, the situation is different than in 1918," reflected Hans-Georg Studnitz, a high-ranking foreign affairs official in Berlin, and no friend of Hitler, two weeks later: "Morale on the home front, the burdens of the air attacks notwithstanding, has remained intact."[126] Soldiers' letters, which were not dictated by higher authorities, showed near-unanimous support for the Führer.[127] The fact is that in the summer of 1944, most Germans could not imagine a future without Hitler.

The expansion of total war after 1943 was horribly lethal. The Red Army incurred extraordinary losses as it drove into Germany; in the final stage of the Soviet offensive, in January–May 1945, over 800,000 soldiers were killed or captured; 300,000 fell in the final push for Berlin. Overall, the majority of Soviet combat deaths occurred in 1943, 1944, and 1945.[128] The United States and Britain also suffered large numbers of battlefield deaths in 1944 and 1945.

Over 135,000 American soldiers died in the eleven months between D-Day and V-E Day, including 19,000 in the Battle of the Bulge on the western front in December 1944–January 1945, the deadliest in American history.

The determination to fight to the bitter end also resulted in most of Germany's military and civilian casualties. It was not Stalingrad but the endgame of the war in 1944–45, guided as it was by the fear of collapse as in 1918, that smashed the Wehrmacht. "Overall, more German soldiers were killed in action between July 20, 1944 . . . and May 8, 1945," when the Third Reich finally surrendered, notes Geyer, "than in the entire previous five years of war. January and February 1945 were the deadliest months of the entire Second World War."[129] The last ninety-eight days of war in 1945 alone cost the lives of 1.4 million German soldiers, about 14,000 every day. Furthermore, the majority of civilian air-raid casualties occurred in 1945, when British and American attacks wrecked one city after another in a grim commitment to force Germany to surrender. The month in which the most bombs were dropped was March 1945. An average of 127 German civilians died every day in air raids in 1944, and more than 1,000 every day in the raids of 1945.[130] It is worth rereading these numbers. Beginning in the fall of 1944, teenage boys and old men drafted into the *Volkssturm* suffered terrible losses whenever they engaged the enemy. Violence continued when German civilians in eastern Germany fled the rapid Soviet advance. As the Russians overran German settlements, they raped tens of thousands of women and girls in an awful process of revenge that lasted until after Germany had surrendered. Bombing, rape, evacuation—this is the horrible battering Germans remembered, although they usually failed to remember their own determination a year or so earlier, in the summer of 1943 or the fall of 1944, in the face of doubt and fear, to fight on. They tended to recollect the war as a series of sudden, dramatic disasters that tore apart the order of peaceful communities when bombs began to fall, or when refugees from bombed-out cities poured in, or when Allied troops appeared.[131]

Neither did German memories dwell on the ferocious attacks that Nazi officials unleashed against their own citizens whom they suspected of sabotage, looting, and desertion. Dead bodies of soldiers shot or hung for refusing to fight were not an uncommon sight in the last weeks of the war. That, as the snide remark put it, "Adolf has now even declared war on us" was one reason why Germans finally rejected the Nazis (though not necessarily the ideas of Nazism). Even so, for all the violence in 1945, there were strikingly few incidents of revenge against Nazi loyalists after the surrender, unlike the slaughter of over 10,000 suspected collaborators in France.[132] Foreign workers, however, increasingly regarded as a fifth column of potential enemies, found themselves subject to extremely harsh treatment. Nazi guards murdered foreign workers held in detention camps and slave laborers in satellite work camps before the final retreat of the German army. In one horrific incident, German authorities executed over 200 individuals, most of them Italians, in a public hanging for having helped themselves to food in the bombed-out ruins of Hildesheim in March 1945. Massacres such as this one took place in semipublic view with German civilians as frequent, unwilling witnesses. They left few traces in postwar histories.[133]

More than 700,000 prisoners who were still alive in the hundreds of concentration and labor camps across the German empire in January 1945 knew that the moment of liberation had finally drawn near. Inmates in Auschwitz could hear the pounding of Russian guns as early as 17 January 1945. But what separated prisoners of war, and Polish or French or German political prisoners, and incarcerated Jews who had survived as slave laborers from freedom was the determination of the Nazis to take as many hostages as possible into the shrinking confines of the German Reich. Just why German authorities went to such extraordinary efforts to retain concentration-camp victims is not clear, and the subordinate SS officials acted out of different motives. Certainly one reason is that the Nazis did not envision the final end and intended to hold onto slave laborers. They also did not want the Red Army to stumble over evidence of the "final solution," which would have complicated Germany's future relations with its client states and neutral countries in the event the tide of war shifted back in Germany's favor. Yet the witnesses left behind at Auschwitz offered damning testimony. Since the Nazis regarded the Jews as dangerous, it was important not to lose them to the Allies, although that vision could hardly be squared with the sight of emaciated, weak survivors. In a massive but uncoordinated effort, Himmler's security service shipped thousands of prisoners from Auschwitz, its satellites, and other camps to transit camps in Buchenwald and Bergen-Belsen in central Germany. These camps became hopelessly overcrowded. Inmates were ravaged by disease and hunger, so that hundreds of people died every day right up to the moment of liberation. Other transports brought people back to Theresienstadt after the camp had been largely emptied by deportations to Auschwitz in the fall of 1944.

Anne Frank, for example, the fifteen-year-old who had fled Frankfurt as a child in 1934 and whose hiding place in Amsterdam the German security police had discovered in 1944, was shipped from Auschwitz to Bergen-Belsen in January 1945 where she and her sister, Margot, died of typhus in March, just weeks before British soldiers liberated the camp. Her mother, Edith, died in Auschwitz in January. Of the other Jews who hid alongside the Franks, Hermann van Pelt was gassed in Auschwitz in October 1944 after an injury left him unable to work; his wife, Auguste, was transported to Auschwitz, then to Bergen-Belsen, and died in Theresienstadt; and the son, Peter, whom Anne believed herself to love, died in Mauthausen in May 1945 after a "death march" from Auschwitz. The dentist Fritz Pfeffer was deported to Auschwitz and then to Sachsenhausen and Neuengamme, where he starved to death at the end of December 1944. Of the eight German Jews arrested in the "Secret Annexe" on 4 August 1944, only Anne's father, Otto Frank, who after the war would find her diary, survived.

Thousands of prisoners traveled on foot in "death marches," this time to the misery that lay in the west. It was these columns that German civilians in southern Germany, and Ruth Kluger as well, glimpsed in March and April 1945. The whole process of moving, guarding, and killing Jews did not come to an end until May. In the end, the death marches claimed the lives of about 250,000 people, the majority of whom were probably Jews.[134]

In the last weeks of the war, a new wave of haphazard deportations rounded up *Mischlinge* as well as Jews in "privileged marriages"; prisoners in Theresienstadt reported clusters of arrivals on 25 April 1945: "Early morning 230 women from Dresden. Afternoon men from Dresden, Poland, and Hungary." Dresden had been largely destroyed in air raids in mid-February, but two months later authorities evidently had resumed evacuations of Jews. "Six hundred and fifty Hungarian and Slovak women from Leipzig" entered the camp on 29 April 1945, the day before Hitler took his life in Berlin. A few transports even arrived from Auschwitz, this time via Buchenwald. Eva Ginzova recorded the arrival of the first of these on 23 April 1945: "I ran to the ghetto straightaway (we're working outside at the moment), to the railway station. They were just getting off the train, if one can call it getting off. Very few could stand on their feet (bones, covered in nothing but skin), others lay on the floor completely exhausted. They'd been traveling for two weeks with hardly anything to eat. They came from Buchenwald and Auschwitz (Oswiecim) . . . Most of them were Hungarians and Poles. I was so upset I thought I would collapse." It was only at this moment that survivors in Theresienstadt understood for the first time the fantastic, horrible scale of the "final solution." Ginzova explained what she had just learned about the workings of the camp when it was still completely functional in 1944: "Every transport that had arrived in Birkenau had had everything taken away and been divided immediately. Children under fourteen, people over fifty, went straight into the gas chambers and were then burned. Moreover, they always selected some more to be gassed from those who remained. And the food was lousy." "The news crashes down on us like a waterfall," wrote Alice Ehrmann on the next day, 24 April: "It is hopeless, trying to grasp everything. I will write pell-mell, like a stuttering of fright and hopelessness. The key word: Auschwitz—aka labor camp Birkenau (death camp Auschwitz, international slaughtering block, sieve)."[135] In Theresienstadt, final liberation, which came a long two weeks later, was accompanied by the full knowledge of death.

The end of the war made possible a complete report on the devastation that the Germans had wrought since 1939: the shattering realization that the communities Jewish survivors had grown up in before the war and remembered so brightly, the children and parents and friends they had loved, and the long-worked bonds of loyalty, trust, and memory had been destroyed. The world learned that the Hungarian and Slovakian Jews the Germans had seized when they occupied the territories of their recalcitrant allies in 1944 had been only the last national groups dispersed and murdered in a process that had claimed the lives of Greek and Italian Jews, Polish, French, and Dutch Jews, German, Austrian, Czech, and Russian Jews, as well as the lives of tens of thousands of Gypsies from across Europe, and Polish patriots and prisoners of war. Much of this information had been available during the war, but the Allies had not managed "the necessary transition from information to knowledge."[136] In sum, World War II was not the fearsome context for pogroms and atrocities. It was something even more terrible: an existential war waged by the National Socialists in order to build a new racial order in which the cultivation of the healthy German body rested on the physical annihilation of Europe's Jews and the destruction of non-German nations throughout eastern Europe.

What we now know as the Holocaust is what made World War II so awfully different and undermined attempts to establish moral symmetry between victors and vanquished as had been the case in previous wars.

Reading Catastrophe

One way to make sense of the war was to theorize, to see the catastrophe it embodied as an example of a larger tendency or pattern. The desire for theory was the desire for insight, consolation, and forgiveness. It was an attempt to find an alternative to National Socialist explanations for the war. But by creating parallels and comparisons, theory usually clouded rather than clarified an understanding of just how and why the Nazis had yoked together life and death. Theory enabled the active verbs of perpetrators to be exchanged for the passive voice of victims.

A remarkable number of Germans seemed to be reading Ernst Jünger, best known for his fictionalized World War I diary, *Storm of Steel,* as the war crashed down on them. They picked up his books, which intertwined themes of technology, nature, and myth, for a variety of reasons, but readers shared the impulse to try to understand the world war. The insights they reached were not always entirely consistent with Nazism. Jünger offered a spectacular reading of modernity in which National Socialism was reduced to a symptom of a much larger reformation of the universe. To read Jünger was to reframe the war as an epic tragedy that exposed an existentialist approach to events. Soldiers found that Jünger recognized the remorseless qualities of the war they were fighting and gave them courage to accept the brutality of the engagement. "What he had seen in his figure of the worker had become fact," noted Willy Reese, who worked hard to acquiesce in his fate to be a soldier-worker on the eastern front. "I've got a lot of books about the war," wrote twenty-six-year-old Heinrich Böll to his wife: "Binding's, Wiechert's, Beumelburg's"; but Jünger's *Storm of Steel* was the most impressive. To Böll, Jünger conveyed the view of the infantryman with absolute clarity: "real and sober, filled with the passion of a man who sees everything and experiences everything with passion and hardship." The conjunction of the "agony of war" with the recognition of "the elemental lusts of men in a fight" authenticated Jünger, who rendered the "elemental," inalterable conditions of the present moment. "In Jünger one finds truths that have been carved out of ice or iron," Böll explained. This was the mental equipment of the wealthy and mighty, he admitted, and ultimately Böll himself identified with the "utterly poor and helpless" people for whom Dostoyevsky spoke. "It is clear where we belong," he affirmed to Annemarie (anticipating his distinction between Nazi buffaloes and anti-Nazi lambs in his postwar novel *Billiards at Half-Past Nine*). Nonetheless, Böll felt drawn to Jünger, whom he brought up repeatedly in his letters home. This was so not because Jünger was like Böll; "I do not believe he knows human ecstasy, the ecstasy of wine, or of love, or of words." Rather, Jünger described the circumstances in which Böll found himself and which he would have to accept. The soldier acknowledged to his wife: "Isn't it an unbelievably difficult and mysterious law that even the most peaceful of men must become murderers when the law demands it! War is totally unparadisical."[137]

This combination of the unparadisical and helplessness, of Jünger and Dostoyevsky, proved compelling because it allowed a moral stance to be taken and also provided an explanation for why moral judgment could not be translated into rehabilitative action. It comforted the weak, who were forced to murder like the strong. This reading of the war was inconsistent with the National Socialist determination to enroll soldiers and civilians into a specifically German struggle for mastery. At the same time, however, the existentialist terms in which the war was described avoided questions of responsibility and aestheticized helplessness and passivity. It provided Böll and many others with philosophical cover. Finally, this *Jüngerschaft* discipleship lifted the war out of the specific context of National Socialism. Readers naturalized war into elements of ice and steel, which did not distinguish between perpetrators and victims. Everyone was a victim because everyone had been positioned by the war to be a perpetrator. In this fearsome world, the Nazis were not named, nor their uniforms seen, for everything had blended with the terrible powers cavorting in the modern age.

Lisa de Boor, a journalist in her forties, the railroad observer quoted at the outset of the chapter, also read Jünger. She was repeatedly drawn to what she rejected, thereby making her own choices subordinate to a more compelling forcefulness that she saw in the action around her. In June 1942 she reported on "*Gardens and Alleys: Pages from a Diary, 1939–1941,* by Ernst Jünger, the best that I have read recently." At the end of the month she was struck by the "fascinating pathos" of Jünger's *On the Marble Cliffs;* but after a few days she gained some distance: "there is a chilling, 'unchristian' wind blowing, there is no human warmth, the title 'marble cliffs' is fitting." The electricity was out in Marburg in October 1942, but de Boor drew closer to the light of the stub of her candle to read "Ernst Jünger's book *The Adventurous Heart,* an ice-cold text." In January 1944 she was immersed in Jünger's *The Worker* and "the demonic, transcendental entities that overpower humankind." These were completely unchristian creatures, but no less powerful and compelling for that fact. What was the attraction to this ice? To some extent, it was the aesthetic of total war without the embrace of the Nazis, German fascism without Hitler. De Boor dramatized her own passivity in order to accept both the necessity of total war and the rigor of likely defeat.[138]

De Boor went on to quote "a comrade of Ernst Jünger's," Gerhard Nebel, who prepared for collective death over life: "Autumn is superior to spring for the same reason that courage in the face of death is more valuable than sheer high-spiritedness." In

May 1944, Ursula von Kardorff conjured up the same mood of farewell and departure, quoting this time from the first lines of *On the Marble Cliffs:* "You all know the wild grief that besets us when we remember times of happiness. How far beyond recall they are, and we are severed from them by something more pitiless than leagues and miles." Like Nossack's "abyss," this was a place where an unnamed but powerful catastrophe had swept away the past and stranded the survivors. Jünger himself observed that the sinking of the *Titanic* provided the key to understanding "our time." This destruction of the past was an estrangement from National Socialism. There was no longer an internal connection to race or sovereignty or German freedom. Yet the destructive forces were completely without provenance—according to de Boor, they were "neither the Jews, nor the freemasons, nor the Jesuits."[139] One after the other, Jünger's readers naturalized calamity so that they no longer recognized protagonists or perpetrators, did not see Jews or Nazis or Russians. What these Germans had come to see was the general condition of dispersion or shipwreck that they believed they shared with all their contemporaries in a new universal.

Strikingly similar passages and readings can be found in the texts written by victims of the Nazis. Dostoyevsky, for example, preoccupied not only Jünger and Böll but also Etty Hillesum, a Jewish inmate in Westerbork, the transit camp in Holland. Writing in Amsterdam and later in Westerbork, Hillesum watched as transports to Auschwitz gradually depopulated the camp. In her diaries, she named Germans as perpetrators and Jews as victims. Nonetheless, she tried on an existentialist reading to make sense of what was happening around her. She repeatedly submerged Germans and Jews into a more general fate: "One moment it is Hitler, the next it is Ivan the Terrible; one moment it is resignation and the next war, pestilence, earthquake or famine." Hillesum addressed the new universal subject in the first person. "God is not accountable to us for the senseless harm we cause one another," she told herself: "We are accountable to Him!" This was her response to the news on the BBC in June 1942 that the Nazis had already murdered hundreds of thousands of Jews in eastern Europe.[140] It is as if the feeling of utter powerlessness was so overwhelming that from the perspective of the victims it absorbed the activism of the perpetrators themselves.

The huge scale of the epochal change that observers imagined was gripping the world in 1945 recalled the Nazis' own determination after 1933 to install a thousand years of "new time" in which questions of politics between Nazis and Social Democrats would be subsumed by much larger necessities requiring an "altered world" of regimes, systems, and administrations so that the old republic looked not so much undesirable as obsolescent.[141] Epochal thinking retrospectively explained the seizure of power in 1933. It also anticipated a whole range of postwar comparisons between twentieth-century regimes that were alike because they were totalitarian, had obliterated the individual in the management of the masses, or proven adept at the administration of things and techniques.

This "civilizational" reading of catastrophe became increasingly authoritative in the 1950s and 1960s. It was picked up by observers in the United States who were trying to understand the subordination of the individual in the huge technological operations of the war in ways that seemed to suggest equivalences among modern war machines. Once the United States dropped atomic bombs on Japan, the catastrophe of Auschwitz was often combined with Hiroshima to create "Auschwitz-Hiroshima," a twinned existential threat to world civilization that loomed in the future. In this way, the historical specificities of Nazism or the Holocaust were subordinated to technocratic developments and military capacities operating on a global scale in a kind of epic modernity that World War II epitomized. The continuity expressed in the serialization of the wars as World War I and World War II had the same effect.[142] Emplotting the years 1914–1945 as a hugely self-destructive thirty years' war or civil war also confiscated the political causes of World

War II and the relentless utopian ambitions of the Nazis. It created equivalencies between the belligerent states, and as a result tended to overlook the central role of racism and antisemitism in the Third Reich. Whatever the merits of these interpretations, they allowed Germans (and others) in the postwar period to see Nazism as a part of longer-term processes that moved through Europe and the United States. They challenged contemporaries in the postwar period to find more humane and cooperative political mechanisms for future conduct, but they did not always pose difficult problems about the nature of political choices and judgments made in the recent past. New generic figures such as the partisan, the survivor, or the administrator were introduced to explain postwar power hierarchies. This had the effect of smoothing out questions of ideological commitment. The structural interpretation of Nazism and Communism as totalitarian systems or the view that the Holocaust was an extreme example of modernist triage worked in similar fashion.[143] Reading Jünger in Germany in 1945 was both scary and consoling.

German readers after 1945 also developed more historically specific explanations of the catastrophe of Nazism. They increasingly saw themselves as victims of a brutal war imposed on them by a politically fanatical minority that had misled and betrayed a patriotic majority and misused the tribulations that most Germans felt had been inflicted on them after World War I. They were appalled at how the war ended rather than how it had started; they focused on Stalingrad and German prisoners of war in the Soviet Union, Dresden and the air war against civilians, and the expulsion of Germans from eastern Europe in 1945. This perspective was obviously politically expedient, since it not only downplayed the active roles that Germans had played in the crimes of the Nazis but turned Germans into victims first. It conceded that Germans might have been complicit, but complicit because they were morally weak, not because they were criminally motivated. The imagery of German victims also allowed postwar Germans to recover a usable past in which Nazism did not compromise entirely the history and culture of Germany. Thus the Wehrmacht was generally regarded as "clean," and Hitler's war against the Soviet Union as fundamentally different in nature from the more conventional wars against Poland (justified because of the Corridor and Danzig) and even France (a hereditary foe). This version of history was not accurate, but it pointed in the right antifascist direction. I want to examine the struggle to rescue the narrative of German history from an unexpected angle in order to underscore the immense desire for a usable German past. The example comes from a true story Victor Klemperer related in his diary in January 1944. I extrapolate from it to illuminate the wider work of memory in Germany in the twenty-five years after the war.[144]

One year after Stalingrad, Klemperer imagined how the war might be represented once it had ended. He transcribed into his diary an account of Horst Weigmann, whose death had been announced in the local paper on 19 January 1944, with a "swastika inside the Iron Cross at the side of the notice." The announcement read: "Ordained by fate, my only dear son, student of chemistry, Lance Corporal Horst-Siegfried Weigmann, volunteer, holder of the Iron Cross, Second Class, participant in the Polish and French campaigns, was suddenly and unexpectedly taken from this life in the midst of his studies at only twenty-four years of age." The death notice was signed "in deep sorrow" by his father, Bruno Weigmann, a musician. As it turned out, some of Klemperer's friends knew the family; "his mother, divorced from his father, was Jewish." She had been among those arrested in what Klemperer refers to as Dresden's "last action." Horst had been discharged from the army for being a *Mischling,* but evidently had been granted an exception to study at the university on account of his distinguished military record. When he discovered that his mother had been arrested, he posed as a Gestapo officer and managed to escort his mother out of prison with the intention of bringing her into the underground. "There are said to be many Jews in hiding, particularly in Berlin," Klemperer noted. At the entrance of the building, however, mother and son ran into an officer who recognized Weigmann and discovered the ruse. Dresden's Nazis sent the mother to Theresienstadt; the son hanged himself in prison. Klemperer went on to juxtapose the suicide and the Iron Cross, commenting that Weigmann fell on "the field of honor" and showed "more courage than any soldier in battle." The example of his brave actions, Klemperer concluded, "will undoubtedly go down in history and literature." Weigmann "will be the hero of plays and novels."[145]

Klemperer's vignette is extraordinary; what might the drama have looked like? Even as Klemperer worried about his own survival, he considered how "plays and novels" would deal with the Third Reich, the eastern front, and the fate of Germany's Jews after the war. As the diaries reveal, Klemperer was not at all clear about the nature of Nazism's hold over the Germans. He closely monitored the "vox populi" he encountered on the streets of Dresden. But with the particulars of Weigmann's story he projected lines of continuity back into the pre-Nazi past. What Klemperer imagined, after the great majority of Dresden's and Germany's Jews had been murdered, was nothing less than a drama of national reconciliation. The *Mischling* son is placed at the center of newly negotiated German-German relations, which restore the heritage of mixed Jewish-Christian marriages even if the mother cannot be saved. It also repudiates the father, who, we can assume, divorced his Jewish wife for political advantage. That the hero dies and his Jewish mother is deported, whereas the "Aryan" father survives, is an equation consistent with wartime realities: the vast numbers deported and killed. Nonetheless, with his sacrifice, the son holds out the possibility that the damage inflicted on Germany's Jews can be healed. In postwar novels and postwar dramas, the *Mischling* will be the hero, applauded and honored by the German public. Rather than being commanded by fate, as the father put it, Weigmann acted in a deliberate, morally commendable way. Even as the story turns on the awful coincidence of recognition at the entrance to the prison, it gestures toward other places (hiding places) overseen by other people (who help Jews), indicating the existence of a genuinely non-Nazi Germany. The righteous action of the son stands in for this uncontaminated area. The price of reconciliation, however, is the rejection of the father. The drama that Klemperer imagined works by linking the depravity of the father with the deportation of the mother. Thousands of German Jews are dead, but so is Germany's militaristic nationalism.

It is important that Klemperer did not necessarily have to reject war service itself; rather he recruited its imagery. To work as a reconciliationist drama, the story refrains from challenging the honor of German soldiers in France or Poland, but rather shames the one-sided representation by the father. It is not the soldier-son who is the hypocrite, but the civilian father who misplaces the swastika inside the Iron Cross. Indeed, the Iron Cross, once the father's Nazi scribbles have been erased, and the son's sacrifice for his mother reinforce each other dramatically. The postwar audiences whom Klemperer implicitly assembles in this literary success story are brought together through the successful combination of the Iron Cross and Jewish valor. It is the German-Jewish *Mischling*, Lance Corporal Horst-Siegfried Weigmann, who becomes the symbol of the new Germany.

Despite the killings he knew about, in Riga, Kiev, and elsewhere, Klemperer imagined reconciliation and did so in 1944 in a format that relied on a national narrative and a cohesive cultural history—Weigmann's story would "go down in history." Indeed, he cross-referenced the diary entry as a *Köpenickiade,* a reference to a Wilhelmine-era farce.[146] There is no mistaking the relentless brutality of the Nazis. Yet the despicable behavior of the father acted as a lightning rod to put to rest larger questions about the complicity of ordinary Germans; they were contained by the father's evil. Klemperer's readiness to imagine a German public that embraces Weigmann's story further underscores the basic good character of the majority. In Klemperer's version, postwar Germans will readily recognize Weigmann as a hero, and they will disqualify the father from the nation. Although both mother and son are dead, the drama presumes that if they were alive they would be accepted by postwar audiences and feel comfortable in their midst. This is the postwar world Klemperer wanted to live in, one in which German culture had not been totally contaminated and the continuities of German history not entirely compromised by the Nazis.

Klemperer's desire was shared by millions of Germans who in the postwar years constructed their own rehabilitative dramas in which good Germans were contrasted with bad Nazis, the "clean" Wehrmacht with the criminal SS, the son with the father. German history after 1943—in the wake of Stalingrad, the war dead, the bombed-out cities, the prisoners in Russia, the expulsion of Germans from Poland and Czechoslovakia in the years 1945–1947— revealed the scars of what Germans had endured during the war and eventually formed the basis for the collective memory of the postwar nation. These popular stories of collective suffering did not—as Klemperer's imaginary version does—leave room for Jews, who simply were not there; and in fact postwar texts were often founded on the suppression of knowledge of the fate of the Jews and their heritage in Germany. However, the histories did envision postwar Germany as a transformed, rehabilitated nation in which the militarism of the past and the cruelty of the fathers had been repudiated. This was in fundamental contrast to the revanchist memories recollected after World War I: Germans in 1945 had no pretensions to refight the war to win advantage; they sought to write a new page and to add it to an old book.

The popular, tendentious narratives of the suffering German nation always leaked. The depictions of burning cities brought up associations of burning synagogues. The violence Germans had suffered could not screen out all knowledge about the violence the Germans themselves had meted out, although Germany's acknowledgment of the violence suffered by all sides often seemed to demonstrate the belief that the moral score at the end of the war was basically even. Traces of guilt emerged in the very urgency with which Germans defended themselves and professed their innocence or their ignorance of anti-Jewish actions. "We didn't know" was a knowing statement because it skirted what people had guessed and had even been told by the Nazis to suspect. What leaked out in the 1950s and 1960s would eventually become the basis for critical evaluations of the past and for the sober, searching attempts to explore the parameters of complicity that we see in Germany today.[147]

Both the *urge* to call up anonymous, demonic forces in the modern age and the *desire* for narrative closure revealed the inadequacy of certain knowledge about the war, about the Nazis' racial program or the Holocaust. Interpretations of catastrophe sidelined and sidetracked. They enveloped people in the dangerous present, but obscured the silences and absences of the past. Murderers and murdered were numbered but infrequently named. Even Klemperer's drama about Weigmann, like Germany's about Stalingrad or Dresden or the *Wilhelm Gustoff* (the ship crammed with thousands of German refugees that a Russian submarine torpedoed in January 1945), missed the Holocaust. But in a backhanded, unintended way, the immense work to produce comprehensibility gestured at the basic incomprehensibility that so many survivors felt. The powerful testimony of Jewish witnesses was accompanied by the fear that the world would not understand what they were saying and by the suspicion that the words they were using could not adequately express either what they wanted to say or what they had experienced. Alice Ehrmann wrote in a stuttering fashion that revealed her shock. The limited capacity of expression outlined what Charlotte Delbo considered to be a "world beyond knowledge" and what historians later suggested were "limits of representation."[148] Not for the first time in history, not for the last perhaps, but this time certainly, the Holocaust destroyed expectations about how the world worked. Many years later one Jewish survivor reflected: "it seems to me that Hitler chopped off part of the universe and created annihilation zones and torture and slaughter areas. You know, it's like the planet was chopped up into a normal [part]—so-called normal: our lives are not really normal—and this other planet, and we were herded onto that planet from this one, and herded back again."[149] Theory and narrative try to bring these lives together into an orbit of understanding, but events slip out from their grasp, and startle. Part of the knowledge about life and death in the Third Reich is the lasting incompleteness of explanation.

Notes

The following abbreviations are used in the notes.

BAB   Bundesarchiv Berlin

NARA National Archives and Record Administration, College Park, Md.

RG   Record Group

USSBS U.S. Strategic Bombing Survey

Introduction

1. Edwin Erich Dwinger, *Der Tod in Polen* (Jena, 1940), pp. 36–37, 69, 90, 123, 136, 153. Jürgen Matthäus, "Die 'Judenfrage' als Schulungsthema von SS und Polizei: 'Inneres Erlebnis' und Handlungslegitimation," in Matthäus, Konrad Kwiet, Jürgen Föster, and Richard Breitman, eds., *Ausbildungsziel Judenmord? "Weltanschauliche Erziehung" von SS, Polizei, und Waffen-SS im Rahmen der "Endlösung"* (Frankfurt, 2003), p. 85. Two years later the German press was told to consider Soviet atrocities in Lwow, or Lemberg, as "basically a normal Jewish-Bolshevik state of affairs [*Normalzustand*]." Quoted in Peter Longerich, *"Davon haben wir nichts gewusst!" Die Deutschen und die Judenverfolgung 1933–1945* (Berlin, 2006), p. 159. For the political role of atrocities, see John Horne and Alan Kramer, *German Atrocities, 1914: A History of Denial* (New Haven, 2004); and Isabel Hull, *Absolute Destruction: Military Culture and the Practices of War in Imperial Germany* (Ithaca, 2004).

2. Dwinger, *Der Tod in Polen,* pp. 113–115.

3. Jeffrey Herf, *The Jewish Enemy: Nazi Propaganda during World War II and the Holocaust* (Cambridge, 2006), pp. 79, 113.

4. Vegas Gabriel Liulevicius, *War Land on the Eastern Front: Culture, National Identity, and German Occupation in World War I* (Cambridge, Eng., 2000), p. 8.

5. Zygmunt Bauman, *Modernity and the Holocaust* (Ithaca, 1989); Peter Fritzsche, "Nazi Modern," *Modernism/Modernity* 3 (January 1996), pp. 1–21.

6. Thomas Childers, *The Nazi Voter: The Social Foundations of Fascism in Germany, 1919–1933* (Chapel Hill, 1983); Richard J. Evans, *The Third Reich in Power, 1933–1939* (New York, 2005); Ian Kershaw, *Popular Opinion and Political Dissent in the Third Reich: Bavaria 1933–1945* (Oxford, 1983); and Kershaw, *The "Hitler Myth": Image and Reality in the Third Reich* (Oxford, 1987).

7. Hannah Arendt, *The Origins of Totalitarianism* (New York, 1973); Detlev Peukert, *Inside Nazi Germany: Conformity, Opposition, and Racism in Everyday Life* (New Haven, 1989).

8. Norbert Frei, *1945 und Wir: Das Dritte Reich im Bewusstsein der Deutschen* (Munich, 2005); Saul Friedländer, *Nazi Germany and the Jews: The Years of Persecution, 1933–1939* (New York, 1997); Robert Gellately, *Backing Hitler: Consent and Coercion in Nazi Germany* (New York, 2001); Ludolf Herbst, *Das nationalsozialistische Deutschland 1933–1945* (Frankfurt, 1996); Claudia Koonz, *The Nazi Conscience* (Cambridge, 2003).

9. Daniel Jonah Goldhagen, *Hitler's Willing Executioners* (New York, 1996).

10. Lothar Bluhm, *Das Tagebuch zum Dritten Reich: Zeugnisse der Inneren Emigration* (Bonn, 1991); Gustav René Hocke, *Das europäische Tagebuch* (Wiesbaden, 1963); and also Ursula von Kardorff, "Vom Tagebuch," *Deutsche Allgemeine Zeitung,* no. 535, 8 Nov. 1942.

11. Tim Mason, *Social Policy in the Third Reich: The Working Class and the "National Community"* (Oxford, 1993).

12. Entry for 24 April 1941 in Victor Klemperer, *I Will Bear Witness, 1933–1941: A Diary of the Nazi Years* (New York, 1998), p. 383.

13. Irmgard Keun, *Nach Mitternacht* (Amsterdam, 1937), p. 92.

14. Theodore Abel, *Why Hitler Came to Power* (New York, 1938), p. 1.

15. Hans Erich Nossack, *The End: Hamburg 1943* (Chicago, 2004), p. 61.
16. Ibid., p. 55.
17. David Schoenbaum, *Hitler's Social Revolution: Class and Status in Nazi Germany, 1933–1939* (New York, 1966), p. 72.
18. See Peter Fritzsche, *Germans into Nazis* (Cambridge, 1998).

1. Reviving the Nation

1. Entry for 11 Sept. 1938 in Victor Klemperer, *I Will Bear Witness, 1933–1941: A Diary of the Nazi Years* (New York, 1998), pp. 267–268.
2. Lieselotte G., diary entry for 22 April 1945, in Ingrid Hammer and Susanne zur Nieden, eds., *Sehr selten habe ich geweint: Briefe und Tagebücher aus dem Zweiten Weltkrieg von Menschen in Berlin* (Zurich, 1992), p. 311; entry for 28 July 1933, Klemperer, *I Will Bear Witness*, p. 27; Erika Mann, *School for Barbarians* (New York, 1938), p. 21. On the greeting in daily life in general, see Andrew Bergerson, *Ordinary Germans in Extraordinary Times: The Nazi Revolution in Hildesheim* (Bloomington, Ind., 2004).
3. Entries for 8 July and 30 Oct. 1933 in Erich Ebermayer, *Denn heute gehört uns Deutschland . . .* (Hamburg, 1959), pp. 155, 195–196; Klaus P. Fischer, *Nazi Germany: A New History* (New York, 1995), p. 343; entry for 6 May 1933 in Karl Windschild, *Mit Finger vor dem Mund: Ballenstedter Tagebuch des Pfarrers Karl Fr. E. Windschild, 1931–1944*, ed. Günther Windschild and Helmut Schmid (Dessau, 1999), p. 75.
4. Entry for 10 April 1933, Klemperer, *I Will Bear Witness*, p. 13.
5. Ian Kershaw, *The "Hitler Myth": Image and Reality in the Third Reich* (Oxford, 1987), pp. 75, 202; entry for 25 Oct. 1940 in William L. Shirer, *Berlin Diary, 1934–1941* (New York, 1942), p. 436.
6. Entries for 2 Sept. 1941 and 17 March 1940, Klemperer, *I Will Bear Witness*, pp. 428, 329; entry for 19 February 1944, "Tagebuch Nr. 8, 18. Nov. 1943–7. April 1945," Nachlass Franz von Göll, Landesarchiv Berlin, E Rep. 200-43, Acc. 3221, Nr. 8.
7. Diary entries for 24 and 26 June 1934 in Theodore Abel, *The Columbia Circle of Scholars: Selections from the Journal (1930–1957)*, ed. Elzbieta Halas (Frankfurt, 2001), pp. 178, 181.

8. Diary entry for 12 June 1935, ibid., p. 226; Theodore Abel, *Why Hitler Came to Power* (New York, 1938), p. 174.

9. Elisabeth Gebensleben to Irmgard Brester, 15 Sept. 1930 and 3 Feb. 1933, in Hedda Kalshoven, ed., *Ich denk so viel an Euch: Ein deutschholländischer Briefwechsel, 1920–1949* (Munich, 1995), pp. 99, 160.

10. Elisabeth Gebensleben to Irmgard Brester, 3 Feb. and 2, 10, and 22 March 1933, ibid., pp. 160–161, 168–169, 184.

11. Elisabeth Gebensleben to Irmgard Brester, 22 March and 4 May 1933, ibid., pp. 182, 197.

12. Eberhard Gebensleben to Karl Gebensleben, 15 March 1933; Irmgard Brester to Elisabeth Gebensleben, 3 April 1933; and Elisabeth Gebensleben to Irmgard Brester, 14 March and 6 April 1933, ibid., pp. 175–178, 188, 190–191.

13. Minna von Alten to Irmgard Brester, 29 Aug. 1940; Irmgard Brester to Minna von Alten, 5 Sept. 1940; and Chef der Kanzlei to Eberhard Gebensleben, 25 Feb. 1944, ibid., pp. 353–354, 421.

14. Entries for 20 March, 20 and 28 April, and 21 May 1933 in Karl Dürkefälden, *"Schreiben wie es wirklich war . . ." Aufzeichungen Karl Duerkefaeldens aus den Jahren 1933–1945,* ed. Herbert and Sibylle Obenaus (Hanover, 1985), pp. 37–38, 43, 52. Karl Windschild's diaries, *Mit Finger vor dem Mund,* reach similar conclusions for Ballenstedt.

15. Entry for 2 May 1933, Dürkefälden, *"Schreiben wie es wirklich war,"* p. 46.

16. Entries for 24 April, 24 and 29 May, 1 and 26 June, and 18 July 1933; and "Januar bis zum 7. Februar 1934," ibid., pp. 42, 44, 53–54, 57, 64, 70, 77–78.

17. Entries for 30 Jan., 9 May, and 18 July 1933, 10 Sept. 1934, and 15 Sept. 1935, Ebermayer, *Denn heute gehört uns Deutschland,* pp. 14, 75, 155, 382–83, 595.

18. Entry for 4 April 1934, ibid., pp. 288–289.

19. Entries for 20 and 21 March 1933, ibid., pp. 44, 47; entry for 9 March 1938 in Erich Ebermayer, *. . . Und morgen die ganze Welt: Erinnerungen an Deutschlands dunkle Zeit* (Bayreuth, 1966), p. 244.

20. See Karl-Heinz Reuband, "Das NS-Regime zwischen Akzeptanz und Ablehunung. Eine retrospektive Analyse von Bevölkerungseinstellungen im Dritten Reich auf der Basis von Umfragedaten," *Geschichte und Gesellschaft* 32 (2006), pp. 315–344.

21. Hans Fallada, *Little Man, What Now?* (1933; reprint, Chicago, 1992); entry for 23 April 1933, Dürkefälden, *"Schreiben wie es wirklich war,"* p. 40.

22. André François-Poncet, *The Fateful Years: Memoirs of a French Ambassador in Berlin, 1931–1938,* trans. Jacques LeClerq (New York, 1949), p. 48; Melita Maschmann, *Account Rendered: A Dossier on My Former Self,* ed. Geoffrey Strachan (London, 1964), pp. 10–14.

23. Berel Lang, "The Nazi as Criminal," in *Post-Holocaust: Interpretation, Misinterpretation, and the Claims of History* (Bloomington, Ind., 2005), p. 13.

24. Ralf Georg Reuth, *Goebbels,* trans. Krishna Winston (New York, 1993), p. 164.

25. Entry for 2 May 1943 in Joseph Goebbels, *Die Tagebücher von Joseph Goebbels. Sämtliche Fragmente,* ed. Elke Fröhlich (Munich, 1994), pt. II, vol. 8, p. 197.

26. Michael Schneider, *Unterm Hakenkreuz: Arbeiter und Arbeiterbewegung 1933 bis 1939* (Bonn, 1999), p. 92; Hans Wendt, *Der Tag der Nationalen Arbeit. Die Feier des 1. Mai 1933* (Berlin, 1933), p. 11.

27. Peter Fritzsche, *A Nation of Fliers: German Aviation and the Popular Imagination* (Cambridge, 1992), pp. 162–170.

28. *Berliner Morgenpost,* no. 104, 2 May 1933. See also Reinhard Döhl, *Das Hörspiel zur NS-Zeit: Geschichte und Typologie des Hörspiels* (Darmstadt, 1992), pp. 132–133.

29. Eberhard Heuel, *Der umworbene Stand: Die ideologische Integration der Arbeiter im Nationalsozialismus 1933–1935* (Frankfurt, 1989).

30. "Wolfgang Diewerge," Berlin Document Center, A2242 SS-153, NARA; Eugen Hadamovsky, *Hilfsarbeiter Nr. 50,000* (Berlin, 1938).

31. "Nach dem 21. Juli bis zum 14. September 1933," in Dürkefälden, *"Schreiben wie es wirklich war,"* pp. 64–66.

32. Detlef Schmiechen-Ackermann, *Nationalsozialismus und Arbeitermilieus: Der nationalsozialistische Angriff auf die proleatrischen Wohnquartiere und die Reaktion in den sozialistischen Vereinen* (Bonn, 1998), pp. 487–491, 536–537.

33. Hans-Ulrich Thamer, *Verführung und Gewalt: Deutschland 1933–1945* (Berlin, 1986), p. 233. See also Vernon L. Lidtke, *The Alternative Culture: Socialist Labor in Imperial Germany* (New York, 1985).

34. Hans-Ulrich Thamer, *Der Nationalsozialismus* (Stuttgart, 2002), p. 14.

35. Robert N. Proctor, *The Nazi War on Cancer* (Princeton, 1999), pp. 7–8, 114; Detlef Peukert, *Max Webers Diagnose der Moderne* (Göttingen, 1989), pp. 69, 110–111. See also Claudia Koonz, *The Nazi Conscience* (Cambridge, 2003).

36. Elisabeth Gebensleben to Irmgard Brester, 15 Sept. 1933, Kalshoven, *Ich denk so viel an Euch,* p. 208.

37. Heinrich Hauser, *Battle against Time: A Survey of Germany of 1919 from the Inside* (New York, 1939), pp. 11–12.

38. No. 61074, 17 June 1945, Schedule B interviews, USSBS, RG 243, box 536, folder 21, NARA.

39. Entry for 4 Sept. 1943, Goebbels, *Die Tagebücher,* pt. II, vol. 9, p. 421; Herwart Vorländer, *Die NSV: Darstellung und Dokumentation einer nationalsozialistischen Organisation* (Boppard, 1988), pp. 51, 59.

40. *The Times* (London), 10 Dec. 1934, quoted in Thomas E. de Witt, "'The Struggle against Hunger and Cold': Winter Relief in Nazi Germany, 1933–1939," *Canadian Journal of History* 12 (1978), p. 369, who gives an excellent general account. *Völkischer Beobachter,* no. 334, 30 Nov. 1938; and *BZ am Mittag,* no. 298, 3 Dec. 1938, both in R43II/564a/86–88, BAB.

41. Hauser, *Battle against Time,* pp. 11–12; Eva Sternheim-Peters, *Die Zeit der grossen Täuschungen. Mädchenleben im Faschismus* (Bielefeld, 1987), p. 86; Vorländer, *Die NSV,* p. 54; Hans Dieter Schäfer, *Das Gespaltenes Bewusstsein: Über deutsche Kultur und Lebenswirklichkeit 1933–1945* (Munich, 1984), pp. 140–141.

42. Clifford Kirkpatrick, *Nazi Germany: Its Women and Family Life* (Indianapolis, 1938), p. 26. In general, Peter Fritzsche, "Machine Dreams: Airmindedness and the Reinvention of Germany," *American Historical Review* 98 (1993), pp. 685–709.

43. Victor Klemperer, *The Language of the Third Reich: LTI, Lingua Tertii Imperii. A Philologist's Notebook,* trans. Martin Brady (1957; reprint, Somerset, N.J., 2000), pp. 5, 226–227.

44. Diary entry for 28 Sept. 1938, Ebermayer, *Und morgen die ganze Welt,* p. 299. See also entry for 9 Aug. 1939, ibid., p. 405. Kershaw reports the same thing in a Wehrmacht report for September 1938; *Popular Opinion and Political Dissent in the Third Reich: Bavaria 1933–1945* (Oxford, 1983), pp. 151–152.

45. Norbert Frei, "People's Community and War: Hitler's Popular Support," in Hans Mommsen, ed., *The Third Reich between Vision and Reality: New Perspectives on German History, 1918–1945* (Oxford, 2001), p. 64.

46. Kershaw, *Popular Opinion*, p. 108. The figures are from Schneider, *Unterm Hakenkreuz*, p. 284.

47. Ludolf Herbst, *Das nationalsozialistische Deutschland 1933–1945* (Frankfurt, 1996), p. 90; entry for 24 Nov. 1936, Klemperer, *I Will Bear Witness*, p. 201. For the figures on women's employment, Jill Stephenson, *Women in Nazi Germany* (London, 2001), p. 54.

48. Norbert Frei, *National Socialist Rule in Germany: The Führer State, 1933–1945* (1987), trans. Simon B. Steyne (Oxford, 1993 [1987]), p. 78. See also Thamer, *Verfolgung und Gewalt*, p. 489.

49. Wolfgang König, *Volkswagen, Volksempfänger, Volksgemeinschaft: "Volksprodukte" im Dritten Reich. Vom Scheitern einer nationalsozialistischen Konsumgesellschaft* (Paderborn, 2004), p. 137.

50. Adam Tooze, *The Wages of Destruction: The Making and Breaking of the Nazi Economy* (New York, 2007), p. 135; Richard J. Evans, *The Third Reich in Power, 1933–1939* (New York, 2005), p. 327.

51. König, *Volkswagen, Volksempfänger, Volksgemeinschaft*, pp. 18, 178.

52. Ian Kershaw, *Hitler 1936–1945: Nemesis* (New York, 2000), p. 434.

53. Entry for 25 June 1943, Goebbels, *Die Tagebücher*, pt. II, vol. 8, p. 528. See also the entry for 25 Jan. 1944, ibid., vol. 11, p. 166.

54. Tim Mason, *Social Policy in the Third Reich: The Working Class and the "National Community"* (Oxford, 1993), p. 159.

55. Franz Janka, *Die braune Gesellschaft: Ein Volk wird formatiert* (Stuttgart, 1997), p. 380.

56. Bernd Stöver, *Volksgemeinschaft im Dritten Reich. Die Konsensbereitschaft der Deutschen aus der Sicht sozialistischer Exilberichte* (Düsseldorf, 1993), p. 271.

57. König, *Volkswagen, Volksempfänger, Volksgemeinschaft*, p. 206.

58. Shelley Baranowski, *Strength through Joy: Consumerism and Mass Tourism in the Third Reich* (Cambridge, Eng., 2004), p. 177.

59. Kristin Semmens, *Seeing Hitler's Germany: Tourism in the Third Reich* (New York, 2005), pp. 120, 46–47, 68; Joshua Hagen, "The Most German of Towns: Creating an Ideal Nazi Community in Rothenburg ob der Tauber," *Annals of the Association of American Geographers* 94 (2004), pp. 207–227. On photo albums, Nachlass

Franz von Göll, Landesarchiv Berlin, E Rep. 200-43, Acc. 3221, Nr. 89.

60. Tooze, *The Wages of Destruction,* p. 163; "Dezember/Januar— Bericht über die Lage in Deutschland (Abgeschlossen am 21 Januar 1935)," in Bernd Stöver, ed., *Berichte über die Lage in Deutschland. Die Meldungen der Gruppe Neu Beginnen aus dem Dritten Reich 1933–1936* (Bonn, 1996), p. 335.

61. Entry for 17 Jan. 1935 in Lore Walb, *Ich, die Alte, ich, die Junge: Konfrontation mit meinem Tagebüchern 1933–1945* (Berlin, 1997), p. 51.

62. "April [1935] Bericht über die Lage in Deutschland," in Stöver, *Berichte über die Lage in Deutschland,* pp. 429–430; Tooze, *The Wages of Destruction,* p. 165.

63. Albert Speer, *Inside the Third Reich,* trans. Richard and Clara Winston (New York, 1970), p. 86; Götz Aly, ed., *Volkes Stimme. Skepsis und Führervertrauen im Nationalsozialismus* (Frankfurt, 2006); Norbert Frei, *1945 und Wir: Das Dritte Reich im Bewusstsein der Deutschen* (Munich, 2005), pp. 116–117.

64. Letter dated 7 June 1943, quoted in Joachim Dollwet, "Menschen im Krieg, Bejahung–und Widerstand?" *Jahrbuch für westdeutsche Landesgeschichte* 13 (1987), p. 289; Stöver, *Volksgemeinschaft im Dritten Reich,* p. 125.

65. Klaus-Michael Mallmann and Gerhard Paul, *Herrschaft und Alltag: Ein Industrierevier im Dritten Reich* (Bonn, 1991), p. 162. See also David Schoenbaum, *Hitler's Social Revolution: Class and Status in Nazi Germany, 1933–1939* (New York, 1965), pp. 77, 286–288.

66. Entry for 8 March 1936, Klemperer, *I Will Bear Witness,* p. 155.

67. Kirkpatrick, *Nazi Germany,* p. 26; Leni Riefenstahl, *Hinter den Kulissen des Reichsparteitagfilms* (Munich, 1935).

68. Broadcast from France, 17 June 1940, in William L. Shirer, *"This Is Berlin": Radio Broadcasts from Nazi Germany, 1938–40* (New York, 1999), p. 328. See also Gustave Flocher, *Marching to Captivity: The War Diaries of a French Peasant 1939–45,* ed. Christopher Hill (London, 1996), p. 128.

69. Schäfer, *Das Gespaltenes Bewusstsein,* p. 84; *Illustrierter Beobachter,* 6 July 1939; Klaus Hesse and Philippe Springer, *Vor alle Augen: Fotodokumente des nationalsozialistischen Terrors in der Provinz* (Essen, 2002), p. 15.

70. Peter Reichel, *Der schöne Schein des Dritten Reiches: Faszination und Gewalt des Faschismus* (Munich, 1991), p. 189.
71. Eric Rentschler, *The Ministry of Illusion: Nazi Cinema and Its Afterlife* (Cambridge, 1996), p. 1.
72. König, *Volkswagen, Volksempfänger, Volksgemeinschaft,* pp. 83–85; Heinz Pohle, *Der Rundfunk als Instrument der Politik* (Hamburg, 1955), p. 249.
73. Hans Richter, "Neuland des Hörspiels," *Rufer und Hörer* 3 (1933), quoted in Döhl, *Das Hörspiel zur NS-Zeit,* p. 137; Kate Lacey, *Feminine Frequencies: Gender, German Radio, and the Public Sphere, 1923–1945* (Ann Arbor, 1996), pp. 97–98.
74. Goebbels in König, *Volkswagen, Volksempfänger, Volksgemeinschaft,* p. 82; Ortwin Buchbender and Reinhold Sterz, eds., *Das andere Gesicht des Krieges: Deutsche Feldpostbriefe 1939–1945* (Munich, 1982), p. 47.
75. Entry for 17 Aug. 1937, Klemperer, *I Will Bear Witness,* p. 233. See also his *Curriculum Vitae* (Berlin, 1989), p. 247. Goebbels also used this expression. See Saul Friedländer, *Nazi Germany and the Jews: The Years of Persecution, 1933–1939* (New York, 1997), p. 143.
76. Adelheid von Saldern, Inge Marssolek, Uta C. Schmidt, Monika Pater, and Daniela Münkel, "Zur politischen und kulturellen Polyvalenz des Radios: Ergebnisse und Ausblicke," in Inge Marssolek and Adelheid von Saldern, eds., *Zuhören und Gehörtwerden I. Radio im Nationalsozialismus* (Tübingen, 1998), p. 370.
77. See the excellent analysis of Monika Pater, "Rundfunkangebote," in Marssolek and von Saldern, *Zuhören und Gehörtwerden I,* pp. 143–146, 185–186.
78. Quoted in Uta C. Schmidt, "Authentizitätsstrategien im nationalsozialistischen Spielfilm 'Wunschkonzert,'" in Daniela Münkel and Jutta Schwarzkopf, eds., *Geschichte als Experiment* (Frankfurt, 2004). See also Hans-Jörg Koch, *Das Wunschkonzert im NS-Rundfunk* (Cologne, 2003), p. 172.
79. Pater, "Rundfunkangebote", pp. 225–238.
80. Goebbels' diary entry for 15 Dec. 1941, quoted in Gerd Albrecht, *Nationalsozialistische Filmpolitik* (Munich, 1982), p. 469.
81. "Meldungen aus dem Reich," 8 March 1940, in Heinz Boberach, ed., *Meldungen aus dem Reich 1938–1945* (Munich, 1986), vol. 3, p. 856; Foerster, "Kriegsgeschichte der EWZ" (1941), R69/40/41,

BAB. See also the monthly reports prepared by the Gaupropaganda-leitung Ostpreussen, NS18/996, BAB.

82. David Welch, *Propaganda and German Cinema, 1933–1945* (New York, 1983), p. 31. Over the 1930s cinema attendance in Great Britain increased from 19 to 30 million a week in a population of some 44 million. In the United States, wartime audiences numbered 90 million a week in a population of 130 million. In Germany, by contrast, there were never more than 20 million weekly visits in a population of some 70 million.

2. Racial Grooming

1. "Aryans" is a nonsensical racial designation, and scare quotes allow me to indicate this fact, but since the designation created fundamental divisions in German society, "Aryans" did, in fact, exist. In order to show how commonplace racial identities became Nazi Germany, I have decided not to scare-quote most appearances of the word.

2. Oscar Robert Achenbach, "Eine Viertelstunde Familienforschung," *Illustrierter Beobachter* 9 (19 May 1934), pp. 812, 814.

3. Udo R. Fischer, "Familienforschung. Ein Gebot der Stunde," *Neues Volk* 1 (July 1933), pp. 20–21; Herbert Fuhst to Reichsstelle für Sippenforschung, 8 Jan. 1937, R1509/565a, BAB. See also the problems surveyed by Andrej Angrick, *Besetzungspolitik und Massenmord. Die Einsatzgruppe D in der südlichen Sowjetunion 1941–1943* (Hamburg, 2003), pp. 440–441.

4. See Nachlass Walter Helfenstein, Landesarchiv Berlin, E. Rep. 200-48/6/108; and *Das Schwarze Korps*, writing against attempts to apply racial principles to dogs, "Grenzen der Kunst, zu organisieren," 28 Sept. 1940.

5. "Anfragen beim Kusteramt," *Neues Volk* 4 (July 1936); "Gedanken um den Ahnenpass," *Völkischer Beobachter,* no. 176, 24 June 1936. On the Jewish great-grandmother, Barbara Sevin, "Mein Leben in Deutschland vor und nach dem 30. January 1933" (1940), p. 158, "My Life in Germany," Houghton Library, bms Ger 91, Harvard University.

6. Christa Wolf, *Patterns of Childhood* (New York, 1980), pp. 57–58, 60.

7. Entry for 28 Sept. 1934 in "Tagebuch 16 Jan 1933–12 März 1938, 4. Buch," Nachlass Franz von Göll, Landesarchiv Berlin, E Rep. 200-43,

Acc. 3221, Nr. 4. See also the entries for 30 July 1933 and 11 and 15 Nov. 1934.

8. "Ahnenpässe," Sammlung F Rep. 240/1, Landesarchiv Berlin.

9. Entries for 29 June 1938, 21 and 22 May 1940 and 4 and 7 December 1941 in Victor Klemperer, *I Will Bear Witness, 1933–1941: A Diary of the Nazi Years* (New York, 1998), pp. 260, 338–339, 447–449.

10. "Dienstleistungen für die Standesbeamten und ihre Aufsichtsbehörden" (1938), Reichsministerium des Innern, R1501/127452, BAB. See also Nancy R. Reagin, *Sweeping the German Nation: Domesticity and National Identity in Germany, 1870–1945* (Cambridge, Eng., 2007), p. 117.

11. Renate Bridenthal, Atina Grossmann, and Marion Kaplan, eds., *When Biology Became Destiny: Women in Weimar and Nazi Germany* (New York, 1984).

12. Based on the number of "hereditary biological peer reviews" prepared by public-health offices between 1935 and 1939. See Johannes Vossen, *Gesundheitsämter im Nationalsozialismus. Rassenhygiene und öffentliche Gesundheitsfürsorge in Westfalen 1900–1950* (Essen, 2001), p. 226; Gisela Bock, *Zwangssterilisation im Nationalsozialismus. Studien zur Rassenpolitik und Frauenpolitik* (Opladen, 1986), p. 192.

13. Richard Overy, *The Dictators: Hitler's Germany, Stalin's Russia* (New York, 2004), p. 209.

14. Ulrich Herbert, *Best: Biographische Studien über Radikalismus, Weltanschauung und Vernunft 1903–1989* (Bonn, 2001), p. 69; Michael Wildt, *Generation des Unbedingten: Das Führungskorps des Reichssicherheitshauptamtes* (Hamburg, 2002), p. 45; Götz Aly, *Hitlers Volksstaat: Raub, Rassenkrieg, und nationaler Sozialismus* (Frankfurt, 2005), p. 14.

15. Vossen, *Gesundheitsämter im Nationalsozialismus,* p. 209; Asmus Nitschke, *Die "Erbpolizei" im Nationalsozialismus: zur Alltagsgeschichte der Gesundheitsämter im Dritten Reich. Das Beispiel Bremen* (Wiesbaden, 1999), p. 84; Bock, *Zwangssterilisation im Nationalsozialismus,* p. 94.

16. Claudia Koonz, *The Nazi Conscience* (Cambridge, 2003), pp. 43–44; Reagin, *Sweeping the German Nation.*

17. Sebastian Haffner, *Geschichte eines Deutschen* (Stuttgart, 2000), p. 138.

18. Wilhelm Frick, *Bevölkerungs- und Rassenpolitik* (Langensalza, 1933), p. 16; Koonz, *The Nazi Conscience,* p. 104.

19. Bock, *Zwangssterilisation im Nationalsozialismus,* pp. 79, 89.
20. *Neues Volk* 1 (July 1933); Walter Gross, "Von der äusseren zur inneren Revolution," *Neues Volk* 2 (August 1934).
21. See, for example, Ludolf Herbst, *Das nationalsozialistische Deutschland 1933–1945* (Frankfurt, 1996), p. 111.
22. *Völkischer Beobachter,* no. 189 (8 July 1933); Koonz, *The Nazi Conscience,* pp. 84–85.
23. *Völkischer Beobachter,* no. 184 (3 July 1933).
24. Entries for 2 and 6 Nov. 1933 in Erich Ebermayer, *Denn heute gehört uns Deutschland . . .* (Hamburg, 1959), pp. 197–198, 200. See also *Völkischer Beobachter,* nos. 307 (3 Nov. 1933) and 310 (6 Nov. 1933).
25. Karl Ludwig Rost, *Sterilisation und Euthanasie im Film des "Dritten Reiches"* (Husum, 1987), p. 43.
26. Christoph Zuschlag, *"Entartete Kunst": Ausstellungen im Nazi-Deutschland* (Worms, 1995), pp. 313, 329; Joshua Hagen, "The Most German of Towns: Creating an Ideal Nazi Community in Rothenburg ob der Tauber," *Annals of the Association of American Geographers* 94 (2004), p. 219; entry for 1 Sept. 1937 in Joseph Goebbels, *Die Tagebücher von Joseph Goebbels. Sämtliche Fragmente,* ed. Elke Fröhlich (Munich, 1994), pt. I, vol. 3, p. 251.
27. Gross, "Von der äusseren zur inneren Revolution"; Walter Gross, *Volk und Rasse* (Berlin, 1936), p. 333; Helmut Hübsch, "Kein Grund zum Verzagen," *Neues Volk* 2 (January 1934). On "Erkenne dich selbst," see also Hans F. K. Günther in Charlotte Köhn-Behrens, *Was ist Rasse?* (Munich, 1934), p. 83.
28. Rost, *Sterilisation und Euthanasie,* pp. 42–43, 40, 45; Koonz, *The Nazi Conscience,* pp. 125–126.
29. Entry for 24 May 1936, Klemperer, *I Will Bear Witness,* p. 166; "Deutschland-Bericht der Sopade" (Jan. 1936), in *Deutschland-Berichte der Sozialdemokratischen Partei Deutschlands (Sopade) 1934–1940. Dritter Jahrgang 1936* (Frankfurt, 1980), p. 26. See also report for Oct. 1936, ibid., p. 1248.
30. Marion Kaplan, *Between Dignity and Despair: Jewish Life in Nazi Germany* (New York, 1998), p. 37; entry for 20 March 1938, Klemperer, *I Will Bear Witness,* p. 252. On German soldiers' impressions of the Soviet Union, see, for example, Stephen G. Fritz, *Frontsoldaten: The German Soldier in World War II* (Lexington, Ky., 1995), pp. 196, 199–200.

31. Elisabeth Brasch, "Mein Leben in Deutschland vor und nach dem 30. January 1933" (1940), "My Life in Germany," Houghton Library, bms Ger 91, no. 35, Harvard University. See also Hans Bender, "Willst du nicht beitreten?" in Marcel Reich-Ranicki, ed., *Meine Schulzeit im Dritten Reich: Erinnerungen deutscher Schriftsteller* (Munich, 1984), pp. 37–38.

32. Wilhelm Möller-Crivitz in Rudolf Benze and Gustav Gräfer, eds., *Erziehungsmächte und Erziehungshoheit im Grossdeutschen Reich als gestaltende Kräfte im Leben des Deutschen* (Leipzig, 1940), p. 43; Brasch, "Mein Leben in Deutschland vor und nach dem 30. January 1933." See also Bender, "Willst du nicht beitreten?" pp. 37–38.

33. "Mutterhände," *Neues Volk* 2 (Feb. 1934), pp. 30–31; on Hitler, entry for 20 April 1939, Klemperer, *I Will Bear Witness*, p. 299.

34. Albrecht Erich Günther, "Das Lager," *Deutsches Volkstum* (1934), p. 810. "Empire of the Camps" is the title of chap. 14 in Overy, *The Dictators*, which refers to concentration, not community, camps. See also Robert Gellately, *Backing Hitler: Consent and Coercion in Nazi Germany* (New York, 2001), pp. 58, 62, 65.

35. Günther, "Das Lager," p. 809; Mertens quoted in Jürgen Schiedeck and Martin Stahlmann, "Die Inszenierung 'totalen Erlebens': Lagererziehung im Nationalsozialismus," in Hans-Uwe Otto and Heinz Sünker, eds., *Politische Formierung und soziale Erziehung im Nationalsozialismus* (Frankfurt, 1991), p. 173.

36. Jutta Rüdiger, ed., *Die Hitler-Jugend und ihr Selbstverständnis im Spiegel ihrer Aufgabengebiete* (Lindhorst, 1983), p. 150; Manfred Seifert, *Kulturarbeit im Reichsarbeitsdienst. Theorie und Praxis nationalsozialistischer Kulturpflege* (Münster, 1996), p. 120.

37. Schiedeck and Stahlmann, "Die Inszenierung 'totalen Erlebens,'" p. 194.

38. Hans-Ulrich Thamer, *Verfolgung und Gewalt. Deutschland 1933–1945* (Berlin, 1986), pp. 407–408.

39. 1938 Sopade report, quoted in Richard J. Evans, *The Third Reich in Power, 1933–1939* (New York, 2005), p. 277; Thamer, *Verfolgung und Gewalt*, p. 407; entry for 2 July 1936, Goebbels, *Die Tagebücher*, pt. I, vol. 2, p. 636.

40. Konrad Warner, *Schicksalswende Europas? Ich sprach mit dem deutschen Volk . . .* (Rheinfelden, 1944), p. 41.

41. Hartmut Lohmann, *"Hier war doch alles nicht so schlimm": Der Landkreis Stade in der Zeit des Nationalsozialismus* (Stade, 1991),

p. 198. See also Dieter Rossmeissl, *"Ganz Deutschland wird zum Führer halten"*: *Zur politischen Erziehung in den Schules des Dritten Reiches* (Frankfurt, 1985), p. 68.

42. Adolf Mertens, *Schulungslager und Lagererziehung* (Berlin, 1937), pp. 62–63; Reagin, *Sweeping the German Nation,* p. 123.

43. Kiran Klaus Patel, *"Soldaten der Arbeit"*: *Arbeitsdienste in Deutschland und den USA* (Göttingen, 2003), p. 220.

44. Hellmut Petersen, *Die Erziehung der deutschen Jungmannschaft im Reichsarbeitsdienst* (Berlin, 1938), pp. 51, 59. See also Paul Seipp, *Formung und Auslese im Reichsarbeitsdienst. Das Ergebnis des Diensthalbjahrs 1934* (Berlin, 1935), pp. 30, 97.

45. Petersen, *Die Erziehung der deutschen Jungmannschaft im Reichsarbeitsdienst,* pp. 53–54.

46. Exit surveys quoted in Seipp, *Formung und Auslese im Reichsarbeitsdienst,* pp. 61–62.

47. Brasch, "Mein Leben in Deutschland vor und nach dem 30. January 1933," pp. 55–62, 71. See also Oskar Rummel, ". . . *Kein held!" Tagebuch Aufzeichnungen 1939–1947* (Würzburg, 1996), pp. 3–24, on his strenuous service in 1939.

48. On *Lager und Kolonne,* see Hans-Ulrich Thamer, *Der Nationalsozialismus* (Stuttgart, 2002), pp. 266–267; and Peter Dudek, "Nationalsozialistische Jugendpolitik und Arbeitserziehung: Das Arbeitslager als Instrument sozialer Disziplinierung," in Otto and Sünker, *Politische Formierung und soziale Erziehung,* p. 152.

49. Entries for 17 June 1933 and 5 Feb. 1937, Klemperer, *I Will Bear Witness,* pp. 19, 212. See also Bock, *Zwangssterilisation im Nationalsozialismus,* pp. 196–197; Koonz, *The Nazi Conscience,* pp. 115, 123; Evans, *The Third Reich in Power,* p. 444; and Vossen, *Gesundheitsämter im Nationalsozialismus,* p. 258.

50. Alfred Mierzejewski, *The Most Valuable Asset of the Reich: A History of the German National Railway,* vol. 2 (Chapel Hill, 2000), p. 37; Rüdiger, *Die Hitler-Jugend und ihr Selbstverständnis,* p. 147.

51. Entry for 6 Feb. 1936 in Lore Walb, *Ich, die Alte, ich, die Junge: Konfrontation mit meinem Tagebüchern 1933–1945* (Berlin, 1997), p. 58. See also Gerhard Remper, *Hitler's Children: The Hitler Youth and the SS* (Chapel Hill, 1989), p. 67; Michael Kater, *Hitler Youth* (Cambridge, 2004); and Melita Maschmann, *Account Rendered: A Dossier on My Former Self,* ed. Geoffrey Strachan (London, 1964), pp. 57–58.

52. See the following articles in *Das Schwarze Korps:* "Frauen sind keine Männer," 12 March 1935; "Hier steht die deutsche Frau!" 9 July 1936; "Vom Umgang mit Frauen," 23 Dec. 1937; "Wir wollen uns kennenlernen," 3 March 1938; "Aus Alt nach Neu," 26 Jan. 1939; and "Ist das unmännlich?" 10 Aug. 1939, with photographs of SS men diapering and feeding babies and pushing baby carriages. See also Gudrun Schwarz, *Eine Frau an seiner Seite: Ehefrauen in der "SS-Sippengemeinschaft"* (Hamburg, 1997).

53. Entry for 23 May 1933, Walb, *Ich, die Alte, ich, die Junge,* p. 31. In general, Irene Guenther, *Nazi Chic: Fashioning Women in the Third Reich* (Oxford, 2004).

54. Andrew Bergerson, *Ordinary Germans in Extraordinary Times: The Nazi Revolution in Hildesheim* (Bloomington, Ind., 2004), pp. 40–43. See also Günter Gaus, "Der Eigensinn der Erinnerungen," in Reich-Ranicki, *Meine Schulzeit im Dritten Reich,* p. 260; Eva Sternheim-Peters, *Die Zeit der grossen Täuschungen. Mädchenerleben im Faschismus* (Bielefeld, 1987), p. 99.

55. Jill Stephenson, *Women in Nazi Germany* (London, 2001), pp. 24, 32; Kater, *Hitler Youth,* pp. 107–111; and Gisela Miller-Kipp, ed., *"Auch Du gehörst dem Führer": Die Geschichte des Bundes Deutscher Mädel (BDM) in Quellen und Dokumenten* (Weinheim, 2001), p. 12.

56. Gisela Otmar, "Ich will mich jetzt nicht davon freisprechen, aber ich habe mich eigentlich wirlich hauptsächlich sportlich betätigt," in Gabriele Rosenthal, ed., *Die Hitlerjugend Generation: Biographische Thematisierung als Vergangenheitsbewältigung* (Essen, 1986), p. 111.

57. Sternheim-Peters, *Die Zeit der grossen Täuschungen,* p. 52; Wolfgang Ayass, *"Asoziale" im Nationalsozialismus* (Stuttgart, 1995), p. 39.

58. Henry Friedlander, *The Origins of Nazi Genocide: From Euthanasia to the Final Solution* (Chapel Hill, 1995), p. 20.

59. Herbert, *Best,* pp. 167, 175.

60. Ayass, *"Asoziale" im Nationalsozialismus,* p. 41; Günter Grass, *Peeling the Onion,* trans. Michael Henry Heim (New York, 2007), p. 92. On lesbians, see Goebbels on Hitler's views in his diary entry for 4 March 1944, Goebbels, *Die Tagebücher,* pt. II, vol. 11, p. 408.

61. Ayass, *"Asoziale" im Nationalsozialismus,* pp. 65, 69, 46.

62. Evans, *The Third Reich in Power,* p. 96. See also Aly, *Hitlers Volksstaat,* p. 27; Ayass, *"Asoziale" im Nationalsozialismus,* p. 62.

63. Holger Berschel, *Bürokratie und Terror. Das Judenreferat der Ge-*

stapo Düsseldorf 1935–1945 (Essen, 2001), p. 147; Tim Mason, *Social Policy in the Third Reich: The Working Class and the "National Community"* (Oxford, 1993), pp. 26–27. See also Robert Gellately, *The Gestapo and German Society: Enforcing Racial Policy, 1933–1945* (Oxford, 1990).

64. Michael Burleigh, *The Third Reich: A New History* (New York, 2000), p. 382.

65. Uwe Mai, *"Rasse und Raum": Agrarpolitik, Sozial- und Raumplanung im NS-Staat* (Paderborn, 2002), p. 57. See also Christopher Dipper, "20 July and the 'Jewish Question,'" in David Bankier, ed., *Probing the Depths of German Antisemitism: German Society and the Persecution of the Jews, 1933–1941* (New York, 2000), p. 497.

66. Bock, *Zwangssterilisation im Nationalsozialismus,* pp. 189–190.

67. Vossen, *Gesundheitsämter im Nationalsozialismus,* pp. 286–303.

68. Ibid., pp. 423, 448, 334. Stephenson, *Women in Nazi Germany,* p. 34, misreads the statistics for Berlin, putting the rate of rejection at 50 rather than 5 percent.

69. No. 62203, 10 July 1945, Schedule B interviews, USSBS, RG 243, box 505, folder 9, NARA; Johannes Vossen, "Das staatliche Gesundheitsamit im Dienst der Rassenpolitik," in Hermann Niebuhr and Andreas Ruppert, eds., *Nationalsozialismus in Detmold: Dokumentation eines stadtgeschichtlichen Projekts* (Bielefeld, 1998), p. 358.

70. Bock, *Zwangssterilisation im Nationalsozialismus,* pp. 216–219, 281.

71. Ibid., pp. 285, 209. On the debate about victims and perpetrators, see also Gisela Bock, "Claudia Koonz: *Mothers in the Fatherland,*" *Bulletin* (German Historical Institute, London) 2 (1989), pp. 16–24; Atina Grossmann, "Feminist Debates about Women and National Socialism," *Gender and History* 3 (1991), pp. 350–358.

72. Friedlander, *The Origins of Nazi Genocide,* pp. xi–xii, 54, 107, 110, 188.

73. Entry for 4 Nov. 1941, Göll, "Tagebuch 17. Febr. 1940–5. Juli 1942, 6. Buch," Landesarchiv Berlin, E Rep. 200-43, Acc. 3221, Nr. 6. See also entry for 21 Oct. 1941 in Lisa de Boor, *Tagebuchblätter. Aus den Jahren 1938–1945* (Munich, 1963), p. 88.

74. Letter to Annemarie Böll, 29 April 1943, in Heinrich Böll, *Briefe aus dem Krieg 1939–1945,* ed. Jochen Schubert (Cologne, 2001), p. 735.

75. Saul Friedländer, *The Years of Extermination: Nazi Germany and the Jews, 1939–1945* (New York, 2007), p. 202. See also Jill Stephenson, *Hitler's Home Front: Württemberg under the Nazis* (London, 2006), p. 149.

76. Saul Friedländer, *Nazi Germany and the Jews: The Years of Persecution, 1933–1939* (New York, 1997), p. 3; Koonz, *The Nazi Conscience*, p. 10; Friedländer, *The Years of Extermination*, p. xix.

77. Victor Klemperer, *The Language of the Third Reich: LTI, Lingua Tertii Imperii. A Philologist's Notebook*, trans. Martin Brady (1957; reprint, Somerset, N.J., 2000), p. 105; Koonz, *The Nazi Conscience*, pp. 55–60.

78. See letters from Hegrebe, 4 April 1934, and Elisabeth Sextrohs, 25 Sept. 1933, in the papers of Paula Tobias, "My Life in Germany," Houghton Library, bms Ger 91, no. 235, Harvard University.

79. Entry for 18 July 1933, Ebermayer, *Denn heute gehört uns Deutschland*, p. 155; Michael Wildt, "Violence against Jews in Germany, 1933–1939," in Bankier, *Probing the Depths of German Antisemitism*, p. 181.

80. Günter von Roden, *Geschichte der Duisburger Juden* (Duisburg, 1986), p. 797; Fritz Stern, *Five Germanys I Have Known* (New York, 2006), p. 94.

81. Raul Hilberg quoted in Koonz, *The Nazi Conscience*, pp. 10–11; Frank Bajohr, *"Aryanisation" in Hamburg: The Economic Exclusion of Jews and the Confiscation of Their Property in Nazi Germany* (New York, 2002), pp. 22–24. See advertisements in *Illustrieter Beobachter*, 27 May, 24 June, and 26 Aug. 1933.

82. Entry for 23 May 1933, Walb, *Ich, die Alte, ich, die Junge*, p. 31. In general, Guenther, *Nazi Chic*.

83. Frances Henry, *Victims and Neighbors: A Small Town in Germany Remembered* (South Hadley, Mass., 1984), p. 56; Kaplan, *Between Dignity and Despair*, p. 37; Friedländer, *Nazi Germany and the Jews: Persecution*, p. 38.

84. Kaplan, *Between Dignity and Despair*, p. 40; Friedländer, *Nazi Germany and the Jews: Persecution*, p. 38; entry for 27 May 1933 in Karl Windschild, *Mit Finger vor dem Mund: Ballenstedter Tagebuch des Pfarrers Karl Fr. E. Windschild, 1931–1944*, ed. Günther Windschild and Helmut Schmid (Dessau, 1999), p. 81.

85. "Deutschland-Bericht der Sopade" (July 1935), in *Deutschland-*

Berichte der Sozialdemokratischen Partei Deutschlands (Sopade) 1934–1940. Zweiter Jahrgang 1935 (Frankfurt, 1980), p. 812.

86. The term is from *The Times* (London), commenting on the Nuremberg Laws on 8 Nov. 1935, quoted in Gellately, *Backing Hitler,* p. 122. Jochen Klepper described these early weeks as a "silent pogrom." See entry for 27 March 1933 in Jochen Klepper, *Unter dem Schatten Deiner Flügel: Aus den Tagebüchern der Jahre 1932–1942* (Stuttgart, 1955), p. 45.

87. Entry for 9 May 1944, Klemperer, *I Will Bear Witness,* p. 312; Joseph Goebbels, "Die Juden sind schuld!" *Das Reich,* 16 Nov. 1941.

88. Entry for 2 Aug. 1935, Klepper, *Unter dem Schatten Deiner Flügel,* p. 273. See also Friedländer, *Nazi Germany and the Jews: Persecution,* pp. 122, 138; Bajohr, *"Aryanisation" in Hamburg,* p. 85; Inge Deutschkron, *Ich trug den gelben Stern* (Munich, 1985), p. 24.

89. Entries for 30 March 1933 and 21 July 1935, Klemperer, *I Will Bear Witness,* pp. 9, 129; Kaplan, *Between Dignity and Despair,* pp. 5–6.

90. Valentin Senger, *No. 12 Kaiserhofstrasse,* trans. Ralph Manheim (New York, 1980), p. 73; Peter Longerich, *Politik der Vernichtung: Eine Gesamtdarstellung der nationalsozialistischen Judenverfolgung* (Munich, 1998), p. 53; "Lagebericht des hannoverschen Regierungspräsidenten an den Reichsminister des Innern für die Monate Dezember 1934/January 1935," 4 Feb. 1935, in Klaus Mlynek, ed., *Gestapo Hannover meldet . . . : Polizei- und Regierungsberichte für das mittlere und südliche Niedersachsen zwischen 1933 und 1937* (Hildesheim, 1986), p. 315.

91. Entries for 12, 19, and 26 Aug. 1935, Windschild, *Mit Finger vor dem Mund,* pp. 267–273.

92. Koonz, *The Nazi Conscience,* p. 185. For a full account of the laws and the racial theories behind them, see Cornelia Essner, *Die "Nürnberger Gesetze" oder die Verwaltung des Rassenwahns 1933–1945* (Paderborn, 2002).

93. David Bankier, *The Germans and the Final Solution: Public Opinion under Nazism* (Oxford, 1992), pp. 76–77; Longerich, *Politik der Vernichtung,* pp. 106–110. See also the entry for 15 Sept. 1935, Windschild, *Mit Finger vor dem Mund,* p. 279.

94. Yehuda Bauer, "Overall Explanations, German Society, and the Jews or: Some Thoughts about Context," in Bankier, *Probing the Depths*

of German Antisemitism, p. 16; Kaplan, *Between Dignity and Despair,* p. 24.

95. Friedländer, *Nazi Germany and the Jews: Persecution,* p. 184.
96. Entry for 30 Jan. 1937, Klepper, *Unter dem Schatten Deiner Flügel,* p. 419.
97. Sternheim-Peters, *Die Zeit der grossen Täuschungen,* p. 20, on her brother. According to SS personnel records in the Berlin Document Center, twenty-three SS officers carried the last name Israel.
98. "Wohin mit den Juden?" *Das Schwarze Korps,* 10 Feb. 1938.
99. Karl Schlögel, *Im Raume Lesen wir die Zeit* (Munich, 2003), p. 127.
100. Entry for 11 Sept. 1938, Klemperer, *I Will Bear Witness,* p. 268; Jonny Moser, "Depriving Jews of Their Legal Rights in the Third Reich," in Walter H. Pehle, ed., *November 1938: From "Reichskristallnacht" to Genocide,* trans. William Templer (Oxford, 1991), p. 128.
101. On the vernacular origins of the term, Dieter Obst, *"Reichskristallnacht": Ursachen und Verlauf des antisemitischen Pogroms vom November 1938* (Frankfurt, 1991), p. 1.
102. On karma, see the entry for 28 Dec. 1941, de Boor, *Tagebuchblätter,* p. 94.
103. Goebbels quoted in Hermann Graml, *Anti-Semitism in the Third Reich,* trans. Tim Kirk (Oxford, 1992), p. 120; and in Friedländer, *Nazi Germany and the Jews: Persecution,* p. 274. The missing entries for 10 and 11 Nov. were recently rediscovered.
104. Heinemann Stern, quoted in Hans Dieter Schäfer, *Das Gespaltenes Bewusstsein: Über deutsche Kultur und Lebenswirklichkeit 1933–1945* (Munich, 1984), p. 146.
105. Swiss consul quoted in Friedländer, *Nazi Germany and the Jews: Persecution,* p. 277; on "Sonderburg," Kaplan, *Between Dignity and Despair,* pp. 124–125; and Henry, *Victims and Neighbors,* p. 117; on Teuchtlingen, Wildt, "Violence against Jews in Germany, 1933–1939," pp. 197–198, 200.
106. For details, Obst, *"Reichskristallnacht."*
107. Friedländer, *Nazi Germany and the Jews: Persecution,* p. 277.
108. Georg Hensel, "Der Sack überm Kopf," in Reich-Ranicki, *Meine Schulzeit im Dritten Reich,* p. 120.
109. Diary entry for 9 Nov. 1938 in Ruth Andreas-Friedrich, *Berlin Under-*

ground, 1938–1945 (New York, 1947), p. 22. This entry, however, appears to be a composite and was probably written after the events of 10 Nov. 1938. In general, Wolf-Arno Kropat, *"Reichskristallnacht": Der Judenpogrom vom 7–10 November 1938– Urheber, Täter, Hintergründe* (Wiesbaden, 1997), pp. 156–165.

110. Entry for 22 Jan. 1939 in Karl Dürkefälden, *"Schreiben wie es wirklich war . . .": Aufzeichungen Karl Dürkefäldens aus den Jahren 1933–1945,* ed. Herbert Obenaus and Sibylle Obenaus (Hanover, 1985), pp. 88–91. On the circulation of stories about the pogrom, see also the entries for 18 Nov. and 6 and 16 Dec. 1938, Windschild, *Mit Finger vor dem Mund,* pp. 459–465.

111. Stern, *Five Germanys I Have Known,* p. 135.

112. On Saarbrücken, Wildt, "Violence against Jews in Germany, 1933–1939," p. 201; on Kiel, entry for 22 Jan. 1939, Dürkefälden, *"Schreiben wie es wirklich war,"* p. 92; on Erfurt, Wolfgang Benz, "The Relapse into Barbarism," in Pehle, *November 1938,* p. 30.

113. See the accounts of Hans Berger, "Erinnerungen an die Kristallnacht und meine Erlebnisse im KZ Buchenwald" (1939 ms.), in Monika Richarz, ed., *Jüdisches Leben in Deutschland. Selbstzeugnisse zur Sozialgeschichte 1918–1945* (Stuttgart, 1982), pp. 323–335; and of the husband of Annemarie Wolfram, which is embedded in her "Mein Leben in Deutschland vor und nach dem 30. Januar 1933" (1940), Houghton Library, bms Ger 91, no. 247, Harvard University.

114. Wildt, "Violence against Jews in Germany, 1933–1939," p. 204.

115. Aly, *Hitlers Volksstaat,* p. 61.

116. See "Eine kleine Auswahl," *Das Schwarze Korps,* 24 Nov. 1938; "Zweite Auswahl," 8 Dec. 1938; "Dritte Auswahl," 15 Dec. 1938. See also Eric Rentschler, *The Ministry of Illusion: Nazi Cinema and Its Afterlife* (Cambridge, 1996), p. 160.

117. "Juden was nun?" *Das Schwarze Korps,* 24 Nov. 1938.

118. Friedländer, *Nazi Germany and the Jews: Persecution,* p. 282.

119. Jürgen Hartmann, "Die Deportation Detmolder Juden 1941–1945," in Niebuhr and Ruppert, *Nationalsozialismus in Detmold,* p. 661.

120. Ian Kershaw, *Hitler 1936–1945: Nemesis* (New York, 2000), p. 153.

121. Diary entries for 16 Jan. and 2 Feb. 1939, Andreas-Friedrich, *Berlin Underground,* pp. 35–36. See also Deutschkron, *Ich trug den gelben Stern,* p. 45.

122. Quoted in Kaplan, *Between Dignity and Despair,* p. 117. The phrase

is from a 6 Feb. 1937 letter of Kurt Rosenberg to Grete and Rudolf Eichenberg. See Oliver Doetzer, *"Aus Menschen werden Briefe": Die Korresondenz einer jüdischen Familie zwischen Verfolgung und Emigration 1933–1947* (Cologne, 2002), p. 1.

123. Hans Winterfeldt, "Deutschland. Ein Zeitbild 1920–1945" (1969 ms.), excerpts in Richarz, *Jüdisches Leben in Deutschland,* pp. 344–345.

3. Empire of Destruction

1. Elsa Morante, *History: A Novel* (New York, 1977), pp. 261, 268–269, 272.
2. Paul Salitter, "Bericht über die Evakuierung von Juden nach Riga vom 11.12–17.12.1941," 26 Dec. 1941, reprinted in Günter von Roden, *Geschichte der Duisburger Juden,* vol. 2 (Duisburg, 1986), p. 872; Hans G. Adler, *Der verwaltete Mensch. Studien zur Deportation der Juden aus Deutschland* (Tübingen, 1974), pp. 581–582.
3. Entry for 14 Aug. 1944 in Victor Klemperer, *I Will Bear Witness 1942–1945: A Diary of the Nazi Years* (New York, 1998), p. 344; photo reproduced in Doris L. Bergen, *War and Genocide: A Concise History of the Holocaust* (Lanham, Md., 2003), p. 177. See also Samuel D. Kassow, *Who Will Write Our History? Emmanuel Ringelblum, the Warsaw Ghetto, and the Oyneg Shabes Archive* (Bloomington, Ind., 2007).
4. Ruth Andreas-Friedrich, *Berlin Underground, 1938–1945* (New York, 1947). Letters were actually found and posted. See, for example, Etty Hillesum's report that she and her fellow prisoners left for Auschwitz "singing," in Etty Hillesum, *An Interrupted Life: The Diaries of Etty Hillesum, 1941–1943* (New York, 1983), p. 13; or Alice Licht's letter found on the railway line between Theresienstadt and Auschwitz, in Inge Deutschkron, *Ich trug den gelben Stern* (Munich, 1985), p. 131.
5. Martin Humburg, *Das Gesicht des Krieges. Feldpostbriefe von Wehrmachtssoldaten aus der Sowjetunion 1941–1944* (Opladen, 1998), pp. 18, 88.
6. Ortwin Buchbender and Reinhold Sterz, eds., *Das andere Gesicht des Krieges: Deutsche Feldpostbriefe 1939–1945* (Munich, 1982), p. 13; Christian Gerlach, *Kalkulierte Morde: Die deutsche Wirtschafts- und*

Vernichtungspolitik in Weissrussland 1941 bis 1944 (Hamburg, 2000), p. 33 n. 89; Walter Bähr and Hans W. Bähr, eds., *Kriegsbriefe gefallener Studenten 1939–1945* (Tübingen, 1952).

7. Albert Neuhaus to Agnes Neuhaus, 8 Sept. 1941 and 9 Feb. 1942, in Karl Reddemann, ed., *Zwischen Front und Heimat: Der Briefwechsel des Münsterischen Ehepaares Agnes und Albert Neuhaus 1940–1944* (Münster, 1996), pp. 304, 409.

8. Letter of A. N., Görlitz, 27 June 1940, quoted in Buchbender and Sterz, *Das andere Gesicht des Krieges*, p. 62; entry for 24 June 1941 in Paulheinz Wantzen, *Das Leben im Krieg. Ein Tagebuch* (Bad Homburg, 2000), p. 407; Klaus Latzel, *Deutsche Soldaten— nationalsozialistischer Krieg? Kriegserlebnis—Kriegserfahrung 1939– 1945* (Paderborn, 1998), p. 297.

9. Letter of A. N., Görlitz, 27 June 1940, quoted in Buchbender and Sterz, *Das andere Gesicht des Krieges*, p. 62.

10. Albert Neuhaus to Agnes Neuhaus, 25 Sept. and 30 Nov. 1941 and 1 March 1942, Reddemann, *Zwischen Front und Heimat*, pp. 323, 362–363, 433.

11. Latzel, *Deutsche Soldaten—nationalsozialistischer Krieg?* p. 134. See also letter of 12 July 1940 in Marlies Tremper, ed., *Briefe des Soldaten Helmut N., 1939–1945* (Berlin, 1988), p. 70.

12. Letter of 12 April 1941, quoted in Latzel, *Deutsche Soldaten— nationalsozialistischer Krieg?* p. 46; ibid., p. 177.

13. Letters of 9 and 10 July 1941, Buchbender and Sterz, *Das andere Gesicht des Krieges*, pp. 73–74. See also Stephen G. Fritz, *Front- soldaten: The German Soldier in World War II* (Lexington, Ky., 1995), pp. 199–200.

14. Buchbender and Sterz, *Das andere Gesicht des Krieges*, p. 26. See also Klara Löffler, *Aufgehoben: Soldatenbriefe aus dem Zweiten Weltkrieg. Eine Studie zur subjektiven Wirklichkeit des Krieges* (Bamberg, 1992), p. 61.

15. Entry for 12 Dec. 1941 in Joseph Goebbels, *Die Tagebücher von Joseph Goebbels. Sämtliche Fragmente*, ed. Elke Fröhlich (Munich, 1994), pt. II, vol. 2, p. 483; *Mitteilungen für die Truppe*, quoted in Marlis G. Steinert, *Hitler's War and the Germans: Public Mood and Attitude during the Second World War*, ed. and trans. Thomas E. J. de Witt (Athens, Ohio, 1977), p. 152.

16. Hans Olte (pseud.), letter of 26 Feb. 1942, Latzel, *Deutsche*

Soldaten—nationalsozialistischer Krieg? p. 92; Albert Neuhaus to Agnes Neuhaus, 4 April and 11 Aug. 1942 and 23 May 1943, Reddemann, *Zwischen Front und Heimat*, pp. 485, 759, 851.

17. Latzel, *Deutsche Soldaten—nationalsozialistischer Krieg?* pp. 273, 90.
18. Hannes Heer, "How Amorality Became Normality: Reflections on the Mentality of German Soldiers on the Eastern Front," in Heer and Klaus Naumann, eds., *War of Extermination: The German Military in World War II, 1941–44* (New York, 2000), pp. 331–332; Kleo Pleyer, *Volk im Feld* (Hamburg, 1943), p. 227; July 1941 letter quoted in Omer Bartov, *Hitler's Army: Soldiers, Nazis, and the War in the Third Reich* (New York, 1991), p. 26; and Hanns Wiedmann, *Landser, Tod, und Teufel: Aufzeichnungen aus dem Feldzug im Osten* (Munich, 1942), p. 11.
19. Joseph Goebbels, "Gespräche mit Frontsoldaten," *Das Reich*, 26 July 1942.
20. Notes dated 23 April and 24 June 1942, Reddemann, *Zwischen Front und Heimat*, pp. 500–501, 548–549.
21. Janina Struck, "My Duty Was to Take Pictures," *The Guardian*, 28 July 2005. See also Dieter Reifarth and Viktoria Schmidt-Linsenhoff, "Die Kamera der Täter," in Hannes Heer and Klaus Naumann, eds., *Vernichtungskrieg: Verbrechen der Wehrmacht 1941–1944* (Hamburg, 1995); Wendy Lower, *Nazi Empire-Building and the Holocaust in Ukraine* (Chapel Hill, 2005), pp. 79–82.
22. Letter of 28 Sept. 1941, quoted in Sven Oliver Müller, "Nationalismus in der deutschen Kriegsgesellschaft 1939 bis 1945," in Jörg Echternkamp, ed., *Die Deutsche Kriegsgesellschaft 1939 bis 1945*, 2 vols. (Munich, 2004), 2: 84.
23. Entry for 26 Nov. 1941 in Anna Haag, "Kriegstagebuch," in *Leben und gelebt werden* (Tübingen, 2003), pp. 252–253. See also David Bankier, *The Germans and the Final Solution: Public Opinion under Nazism* (Oxford, 1992), pp. 108–111, 115; Hans Mommsen, "What Did the Germans Know about the Genocide of the Jews?" in Walter H. Pehle, ed., *November 1938: From "Reichskristallnacht" to Genocide*, trans. William Templer (Oxford, 1991), pp. 187–221.
24. Walter Kempowski, *Das Echolot: Ein kollektives Tagebuch 16.2–28.2.1943* (Munich, 1997), pp. 271, 127; Uwe Timm, *In My Brother's Shadow: A Life and Death in the SS*, trans. Anthea Bell (New York, 2005), p. 25.

25. On Austerlitz, Jean-Marc Dreyfus, "'Almost Camps' in Paris: The Difficult Description of Three Annexes of Drancy—Austerlitz, Lévitan, and Bassano, July 1943 to August 1944," in Jonathan Petropoulos and John K. Roth, eds., *Gray Zones: Ambiguity and Compromise in the Holocaust and Its Aftermath* (New York, 2005), p. 228.

26. Alexander Rossino, *Hitler Strikes Poland: Blitzkrieg, Ideology and Atrocity* (Lawrence, Kans., 2003), pp. 2–9; Lower, *Nazi Empire-Building and the Holocaust,* pp. 3, 6.

27. A. J. P. Taylor, *The Origins of the Second World War* (New York, 1996); Gerhard L. Weinberg, *A World at Arms: A Global History of World War II* (Cambridge, Eng., 1994), especially pp. 54–55, 176–181.

28. Norman Goda, *Tomorrow the World: Hitler, Northwest Africa, and the Path toward America* (College Station, Tex., 1998).

29. Rossino, *Hitler Strikes Poland,* pp. 9–10.

30. Entry for 5 Sept. 1939 in the war diary of Gerhard M., in Heinrich Breloer, ed., *Mein Tagebuch: Geschichten vom Überleben 1939–1947* (Cologne, 1984), p. 34; Rossino, *Hitler Strikes Poland.*

31. Peter Longerich, *"Davon haben wir nichts gewusst!" Die Deutschen und die Judenverfolgung 1933–1945* (Berlin, 2006), p. 149, on *Der Angriff,* 24 and 26 Oct. 1939; Rossino, *Hitler Strikes Poland,* pp. 72, 154–169; Christopher R. Browning, *The Origins of the Final Solution: The Evolution of Nazi Jewish Policy, September 1939–March 1942* (Lincoln, Neb., 2004), p. 17. Widely used as a training manual, Edwin Erich Dwinger's *Der Tod in Polen: Eine volksdeutsche Passion* (Jena, 1940) is the key example of the propaganda.

32. Melita Maschmann, *Account Rendered: A Dossier on My Former Self,* ed. Geoffrey Strachan (London, 1964), p. 59; Rossino, *Hitler Strikes Poland,* p. 202.

33. Quote from Alvensleben, Ian Kershaw, *Hitler 1936–1945: Nemesis* (New York, 2000), pp. 242–243; instructions quoted in Elizabeth Harvey, *Women and the East: Agents and Witnesses of Germanization* (New Haven, 2003), p. 80; entries for 14, 15, and 16 Oct. 1939 in Zygmunt Klukowski, *Diary of the Years of Occupation 1939–44* (Urbana, 1993), pp. 40–42. See also entries for 12 Sept. and 3 and 4 Oct. 1939 in Alan Adelson, ed., *The Diary of David Siera-*

kowiak: Five Notebooks from the Łódź Ghetto (New York, 1996), pp. 37, 46–47.

34. Entry for 19 Sept. 1939 in Franz Halder, *The Halder War Diary, 1939–1942,* ed. Charles Burdick and Hans-Adolf Jacobsen (Morato, Calif., 1988), p. 57; Alvensleben quoted in Richard Breitman, *The Architect of Genocide: Himmler and the Final Solution* (New York, 1991), p. 95; Martin Cüppers, *Wegbereiter der Shoah: Die Waffen SS, der Kommandostab Reichsführer-SS und die Judenvernichtung* (Darmstadt, 2005), p. 53; Czeslaw Madajczyk, *Die Okkupationspolitik Nazideutschlands in Polen 1939–1945* (Berlin, 1987), p. 15.

35. Browning, *Origins of the Final Solution,* p. 69.

36. Entry for 5 Nov. 1940, Goebbels, *Die Tagebücher,* pt. I, vol. 4, p. 387; and Goebbels in *Das Reich,* 5 Jan. 1941. See also Michael Wildt, *Generation des Unbedingten: Das Führungskorps des Reichssicherheitshauptamtes* (Hamburg, 2002).

37. Untitled document, probably from early 1940, R49/3073/21, BAB; Browning, *Origins of the Final Solution,* p. 13.

38. Hanns Johst, *Ruf des Reiches, Echo des Volkes* (Munich, 1940), pp. 8, 24, 33, 37, 61–63, 68–69; Pohl to Brandt, 23 Nov. 1944, file for Hanns Johst, Berlin Document Center, A3343, SSO-140A, NARA.

39. Entry for 5 Nov. 1940, Goebbels, *Die Tagebücher,* pt. I, vol. 4, p. 387.

40. Karl Schlögel, *Im Raume Lesen Wir die Zeit* (Munich, 2003), p. 54; Götz Aly and Susanne Heim, *Architects of Annihilation: Auschwitz and the Logic of Destruction* (1991; reprint, Princeton, 2002), p. 81.

41. Merkblatt für den Polizeibeamten zur Durchführung der Evakuierungen von polnischen Hofbesitzern," 9 May 1940, R75/3/7, BAB; "Verlauf der Evakuierung und Ansiedlung am 30.3.40," R75/3/5, BAB. See the spooked recollections of a Polish woman who had worked in Posen as a maid for a family from Riga: "Franziska E," in Annekatrein Mandel, *Zwangsarbeit im Kinderzimmer: "Ostarbeiterinnen" in deutschen Familien von 1939 bis 1945* (Frankfurt, 1994), pp. 20–21.

42. Isabel Heinemann, *"Rasse, Siedlung, deutsches Blut": Das Rasse- und Siedlungshauptamt der SS und die rassenpolitische Neuordnung Europas* (Göttingen, 2003), p. 289.

43. Memorandum prepared by the Reichsführer SS and Reichskommissar

für die Festigung deutschen Volkstums, 16 Feb. 1942, R5/6774, BAB; Harvey, *Women and the East,* p. 84.

44. Madajczyk, *Die Okkupationspolitik Nazideutschlands,* pp. 77–78, 80; Sophie Jaki, "Unsere letzten Tagen in Stanislau," R69/161/15–18, BAB. In general, see Mechthild Rössler and Sabine Schleiermacher, eds., *Der "Generalplan Ost": Hauptlinien der nationalsozialisten Planungs- und Vernichtungspolitik* (Berlin, 1993).

45. Himmler quoted in Aly and Heim, *Architects of Annihilation,* pp. 86, 82–83; Harvey, *Women and the East,* p. 239.

46. Götz Aly, *"Final Solution": Nazi Population Policy and the Murder of the European Jews* (London, 1999), pp. 76, 123; "Auszüge aus Briefen und Karten baltendeutscher Rückwanderer," R69/1223/12–18, BAB.

47. Aly and Heim, *Architects of Annihilation,* p. 89.

48. Aly, *"Final Solution,"* pp. 207–208.

49. Harvey, *Women and the East,* pp. 90, 155.

50. Ibid., pp. 31, 190; and generally R49/3046, /3057, /3062, BAB. See also Martha Wegmann, "Allgemeine Stimmung der Siedler," Kreis Grätz, 9 Nov. 1942, R49/3062/4, BAB, as well as reports from Kreis Samter by Hermine Bungerberg, 2 Sept. 1942, R49/3062/11; from Ostrowo by Else Reichert, January 1943, R49/3062/12; and from Kreis Litzmannstadt-Land by Erna Berg, 1 March 1943, R49/3062/111. See also "In der neuen Heimat," *Der Arbeitsmann,* 20 Dec. 1941, NS5VI/19298, BAB.

51. "Eine moderne Völkerwanderung," *Der Neue Tag* (Prague), 27 May 1940, quoted in Adler, *Der verwaltete Mensch,* p. 171.

52. Irene Körner, "Bericht über meine Kindergartenarbeit im Kreise Leslau Warthegau" (1940); and Anni Klingel and Annerose Eberhardt, "Bericht über die Tätigkeit im Kindergarten zu Krosniewice" (1941?), R49/3051/1–11, /109–110, BAB; Wilhelm Hess, "Erlebnisbericht für die Kriegsgeschichte der EWZ," 25 May 1942, R69/40/60, BAB.

53. Helmut Koschorke, *Polizei greift ein! Kriegsberichte aus Ost, West, und Nord* (Berlin, 1941), p. 30; Harvey, *Women and the East,* p. 245.

54. Körner, "Bericht über meine Kindergartenarbeit"; Walter Hebenbrock, *Mit der NSV nach Polen* (Berlin, 1940), pp. 23–24.

55. Harvey, *Women and the East,* pp. 131–132.

56. Entries for 13 July and 20 July 1943 in Annemarie Landenberger, *Als*

Hamburger Lehrerin in der Kinderlandverschickung: Tagebuch 1943 (Hamburg, 1992), pp. 42, 46.

57. *Das Generalgouvernement: Reisehandbuch von Karl Baedeker* (Leipzig, 1943), pp. 50, 129; entry for 10 Jan. 1943 in Liselotte Orgel-Purper, *Willst Du meine Witwe werden? Eine deutsche Liebe im Krieg* (Berlin, 1995), p. 65.

58. Teacher from Thüringen quoted in Harvey, *Women and the East,* p. 278; Lower, *Nazi Empire-Building and the Holocaust,* p. 201; Andrej Angrick, *Besatzungspolitik und Massenmord: Die Einsatzgruppe D in der südlichen Sowjetunion 1941–1943* (Hamburg, 2003), p. 292.

59. Entry for 8 March 1945, Goebbels, *Die Tagebücher,* pt. II, vol. 15, p. 450.

60. Entries for 2 and 22 June 1940, ibid., pt. I, vol. 4, pp. 187, 213; "Eine neue Gründerzeit?" *Das Schwarze Korps,* 25 July 1940.

61. Ulrich Herbert, *Hitler's Foreign Workers: Enforced Foreign Labor in Germany under the Third Reich,* trans. William Templer (Cambridge, Eng., 1997), p. 107; entry for 30 Nov. 1941, Goebbels, *Die Tagebücher,* pt. II, vol. 2, p. 402.

62. Entry for 13 Dec. 1940, ibid., pt. I, vol. 4, p. 431; entry for 7 Oct. 1940, Wantzen, *Das Leben im Krieg,* p. 269; and Hans Hoeschen, *Zwischen Weichsel und Volga* (Gütersloh, 1943), p. 8.

63. No. 62792, 25 July 1945, Schedule B interviews, USSBS, RG 243, box 512, folder 32, NARA; Norbert Frei, *1945 und Wir: Das Dritte Reich im Bewusstsein der Deutschen* (Munich, 2005), p. 118.

64. Kershaw, *Hitler 1936–1945,* pp. 345, 335.

65. Entry for 25 Feb. 1944, Goebbels, *Die Tagebücher,* pt. II, vol. 11, p. 348.

66. Adam Tooze, *The Wages of Destruction: The Making and Breaking of the Nazi Economy* (New York, 2007), pp. 476–480. See also Gerlach, *Kalkulierte Morde,* pp. 49–50.

67. Jörg Echternkamp, "Im Kampf an der inneren und äusseren Front. Grundzüge der deutschen Gesellschaft im Zweiten Weltkrieg," in Echternkamp, *Die Deutsche Kriegsgesellschaft,* 1: 58.

68. Peter Longerich, *Politik der Vernichtung: Eine Gesamtdarstellung der nationalsozialistischen Judenverfolgung* (Munich, 1998), pp. 299–301.

69. Entry for 22 June 1941, Goebbels, *Die Tagebücher,* pt. I, vol. 4,

pp. 710–711, 719–720. On the film, see entry for 30 July 1940, ibid., p. 259; and "'Vom Winde verweht,'" *Das Reich,* 29 Oct. 1944. On German reactions, see interviews collected in USSBS, RG 243, NARA.

70. Dölker-Rehder and A. N. diary excerpts for 22 June 1941, Kempowski, *Das Echolot,* pp. 20–21, 46; Agnes to Albert Neuhaus, 6 July 1941, Reddemann, *Zwischen Front und Heimat,* p. 253.

71. Entry for 22 June 1941, Klemperer, *I Will Bear Witness,* p. 390. See also Angrick, *Besetzungspolitik und Massenmord,* p. 37.

72. Entry for 29 June 1941, Andreas-Friedrich, *Berlin Underground,* p. 69. On Dietrich, see Aristotle A. Kallis, "Der Niedergang der Deutungsmacht. Nationalsozialistische Propaganda im Kriegsverlauf," in Echternkamp, *Die Deutsche Kriegsgesellschaft,* 2: 209.

73. Christa Wolf, *Patterns of Childhood* (New York, 1980), p. 172. On *Erlebnisgemeinschaft,* see Birthe Kundrus, "Totale Unterhaltung? Die kulturelle Kriegführung 1939 bis 1945 im Film, Rundfunk und Theater," in Echternkamp, *Die Deutsche Kriegsgesellschaft,* 2: 116.

74. Entry for 16 June 1941, Goebbels, *Die Tagebücher,* pt. I, vol. 4, p. 695; Smith quoted in Ernest K. Bramsted, *Geobbels and National Socialist Propaganda, 1925–1945* (East Lansing, 1965), p. 246.

75. Entries for 17 Aug. and 8 Sept. 1941 in Lore Walb, *Ich, die Alte, ich, die Junge: Konfrontation mit meinem Tagebüchern 1933–1945* (Berlin, 1997), pp. 227–228; Harry W. Flannery, *Assignment to Berlin* (New York, 1942), p.380; entry for 11 Aug. 1941, Halder, *War Diary,* p. 506. Germans often used the phrase "wir siegen uns todt" (we are beating ourselves to death) to describe their predicament in Russia. See the postwar interviews conducted by the USSBS, RG 243, NARA.

76. Speech quoted in Ian Kershaw, *The "Hitler Myth": Image and Reality in the Third Reich* (Oxford, 1987), p. 174; Howard K. Smith, *Last Train from Berlin* (New York, 1942), pp. 88–90.

77. *Völkischer Beobachter,* 10 Oct. 1941; entry for 9 Oct. 1941, Klemperer, *I Will Bear Witness,* p. 439. See also entry for 24 Sept. 1941, Goebbels, *Die Tagebücher,* pt. II, vol. 1, p. 481.

78. Entry for 1 Jan. 1942 in Lili Hahn, . . . *bis alles in Scherben fällt. Tagebuchblätter 1933–1945* (Cologne, 1979), p. 430; Goebbels quoted in *Völkischer Beobachter,* 21 Dec. 1941.

79. Göring quoted in Jost Dülffer, *Deutsche Geschichte 1933–1945: Führerglaube und Vernichtungskrieg* (Stuttgart, 1992), p. 125.

80. Longerich, *Politik der Vernichtung*, p. 269.
81. Aly, *"Final Solution,"* p. 59. See also Wolf Gruner, "Von der Kollektivausweisung zur Deportation der Juden aus Deutschland (1938–1945): Neue Perspektiven und Dokumente," in Birthe Kundrus and Beate Meyer, eds., *Deportation der Juden aus Deutschland: Pläne, Praxis, Reaktionen 1938–1945* (Göttingen, 2004), pp. 39, 40.
82. Browning, *Origins of the Final Solution*, pp. 69, 83.
83. Aly, *"Final Solution,"* p. 92; Browning, *Origins of the Final Solution*, pp. 85–86.
84. Longerich, *Politik der Vernichtung*, p. 274.
85. Aly, *"Final Solution,"* pp. 109, 125.
86. Longerich, *Politik der Vernichtung*, pp. 324, 342–343; Gerlach, *Kalkulierte Morde*, pp. 536–537.
87. Longerich, *"Davon haben wir nichts gewusst!"* pp. 159–160.
88. Himmler quoted in Lower, *Nazi Empire-Building and the Holocaust*, pp. 8, 76; Wendy Lower, "'Anticipatory Obedience' and the Nazi Implementation of the Holocaust in the Ukraine: A Case Study of Central and Peripheral Forces in the Generalbezirk Zhytomyr, 1941–144," *Holocaust and Genocide Studies* 16 (spring 2002), pp. 1–22.
89. Browning, *Origins of the Final Solution*, p. 309; Kershaw, *Hitler 1936–1945*, p. 400; entry for 5 July 1941 in H. R. Trevor-Roper, ed., *Hitler's Secret Conversations, 1941–1944* (New York, 1972), p. 4.
90. Longerich, *Politik der Vernichtung*, p. 372; Saul Friedländer, *The Years of Extermination: Nazi Germany and the Jews 1939–1945* (New York, 2007), pp. 238–239.
91. Longerich, *Politik der Vernichtung*, p. 385.
92. Gerlach, *Kalkulierte Morde*, p. 574.
93. Kershaw, *Hitler 1936–1945*, p. 468. See also Wolfgang Scheffler, "Die Einsatzgruppe A 1941/42," in Peter Klein, ed., *Die Einsatzgruppen in der besetzten Sowjetunion 1941/42. Die Tätigkeits- und Lageberichte des Chefs der Sicherheitspolizei und des SD* (Berlin, 1997), p. 35; Christian Gerlach, "Die Einsatzgruppe B 1941/42," ibid., pp. 58–59.
94. Sybille Steinbacher, "In the Shadow of Auschwitz: The Murder of the Jews of East Upper Silesia," in Ulrich Herbert, ed., *Nationalsocialist Extermination Policies: Contemporary German Perspectives and Controversies* (New York, 2000), pp. 287–288.

95. Longerich, *Politik der Vernichtung*, p. 391; G. F. Krivosheev, *Soviet Casualties and Combat Losses in the Twentieth Century* (London, 1997), p. 96.

96. See also John Garrard and Carol Garrard, *The Bones of Berdichev: The Life and Fate of Vasily Grossman* (New York, 1996).

97. Hartmut Rüss, "Wer war verantwortlich für das Massaker von Babij Jar?" *Militärgeschichtliche Mitteilungen* 57 (1998), pp. 483–508; "Operational Situation Report USSR No. 97," entry for 28 Sept. 1941, in Yitzchak Arad, Shmuel Krakowski, and Shmuel Spector, eds., *The Einsatzgruppen Reports: Selections from the Dispatches of the Nazi Death Squads' Campaign against the Jews, July 1941–January 1943* (New York, 1989), p. 165.

98. This was in fact the explicit premise of an SS workshop on fighting partisans held at the end of September 1941. See Gerlach, *Kalkulierte Morde*, p. 566.

99. Quoted in Wolfram Wette, *The Wehrmacht: History, Myth, Reality*, trans. Deborah Lucas Schneider (Cambridge, 2006), pp. 117–118.

100. Testimony of the driver Höfer in Michael Berenbaum, ed., *Witness to the Holocaust* (New York, 1997), pp. 138–139.

101. Longerich, *Politik der Vernichtung*, pp. 378, 377.

102. Entry for 11 Oct. 1941 in Willy Cohn, *Als Jude in Breslau 1941*, ed. Joseph Walk (Gerlingen, 1984), p. 106; Karl Dürkefälden, "*Schreiben wie es wirklich war . . .*" *Aufzeichungen Karl Dürkefäldens aus den Jahren 1933–1945,* ed. Herbert Obenaus and Sibylle Obenaus (Hanover, 1985), pp. 107, 110; entry for 19 April 1942, Klemperer, *I Will Bear Witness*, p. 41; Wette, *The Wehrmacht*, p. 112.

103. Entries for 23 July 1941 and 5 April 1943 in Kazimierz Sakowicz, *Ponary Diary 1941–1943: A Bystander's Account of a Mass Murder* (New Haven, 2005), pp. 13, 81. See also Christopher R. Browning, *Ordinary Men: Reserve Police Battalion 101 and the Final Solution in Poland* (New York, 1992), p. 152; Scheffler, "Die Einsatzgruppe A 1941/42," p. 36.

104. *True to Type: A Selection from Letters and Diaries of German Soldiers and Civilians Collected on the Soviet-German Front* (London, n.d. [1943]), p. 29.

105. Bernd Boll and Hans Safrian, "On the Way to Stalingrad: The 6th Army in 1941–42," in Heer and Naumann, *War of Extermination*, p. 249; Hannes Heer, "Killing Fields: The Wehrmacht and the Holocaust in Belorussia, 1941–42," ibid., p. 66; Erich Mirek, "Enthüllung

Faschistischer Grausamkeiten," in *In den Wäldern Belorusslands: Erinnerungen sowjetischer Partisanen und deutscher Antifaschisten* (Berlin, 1977), p. 126.

106. Jürgen Matthäus, "Operation Barbarossa and the Onset of the Holocaust, June–December 1941," in Browning, *Origins of the Final Solution*, p. 297.

107. Heydenrich quoted in *True to Type*, p. 31; company commander quoted in Heer, "Killing Fields," p. 62; Thomas Kühne, *Kameradschaft: Die Soldaten des nationalsozialistischen Krieges und das 20. Jahrhundert* (Göttingen, 2006), p. 174. In addition, see Browning, *Ordinary Men*.

108. Angrick, *Besatzungspolitik und Massenmord*, pp. 79–80; Scheffler, "Der Einsatzgruppe A 1941/42," p. 30; Longerich, *Politik der Vernichtung*, pp. 304–310; Rossino, *Hitler Strikes Poland*, pp. 27–57; and Jürgen Matthäus, Konrad Kwiet, and Jürgen Förster, eds., *Ausbildungsziel Judenmord? "Weltanschauliche Erziehung" von SS, Polizei, und Waffen-SS im Rahmen der "Endlösung"* (Frankfurt, 2003).

109. Harald Welzer, *Täter: Wie aus ganz normalen Menschen Massenmörder werden* (Frankfurt, 2005), p. 40.

110. Fritz Jacob to Rudolf Quener, 5 May and 21 June 1942, quoted and discussed in Frank Bajohr, "'. . . dann bitte keine Gefühlsduseleien.' Die Hamburger und die Deportationen," in Forschungsstelle für Zeitgeschichte, Hamburg, ed., *Die Deportationen der Hamburger Juden 1941–1945* (Hamburg, 2002), pp. 20–21.

111. Kempowski, *Das Echolot*, p. 88. Generally, Hannes Heer, *Tote Zonen: Die deutsche Wehrmacht an der Ostfront* (Hamburg, 1999), pp. 120–123.

112. Goebbels' diary entry for 19 Aug. 1941, quoted in Christopher R. Browning, *Nazi Policy, Jewish Workers, German Killers* (Cambridge, Eng., 2000), p. 35.

113. Himmler to Greiser, 18 Sept. 1941, NS19/2655, BAB. See Tobias Jersak, "Entscheidungen zu Mord und Lüge. Die deutsche Kriegsgesellschaft und der Holocaust," in Echternkamp, *Die Deutsche Kriegsgesellschaft*, 1: 304–310; Philippe Burrin, *Hitler and the Jews: The Genesis of the Holocaust* (London, 1994); Peter Witte, "Two Decisions concerning the Final Solution to the Jewish Question," *Holocaust and Genocide Studies* 9 (1995), p. 330.

114. Browning, *Origins of the Final Solution*, p. 371; Witte, "Two Decisions concerning the Final Solution," pp. 321, 329.

115. Himmler quoted in Browning, *Origins of the Final Solution,* p. 325; Himmler to Uebelhoer, 9 Oct. 1941, NS19/2655/38–39, BAB.

116. The opening line in Adler, *Der verwaltete Mensch,* p. 3.

117. Gustavo Corni, *Hitler's Ghettos: Voices from a Beleaguered Society, 1939–1944* (London, 2002), pp. 35, 37; Max Kaufmann, *Churbn Lettland. Die Vernichtung der Juden Lettlands* (1947; reprint, Konstanz, 1999), pp. 93–116.

118. Christian Gerlach, "The Wannsee Conference, the Fate of German Jews, and Hitler's Decision in Principle to Exterminate All European Jews," *Journal of Modern History* 70 (1998), pp. 769–771; Browning, *Origins of the Final Solution,* p. 399; Jersak, "Entscheidungen zu Mord und Lüge," pp. 335–337.

119. Gerlach, "The Wannsee Conference, the Fate of German Jews," p. 798; Longerich, *Politik der Vernichtung,* pp. 467–471. See also entry for 30 May 1942, Goebbels, *Die Tagebücher,* pt. II, vol. 4, p. 406.

120. Raul Hilberg, *The Destruction of the European Jews* (New Haven, 2003), pp. 448, 628; Eichmann quoted in Aly, *"Final Solution,"* p. 265.

121. Ruth Kluger, *Still Alive: A Holocaust Girlhood Remembered* (New York, 2001), p. 70. See also Sybille Steinbacher, *Auschwitz: A History* (New York, 2005), p. 109.

122. Browning, *Origins of the Final Solution,* p. 370.

123. Entry for 13 Dec. 1941, Goebbels, *Die Tagebücher,* pt. II, vol. 2, pp. 498–499; Browning, *Origins of the Final Solution,* pp. 407–409.

124. Elisabeth Freund, "Zwangsarbeit Berlin 1941" (ms. dated Havana, December 1941), in Monika Richarz, ed., *Jüdisches Leben in Deutschland. Selbstzeugnisse zur Sozialgeschichte 1918–1945* (Stuttgart, 1982), p. 381; Smith, *Last Train from Berlin,* p. 197. See also Jeffrey Herf, *The Jewish Enemy: Nazi Propaganda during World War II and the Holocaust* (Cambridge, 2006).

125. Goebbels, "Die Juden sind schuld!" *Das Reich,* 16 Nov. 1941.

126. Ibid.; entry for 28 Oct. 1941, Goebbels, *Die Tagebücher,* pt. II, vol. 2, pp. 193–195.

127. Newspaper quoted in entry for 3 Oct. 1941, Haag, *Leben und gelebt werden,* p. 245.

128. Entries for 25 and 28 Sept. and 19 Oct. 1941, Wantzen, *Das Leben im Krieg,* pp. 551, 567, 594; Ursel, letter of 23 Sept. 1941 in Jürgen

Reulecke and Anatoly Golovchansky, eds., *"Ich will raus aus diesem Wahnsinn": Deutsche Briefe von der Ostfront 1941–1945* (Wuppertal, 1991), p. 35. According to Longerich, *"Davon haben wir nichts gewusst!"* p. 197, similar rumors were reported in Minden. This "local knowledge" would become propaganda soon enough. See Maurer, "Wie sich die Juden tarnen," *Der Stürmer,* 20 Nov. 1941.

129. Entries for 24 Jan., 13 Feb., and 24 March 1942, Goebbels, *Die Tagebücher,* pt. II, vol. 3, pp. 177–178, 298, 535; and entries for 2 and 17 April and 14 May 1942, ibid., vol. 4, pp. 40–41, 117–18, 288. See also Georges Bonnet, *Dans la tourmente 1938–1948* (Paris, 1971), pp. 241–243; Ron Roizen, "Herschel Grynszpan: The Fate of a Forgotten Assassin," *Holocaust and Genocide Studies* 1 (1986), pp. 217–228; and Gerald Schwab, *The Day the Holocaust Began: The Odyssey of Herschel Grynszpan* (New York, 1990).

130. Entry for 10 May 1943, Goebbels, *Die Tagebücher,* pt. II, vol. 8, p. 261. In general, Herf, *The Jewish Enemy.*

131. Heinrich Himmler, "Rede des Reichsführer-SS bei der Gruppenführertag in Posen am 4. Oktober 1943," NS19/4010, BAB.

132. Hilberg, *Destruction of the European Jews,* p. 423.

133. "Hitler and the Beginning of the Systematic Murder of European Jewry in Spring 1942," "Holocaust Denial on Trial," http://www .hdot.org/evidence/pl118.asp; Wolf to Ganzmüller, 13 Aug. 1942, NS19/2655/64, BAB.

134. Browning, *Nazi Policy, Jewish Workers,* p. 57; Longerich, *Politik der Vernichtung,* pp. 488–489; Charlotte Delbo, *Auschwitz and After,* trans. Rosette C. Lamont (New Haven, 1995), p. 4.

135. Longerich, *Politik der Vernichtung,* pp. 497, 508; Danuta Czech, *Auschwitz Chronicle, 1939–1945* (New York, 1990), pp. 198–199.

136. Himmler to Chef des SS-Wirtschafts-Verwaltungshauptamtes Obergruppenführer Pohl and Chef des Hauptamtes Volksdeutsche Mittelstelle SS-Obergruppenführer Lorenz, 24.10.42, NS19/1801/ 175, BAB; Steinbacher, *Auschwitz,* p. 128; Andrezj Strzelecki, "The Plunder of Victims and Their Corpses," in Yisrael Gutman and Michael Berenbaum, *Anatomy of the Auschwitz Death Camp* (Bloomington, Ind., 1994), p. 256.

137. Sybille Steinbacher, *"Musterstadt" Auschwitz: Germanisierungspolitik und Judenmord in Ostoberschlesien* (Munich, 2000), p. 240, and also pp. 185–187, 242, 245; Gudrun Schwarz, *Eine Frau an seiner*

Seite: Ehefrauen in der "SS-Sippengemeinschaft" (Hamburg, 1997). See also *Das Generalgouvernement,* p. 10.

138. Norbert Frei, "Auschwitz und die Deutschen," in *1945 und Wir,* p. 157, quoting Marianne B's diary entry and its original emphases from September 1943.

139. Himmler quoted in Longerich, *Politik der Vernichtung,* p. 506.

140. Christian Gerlach and Götz Aly, *Das letzte Kapitel: Realpolitik, Ideologie, und der Mord an den ungarischen Juden 1944/45* (Stuttgart, 2002). On the hotline, Tooze, *The Wages of Destruction,* p. 671.

141. Peter Steinberg, *Journey to Oblivion: The End of the East European Yiddish and German Worlds in the Mirror of Literature* (Toronto, 1991), pp. 9–10.

142. Vegas Gabriel Liulevicius, *War Land on the Eastern Front: Culture, National Identity, and German Occupation in World War I* (Cambridge, Eng., 2000), p. 8.

143. Tony Judt, "From the House of the Dead," in *Postwar: A History of Europe since 1945* (New York, 2005).

144. See Wolfgang Benz, ed., *Dimensionen des Völkermordes: Die Zahl der jüdischen Opfer des Nationalsozialismus* (Munich, 1991).

4. Intimate Knowledge

1. Entry for 10 March 1943 in Lisa de Boor, *Tagebuchblätter. Aus den Jahren 1938–1945* (Munich, 1963), p. 135.

2. Willy Peter Reese, *A Stranger to Myself. The Inhumanity of War: Russia, 1941–1944,* trans. Michael Hofmann (New York, 2005), p. 108; entry for 6 Sept. 1943 in Joseph Goebbels, *Die Tagebücher von Joseph Goebbels. Sämtliche Fragmente,* ed. Elke Fröhlich (Munich, 1994), pt. II, vol. 9, p. 435.

3. Entry for 1–3 Jan. 1943, de Boor, *Tagebuchblätter,* p. 127. See also entry for 30 Nov. 1944 in Ursula von Kardorff, *Berliner Aufzeichnungen: Aus den Jahren 1942 bis 1945,* ed. Peter Hartl (1962; reprint, Munich, 1992), p. 264; and entries for 11 Sept. 1943 and 30 Nov. 1944 in "Tagebuch 6. Juli 1942–17. Nov. 1943. 7. Buch," Nachlass Franz von Göll, Landesarchiv Berlin, E Rep. 200-43, Acc. 3221, Nrs. 7, 8. On foreign labor, see Ulrich Herbert, *Hitler's Foreign Workers: Enforced Foreign Labor in Germany under the Third Reich,* trans. William Templer (Cambridge, Eng., 1997).

4. Alfred Mierzejewski, *The Most Valuable Asset of the Reich: A History of the German National Railway,* 2 vols. (Chapel Hill, 2000), 2: 127; Primo Levi, *The Drowned and the Saved* (New York, 1988), p. 107.

5. Hanns Johst, *Ruf des Reiches, Echo des Volkes* (Munich, 1940), pp. 5–6.

6. Entry for 2–5 Feb. 1941, de Boor, *Tagebuchblätter,* p. 70; René Schindler, *Ein Schweizer erlebt das geheime Deutschland* (Zurich, 1945), pp. 7–8; entries for 27–30 July and "End of August" 1943, de Boor, *Tagebuchblätter,* pp. 149, 152.

7. Karola Fings, "Sklaven für die 'Heimatfront.' Kriegsgesellschaft und Konzentrationslager," in Jörg Echternkamp, ed., *Die Deutsche Kriegsgesellschaft 1939 bis 1945,* 2 vols. (Munich, 2004), 1: 220, 248, 260; Gerald Reitlinger, *The Final Solution* (New York, 1953), p. 486; Adam Tooze, *The Wages of Destruction: The Making and Breaking of the Nazi Economy* (New York, 2007), p. 519.

8. Charlotte Delbo, *Auschwitz and After,* trans. Rosette C. Lamont (New Haven, 1995), pp. 182–184.

9. Christopher Browning, *Ordinary Men: Reserve Police Battalion 101 and the Final Solution in Poland* (New York, 1992), pp. 67, 105; Marlis G. Steinert, *Hitler's War and the Germans: Public Mood and Attitude during the Second World War,* ed. and trans. Thomas E. J. de Witt (Athens, Ohio, 1977), p. 145.

10. Martin Doerry, *"Mein verwundetes Herz": Das Leben der Lilli Jahn 1900–1944* (Stuttgart, 2002), pp. 156, 216, 242–243.

11. Another example of diverging narratives is Hertha Feiner's attempt to get her half-Jewish daughters, who declared themselves to be Christians, to understand that only by returning to Berlin from boarding school in Switzerland could they save their mother, who would then live in a "mixed" household. See letter of 19 June 1942 in Hertha Feiner, *Vor der Deportation. Briefe an die Töchter Januar 1939– Dezember 1942* (Frankfurt, 1993), p. 114. In *Pawels Briefe. Eine Familiengeschichte* (Frankfurt, 1999), Monika Maron expressed astonishment at how quickly her family had forgotten about its Jewish origins in Poland at the turn of the century, the sad letters to deported grandparents in the years 1939–1942, and, more generally, the poverty of tenement life in pre-1933 Berlin.

12. "Piskowitz, February 19, Monday afternoon," in Victor Klemperer, *I*

Will Bear Witness 1942–1945: A Diary of the Nazi Years (New York, 1998), p. 415; Inge Deutschkron, *Ich trug den gelben Stern* (Munich, 1985).

13. Ruth Kluger, *Weiter leben* (Gottingen, 1992), p. 171; idem, *Still Alive: A Holocaust Girlhood Remembered* (New York, 2001), p. 146.

14. Entries for 15, 18, 22, 23, and 25 Sept. 1941, Klemperer, *I Will Bear Witness*, pp. 429, 433, 435–436.

15. Elisabeth Freund, "Zwangsarbeit Berlin 1941," in Monika Richarz, ed., *Jüdisches Leben in Deutschland. Selbstzeugnisse zur Sozialgeschichte 1918–1945* (Stuttgart, 1982), p. 381. Ursula von Kardorff's story from 3 March 1943 is similar. She tells of a worker "who gave up his seat to a Jew in the streetcar: 'Sit down you old shooting star,' he said, and when a party member complained, went at him: 'I decide where to put my ass.'" See *Berliner Aufzeichnungen*, p. 72.

16. Entry for 19 Aug. 1941, Goebbels, *Die Tagebücher*, pt. II, vol. 1, p. 266.

17. This was the vague formulation used by the Union of Jewish Communities in Württemberg in November 1941. See Karl Heinz Mistele, *The End of the Community: The Destruction of the Jews of Bamberg, Germany 1938–1942*, trans. Jacob Feuchtwanger (Hoboken, 1995), pp. 116–117.

18. Freund, "Zwangsarbeit Berlin 1941," p. 383; entry for 28 Nov. 1941, Klemperer, *I Will Bear Witness*, p. 446.

19. Quoted from an undated memo (probably 1942) written by Berlin's Jewish community, in Hans G. Adler, *Der verwaltete Mensch. Studien zur Deportation der Juden aus Deutschland* (Tübingen, 1974), p. 403. See also p. 399.

20. Angelika Eder, "Die Deportationen im Spiegel lebensgeschichtlicher Interviews," in Forschungsstelle fur Zeitgeschichte, Hamburg, ed., *Die Deportationen der Hamburger Juden 1941–1945* (Hamburg, 2002), p. 48.

21. Deutschkron, *Ich trug den gelben Stern*, pp. 99–100; Alfred Kaufmann quoted in Monica Kingreen, "'Wir werden darüber hinweg kommen': Letzte Lebenszeichen deportierter hessischer Juden. Eine dokumentarische Annäherung," in Birthe Kundrus and Beate Meyer, eds., *Deportation der Juden aus Deutschland: Pläne, Praxis, Reaktionen 1938–1945* (Göttingen, 2004), p. 99.

22. Beate Meyer, "Handlungsspielräume regionaler jüdischer Repräsen-

tanten (1941–1945): Die Reichsvereinigung der Juden in Deutschland und die Deportationen," in Kundrus and Meyer, *Deportation der Juden aus Deutschland,* pp. 76–77; entries for 16, 17, and 19 Oct. 1941 in David Sierakowiak, *The Diary of David Sierakowiak: Five Notebooks from the Łódź Ghetto* (New York, 1996), pp. 141–142; Saul Friedländer, *The Years of Extermination: Nazi Germany and the Jews 1939–1945* (New York, 2007), p. 312.

23. Ministry of the Interior, Schnellbrief to all Staatspolizei(leit)stellen, 24 March 1942, R58/276/332, BAB.

24. Letter of Selma Fleischer, 27 April 1942, in Hanne Hiob and Gerd Keller, eds., *"Wir verreisen . . ."In die Vernichtung. Briefe 1937–1944* (Hamburg, 1993), p. 81; entry for 26 June 1942, Klemperer, *I Will Bear Witness,* p. 87.

25. Entries for 22 Dec. 1941 and 19 May 1942, Klemperer, *I Will Bear Witness,* pp. 451, 55.

26. Letters of Selma Fleischer, 7 Dec. 1941 and 18 Aug. 1942, and letter of Nanny Fleischer, 14 Oct. 1941, in Hiob and Keller, *"Wir verreisen,"* pp. 68, 96, 100.

27. Kingreen, "'Wir werden darüber hinweg kommen,'" pp. 87–88, 95; Alexandra Garbarini, *Numbered Days: Diaries and the Holocaust* (New Haven, 2006), p. 65; for Leipzig, Marion Kaplan, *Between Dignity and Despair: Jewish Life in Nazi Germany* (New York, 1998), p. 187; Adler, *Der verwaltete Mensch,* pp. 408, 581.

28. See, for example, entries for 23 May and 11 June 1942, Klemperer, *I Will Bear Witness,* pp. 57–58, 73; and entry for 16 Oct. 1942, ibid., p. 155.

29. Entries for 17 Jan. 1944 and 27 Feb. 1943, ibid., pp. 290, 203–204.

30. Entries for 15 Sept. and 24 Oct. 1944, ibid., pp. 358, 371.

31. Kurt Lindenberg quoted in Beate Kosmala, "Zwischen Ahnen und Wissen: Flucht vor der Deportation (1941–1943)," in Kundrus and Meyer, *Deportation der Juden aus Deutschland,* p. 154; Garbarini, *Numbered Days,* p. 114.

32. Kosmala, "Zwischen Ahnen und Wissen," p. 136.

33. Kaplan, *Between Dignity and Despair,* pp. 180, 184; Lothar Bembenek and Horst Dickel, *Ich bin kein deutscher Patriot mehr, jetzt bin ich Jude: Die Vertreibung jüdischer Bürger aus Wiesbaden (1933–1947)* (Wiesbaden, 1991), p. 128. See also Monika Richarz, "Einführung," in Richarz, *Jüdisches Leben in Deutschland,* p. 65.

34. Schindler quoted in Kosmala, "Zwischen Ahnen und Wissen," p. 142;

Raul Hilberg, *The Destruction of the European Jews* (New Haven, 2003), p. 483.

35. See entries for 20 Oct. and 25 Nov. 1941 and 25 Jan. and 10 Dec. 1942 in Jochen Klepper, *Unter dem Schatten Deiner Flügel: Aus den Tagebüchern der Jahre 1932–1942* (Stuttgart, 1955), pp. 969–970, 992, 1029, 1133.

36. Kosmala, "Zwischen Ahnen und Wissen," pp. 138–139; Lindenberg quoted in ibid., p. 150.

37. Kingreen, "'Wir werden darüber hinweg kommen,'" p. 109. When Sweden, Switzerland, and Denmark began to raise questions about the Nazis' anti-Jewish policies at the end of 1943, after Danish Jews had been deported to Theresienstadt, it was to a tidied-up camp that their representatives and officials of the International Red Cross were escorted on 23 June 1944. Believing the lie that Theresienstadt was an *Endlager,* not a transit camp, and impressed by the sight of children playing in the "kindergarten," the investigators took photographs and returned home "pleasantly surprised." They passed up the opportunity to inspect what the Germans had set aside as a "family camp" in Auschwitz-Birkenau, in which 5,000 inmates were held back from gassing and slave labor, and could write and receive mail (addressed to "Birkenau, bei Neuberun, Ost Oberschlesien"). Its function was certainly to deceive residents in Theresienstadt, who had more contact with the outside world, about the nature of deportations to Auschwitz. It was probably also established in the event of international inspections. Once the second "family camp" had served its function, it was disassembled and its inhabitants sent to the gas chambers on 7 July 1944. See the correspondence in R58/89, BAB, and especially the 27 June 1944 report by Dr. Rossel, R58/89/24. On the family camp, Nili Keren, "The Family Camp," in Yisrael Gutman and Michael Berenbaum, eds., *Anatomy of the Auschwitz Death Camp* (Bloomington, Ind., 1994); and Mark Roseman, *A Past in Hiding: Memory and Survival in Nazi Germany* (New York, 2000). For the address, Martin Gilbert, "What Was Known and When," in Gutman and Berenbaum, *Anatomy,* p. 548.

38. Deutschkron, *Ich trug den gelben Stern,* p. 119; entry for 17 Jan. 1943, Klemperer, *I Will Bear Witness,* p. 117.

39. On the complaints, Rissen to Brandt, 4 March 1943, NS19/3492/6, BAB.

40. Entry for 18 April 1943, Goebbels, *Die Tagebücher,* pt. II, vol. 8, p. 126; entry for 26 April 1943 in Victor Klemperer, *Ich will Zeugnis ablegen bis zum letzten. Tagebücher 1942–1945* (Berlin, 1995), p. 361.

41. See the remarkable document written by Ernst Krombach, dated 22 Aug. 1942, discussed and quoted in Roseman, *A Past in Hiding,* pp. 182–196.

42. Quoted in Sandra Ziegler, *Gedächtnis und Identität der KZ-Erfahrung. Niederländische und deutsche Augenzeugenberichte des Holocaust* (Würzburg, 2006), p. 38.

43. Ibid., p. 214.

44. Garbarini, *Numbered Days,* p. 84. See also David Engel, "'Will They Dare?': Perceptions of Threat in Diaries from the Warsaw Ghetto," in Robert Moses Shapiro, ed., *Holocaust Chronicles: Individualizing the Holocaust through Diaries and Other Contemporaneous Personal Accounts* (Hoboken, 1999), pp. 78–79.

45. Entry for 27 May 1943, Klemperer, *I Will Bear Witness,* p. 61; Klüger, *Weiter leben,* p. 139.

46. See entries for 28 Aug., 21 Sept., and 1 Nov. 1942 in Abraham Lewin, *A Cup of Tears: A Diary of the Warsaw Ghetto* (Oxford, 1988), pp. 171, 184, 197, and also 38–40; Margarete Holländer quoted in Garbarini, *Numbered Days,* p. 91.

47. Garbarini, *Numbered Days,* p. 2; Alexandra Zapruder, ed., *Salvaged Pages: Young Writers' Diaries of the Holocaust* (New Haven, 2002), p. 306.

48. See the appendices and preface to Irène Némirovsky, *Suite Française,* trans. Sandra Smith (New York, 2006), pp. 351, 394.

49. Entry for 4 Feb. 1944 in Ruth Andreas-Friedrich, *Berlin Underground, 1938–1945* (New York, 1947), p. 116.

50. Christel Beilmann quoted in Tobias Jersak, "Eintscheidungen zu Mord und Lüge. Die deutsche Kriegsgesellschaft und der Holocaust," in Echternkamp, *Die Deutsche Kriegsgesellschaft,* p. 349. See also Sybille Steinbacher, *"Musterstadt" Auschwitz: Germanisierungspolitik und Judenmord in Ostoberschlesien* (Munich, 2000), p. 190.

51. On *verarbeitet,* see Hellmuth von Moltke, quoted in Peter Longerich, *"Davon haben wir nichts gewusst!" Die Deutschen und die Judenverfolgung 1933–1945* (Berlin, 2006), p. 229; for "pieces," Primo Levi, *Survival in Auschwitz* (New York, 1986), p. 16; for "cargo," Gitta Sereny, *Into That Darkness* (New York, 1974), p. 201.

52. Entry for 27 Dec. 1944, von Kardorff, *Berliner Aufzeichnungen,* p. 272.

53. Quoted in Longerich, *"Davon haben wir nichts gewusst!"* pp. 195–196.

54. Frank Bajohr, "'. . . dann bitte keine Gefühlsduseleien.' Die Hamburger und die Deportationen," in Forschungsstelle fur Zeitgeschichte, Hamburg, *Die Deportationen der Hamburger Juden,* pp. 15–16; Götz Aly, *Hitlers Volksstaat: Raub, Rassenkrieg, und nationaler Sozialismus* (Frankfurt, 2005), pp. 139–140.

55. Entry for 27 April 1942, Goebbels, *Die Tagebücher,* pt. II, vol. 4, p. 184; on Nuremberg, Meyer, "Handlungsspielräume regionaler jüdischer Repräsentanten," p. 77; on Stuttgart, Roland Müller, *Stuttgart zur Zeit des Nationalsozialismus* (Stuttgart, 1988), p. 405; and on Bad Neustadt, Herbert Schultheis, *Juden in Mainfranken 1933–1945* (Bad Neustadt, 1980), pp. 467–468.

56. Entries for 6 and 23 Nov. and 15 Dec. 1941 and 8 Aug. 1942 in Paulheinz Wantzen, *Das Leben im Krieg. Ein Tagebuch* (Bad Homburg, 2000), pp. 610, 639, 651–652, 916.

57. Entry for 8 Dec. 1941, Andreas-Friedrich, *Berlin Underground,* p. 75; Deutschkron, *Ich trug den gelben Stern,* pp. 99–100, 119; Longerich, *"Davon haben wir nichts gewusst!"* pp. 190–191.

58. Quoted in ibid., pp. 219–220. See also Adler, *Der verwaltete Mensch,* p. 332.

59. Frank Bajohr, "Über die Entwicklung eines schlechten Gewissens: Die deutsche Bevölkerung und die Deportationen 1941–1945," in Kundrus and Meyer, *Deportation der Juden aus Deutschland,* p. 190.

60. Düsseldorf Gestapo officer Hermann Waldbillig quoted in Holger Berschel, *Bürokratie und Terror. Das Judenreferat der Gestapo Düsseldorf 1935–1945* (Essen, 2001), p. 119; Bajohr, "Über die Entwicklung eines schlechten Gewissens," p. 184. For verbal assaults in Bad Neustadt, Schultheis, *Juden in Mainfranken 1933–1945,* p. 467.

61. No. 62147, 4 July 1945, Schedule B interviews, USSBS, RG 243, box 505, folder 11, NARA; no. 62136, 11 July 1945, ibid., folder 9.

62. Christopher Browning, *The Origins of the Final Solution: The Evolution of Nazi Jewish Policy, September 1939–March 1942* (Lincoln, Neb., 2004), p. 387; Paul Salitter, "Bericht über die Evakuierung von Juden nach Riga vom 11.12–17.12.1941" (26 Dec. 1941), in Günter

von Roden, *Geschichte der Duisburger Juden* (Duisburg, 1986), pp. 872–873.

63. Meyer, "Handlungsspielräume regionaler jüdischer Repräsentanten," p. 77; Arnd Müller, *Geschichte der Juden in Nürnberg* (Nuremberg, 1968), pp. 247–248.

64. Jürgen Hartmann, "Die Deportation Detmolder Juden 1941–1945," in Hermann Niebuhr and Andreas Ruppert, eds., *National-sozialismus in Detmold: Dokumentation eines stadtgeschichtlichen Projekts* (Bielefeld, 1998), p. 668.

65. Franziska Becker, *Gewalt und Gedächtnis: Erinnerungen an die nationalsozialistische Verfolgung einer jüdischen landgemeinde* (Göttingen, 1994), pp. 77–78, 83.

66. Entry for 11 Dec. 1942, Klemperer, *I Will Bear Witness*, p. 173; Aly, *Hitlers Volksstaat*, p. 150. See also Jean-Marc Dreyfus, "'Almost Camps' in Paris: The Difficult Description of Three Annexes of Drancy—Austerlitz, Lévitan, and Bassano, July 1943 to August 1944," in Jonathan Petropoulos and John K. Roth, eds., *Gray Zones: Ambiguity and Compromise in the Holocaust and Its Aftermath* (New York, 2005), pp. 224–225.

67. Frank Bajohr, *"Aryanisation" in Hamburg: The Economic Exclusion of Jews and the Confiscation of Their Property in Nazi Germany* (New York, 2002), p. 279.

68. Longerich, *"Davon haben wir nichts gewusst!"* pp. 284–285.

69. No. 70, Schedule B interviews, USSBS, RG 243, box 502, folder 2, NARA.

70. No. 62040, 3 July 1945, ibid., box 506, folder 14; 28 April 1945, ibid., box 509, folder 29.

71. No. 60355, 11 June 1945, ibid., box 533, folder 105.

72. Entry for 4 Feb. 1944, Andreas-Friedrich, *Berlin Underground*, p. 117.

73. Karl Dürkefälden, *"Schreiben wie es wirklich war . . ." Aufzeich-ungen Karl Dürkefäldens aus den Jahren 1933–1945*, ed. Herbert Obenaus and Sibylle Obenaus (Hanover, 1985), pp. 108–111.

74. Entry for 27 Dec. 1944, von Kardorff, *Berliner Aufzeichnungen*, p. 272; Filip Müller, *Eyewitness Auschwitz: Three Years in the Gas Chambers* (New York, 1979), p. 129. See also Nicholas Stargardt, *Witnesses of War: The Third Reich through Children's Eyes* (London, 2004), p. 221.

75. Schindler, *Ein Schweizer erlebt das geheime Deutschland,* p. 57.

76. Frank Stern, *The Whitewashing of the Yellow Badge: Antisemitism and Philosemitism in Postwar Germany* (New York, 1992), pp. 117–118, 121.

77. Dürkefälden, *"Schreiben wie es wirklich war,"* p. 110. See also Browning, *Ordinary Men,* p. 58.

78. Goebbels' diary entry for 2 March 1943, quoted in Bajohr, "Über die Entwicklung eines schlechten Gewissens," p. 194.

79. Entry for 29 Nov. 1942 in Lore Walb, *Ich, die Alte, ich, die Junge: Konfrontation mit meinem Tagebüchern 1933–1945* (Berlin, 1997), p. 253.

80. Böll to Annemarie, 14 Dec. 1942 and 29 Jan. 1943, in Heinrich Böll, *Briefe aus dem Krieg 1939–1945,* ed. Jochen Schubert (Cologne, 2001), pp. 573–574, 599.

81. Hugo B., diary entry for 27 Sept. 1942, in Ingrid Hammer and Susanne zur Nieden, eds., *Sehr selten habe ich geweint: Briefe und Tagebücher aus dem Zweiten Weltkrieg von Menschen in Berlin* (Zurich, 1992), p. 333; Jay Winter, *Dreams of Peace and Freedom: Utopian Moments in the Twentieth Century* (New Haven, 2006), p. 142. In general, Michael Geyer, "Endkampf 1918 and 1945: German Nationalism, Annihilation, and Self-Destruction," in Alf Lüdtke and Bernd Weisbrod, eds., *No Man's Land of Violence: Extreme Wars in the Twentieth Century* (Göttingen, 2006), p. 44.

82. Susanne zur Nieden, *Alltag im Ausnahmezustand. Frauentagebücher im zerstörten Deutschland 1943–1945* (Berlin, 1993), p. 199. See also Norbert Frei, "Auschwitz und die Deutschen," in *1945 und Wir: Das Dritte Reich im Beuwsstein der Deutschen* (Munich, 2005), p. 158.

83. Entry for 27 Dec. 1941, Walb, *Ich, die Alte, ich, die Junge,* p. 238.

84. Letter of 6 Aug. 1943 in Marlies Tremper, ed., *Briefe des Soldaten Helmut N., 1939–1945* (Berlin, 1988), pp. 171–172; and entry for 28 July 1943, Goebbels, *Die Tagebücher,* pt. II, vol. 9, p. 186.

85. Karl Kretschmer to his wife and children, 15 Oct. 1942, reprinted in Ernst Klee, Willi Dressen, and Volker Riess, eds., *"The Good Old Days": The Holocaust as Seen by Its Perpetrators and Bystanders,* trans. Deborah Burnstone (New York, 1991), pp. 167–168.

86. Entry for 27 Jan. 1945, "Tagebuch Nr. 8, 18. Nov. 1943–7. April 1945," Nachlass Franz von Göll, Landesarchiv Berlin, E Rep. 200-43, Acc. 3221, Nr. 8.

87. Lieselotte G., diary entry for 12 April 1945, in Hammer and zur Nieden, *Sehr selten habe ich geweint,* p. 309. See also Saul Padover, *Experiment in Germany: The Story of an American Intelligence Officer* (New York, 1946), pp. 111–118; and Karl-Heinz Reuband, "Das NS-Regime zwischen Akzeptanz und Ablehunung. Eine retrospektive Analyse von Bevölkerungseinstellungen im Dritten Reich auf der Basis von Umfragedaten," *Geschichte und Gesellschaft* 32 (2006), pp. 315–344.

88. Reese, *A Stranger to Myself,* p. 46.

89. Entry for 24 Nov. 1941, excerpted in *True to Type: A Selection from Letters and Diaries of German Soldiers and Civilians Collected on the Soviet-German Front* (London, n.d. [1943]), p. 35. See also Christoph Rass, "Das Sozialprofil von Kampfverbänden," in Echternkamp, *Die Deutsche Kriegsgesellschaft,* 1: 664.

90. Letter of 19 Nov. 1941, quoted in Ortwin Buchbender and Reinhold Sterz, eds., *Das andere Gesicht des Krieges: Deutsche Feldpostbriefe 1939–1945* (Munich, 1982), p. 87.

91. Entry for 9 March 1942, diary of Friedrich Schmidt, secretary for the secret field police, 626th Group, 1st Tank Army, in *True to Type,* p. 51; entry for 20 Sept. 1943, Goebbels, *Die Tagebücher,* pt. II, vol. 9, p. 542.

92. Diary entry for 16 March 1945, quoted in Wolfram Wette, "Das Russlandbild in der NS-Propaganda: Ein Problemaufriss," in Hans-Erich Volkmann, ed., *Das Russlandbild im Dritten Reich* (Cologne, 1994), p. 72.

93. Goebbels diary entry for 20 Dec. 1941, quoted in Walter Kempowski, *Das Echolot: Barbarossa '41* (Munich, 2002), p. 540; "Introduction," in Hannes Heer and Klaus Naumann, eds., *War of Extermination: The German Military in World War II, 1941–44* (New York, 2000), p. 3.

94. Reese, *A Stranger to Myself,* pp. xv, 53; Omer Bartov, *Hitler's Army: Soldiers, Nazis, and War in the Third Reich* (New York, 1992), p. 6.

95. Entry for 3 July 1942, Goebbels, *Die Tagebücher,* pt. II, vol. 5, p. 47; Wolfram Wette, *Die Wehrmacht: Feindbilder, Vernichtungskrieg, Legenden* (Frankfurt, 2002), p. 130; Hans-Heinrich Nolte, "Partisan War in Belorussia, 1941–1944," in Roger Chickering, Stig Förster, and Bernd Greiner, eds., *A World at Total War: Global Conflict and the Politics of Destruction, 1937–1945* (Cambridge, Eng., 2005),

p. 275. Generally, Christian Gerlach, *Kalkulierte Morde: Die deutsche Wirtschafts- und Vernichtungspolitik in Weissrussland 1941 bis 1944* (Hamburg, 2000).

96. Quoted in Stefan Schmitz, "'Wir wohnten im Verfall der Seele.' Um Umgang mit Leid und Schuld," in Willy Peter Reese, *Mir selbser seltsam fremd. Die Unmenschlichkeit des Krieges. Russland 1941–44* (Munich, 2003), pp. 242–244. For more on Reese, see Harald Welzer, *Täter: Wie aus ganz normalen Menschen Massenmörder werden* (Frankfurt, 2005).

97. Private Alfred G. quoted in Müller, "Nationalismus in der deutschen Kriegsgesellschaft," p. 57; Mielert quoted in Stephen G. Fritz, *Frontsoldaten: The German Soldier in World War II* (Lexington, Ky., 1995), p. 189.

98. Zur Nieden, *Alltag im Ausnahmezustand*, pp. 86 and 149, 200.

99. Ernest K. Bramsted, *Goebbels and National Socialist Propaganda, 1925–1945* (East Lansing, 1965), p. 250.

100. Entry for 3 Oct. 1942 in Lili Hahn, *. . . bis alles in Scherben fällt. Tagebuchblätter 1933–1945* (Cologne, 1979), p. 467; *Das Schwarze Korps*, 22 Feb. 1945.

101. Albert Speer relating Hitler's views, *Inside the Third Reich*, trans. Richard and Clara Winston (New York, 1970), p. 256; no. 62959, 28 July 1945, Schedule B interviews, USSBS, RG 243, box 506, folder 30, NARA.

102. Entries for 13 July 1941 and 27 March 1942, Klemperer, *I Will Bear Witness*, pp. 419, 34; entries for 9 Jan., 11 and 29 Aug., and 3 Sept. 1941, and 9 July 1942, Wantzen, *Das Leben im Krieg*, pp. 331, 477, 496, 526, 891–893; entry for 6 Sept. 1943, Goebbels, *Die Tagebücher*, pt. II, vol. 9, p. 434; and entry for 29 Nov. 1943, ibid., vol. 10, pp. 381–382. See also Ian Kershaw, *The "Hitler Myth": Image and Reality in the Third Reich* (Oxford, 1987), pp. 188–189.

103. Entry for 23 March 1943, Goebbels, *Die Tagebücher*, pt. II, vol. 7, p. 631; entry for 24 Dec. 1943, ibid., vol. 10, p. 542. On the vodka, entry for 13 May 1943 in Zygmunt Klukowski, *Diary of the Years of Occupation, 1939–44* (Urbana, 1993), p. 252. See also Ian Kershaw, *Hitler 1936–1945: Nemesis* (New York, 2000), p. 534.

104. Entry for 23 Jan. 1943, Goebbels, *Die Tagebücher*, pt. II, vol. 7, pp. 174–175; Geyer, "Endkampf 1918 and 1945," pp. 52–53.

105. Entry for 2 Feb. 1943, Goebbels, *Die Tagebücher*, pt. II, vol. 7, p. 240;

Frank Biess, *Homecomings: Returning POWs and the Legacies of Defeat in Postwar Germany* (Princeton, 2006), p. 27.

106. Bramsted, *Goebbels and National Socialist Propaganda*, p. 229.

107. Paul Fussell, quoted in Thomas Childers, "'Facilis descensus averni est': The Allied Bombing of Germany and the Issue of German Suffering," *Central European History* 38 (2005), pp. 103–104. See also Stephen G. Fritz, *Endkampf: Soldiers, Civilians, and the Death of the Third Reich* (Lexington, Ky., 2004).

108. On suicides, Richard Bessel, "The War to End All Wars: The Shock of Violence in 1945 and Its Aftermath in Germany," in Lüdtke and Weisbrod, *No Man's Land of Violence*, p. 78. See also Lieselotte G., diary entry for 29 April 1945, in Hammer and zur Nieden, *Sehr selten habe ich geweint*, p. 312.

109. Tooze, *The Wages of Destruction*, pp. 603–604.

110. Entry for 8 Nov. 1943, zur Nieden, *Alltag im Ausnahmezustand*, p. 148.

111. Bartov, *Hitler's Army*, p. 9. See also Joseph B. Perry, "The Madonna of Stalingrad: The (Christmas) Past and West German National Identity after World War II," *Radical History Review* 83 (2002), pp. 7–27.

112. Bernd Boll and Hans Safrian, "On the Way to Stalingrad: The 6th Army in 1941–42," in Heer and Naumann, *War of Extermination*.

113. Günter Moltmann, "Goebbels' Rede zum Totalen Krieg am 18. Februar 1943," *Vierteljahrshefte für Zeitgeschichte* 12 (1964), p. 22; Jeffrey Herf, *The Jewish Enemy: Nazi Propaganda during World War II and the Holocaust* (Cambridge, 2006), p. 192.

114. Konrad Warner, *Schicksalswende Europas? Ich sprach mit dem deutschen Volk* . . . (Rheinfelden, 1944), pp. 23–24; Schindler, *Ein Schweizer erlebt das geheime Deutschland*, p. 63.

115. Nicholas Stargardt, "Opfer der Bomben und der Vergeltung," in Lothar Kettenacker, ed., *Ein Volk von Opfern? Die neue Debatte um den Bombenkrieg 1940–45* (Berlin, 2003), p. 69. See also Holger Schlüter, "Terrorinstanz Volksgerichtshof," in Götz Aly, ed., *Volkes Stimme. Skepsis und Führervertrauen im Nationalsozialismus* (Frankfurt, 2006), pp. 88–90.

116. Entry for 9 May 1943, Wantzen, *Das Leben im Krieg*, p. 1093.

117. Tooze, *The Wages of Destruction*, pp. 608–609; Heinrich Himmler, "Rede vor den Reichs- und Gauleitern in Posen am 6.10.1943," in

Bradley F. Smith and Agnes F. Peterson, eds., *Heinrich Himmler. Geheimreden 1933 bis 1945* (Frankfurt, 1974), p. 170.

118. Quoted in Hans-Ulrich Thamer, *Verfolgung und Gewalt: Deutschland 1933–1945* (Berlin, 1986), p. 679. See also the reflections of Ludolf Herbst, *Das nationalsozialistische Deutschland 1933–1945* (Frankfurt, 1996), p. 453; and Tooze's analyses of Speer and Himmler at the October 1943 Gauleiter meeting at Posen, in *The Wages of Destruction*, pp. 605–611.

119. Entry for 25 Jan. 1944, Goebbels, *Die Tagebücher*, pt. II, vol. 11, p. 166.

120. No. 62859, 7 July 1945, Schedule B interviews, USSBS, RG 243, box 509, folder 32, NARA.

121. Geyer, "Endkampf 1918 and 1945," pp. 57, 60; Erhard Schütz, "Flieger-Helden und Trümmer-Kultur. Luftwaffe und Bombenkrieg im nationalsozialistischen Spiel- und Dokumentarfilm," in Manuel Köppen and Schütz, eds., *Kunst der Propaganda. Der Film im Dritten Reich* (Bern, 2007), p. 129. On the Berlin group, entry for 20 April 1945, in *Anonyma: Eine Frau in Berlin. Tagebuchaufzeichnungen vom 20. April bis zum 22. Juni 1945.* (Berlin, 2002), pp. 14–17. On "terror" among anti-Nazis, see entries for 6 and 31 Jan. 1945, Göll, "Tagebuch Nr. 8, 18. Nov. 1943–7. April 1945"; entry for 27–30 July 1943, de Boor, *Tagebuchblätter*, p. 149; entries for 18 Sept. 1944 and 12 April 1945 in Emilie Braach, *Wenn meine Briefe Dich erreichen könnten. Aufzeichnungen aus den Jahren 1939–1945*, ed. Bergit Forchhammer (Frankfurt, 1987), pp. 199, 226.

122. See, for example, the case of Marianne Strauss in Roseman, *A Past in Hiding;* as well as Ralph Giordano, "Ein Volk von Opfern?" in Lothar Kettancker, ed., *Ein Volk von Opfern? Die neue Debatte um den Bombenkrieg 1940–1945* (Berlin, 2003), pp. 166–168.

123. No. 60898, 21 June 1945, Schedule B interviews, USSBS, RG 243, box 537, folder 26, NARA.

124. Entry for 1 Jan. 1944, Goebbels, *Die Tagebücher*, pt. II, vol. 11, pp. 33–34. On Hitler's overestimation, see entry for 7 July 1944, ibid., vol. 13, p. 56; also Speer, *Inside the Third Reich*, pp. 485–486. See also Hans Fritsch, 14 Jan. 1945, quoted in Walter Kempowski, *Das Echolot: Fuga Furiosa. Ein kollektives Tagebuch, Winter 1945* (Munich, 1999), p. 145.

125. Warner, *Schicksalswende Europas?* pp. 46, 93–94; Schindler, *Ein Schweizer erlebt das geheime Deutschland,* pp. 34, 65–66; Geyer, "Endkampf 1918 and 1945," pp. 40–41.

126. Entry for 8 Aug. 1944 in Hans-Georg Studnitz, *Als Berlin brannte. Diarium der Jahre 1943–1945* (Stuttgart, 1963), p. 192. See also Jay W. Baird, *The Mythical World of Nazi War Propaganda* (Minneapolis, 1974), pp. 233–235.

127. Müller, "Nationalismus in der deutschen Kriegsgesellschaft," p. 44. See also Kershaw, *Hitler 1936–1945,* p. 699; and Bartov, *Hitler's Army,* pp. 144, 172–173.

128. G. F. Krivosheev, *Soviet Casualties and Combat Losses in the Twentieth Century* (London, 1997), p. 96.

129. Geyer, "Endkampf 1918 and 1945," p. 37.

130. Tooze, *The Wages of Destruction,* pp. 649–650; Jörg Friedrich, *The Fire: The Bombing of Germany, 1940–1945* (New York, 2006), p. 144.

131. Klaus Naumann, *Der Krieg als Text: Das Jahr 1945 im kulturellen Gedächtnis der Presse* (Hamburg, 1998).

132. Entry for 23 April 1945, "Tagebuch Nr. 9, 8 Apr. 1945–3 Okt. 1946," Nachlass Franz von Göll, Landesarchiv Berlin, E Rep. 200-43, Acc. 3221, Nr. 9; entry for 1 Feb. 1945, Studnitz, *Als Berlin brannte,* p. 243. See also Herbert R. Lottman, *The Purge: The Purification of the French Collaborators after World War II* (New York, 1986).

133. Robert Gellately, *Backing Hitler: Consent and Coercion in Nazi Germany* (New York, 2001), p. 239. See also Herbert, *Hitler's Foreign Workers,* pp. 361–362.

134. Yehuda Bauer, "The Death Marches, January–May 1945," *Modern Judaism* 3 (Feb. 1983), pp. 1–21.

135. Zapruder, *Salvaged Pages,* pp. 187, 416–417.

136. Bauer, "The Death Marches, January–May 1945," p. 13.

137. Reese, *A Stranger to Myself,* p. 70; Böll to Annemarie, 19 July 1944 and 18 March, 28 April, and 14 Feb. 1943, in Böll, *Briefe aus dem Krieg,* pp. 1091–92, 653, 733, 616.

138. Entries for mid-June, late June, and 10 Oct. 1942, 11–12 Sept. 1943, and 8–15 Jan. 1944, de Boor, *Tagebuchblätter,* pp. 110–111, 119, 154, 167.

139. Entry for 10 May 1944, von Kardorff, *Berliner Aufzeichnungen,*

p. 186; entry for 7 Feb. 1945 in Ernst Jünger, *Strahlungen* (Munich, 1955), p. 471; entry for 8–15 Jan. 1944, de Boor, *Tagebuchblätter,* p. 167. See also Thomas Nevin, *Ernst Jünger and Germany: Into the Abyss, 1914–1945* (Durham, N.C., 1996), pp. 198, 204.

140. Entries for 10 July and 29 June 1942 in Etty Hillesum, *An Interrupted Life: The Diaries of Etty Hillesum 1941–1943* (New York, 1983), pp. 146, 127. See also entry for 24 May 1942, "Frieda and Max Reinach Diary," RG-10.249, Acc. 1999.A.0215, U.S. Holocaust Memorial Museum, Washington, D.C.

141. Edmund Schultz and Ernst Jünger, eds., *Die veränderte Welt: Eine Bilderfibel unserer Zeit* (Breslau, 1933).

142. Enzo Traverso, *À feu et à sang: De la guerre civile européenne* 1914–1945 (Paris, 2007); Dan Diner, "The Destruction of Narrativity: The Holocaust in Historical Discourse," in Moishe Postone and Eric Santner, eds., *Catastrophe and Meaning: The Holocaust and the Twentieth Century* (Chicago, 2003), pp. 69, 72.

143. Eva Horn, "'*Waldgänger,*' Traitor, Partisan: Figures of Political Irregularity in West German Postwar Thought," *New Centennial Review* 4 (2004), pp. 125–143; Zygmunt Bauman, *Modernity and the Holocaust* (Ithaca, 1989).

144. See Peter Fritzsche, "What Exactly Is *Vergangenheitsbewältigung?* Narrative and Its Insufficiency in Postwar Germany," in Anne Fuchs, Mary Cosgrove, and Georg Grote, eds., *German Memory Contests: The Quest for Identity in Literature, Film, and Discourse since 1990* (Rochester, N.Y., 2006), pp. 25–40.

145. Entry for 23 Jan. 1944, Klemperer, *I Will Bear Witness,* pp. 291–292. On half-Jewish Wehrmacht soldiers, see Bryan Mark Rigg, *Hitler's Jewish Soldiers: The Untold Story of Nazi Racial Laws and the Men of Jewish Descent in the German Military* (Lawrence, Kans., 2002). Postwar trials of policemen in Dresden shed more light on this incident. On 8 January 1944 Weigmann did assume an identity as an SS officer, but was found out before he could reach his mother. He was dead the next day, most likely on account of injuries received after being beaten up. Apparently his mother, Toni Weigmann, who was sent to Theresienstadt, survived. See http://www1.jur.uva.nl/junsv/Excerpts/ddr1003004.htm.

146. Klemperer, *Ich will Zeugnis ablegen bis zum letzten,* p. 447.

147. Bernd Weisbrod, "Der 8. Mai in der deutsche Erinnerung," *Werkstatt*

Geschichte 13 (1996), pp. 72–81; Longerich, *"Davon haben wir nichts gewusst!"*

148. Delbo, *Auschwitz and After,* pp. 230–231; Saul Friedländer, ed., *Probing the Limits of Representation: Nazism and the "Final Solution"* (Cambridge, 1992).

149. Quoted in Lawrence L. Langer, *Holocaust Testimonies: The Ruins of Memory* (New Haven, 1991), pp. 53–54.

Index